Engineering Communism

STEVEN T. USDIN

Engineering Communism

HOW TWO AMERICANS SPIED FOR
STALIN AND FOUNDED THE
SOVIET SILICON VALLEY

Yale University Press
New Haven
& London

Set in Sabon type by Keystone Typesetting, Inc.
Printed in the United States of America by
Vail-Ballou Press, Binghamton, New York.

Library of Congress Cataloging-in-Publication Data

Usdin, Steven T., 1961–
Engineering communism : how two Americans spied for Stalin and founded the Soviet Silicon Valley / Steven T. Usdin.
p. cm.
Includes bibliographical references and index.
ISBN-13: 978-0-300-19552-1

1. Berg, Iosef Veniaminovich, 1916–1998. 2. Staros, Filipp Georgievich, 1918–1979. 3. Spies — United States — Biography. 4. Electric engineers — Soviet Union — Biography. 5. Communists — United States — Biography. 6. Espionage, Soviet — United States — History — 20th century. 7. Zelenograd (Russia) — History. 8. Technology transfer — Soviet Union. I. Title.
UB271.S652B47 2005
327.1247073'0922 — dc22

2005015436

A catalogue record for this book is available from the Library of Congress and the British Library.

The paper in this book meets the guidelines for permanence and durability of the Committee on Production Guidelines for Book Longevity of the Council on Library Resources.

To Elena and Maxime

Contents

Preface

In September 1990, while in Moscow researching an article on Soviet-American technology transfer, I was introduced to a Russian scientist named Joseph Berg. The American business consultant who arranged our meeting told me Berg had developed an innovative system for producing integrated circuits. In our initial conversation, I asked Berg, a tall, gregarious, and obviously very intelligent man who appeared to be well past seventy, how he came to speak English so well. "Well, we have good schools here," was his first response. I pointed out that no school could produce such a classic Brooklyn accent. Berg then explained that he had grown up in a neighborhood in Johannesburg with a lot of Americans. Berg's story didn't add up, but it was a time, the last months of the Soviet Union, when many people were reinventing themselves.

Although we'd known each other for only an hour, Berg invited me to accompany him to a lunch meeting at a hotel near the Kremlin, where he introduced me to a tall, elegant man, one of the USSR's foremost rocket engine designers. After lunch, Berg asked me to join him in the back seat of a Volga sedan to visit a place he said few Americans had seen. We traveled north, up Gorky Street to the Leningrad highway toward the airport, then veered off, passed through some villages, and after about forty-five minutes came to a large city, home to over 200,000 people. The car passed Futurist style buildings, a movie theater named Elektron, billboards displaying the faces of model workers, and factories with illuminated Communist slogans stuck onto their roofs before stopping near a large statue of Lenin. The statue stood in front of a modern office building with a somewhat mysterious sign, "*Nauchni Tsentr,*" on its roof. It was the "Scientific Center," Berg told me, the brain center of the Soviet microelectronics and computer industry, and we were in a satellite city called Zelenograd, the Soviet Union's version of Silicon Valley.

Perhaps out of modesty — or caution — Berg didn't tell me anything about his role in creating Zelenograd and the Scientific Center. He did describe some of the work being done there, how shiny silicon cylinders were trucked into Zelenograd and sophisticated microelectronic devices, including microchips and computers, were shipped out. Most of the activities taking place at that time in the Center and the other buildings in Zelenograd were strictly classified, and Berg was taking a substantial risk in bringing a foreigner whom he barely knew to the city.

The next weekend I accepted Berg's invitation to attend a "musicale" at his apartment in Leningrad. The event was memorable because of the excellent classical music, lively conversation — and the fact that half of the people who called Berg to confirm the timing of the event said they were staying home when he informed them that an American journalist would be present. They worked in defense plants, Berg told me, and were afraid that socializing with a foreigner would cause trouble. I later learned that when they arrived at work on Monday, several of the people who attended the party had to file a written report with the "first department," the KGB security office, revealing that they had been in contact with a foreigner. (Although the name of the Soviet intelligence service changed several times from 1917 to 1992, the organization's mission was constant, and its structure changed little. For the sake of simplicity, in the following pages all these organizations are referred to as the KGB, the Russian abbreviation for Committee for State Security.)

I didn't learn for several months, until a friend brought a five-year-old article to my attention, that Berg had another identity, that in the United States he was known as Joel Barr, and that he was closely linked with Julius Rosenberg, who had been executed as a Soviet spy.

Although almost half a century separated our births, Joel Barr and I formed a close friendship that endured for the remainder of his life. I stayed with him several times in Leningrad (and St. Petersburg, as it came to be known), and he lived with me for weeks or months at a time in Washington, D.C., becoming a part of my family. Barr and I started work on his autobiography several times, but the project always flew off the rails as he became more interested in fantasizing about how things could and should have been and less concerned about what really happened. I abandoned the project altogether after receiving news of his death in June 1998. The idea resurfaced about six months later when a surprise package containing over 3,000 pages of the FBI's files on Barr arrived on my doorstep. Then I remembered that in 1995 Barr and I had on a whim walked into FBI headquarters in the J. Edgar Hoover Building to request the files under the Freedom of Information Act.

It took a couple of years for the idea to gel in my mind; finally, in 2002, I started to research this book seriously, traveling to Russia to interview his former co-workers and friends, and to the Czech Republic to visit his relatives and obtain records from the archives of the Communist regime's secret police. The book also includes material from hundreds of hours of interviews and informal discussions with Barr from 1990 to 1998.

Barr's story cannot be told separately from that of Alfred Sarant, the man whom Barr recruited into espionage in New York and who was Barr's senior partner in Leningrad and Moscow as they tried to reshape the face of Soviet technology. This book dwells more on Barr's life simply because I knew him well.

I had three goals when I set out to write *Engineering Communism*. The first was to tell a remarkable story that combines espionage, the Cold War, and tangled dramas of love and betrayal. On the personal level, Barr and Sarant were extraordinary in part because, unlike virtually every other defector from the West to the Soviet Union, they led happy, productive lives there. Many other spies who escaped to the USSR were despised and distrusted by their Soviet counterparts; few adjusted to life in the totalitarian society they had risked their lives for; and quite a few drank themselves to death.

The second task I set for myself was to offer some insight into why the Soviet Union failed to harness its tremendous human talent and abundant natural resources to create technologies comparable to those that blossomed in other developed countries in the second half of the twentieth century. Walking in Zelenograd or talking with Russian scientists and engineers in their seventies and eighties about their space program, I'm always vividly reminded of the tremendous sacrifices of the 1940s, the hopeful idealistic commitment and optimism of the 1960s, and how these hopes were dashed in the dreary 1970s and 1980s. Berg's and Sarant's experiences put these dreams and disappointments into perspective.

The third goal was to explain why Barr became an ardent Communist willing to risk everything to help the Soviet Union. Barr's motivations, similar to those of other Americans of his generation who spied for the Soviet Union, could provide an idea of a mindset that is hard to fathom today, one that was shaped by a world that has vanished.

Barr never explicitly admitted his espionage activities, and as far as I know neither did Sarant. In contrast to his adamant public denials, in private conversations with me Barr simply declined to discuss specific questions about spying. He acknowledged that Julius Rosenberg passed some information to the Soviet Union, but he denied that it included any atomic secrets. Barr did, however, talk about why he, Sarant, and Rosenberg felt a greater loyalty to the Soviet Union than to the United States and why they considered it acceptable to pass on secret information to the USSR. He felt that this loyalty was appropriate because the Soviet Union was the only nation on earth trying to build the communist utopia he fervently believed in, and that it justified passing secret information to the USSR during World War II, when the United States and the USSR were allies in the fight against fascism, and after the war, when he feared the United States would use its monopoly on atomic weapons to destroy the Soviet experiment.

Not only a wealth of circumstantial evidence, but also compelling data from decrypted messages sent by Soviet intelligence operatives — fruits of a U.S. Army operation codenamed "Venona" — and several other sources directly confirm Barr's and Sarant's espionage. The memoirs of Alexander Feklisov, a retired KGB officer who says he was Barr's and Rosenberg's case officer during World War II, are credible, as are KGB files that were fleetingly unveiled to a historian, Allen Weinstein, and his assistant, Alexander Vassiliev, a former KGB officer.

Barr himself wrote some of the most compelling evidence. These are his notes, scribbled into an address book, describing what can only have been clandestine meetings with a professional intelligence service. The logistical details of these meetings are almost identical with those described by Americans who contemporaneously spied for the KGB.

In the course of researching this book, I ran into individuals in Russia and the United States who tried to convince me either not to write it or to skew it to support their political beliefs. In Russia, some engineers and patriots are infuriated by the notion that two Americans played a catalytic role in creating Soviet microelectronics. They feel this somehow denigrates the skills and accomplishments of the homegrown engineers who labored in the USSR.

In the United States, I encountered historians on the political left who cryptically cautioned me to tread carefully because I was touching "sensitive" topics. It didn't become apparent to me what this meant until Morton Sobell, the Rosenbergs' codefendant who spent almost two decades in federal prisons, told me that it was "pointless to uncover and write the truth if it doesn't serve 'the cause.'" On the right, I encountered commentators who cited Barr's case as vindication of Joseph McCarthy and evidence of widespread treason among American politicians and civil servants.

Despite my affection for Barr, I have attempted to provide an unvarnished version of his and Sarant's lives, and to leave it to others to decide whether they were heroes, villains, idealists, fools, or a combination of all of these. I will, however, address some of the political implications of this book.

The fact is that two Americans founded and briefly led the Soviet micro-electronics industry. This doesn't mean that Russians couldn't have done something similar, or even better. It is also impossible to know what would have happened if Barr and Sarant had remained in high positions longer than they did. They imagined that a few more years would have been enough to put the Soviet Union on track to leapfrog ahead of the United States, that the first personal computer would have been created in a suburb of Moscow, not Silicon Valley. They were almost certainly wrong: their achievements were exceptions that stood in sharp contrast to a dysfunctional system that crushed innovation and stifled independent scientific or artistic expression.

The notion that the truth should be skewed or suppressed in order to serve a cause is repugnant and in my view shameful. Some of the individuals who expressed concern about the "sensitivity" of American Communist espionage in general, and the Rosenberg case in particular, cited the excesses of Mc-Carthyism. Enough time has passed, I hope, for students of American history to hold two notions in their heads at the same time: Joseph McCarthy was a demagogic bully who did great damage to his country; the Communist Party of the United States was a subsidiary of the Communist Party of the Soviet Union that actively engaged in and supported espionage. McCarthy ranted about Barr and Sarant, but the only new information about them allegedly uncovered by his "investigations" was false. His contention that their former colleagues at the U.S. Army Signal Corps Laboratories continued to spy for the Soviet Union into the 1950s was incorrect, and it led to the pointless persecution of many innocent people.

Barr's story adds color and depth to the portraits that have been painted of Julius and Ethel Rosenberg. No one who looks at the evidence can seriously doubt that Julius Rosenberg was a source of secret information to the KGB, as well as the recruiter and leader of a remarkably successful espionage ring. Ethel was aware of her husband's espionage and actively supported it — for example, by recruiting her brother to spy on the Manhattan Project.

I have uncovered new details about the significance of the technologies the Rosenberg ring supplied to the USSR. Although there is room for disagreement about the value of the atomic information Rosenberg conveyed to the

KGB, there can be no doubt that the specifications about radar, the proximity fuse, jet engines, and analog computers that he, Barr, Sarant, Sobell, and their comrades provided were extremely valuable to the USSR, especially during the early years of the Cold War.

While researching and writing this book, I received valuable assistance and encouragement from many people in the United States, Russia, and the Czech Republic, including some who for reasons of space limitations are not acknowledged below.

I couldn't have even begun without the assistance of my wife, Elena Gerasimov, who helped in every phase: research, translation, writing, and editing.

Ken Jacobson read the entire manuscript and made innumerable valuable suggestions regarding both content and presentation. Carl Feldbaum provided insightful comments on the manuscript.

Kirill Chashchin and Vadim Altskan helped me with research in the former Soviet Union. I also appreciate the assistance of William Benson, John Haynes, and Ron Radosh for their advice and help with American sources. Jan Frolik, Director of the Archive Division of the Interior Ministry of the Czech Republic, was efficient and helpful. Madeline Vadkerty and Peter Kolarik helped translate Czech documents.

Joel Barr's family — his wife, Vera Bergova, and their children, Robert, Vivian, Anton, and Alena — were generous with their time and memories, as was Alfred Sarant's daughter, Kristina Staros. Henry Eric Firdman helped immensely, especially with the technical details of Sarant's and Barr's accomplishments in the Soviet Union.

I thank two of Barr's comrades from the 1930s and 1940s, Morton Sobell and William Danziger, for sharing their views, recognizing that they may not be pleased by some aspects of this book.

Other friends who helped include Karen Bernstein and David Flores, Sergei and Lyudmilla Gerasimov, and Lev Borshevsky.

Any errors I have made in spite of all the assistance I received are, of course, entirely my responsibility.

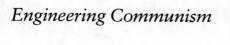

Engineering Communism

Initiation

Nikita Khrushchev, a baggy suit hanging loosely over his pear-shaped body and a neat row of medals pinned over his right breast, hugged Philip Staros and drew Joseph Berg close. The first secretary of the Communist Party took a step back and pointed at the men crowded around him — the commander-in-chief of the Soviet Navy, the top military brass in charge of the defense industry, and the leadership of the Communist Party in Leningrad. "If any of these *bureaucrats* gets in your way, if you need anything at all, let me know and I'll personally take care of it," Khrushchev growled. It was an extraordinary offer, granting the leaders of an obscure R&D outfit with a few hundred employees direct access to the most powerful man in the nation. But, coming at the end of a day when the two engineers had achieved recognition almost beyond their wildest dreams, it seemed natural.[1]

Khrushchev had just approved Staros and Berg's plan to invest hundreds of millions of rubles to build an entire city on the outskirts of Moscow. The new city would be devoted to researching and producing a new generation of electronics technology, from integrated circuits to digital computers — a secret Soviet version of the Silicon Valley that was forming about the same time in California. He'd made it clear that Staros and Berg would be in charge and could rely on the full might of the Soviet state to support the project. They would also have the freedom to recruit the best and the brightest, as well as the authority to cut through the red tape that strangled most Russian efforts to innovate.

It was the afternoon of May 4, 1962, and Khrushchev was wrapping up a visit to Design Bureau-2 (KB-2) in Leningrad. A few hours earlier, Berg and Staros had pressed their noses to the window of the bureau's offices in the Palace of Soviets, looking down on Moscow Square as Khrushchev and his entourage spilled out of black limousines. Bulky military leaders and their thin aides disappeared from view as they entered the massive, neoclassical Stalinist-style edifice. They entered the largest office building in Leningrad under signs proclaiming: "The USSR is a socialist state of workers and peasants" and "Long Live Leninism!"

Khrushchev stepped off the elevator on the third floor and was quickly introduced to the Design Bureau's director, Staros, and its chief engineer, Berg. The officials accompanying Khrushchev — especially Dmitriy Ustinov, head of the Military Industrial Commission (VPK), a powerful body that controlled Soviet defense R&D and production, and Admiral Sergei Gorshkov, the commander-in-chief who was determined to harness technology to achieve Peter the Great's dream of creating a world-class Russian Navy — were already well acquainted with Staros and Berg.

Speaking in a more refined Russian than Khrushchev, with just a trace of an unidentifiable accent, maybe Byelorussian, Staros started the tour, guiding the group into a large hall that looked and even smelled like the future. The men passed by a score of pretty young women wearing white lab coats, hats, and gloves, seated behind gleaming counters, peering into microscopes and expertly manipulating mysterious tiny objects. As they walked, Staros described the physical properties of certain elements that could be coaxed into switching from conductors to nonconductors of electricity, and how an entire industry was being built around these *poluprovotniki* (semiconductors). He predicted that Soviet power would soon rest on the nation's ability to create diminutive components and microelectronic devices incorporating them, not on the huge dams and steel plants that dominated Five-Year Plans. If resources were shifted to the miniature world in which advances were measured in microns and milliseconds, Russia would transform itself into the dominant world power in the coming decade, he promised.

Next, Staros and Berg flattered and surprised Khrushchev, who was far more comfortable on a collective farm than in a high-tech lab, with a demonstration of a computer database that responded to queries by spitting out basic information about the Soviet leader. The delegation viewed colorful posters, more like an American advertising campaign than a typical Soviet technology briefing, depicting industrial and especially military advances that could be achieved if the USSR pursued a vigorous program to develop microelectronics — a word that Staros had literally introduced into the Russian language. The pictures promised networks of spy satellites beaming detailed pictures of North American military installations to Russia, antiaircraft missiles defending the Soviet Union, and guided rockets capable of reaching targets in North America. All of this would flow from the Center for Microelectronics, Staros and Berg's modest name for the new enterprise they asked Khrushchev to create. Modeled on America's Bell Laboratories, but a hundred times larger, the Center would surpass anything existing or contemplated in the West, enabling the Soviet Union to shoot past the capitalist countries in the race to automate industry, Staros confidently predicted.

The visit to KB-2 was timed perfectly for Berg and Staros, at the apogee of Khrushchev's exuberance over technology: two years after Soviet missiles had shot a U-2 spy plane out of the sky, signaling the USSR's ability to marshal high technology in the defense of its borders; a year after Yuri Gagarin had won the race to be the first man in space, lending credibility to Russia's claims to global scientific and technological preeminence; and a few weeks after Khrushchev had conceived the idea to "throw a hedgehog down Uncle Sam's pants" by placing nuclear-tipped missiles in Cuba. Staros and Berg's vision of racing ahead of America, the "main adversary," in Soviet military parlance, was enticing. But the Soviet leader was most enthralled by a tiny radio, no bigger than a hearing aid, which KB-2 had presented to him as a memento of the visit. At the beginning of the visit, Staros placed the radio in Khrushchev's ear while Berg, who had overcome his partner's skepticism to create the "Era" receiver, watched from behind. Their joy over his enthusiasm turned to irritation when the first secretary kept the Era turned on for the entire afternoon. All the sophisticated talk about microns and circuits was impossible for him to evaluate, but the radio was tangible proof that these two young engineers who shared his romantic passion for the Communist cause were the real thing.[2]

Khrushchev loved a good toy, he liked engineers — as a young man he'd dreamed of becoming one — and he trusted Staros and Berg. They had risked their lives to help defend the USSR against Nazi Germany during the Great Patriotic War, had recently made impressive technological breakthroughs, and, perhaps most important, had created an atmosphere of infectious can-do optimism at KB-2 that stood in sharp contrast to the sycophancy and fear that surrounded most Soviet administrators.

KB-2 was named after KB-1, a top-secret design bureau created by Sergo Beria, the son of the feared head of Stalin's intelligence services, Lavrenty Beria, that had developed Moscow's antiaircraft system. By 1962 the Berias were gone, the father shot on Khrushchev's orders in 1953 and the son exiled to a mid-level engineering job in the provinces, but the cult of concealment that permeated Stalinist Russia had not disappeared. Almost everything related to KB-2's activities was a state secret, even its existence, so it was routine to classify as secret the document ordering the transformation of the muddy fields adjacent to Kryukovo, a sleepy village on the outskirts of Moscow, into Zelenograd (Green City), a new metropolis dedicated to realizing Staros and Berg's dreams of a high-tech launchpad for Soviet dominance of the coming computer age.[3]

Nothing about Zelenograd was more secret than the real identities of the two engineers who conceived it, the fathers of the Soviet microelectronics industry. Berg's own wife didn't learn his real name, birth date, or nationality for more than twenty years after their marriage. Khrushchev was among no more than a dozen people outside the KGB who knew that Berg and Staros were Americans who had slipped under the Iron Curtain a few steps ahead of the FBI, that their real names were Joel Barr and Alfred Sarant, and that they were intimately connected to one of the most controversial espionage trials of the twentieth century.

Barr's story began, as it ended, in Russia, in the pursuit of a better life in a more just society. His father, Benjamin Zbarsky, was born in 1886 in Lubny, Ukraine, a small city on the fringe of the Russian empire. To an extent that is difficult to imagine today, ethnicity shaped an individual's destiny in tsarist Russia, especially for Jews like the Zbarskys. "At no time could the life of the Jews in Russia have been described as comfortable," according to Irving Howe, a sociologist whose background and early years resembled Barr's. "Rarely were the Jews able to ease their guard against blows from above and below, bureaucrats and folk, and never could they see themselves as citizens like all others. Their role as pariahs, the stiff-necked enemies of Christ, was fixed both in official doctrine and popular legend. Repression took the forms of economic harassment and legal humiliation, sometimes pogroms and accusations of ritual blood murder," Howe added.[4] Sholem Aleichem, the chronicler of Yiddish life, served as official rabbi in Lubny shortly before Benjamin was born and witnessed a particularly vicious pogrom there in March 1881.

The Zbarskys were prosperous participants in a vibrant, but intensely introverted, Yiddish culture. Benjamin's father, Isidore, was a rabbi and the owner of a sawmill; Benjamin's two older sisters were physicians. The family was swept up in the tumultuous social and political events of the early twentieth century, first encouraged by Tsar Nicholas II's declaration of religious tolerance in 1903, and then threatened by the widespread pogroms that ravaged the south and southwest of Russia from 1903 to 1905. Hopes rose again in the summer of 1905, when the tsar promised political liberalization in an effort to quell rising anger over the loss of the Russo-Japan War, only to be dashed again in the autumn when Leon Trotsky and the Mensheviks overplayed their hand, launching a feeble, easily crushed attempt to establish a Soviet government. Benjamin's sisters participated in the strikes and demonstrations in Moscow that precipitated the failed Revolution of 1905.

The form of reaction varied throughout the empire, but in most places the tsar's authority was reinforced violently. In Ukraine, the assertion of Romanov rule was accompanied by pogroms. Benjamin Zbarsky probably participated in the defense committee that the Jewish population of Lubny organized in 1905. The committee repelled an attack, but it was obvious that the violence could recur without warning, and the next time it might be devastating. Zbarsky didn't wait to find out. He married Rebecca Dobrowolsky, a fifteen-year-old orphan, and late that year joined a wave of Jewish immigration from Russia to the United States.

Like countless immigrants before and after them, Benjamin and Rebecca Zbarsky were anglicized on Ellis Island: by the time the couple reached Manhattan, they were Mr. and Mrs. Barr. The Barrs settled in Brooklyn, on the bottom rung of the economic ladder, and for decades, every time they climbed a bit higher, they were knocked back down. Living in a series of cramped apartments in densely populated neighborhoods, the Barrs and their neighbors relived the claustrophobic intimacy, and retained many of the traditions and habits, of the East European shtetels.

The Barrs' first child, Bernard, was born in 1912; their second, Joyel, arrived on New Year's Day 1916. The next April, Benjamin, who was working as a builder, was naturalized as a U.S. citizen. When the Barrs' third son, Arthur, was born on October 17, 1917, the tenements of Brooklyn and the Lower East Side of Manhattan were buzzing with news of the fall of the tsar, and two weeks later with news of Ukraine's declaration of independence. Over the next few years, as Russia boiled, there were discussions in nearly every immigrant household about returning from the New World to the new world that was taking shape in their homeland. Although thousands of Jews returned, the majority, like the Barrs, had already grown roots in America and remained there.[5]

A thin, unathletic kid, Joyel was beaten up by street gangs of older, tougher boys on his way to and from Public School 156. He grew up believing in a stern and vengeful God, terrified that he would be struck down for minor transgressions of the strict rules his father and the rabbis taught, or for the gradually accumulating doubts that turned into a lifelong antipathy to religion. Joyel went through the motions of a bar mitzvah in 1929, but by that time he'd already rejected Judaism and begun to absorb the tenets of another all-encompassing belief system: Communism. Embarrassed by the foreign and effeminate sound of his name, he changed Joyel to Joel.[6]

While attending Tilden High School in East Flatbush, Joel developed a fascination with technology, building a telescope and a ham radio from scrounged parts. He read voraciously, absorbing all he could about science, and also studying the pamphlets, newspapers, and tracts distributed by various socialist and Communist factions. The streets, where Barr and other boys spent a great deal of time, provided a panorama of practical politics. Speakers on soapboxes castigated the exploiting class, and as the Depression deepened, banks closed their doors, businesses folded, and the crowds of unemployed men grew larger. There was nothing abstract about the collapse of capitalism; Barr saw the human toll all around him, particularly in his own family.

As Joel was growing more confident and outgoing, putting the terrors of bullies and religion behind him, Benjamin was sliding into despair. During Joel's high school years his father, who had lost his job as a salesman for the New York Life Insurance Company in 1929, suffered a series of increasingly humiliating financial setbacks. First his car was repossessed. Not only wasn't there enough money to make the car payments, but it was getting hard to put food on the table. "If someone were to ask me now what is the main element which formed my character, I would say the poverty that we lived in," Barr said six decades later. He remembered going hungry, that "living on relief was a tremendous blow to our egos. There was a joy in getting a big bag of groceries once a week, but it left scars on our characters."[7]

One day in the early 1930s Joel returned home to see his family's belongings on the sidewalk, guarded by his crying mother. Joel was at home a half-year later when beefy marshals arrived early in the morning to haul the furniture into the streets in front of another Brooklyn apartment building. The evictions made a tremendous impression. Joel spoke of them vividly sixty years later, citing the incidents as turning points that convinced him of the cruelty of capitalism. "It was a tremendously harrowing scene, when the marshal came and put the furniture out on the street," Barr recalled. The family lived in a series of apartments, staying one step ahead of the law. "These places were substandard by any standard, with no toilet in the apartment, no hot water, only a coal stove for heat. The El [elevated train] going right by our windows meant that every few minutes you had to stop talking."

Barr's family wasn't unique. Every day on the way to school, Joel passed men who a few years earlier had been professionals with good incomes but were now reduced to selling apples on street corners and standing in soup lines. For the poor anywhere in America in the 1920s and 1930s, it was difficult to believe that capitalism was the path forward to a prosperous future. In the tenements and sweatshops of Brooklyn, the Lower East Side, and Harlem, it was particularly easy for the children of East European immigrants to put their faith in Communism, the force that appeared to be transforming Russia, the most backward region in Europe, into a progressive, egalitarian nation. The Barrs read and believed reports that the Soviet Union's planned economy had inoculated it against the Depression and drew conclusions from the presence of a number of Jews in the new government's leadership, in stark contrast to the WASPs who constituted American "society" and its political elite. Benjamin Barr was not alone when he decided that Russian Communism was the only viable alternative to the militaristic fascism that was infecting Europe.

It seemed clear to Barr and to many of his classmates at Tilden High that the world was dividing into two opposed camps, Communism and fascism, and there wasn't any doubt about which was better. Barr, living in poverty, alienated both from parents who retained the accents and manners of their homelands and from mainstream American culture, felt there was plenty of evidence that America was on the wrong side of the struggle. In addition to his own family's bitter experiences, he heard Henry Ford and Father Coughlin speaking on the radio about their hatred for Jews, read about the bosses' violent union-busting, and witnessed segregation that made blacks third-class citizens. From the streets of Brooklyn in the early 1930s, it looked as though America was heading toward social and economic catastrophe that would turn out like Germany's in the 1920s — or Russia's in 1917.

Speaking about it decades later, Barr and many others who grew up in New York during the Depression used the same expression when asked how they first learned about Communism. "It was in the air," they said. The *Daily Worker* was sold on street corners and slipped under apartment doors along with other leftist literature. There were Young Communist League chapters in high schools. Barr knew kids at Tilden who were members of the school's YCL chapter, and although he didn't join, he was tempted. The party was exciting for romantic teenage boys, combining the comradeship of a club, the thrill of shared secrets — its origins in the Russian underground were preserved through the use of "party names" and covert meetings — and a sense of belonging to an elite.

The contrast between the poverty and hopelessness of Depression-era New York and the fantastic Soviet world depicted in the *Daily Worker* and especially Russian films, a world in which workers ascended from the Donbas coal mines, washed up, and attended operas in the evenings, could not have been more stark. When anyone tried to convince Barr that life in the "workers' paradise" was hell, that there were famine in rural Ukraine and bloody repression in the cities — facts that were reported in some newspapers at the time, while many, including the *New York Times*, reported rosy propaganda — he'd reject the heresy as capitalist lies. For every person who returned from Russia with tales of terror and starvation, there were ten like George Bernard Shaw who extolled the virtues of the Soviet experiment.[8]

Barr's family and those of his friends rarely if ever traveled beyond New York's five boroughs and the adjacent areas of New Jersey. Intellectually and emotionally they were more closely connected with Moscow and Kiev than with Minneapolis or Oklahoma City. Barr was ignorant of how the vast majority of Americans lived. The Communist literary figure Lionel Abel reflected the mood of a large portion of the city's intelligentsia when he said that in the 1930s "Politically, New York became the most interesting part of the Soviet Union. For it became the one part of that country in which the struggle between Stalin and Trotsky could be openly expressed. And was! And how!"[9]

Even at the height of its influence, the Communist Party of America was marginal on a national scale, never attracting more than 105,000 votes. This wasn't how it looked to Barr, however. Membership was concentrated in New York, where the vast majority consisted of the children of Jewish East European immigrants. Most of the people Barr knew as a teenager were sympathetic to Communism, even if they weren't party members, and the biggest crowds he'd ever seen were the tens of thousands who attended Communist rallies and scuffled with socialists and the police in Union Square on May Day. From Barr's vantage point, Communism wasn't a fringe movement at all. Rather, it was a vehicle that would carry him from his mother's world of superstitious religion, Russian folk traditions, and a hazy image of America viewed from the bottom of society into a dynamic future.[10]

Soviet Communism was born from the Russian people's war weariness, and from the start it preached that armed conflicts — except of course those to defend the revolution — were provoked to enrich arms merchants and other capitalists at the expense of the working classes. Antipathy to militarism and distrust of government were not limited to Communists; the generation born during and just after World War I on both sides of the Atlantic came naturally to its antiwar philosophy. When Barr's graduating class at Tilden High School was asked in 1932 to sign a pledge of loyalty to federal and state governments, which they accurately interpreted as a commitment to obey orders to fight, they balked. Barr joined about 100 of the 500 graduating seniors who objected to promising "absolute and unconditional" loyalty to government. When the principal explained that the pledge was just a formality, and that anyone who persisted in rejecting it would not receive a diploma, Barr and all his peers reluctantly signed the paper.[11]

Harking back to their first encounter with college, the 1938 City College of New York (CCNY) yearbook reminded members of Barr's graduating class how their college life had begun in February 1934. "Nervous and naked, we coughed and bent ten times, had our chests tapped and our blood-pressure taken. We underwent a psychological test that asked us to fill in without thinking the space after 'My stomach ____.' " "*Is empty,*" Barr, who stood six feet tall, weighed less than 140 pounds, and looked like a walking skeleton, might have answered.

Looking around as he stood stripped to his briefs, waiting for a doctor to declare him physically fit to endure the rigors of college life, Barr found that he had a lot in common with the other boys in line. Most came from poor families (one of the most attractive aspects of the college was the free tuition), many were the sons of immigrants, and a high proportion were extremely intelligent. Intellectually, City College boys (girls were not admitted) were on a par with their more affluent peers at Ivy League colleges, but in other ways they were quite different.

Even if he could have afforded the tuition, Barr, like most of his classmates, would probably not have been accepted at Yale, Harvard, or other elite colleges, which had unwritten but strictly enforced quotas on Jews. In the 1920s and 1930s, the wealthy neighborhoods, social clubs, and white-shoe law firms that the parents of Ivy League students inhabited, and their children were groomed to join, were tightly closed to the children of poor immigrants who attended CCNY, regardless of their talent. Friendships forged on the playing fields at private schools like St. Paul's and Andover, and later in college dorms and over meals in elegant dining halls, prepared the Ivy Leaguers for respectable positions in business and government. City College kids commuted to school on the subway, ate lunch out of paper bags, and didn't expect to have jobs when they graduated.

"Going to school in the thirties was strictly an act of faith or a manifestation of love of learning for its own sake," recalled Morton Sobell, one of Barr's close friends at CCNY. "We were all aware that the large corporations did not hire City College engineering graduates. For one thing, we were considered too radical; for another, most students were Jewish (to many people, this was redundant). The large corporations openly practiced discrimination against Jews and Blacks at this time." Bill Danziger, a friend of Sobell's at Stuyvesant High School who was also a member of Barr's social circle at CCNY, remembered that at the time he chose to study engineering in college he'd never met or heard of anyone who was employed as an engineer.[12]

Students in the Ivy League staged polite debates on abstract topics, modeled on the Oxford Union. For Barr and his friends, college life was a nonstop debate, argued as if one's life depended on it, often conducted at a shout and occasionally turning into a brawl.

CCNY had a well-deserved reputation in the 1930s as the nation's most radical campus. It featured both a Marxist Cultural Society and a very active branch of the Young Communist League. As at other colleges, there were two main political groupings at CCNY, but they weren't Democrats and Republicans. The major political tension on campus was between pro-Stalin Communists and a minority of Trotskyites. No American college came close to matching CCNY's level of activism until the upheavals of the late 1960s. Looking back half a century later, Irving Howe remembered that during the period when Barr attended, there was an "atmosphere of perfervid, overly heated, overly excited intellectuality" at CCNY.[13]

For the most part, the caliber of the faculty did not match the acuity of the student body. Although Barr and his peers were largely self-taught, the lack of academic leadership did not reduce the rigor of their education. Most of the learning at CCNY took place in informal settings, particularly in alcoves in the school cafeteria. As Howe reported, in "the years between the world wars, City College took on a legendary character, a school at once grubby and exalted: the passionate alcoves where revolutionary position-takers argued 'the correct line.'" Although they hung out in the cafeteria, Barr and his comrades couldn't the afford dime hot dogs — it was front-page news in the CCNY student newspaper when the price was halved to a nickel in November 1936 — so the young revolutionaries brought home-cooked meals packed by their mothers.[14]

For a politically conscious student like Barr, choosing which alcove to affiliate himself with was at least as important as selecting a major. He picked alcove 2, known throughout CCNY as "the Kremlin" because it was home to pro-Stalin Communists and electrical engineering. Leon Wofsy, who entered CCNY in 1938 a few months before Barr graduated, painted in his memoir a portrait of life in alcove 2 that applied also to the preceding four years. "There were no formal speeches, just questions and answers, and dialogue open to anyone who cared to debate — anyone, that is, except the Trotskyists whose hangout was next door in Alcove 1. In my eyes, Trotskyists were almost as evil as fascists, and fraternizing would have been a sin. Looking back, we young Communists brought together a strange mixture of lively, logical minds and dogmatic beliefs. We were tireless activists and effective social critics, ready to question anything except our faith in Soviet socialism."[15]

Soon after his induction into CCNY's Kremlin, Barr developed a close friendship with another electrical engineering student who was even more passionate about politics. Julius Rosenberg had grown up on the Lower East Side of Manhattan and as a teenager had seriously considered becoming a rabbi. He later said that he converted to Communism when instructors at the Downtown Talmud Torah refused to join him at protests against the imprisonment of a labor organizer and in support of the Scottsboro Boys, black men who had been falsely charged and imprisoned for the rape of two white women. Rosenberg studied Marxism with the intensity of a talmudic scholar, and he didn't let the requirements of the engineering curriculum interfere with his political education.[16]

At least half of the 100 students in the electrical engineering class of 1938 considered themselves Communists. Rosenberg was the commissar of an informal cell drawn from the engineering school that included Barr, Sobell, Max Elichter, Danziger, and Bill Perl (at the time, his last name was Mutterperl; William and his brother Samuel legally changed their last names to Perl in 1945). They had a lot in common: all were poor and Jewish, and their fathers had emigrated from Russia in the final decades of the nineteenth century. At CCNY they shared a dream of using engineering knowledge to build Communism, which in their view meant helping the Soviet Union and transforming the United States into a Soviet America.[17]

Most of the other members of his circle were brighter than Rosenberg, but none could match his single-minded commitment to Communism. Rosenberg, "Julie" to his friends, was the group's undisputed ideological guide. He lacked Perl's academic brilliance and Barr's charm or self-confidence, but he was a ferocious defender of the Stalinist orthodoxy that bound the group together. "Fellow students who chanced to disagree with him found him a doctrinaire and inflexible opponent; however, his friends admired his ability to verbally demolish the occasional Trotskyist troublemaker bold enough to venture into their alcove. Julie was to be affectionately remembered as a stalwart who never missed a leafleting session, a demonstration, or a meeting."[18]

The electrical engineering program at CCNY was less than a decade old when Barr and his friends enrolled. It was obvious to them that society was on the cusp of a major technological transformation and that it would be powered by electricity. They were also convinced that capitalists were holding back progress. A regular column in the *Daily Worker,* "Laboratory and Shop: Notes on Science and Technology," influenced Barr. The July 4, 1934, column reflected his sentiments. "At present, American workers and farmers could enjoy the highest standard of living in the history of mankind . . . if they would cut the fetters that capitalism has clamped upon technological change. A technological revolution is maturing which would ensure plenty to all of mankind, but this revolution in technique has come up against the barriers of capitalist social relations. It cannot come to fruition unless it is preceded by the overthrow of capitalism." The article concluded: "Capitalism cannot push through the revolution in technique. It calls a halt on scientific advance; it diverts science into the channels of war. The complete technological revolution can only take place in the Soviet Union. It will take place in America only under a Soviet system."[19]

Electrical engineering students had to suffer through two years of humanities courses before moving on to technical subjects. Although the teaching was indifferent, the tests were extremely tough; only a tenth of the students who entered the engineering school made it to graduation. Barr found time, however, for politics, particularly the antifascist and antiwar movements that were the meeting ground for Communist and more mainstream leftists. On April 13, 1934, he joined about 800 students at the CCNY flagpole for an antiwar strike that had been prohibited by the college administration. New York police and instructors from the hated Military Science Department forcefully broke it up. The melee was a warm-up for the next major political campus political confrontation.

CCNY students were outraged when they learned in September 1934 that the college president, Frederick Robinson, had invited a group of Italian students to visit the campus to address an assembly. The gesture was considered an expression of support for Il Duce, but Robinson refused to comply with the students' demands that he cancel the assembly. On the morning of October 9 a "mass anti-fascist picket line" was formed outside the hall where the Italians were scheduled to speak. Inside, Robinson's welcoming remarks provoked boos and hisses, leading him to exclaim that the students' behavior "was worse than that of a guttersnipe." When a CCNY student grabbed the microphone and began to address "the enslaved, tricked Italian students laboring under Fascism," a faculty member attacked him. City College students jumped to his defense, the Italians intervened on the faculty's side, and "a riot resulted," the CCNY yearbook reported. "Two thousand students who had jammed the Great Hall were involved in the subsequent disorder. The visiting students were led out through a back way to the president's office." Barr and Rosenberg joined the throng who marched through the campus. The next day they were among the students sporting "I'm a guttersnipe" buttons.[20]

Barr enthusiastically read two monthly magazines, *New Masses,* a literary journal, and *Soviet Russia Today,* which was filled with photos and stories about heroic teams building hydroelectric dams and the successes of collectivized farms (at a time when in reality there was mass starvation in the Ukraine, so bad that there were isolated instances of cannibalism) and occasionally printed elaborate procommunist essays by American intellectuals. In the September 1934 issue, for example, Roger Baldwin, founder and director of the American Civil Liberties Union, responded to critics who wondered how he could support civil liberties in the United States and "at the same time support the proletarian dictatorship of the Soviet Union." He argued that while dictatorship was bad in principle, it was acceptable in the Soviet Union, which "has already created liberties far greater than exist elsewhere in the world. They are liberties that most closely affect the lives of the people — power in the trade unions, in peasant organizations, in the cultural life of nationalities, freedom of women in public and private life, and a tremendous development of education for adults and children." The champion of civil liberties proclaimed that "when the power of the working class is once achieved, as it has been only in the Soviet Union, I am for maintaining it by any means whatsoever."[21]

Baldwin's response to personally meeting individuals who had been brutally repressed by the Soviet secret police was incredible. "While I sympathized with personal distress I just could not bring myself to get excited over the suppression of opposition when I stacked it up against what I saw of fresh, vigorous expressions of free living by workers and peasants all over the land. And further, no champion of a socialist society could fail to see that some suppression was necessary to achieve it." America's leading civil liberties advocate also stated: "While I have some reservations about party policy in relation to internal democracy, and some criticisms of the unnecessary persecution of political opponents, the fundamentals of liberty are firmly fixed in the USSR. And they are fixed on the only ground on which liberty really matters — economic. No class to exploit the workers and peasants; wide sharing of control in the economic organizations; and the wealth produced is common property." Baldwin concluded: "And if American champions of civil liberty could all think in terms of economic freedom as the goal of their labors, they too would accept 'workers' democracy' as far superior to what the capitalist world offers to any but a small minority. Yes, and they would accept — regretfully, of course — the necessity of dictatorship while the job of reorganizing society on a socialist basis is being done."[22]

Despite their extraordinarily limited experience of the world, Barr and his comrades imagined they had a deep understanding of politics, international relations, and economics. Their confidence was rooted in the conviction that they were privy to secret information unavailable to the common people, who relied on the likes of William Randolph Hearst's newspapers for information. Barr's circle tore their opinions straight from the pages of the *Daily Worker.* The Marxist interpretation provided a sense of superiority from knowing the "real" story behind the news, and the constant discussion of conflicts, of the world being on the brink, teetering between catastrophe and redemptive revolution, turned current events into an absorbing drama.

Barr, Rosenberg, and their comrades' images of the Soviet workers paradise were formed at the Acme Theater, around the corner from the headquarters of the Communist Party, the *Daily Worker,* the Workers' Bookstore, the Young Communist League headquarters, and near a score of other leftist organizations that occupied the space around Union Square. The films ranged from crude pseudodocumentaries along the lines of *Kolkhoz, Life on the Cooperative Farms* to cinematic classics like Sergei Eisenstein's *Alexander Nevsky,* a call to arms against Nazi Germany thinly veiled as a historical epic.

Walking into the twilight after a matinee at the Acme, past men and women on soapboxes extolling the virtues of Communism, socialism, and other isms, Barr retained the powerful images. He completely suspended any sense of disbelief regarding claims about the positive attributes of the USSR, endowing anything connected with the Soviet state with almost mystical reverence. This adulation of everything Soviet led Barr to Pier 8, at the foot of 39th Street in Brooklyn, on April 4, 1934. A rusty freighter, the *Kim,* was making the first call in the Port of New York by a Russian vessel since the revolutions of 1917, and Barr was eager to see the ship. The sight of the red flag bearing the Soviet Union's hammer and sickle was thrilling, but he was disappointed that the crew did not allow him or the other young men who shouted fraternal greetings from the American branch of the international Communist movement to board. Nonetheless, Barr stood for an hour on the pier watching the sailors at work, imagining that he was in the presence of "Soviet man," a higher form of being.[23]

The attention of New York's Reds was drawn to the docks again in July 1935, this time in a less than celebratory mood. Outraged by America's continuing trade with Nazi Germany, a group of Communists, led by merchant mariners, mingled with the crowd of people bidding farewell to passengers on the *Bremen.* Just after the loudspeakers announced the final call for visitors to clear the decks, one of the Communists blew a whistle, signaling the comrades to start scuffling with the crew. A plainclothes New York cop drew his gun, and a member of the German crew, thinking he was one of the rioters, grabbed it and shot him in the buttocks. A Communist longshoreman broke free from crowd, climbed up the mast, grabbed the swastika flag, and threw it into the Hudson.

The storming of the *Bremen,* which was widely reported in the mainstream media and the Communist press, quickly became an iconic event for the party faithful, a Red version of the Boston Tea Party. It impressed Rosenberg so much that years later he told his impressionable brother-in-law, David Greenglass, that he'd led the raid, a gross exaggeration: at most he was a minor participant. The incident also impressed the Nazis, prompting the drafting of legislation forbidding Jews to display the Nazi flag.[24]

During his first year at CCNY, Barr found time to attend free concerts and become acquainted with, then enthralled by, the classical canon. Any money that he could scrounge was spent on recordings of Bach and Beethoven. For Barr, a personal connection to culture was an essential part of Communism. The American Communist movement had during Barr's high school years promoted the careers of writers who came to dominate the nation's literary landscape: John Dos Passos served as a contributing editor at the *Daily Worker* and *New Masses,* while Communist journals published Langston Hughes, Erskine Caldwell, and Sherwood Anderson. Many prominent writers had broken from the party by 1935, but the intimate link between the arts and radical politics remained.

Barr felt that through his connection with the Communist Party's political and cultural activities he was participating in a broad social movement. Politically, he assumed that Communists were articulating ideas that President Roosevelt and many in his inner circle secretly subscribed to but were too timid to admit publicly, that the party was pushing the boundaries forward by advocating socialist policies, creating space for the New Deal's more modest abridgements of raw capitalism. Opposition to Communism from the CCNY administration and the mainstream press served only to reinforce his beliefs. What better validation could a young revolutionary have than the disapproval of older men in positions of authority? Of course, Barr thought, reactionary elements would fight like hell against the workers.[25]

The pervasive racism in American society, from the upsurge in lynchings in the South to the less violent repression and casual bigotry that characterized daily life throughout the nation, provided a moral underpinning for Communism and reinforced Barr's notion that there were fascist tendencies in American society. On a frigid day in December 1933, four young Communists chained themselves together around a traffic-light pole at Broadway and 47th Street to demand the release of the Scottsboro Boys. One of those arrested was Jack Rosenberg (no relation to Julius), a twenty-one-year-old needleworker who lived on Barr's block in Brooklyn. Barr was impressed by the action, but he wasn't drawn to this kind of physical confrontation.

Julius Rosenberg was deeply affected by an experience that occurred about this time. One day while he was working as a soda jerk at Hoffman's Drug-store, a black man who had been hit by a bus was carried into the store, where he bled to death waiting for an ambulance that took almost an hour to arrive. For Rosenberg and his friends, this was concrete proof of the moral superiority of the Communist Party, which unlike the Democrats or Republicans strongly opposed racism. The Communists fomented a race riot that convulsed Harlem in March 1935, leaving many shop windows shattered; Hoffman's was spared when its Jewish proprietor told the crowd that he employed blacks.[26]

Barr's entry into CCNY coincided with the ascent of a Kansas farmer, Earl Browder, to the leadership of the Communist Party of America (CPUSA), and with the start of the golden age of the Communist movement in America. Just as Barr began debating the politics of the day in CCNY's Kremlin, the party veered sharply from its harsh rhetoric of the late 1920s and early 1930s, when Franklin Roosevelt was denigrated as a fascist, socialists were labeled "social-fascists," and the party's goal was to hijack the labor movement by creating Red unions that could wrest control from the more mainstream American Federation of Labor. Browder, whose midwestern roots put an all-American face on a party that was increasingly dominated by New York Jews, and whose stolid demeanor belied his radical agenda, was an ideal choice to lead the party. Following instructions from Moscow, which had come to view promoting America's role as a potential counterweight to the Nazi threat a much more valuable role for the party than pursuing fantasies of a Soviet States of America, Browder launched the Popular Front under the slogan "Communism Is Twentieth Century Americanism."

There was seemingly no limit to the extent to which the CPUSA would go to Americanize itself under the Popular Front banner. Public references to Marx and Lenin were dropped in favor of American revolutionaries — it was no accident that the Communists who traveled to fight fascism in Spain were called the Abraham Lincoln Brigade. Unintentionally, the Popular Front was a two-way street: while it made the party more palatable to Main Street America, it did at least as much to introduce its members to the broader culture. The party embraced the songs of Woody Guthrie, and young Communists like Rosenberg became some of the most ardent, and most unlikely, fans of American folk music (Barr resisted this fad, remaining devoted to classical music). Communist Party members joined noncommunist ant-fascist organizations, learned the ins and outs of the electoral process, and claimed to respect democratic procedures. As the party Americanized, it also became more firmly rooted in New York; the proportion of Jews grew from about 15 percent in the mid-1920s to about half in the 1930s and 1940s.[27]

Reserve Officer Training Corps (ROTC), symbolizing universities' complicity with militarism, were among the Communist student movement's top targets in the early 1930s, and CCNY was no exception. "To the freshman who this term enters our halls for the first time, *The Campus* has this word — Do not enroll in the R.O.T.C.," an editorial on the front page of the official undergraduate newspaper implored on September 19, 1935, under the headline "Out, Damned Spot!" It added: "Military Science, which teaches the fine art of killing your fellow man, has no place in the curriculum of an institution of higher learning. With the powers of Europe choosing up sides for a new game of war, it is more important than ever before that students and faculty unite in removing Military Science from [the curriculum]. It is the duty of every college student, on whom superior education places the responsibility of leadership, to oppose militarism, and its encroachment into the field of education."[28]

The party's position on pacifism evolved as Moscow's concerns about fascism became more acute. An underground Communist Party newspaper written and published by CCNY teachers urged students to "Support Student Anti-War Strike!" It noted Hitler's rearmament of Germany and accused England of plotting with Germany to organize an attack on the USSR. Exhorting CCNY students and faculty to oppose efforts to rearm the United States, the article stated: "In the last war, thirty-one students and two instructors of the City College were killed, and an untold number wounded, all for the greater glory of [J. P.] Morgan and finance capital. Shall we again allow ourselves to be led into another imperialist slaughter? Imperialist war is a 'rich man's war and the poor man's fight.' "[29]

In April 1935, in accord with the party's antiwar position, Rosenberg and Barr were among the 3,500 students who crowded into CCNY's Great Hall to pledge not to support the United States in any war it might conduct and to demand the abolition of the ROTC and the Civilian Conservation Corps, the transfer of funds from military to educational purposes, and a boycott of all Italian and German goods. In the first of many turns in the "party line" that he would faithfully execute, soon after this event Barr and the other alcove 2 partisans shifted from antiwar activism to advocating collective security.

Nineteen thirty-six was a turning point for Barr and his circle: they started real engineering classes, became embroiled in serious political activity, and joined the Young Communist League. At YCL meetings, held off-campus on Friday nights, the rising political storm in Europe was discussed and the latest "line" (which on all important topics was disseminated from Moscow) was communicated. Outsiders were welcome at the meetings, but many found the party's version of "discipline" — unquestioning obedience — as well as the emphasis on obscure doctrines hard to swallow.

Communist proselytizing wasn't reserved for off-campus YCL meetings, Barr recalled. "I was constantly trying to demonstrate to the other students the inevitableness of the socialist revolution in America. It seemed to me that there were no arguments that could prove we were wrong. The existence of Russia was the thing that bolstered up our whole philosophy, because if the Russians had done it, why couldn't the Americans do it?"

"We were absolutely convinced that the revolution in the United States was inevitable," Barr remembered. "To me a very, very important factor was that the world had been going from one financial crisis to the next and the Soviet Union was out of this system. They had no unemployment. These arguments for us were very solid and explained everything."[30]

The spring of 1936 saw the flowering of the Popular Front strategy. Barr met up with the other members of the CCNY YCL contingent in the garment district at 9:00 A.M. on May 1, marched in a column of about 20,000 people down Eighth Avenue, and turned onto 30th Street, where they merged with another 20,000 marchers. By the time they reached Union Square, the mass had swelled to at least 45,000, and there were tens of thousands of New Yorkers cheering from the streets and fire escapes. For the first time in years, as a result of the new spirit of comity, New York's May Day parade wasn't marred by violence between Communists and socialists vying for possession of Union Square. The next month, Columbia Broadcasting and the National Broadcasting Company broadcast nominating speeches at the Communist Party's presidential convention on national radio.

Barr spent the summer of 1936 at Camp Unity, a Communist summer retreat about sixty miles from New York City in Wingdale, New York, that featured political discussions and swimming by day and music at night. The camp was interracial during an era when African Americans were paid to perform in clubs that they were barred from patronizing and few whites socialized with blacks. The Communist Party's most prominent black, Paul Robeson, performed at the camp, as did many other black musicians, such as the jazz trumpeter Dizzy Gillespie, who carried a Communist Party membership card in his wallet, although he later claimed to have joined to further his career, not out of political conviction.[31]

Barr was sitting at a campfire when Camp Unity's music director played some music he'd written that afternoon. It was the first performance of "Joe Hill," one of the most popular folk songs of the period, celebrating a labor organizer who was reputed to have shouted, "Don't mourn, organize!" just before he was executed on trumped-up charges.[32]

Sobell, a real "Red diaper baby" who grew up watching his mother chair Communist Party meetings in the family's apartment, spent every summer while he and Barr attended CCNY at Camp Unity. Sobell's uncle managed the camp and hired him to wire the cabins for electricity and help with maintenance.

The relaxation of a rural retreat and the warm feelings Barr and Sobell enjoyed from being surrounded by people who shared their intense commitment to what they referred to as "progressive" politics were tinged with a sense of danger. They imagined themselves as revolutionary outlaws. Much of the revolutionary fervor was delusional; because they had little experience of life outside New York, where the CPUSA was concentrated, Barr and his comrades had a greatly exaggerated impression both of the party's ability to influence national politics and of mainstream America's concern about Communism. There was, however, a kernel of truth about the camp's reputation as a conspiratorial conclave. The party used it as a venue for secret "national schools" in which carefully selected comrades received intensive instruction in subjects such as infiltrating and covertly seizing control over labor unions.[33]

When college resumed in September, Barr and his comrades quickly turned more serious as the situation in Europe deteriorated. There was a great deal of talk about leaving the security of alcove 2 for the battlefields of Spain, and there was a growing frustration with FDR, as well as the leaders of Great Britain and France, for refusing to lift the arms embargo in the face of German and Italian intervention in support of Franco.

A straw poll of CCNY students and faculty in November 1936 reflected the radicalism of the campus, as well as its isolation from the rest of the country. In similar polls taken at colleges across the country, just less than half of the students (48.3 percent) expressed support for FDR, while 44 percent said they wanted the Republican, Alf Landon, as their next president. The small difference, probably within the margin of error, shows that most campuses were far from hotbeds of radical rebellion. FDR received a more decisive plurality at CCNY, with 63 percent of the votes. More significantly, most of the remaining support was directed to the president's left: the Stalinist candidate, Earl Browder, came in second, with 504 votes, representing 23 percent of poll participants; and Norman Thomas, the Socialist Party candidate, received 12 percent of the votes. Only 78 students, 3.5 percent, registered support for Landon. Among the faculty, FDR was the overwhelming favorite, while Browder and Thomas received more support than Landon. Support for Browder was probably understated, as the Communist Party tacitly supported reelection of the president.[34]

The political sympathies of the faculty were displayed in an underground newspaper they published from 1935 to 1939, *Teacher and Worker,* whose masthead stated that it was "issued monthly by the Communist Party unit of the City College." *Teacher and Worker* featured articles extolling the virtues of the USSR and promoting the CPUSA. One issue featured a quotation from a tract by Sidney and Beatrice Webb: "If by autocracy or dictatorship is meant government without prior discussion and debate, either by public opinion or in private session, the government of the U.S.S.R. is in that sense actually less of an autocracy or a dictatorship than many a parliamentary cabinet." The *Teacher and Worker* also quoted Earl Browder's remark that "Americanism, as we understand it, means to appropriate for our country all the best achievements of the human mind in all lands. We are the Americans, and Communism is the Americanism of the Twentieth Century."[35]

Ironically, CCNY's Communist teachers, who were educating men who would become some of the Soviet Union's most effective espionage agents, lashed out at alleged spies. In the summer of 1937 a *Teacher and Worker* article headlined "Beware the Spy!" complained that "shedding crocodile tears, the world's capitalist press has depicted the executions of traitorous Soviet generals as the first step in the general decline of the Soviets. Intelligence, well-informed study of the matter and its international ramifications all indicate the contrary. By ridding itself of these Soviet Benedict Arnolds, the Soviet Union has immeasurably strengthened itself and weakened its enemies." The article concluded: "Every revolution sooner or later spews forth its highly-placed traitors."[36]

The rising tide of fascism was topic number one on the City College campus in the winter of 1936. "Francisco Franco, Benito Mussolini, and Adolf Hitler were burned in effigy at 12:40 P.M. yesterday, as 500 College anti-fascists collaborated with 150 neighborhood children in the production of long, lusty, approving cheers intended as an appropriate requiem to the rapidly departing souls of the fascist leaders. To the tunes 'Fry Fascist Franco,' 'Defend Spanish Democracy,' and 'Hitler, Mussolini — Hands Off Spain,' a three-headed, kerosene-saturated, uniformed figure of sawdust and rags burned to ashes atop Lewisohn Stadium's iron fence facing Convent Avenue," *The Campus,* CCNY's official student newspaper, reported on December 4, 1936. Student groups dominated by the Communist Party had organized the demonstration. Communists were struggling to reconcile their opposition to war or military preparations with their strong support for the fight against Franco.

Barr, Sobell, Danziger, and most of the other members of their circle were dedicated to the Communist cause, but they were at least as passionate about electrical engineering. Julius Rosenberg was an exception; he had little interest in or talent for engineering, devoting most of his time and intellect to politics. A contributor to the 1938 issue of *The Microcosm,* CCNY's yearbook, had students like him in mind when he wrote:

Bio, chem., and engineering;
Dialectics flags and cheering;
Labs are dull, and often stink;
A rally's more healthy, Marxists think.
Science yields knowledge, highly touted,
Meetings yield knowledge, loudly shouted.
One's exciting, the other terse;
Whichever you like, the other's worse.

In 1937 Rosenberg organized and became the leader of a branch of the YCL called the Steinmetz Club, which consisted entirely of electrical engineering students. The society was named after Charles Proteus Steinmetz (1865–1923), a German-American genius credited with fundamental discoveries that made modern industry possible. His work on alternating current made it possible to transmit electricity across great distances; without his discovery of the laws of hysteresis, electric motors and generators couldn't have been developed; and without its patents on Steinmetz's inventions, the General Electric Company wouldn't have become one of the world's leading industrial conglomerates. As impressed as they were with their hero's technical achievements, the YCL engineers were even more enthusiastic about his radical politics. Steinmetz had been an early Zionist and enthusiastic cheerleader for Bolshevism. He had written to Lenin offering to help electrify the Soviet Union, and behind his desk at GE he had kept a framed, autographed photo sent in response by the founder of the Soviet Union.[37]

Steinmetz was also a spokesman for the Technocracy movement, which taught that large industrial corporations like GE could be transformed into the beating hearts of a socialist economy, and that advances in engineering and technology for the first time in human history made rational, centralized economic planning possible. Though he clung tightly to the shifting Communist Party line throughout his life, Barr's personal views remained rooted in Steinmetz's Technocracy. The ruin caused by the Depression and the success of government programs like the Tennessee Valley Authority convinced him that central planning was superior to the random cruelty of capitalism, which crushed the life out of men like Benjamin Barr. Joel Barr thought that a planned economy directing large enterprises with tightly integrated R&D and manufacturing capabilities would produce technological innovations that would raise everyone's standard of living.[38]

Rosenberg edited the Steinmetz Club's underground newsletter, *The Integrator,* which argued forcefully for U.S. intervention to stop the spread of fascism. "The heroic fight being waged by the desperate Chinese and Spanish peoples brings to mind the fact that the second World War is already at hand," *The Integrator* told its readers in October 1937. "Not satisfied with the rape of Ethiopia, Italian Fascism, this time together with German Fascism, is striving on an ever widening scale to conquer Spain. Japanese imperialism is playing its part in igniting the new conflagration which may ultimately involve the entire world, no nation excepted."[39]

By 1938 the threat posed by Hitler was crystal clear on the CCNY campus, even if many people in the United States believed Nazism was purely a European concern. In January the school newspaper put out a gag issue, but instead of the sophomoric sex jokes and slapstick humor that had characterized parodies in previous years, this one simulated a takeover of CCNY by "Fooshists." The paper, temporarily renamed *Mein Kampfus,* poked fun at Nazi notions of racial purity, but the jokes had a sharp edge. Under the headline "Dissenters, Listen!" it reported: "All students and members of the faculty who unfortunately find themselves in disagreement with the tenets and ideals of Fooshism are requested to assemble for a few moments in the Exercising Hall today at 3 P.M. The Machine-Gun Brigade of the Central Committee will inspect them and make provisions for their future. The students are requested to bring fifty cents with them to cover expenses, and to have with them identification marks and the names and addresses of nearest relatives."[40]

Even as they were certain war was on the way, Barr and his friends faced a more immediate problem: finding work. Sitting at their lab benches they discussed over sandwiches the deteriorating international situation and their bleak employment prospects, and daydreamed about emigrating to the Soviet Union, where engineering skills would, they thought, surely be in great demand.[41]

Potential salvation came in the spring of 1938, in the form of news that the federal government was offering jobs to qualified engineers. Immediately after they finished their CCNY final exams, members of the Steinmetz Club took over a room at the American Labor Party in upper Manhattan for a week to cram for the Civil Service test.

As Barr's four years at CCNY were drawing to an end, the Communist Party of America was at the height of its popularity, and New York was its epicenter. Candidates with close ties to the party, the black leader Adam Clayton Powell and Vito Marcantonio, had been elected to Congress. The party regularly filled Madison Square Garden to capacity. On May Day 1938, 50,000 people, led by Spanish War veterans from the Abraham Lincoln Brigade, roared down Fifth Avenue and Broadway to Union Square. "They kept pouring in past the flag-bedecked reviewing stand when a drizzle began to fall in mid-afternoon, they were still pouring in when the sun came out again before sunset and they kept it up until the last marcher passed the stand. Representatives of more than 650 organizations, A.F. of L. and C.I.O. unions, peace groups, Spanish war veterans, Negro groups, religious groups, and countless spectators cheered Congressman John T. Bernard to the echo when the Minnesota Farmer-Laborite called for a united front 'to crush the monster of fascism,'" the *Daily Worker* gushed.[42]

A month later, all the members of the Steinmetz Club except their leader graduated. Elitcher, who received an award that was given each year to a deserving student in the School of Technology, and Danziger were quickly given jobs in Washington, at the Navy's Bureau of Ordnance, where Sobell joined them a few months later.[43]

Even with his friends helping on homework assignments, Julius couldn't keep up, graduating in February 1939, six months behind, and near the bottom of his class. Bill Perl, who started college contemporaneously with Rosenberg, received his master's degree in electrical engineering at the same ceremony. Rosenberg was at the head of the pack, however, when most of the members of the Steinmetz Society made the transition from the YCL to become members of the Communist Party of America in early 1939.

His family's suffering in the depth of the Depression had sparked Barr's faith in Communism, but as in the cases of Rosenberg, Sobell, Danziger, Elitcher, and Perl, it was fortified by the party's strong antifascist position. Barr's confidence in the moral superiority of the Soviet Union was enhanced by the contrast between Stalin's intervention in the Spanish Civil War and the capitalist powers' refusal to fight Franco. Barr felt that he was riding a wave that would soon sweep away all the inequities of capitalism, clearing the way for a new society in which the Soviet Union's proclaimed ideals would be fused with America's industrial power. He had no way of knowing that the wave had crested, that this moment was the height of Communist power and influence in American society.

The packed party meetings at Madison Square Garden thrilled Barr and Rosenberg. The size and enthusiasm of the crowds made it easy to overlook the fact that they belonged to a fringe movement that most Americans were barely aware of. At one such meeting on July 5, 1939, Browder ridiculed the notion that Stalin might conclude a treaty with Hitler. "There is as much chance of Russo-German agreement as of Earl Browder being elected President of the Chamber of Commerce," he said.[44]

Browder soon had to eat those words. The Popular Front, which had attracted tens of thousands of people into the party and won the sympathy of hundreds of thousands, came to an abrupt end on August 21, 1939, when the Nazi-Soviet Pact was reported on the front page of the *New York Times*.

Overnight, Barr and his comrades abandoned their demands for embargoes on Germany and Italy. The about-face was a rude introduction to Realpolitik, a renunciation of everything that had animated their student lives. Many people, especially "fellow travelers" who supported its battles against fascism abroad and racism at home, were horrified when the CPUSA removed its Popular Front mask, revealing an organization completely subservient to the Soviet Union, devoid of capacity for independent action and eager to jettison moral principles if they conflicted with the Kremlin's dictates.[45]

Thousands of people quit the party, but the resolve of those who remained was stiffened. "Stalin's pact with Hitler was really a blow," Barr remembered in 1992. He and his CCNY comrades stayed calm, though, comforted by confidence in Stalin's omniscience. "I was well aware that the Communist Party USA was following the lead of the Russian Communist Party, often subordinating the needs of the American workers to the interests of the Soviet Union," Sobell, whose views were similar to Barr's, wrote in his memoir, describing his response to the Soviet alliance with Nazi Germany. "I also believed that the security of the Soviet Union was a paramount concern at this time since, if the USSR were overthrown, the parties of all the other countries would be immeasurably weakened. From any long-range point of view the interests of the USSR seemed to coincide with those of the workers of all other countries, but this didn't resolve the short-range problems that arose to plague me from time to time. If forced to argue I could support almost any position, but in my heart I felt that the party was the way. It was, I suppose, a matter of faith."[46]

In fact the Americanization of the CPUSA had been a pose from the start. Throughout the Popular Front period the party was funded and dominated by the Soviet Union, and its embrace of moderate labor unions and apparent willingness to play by democratic rules were ruses. Contrary to the image it presented to the world, the CPUSA was always a subsidiary of the Soviet party. Its leaders were selected in Moscow, and, despite its democratic rhetoric, they could be and were dismissed when men in the Kremlin decided their time was up.

The subjugation of the CPUSA to Moscow's needs started at the top, with Browder, the public face of the Popular Front. His role as one of the most important operatives for Soviet intelligence in the United States was so obvious that it didn't seem credible, even to cynical law enforcement professionals. Declassified Soviet intelligence documents reveal that Browder's covert activities started in the late 1920s, with subversion assignments in the Philippines and Shanghai. His brother and sister were also longtime covert agents for the Soviet Communist Party. Starting in 1933, when he returned from Asia, and for the next decade, the self-educated Kansan was a central figure in Soviet espionage in America.[47]

At the very time that Browder was posing as a patriot, extolling the virtues of Jeffersonian democracy, he was recruiting and running an intelligence network with strands that enveloped the White House, the State Department, and industry. Browder bamboozled many of his American agents, telling them that they were working for the CPUSA or the international Communist movement, not the USSR.[48] Rank-and-file party members like Barr and Rosenberg had no idea that Browder recruited spies for Soviet intelligence, or of the extent to which the CPUSA was a subsidiary of the Soviet Communist Party. Even when the country turned against it, revolted by the USSR's alliance with Germany, the party continued, with some success in strongholds like New York, to run members for elective office.

In August 1939, Barr, along with thousands of other Communists who lived in Brooklyn, took what seemed at the time an innocuous action, signing a petition to place Peter Cacchione's name on the ballot as a Communist Party candidate for City Council. That petition was a time bomb; by putting his signature on it Barr ensured that he would be among those caught by its shock wave years later.[49]

Washington, Spring 1940

A bitterly cold wind greeted Joel Barr as he stepped off the Silver Meteor, a gleaming, streamlined high-speed train that embodied the engineering ideals he admired, at Union Station on April 12, 1940. It was the start of a rare spring snowstorm that treated Washingtonians to the unusual sight of snowflakes mixed with cherry blossom petals. He wore a jacket that was too light for the unseasonable weather. In its pocket was a palm-sized address book.

The address book contained two Washington contacts: the Civil Aeronautics Authority (CAA) office where he was to be employed, and a local party member who would serve as Barr's introduction to the city's community of underground Communists. Julius Rosenberg had provided the latter, along with an admonition to behave in Washington as if he were behind enemy lines, to be especially careful about hiding his political sympathies from all but trusted comrades.[1]

While Barr and his comrades could openly express their political convictions at CCNY, and in New York generally, circumstances were quite different in Washington. The prohibition against government workers' engaging in political activities was vigorously enforced against Communists. For several years, the FBI and the Civil Service Commission, acting on a shaky legal basis, had been quietly searching out and firing government employees with links to Communism. In August 1939 they received a legislative mandate to pursue the task openly and energetically. The Hatch Act barred government employment of anyone who belonged to an organization, such as the CPUSA, that advocated the overthrow of the U.S. government. Barr would have to keep his party membership secret in order to stay employed.[2] The Hatch Act was part of a broad effort to clamp down on the Soviet Union and its supporters. Congress, afraid that the USSR could become a conduit for intelligence, raw materials, and armaments to Germany and Italy, had imposed restrictions on exports to Russia. The move, combined with the arrests of Browder and other top CPUSA leaders, convinced Barr that the capitalists who controlled America were committed to stamping out Communism both at home and abroad.

Sobell, Danziger, Elitcher, and Perl were also in Washington, but Barr didn't have their addresses, and, perhaps to avoid attracting the attention of the government detectives that he and other Communists imagined were lurking behind every corner in the nation's capital, he made no effort to contact them. Instead of bunking with his old college friends, Barr settled into a cheap boardinghouse on K Street, N.W., two blocks from the Carnegie Library.

Barr considered his day job, making mechanical drawings for the CAA, at most a distraction from his real missions: coming up with an invention to rival the accomplishments of his hero, Charles Proteus Steinmetz, and furthering the Communist cause, preferably through some kind of bold, heroic action. Within a few weeks of arriving in Washington, Barr felt he was making progress on both fronts. The notebook he kept within reach at all times was starting to fill up with scribbled brainstorms. In addition, he'd connected with an underground CPUSA cell and was looking forward to getting firsthand experience with clandestine party work.

Proximity to the seat of power increased the sense of drama Barr felt during his first underground mission. After standing in the basement of a bookstore on Capitol Hill one evening in May 1940 helping a comrade crank a mimeograph machine, he waited nervously for the paper to dry, then walked out into the darkness and hurried home with scores of identical pages in his briefcase and a world of worry in his head. Following a sleepless night, Barr quickly dressed, walked outside, and boarded a streetcar. If they noticed him at all, the other passengers may have wondered why the tall, thin man carrying a cheap briefcase was sweating profusely on a cool morning. Barr struggled to hold himself to a normal pace as he covered the few blocks to his office. It was early, at least an hour before any of the other employees in his section would arrive, but he knew that the janitor would have already unlocked the building. There was no security guard — in those days Washington was an open city; the gates to the White House grounds were open to the public during daylight hours, as were the doors to Congress — so no one observed the junior draftsman as he slipped inside and, heart pounding, climbed the stairs to the large, open drafting room. He raced around the tables, placed a couple of the mimeographed pages on each, dumped a pile in the men's room, and then hastily returned home, showered, changed clothes, and retraced his early-morning route.[3]

That morning, Barr kept his head in his work, trying to conceal furtive glances around the room to see if anyone was observing him, or if his colleagues were reading the flyers he'd gone to so much trouble to deliver. They were solicitations to join the Federation of Architects, Engineers, Chemists, and Technicians (FAECT), which was launching a recruitment campaign in Washington. It is unlikely that anyone paid much attention to the caper; in any case, Barr's role in it remained undetected. Looking back on the incident decades later, Barr laughed at his fear, at how an event trivial in light of the risks he incurred later had seemed so significant at the time. But he also remembered that the fear had been justified. The last thing the Civil Service wanted was for its members to join a Communist-dominated union, and the cost of detection would almost certainly have been dismissal and the real possibility that other employers, reluctant to accept a radical union organizer, would shun him.

The FAECT never attracted enough followers to make an impact on labor conditions, but it served the "progressive" cause in other ways. Although neither Barr nor the U.S. government knew it at the time, KGB agents used the FAECT as a recruitment pool, a source of potential agents who were likely to be sympathetic to the Soviet cause and to have access to valuable scientific and technical information.[4]

Communism functioned as a lens that shaped Barr's perspective on life. More than just an intellectual prism, it was the center of his world. Like many CPUSA members, Barr had few friends outside the party. In addition to a gentle introduction to covert operations, Barr's Communist Party cell arranged something in the spring of 1940 that was more exciting for a twenty-four-year-old living apart from his parents for the first time: a romantic encounter. About a week after proving his revolutionary credentials by distributing the FAECT flyers at the CAA, Barr was singing in the shower of an apartment that a sympathetic comrade had made available for a blind date when, by prearrangement, Elaine Goldfarb, a twenty-year-old party member, quietly let herself in. She draped her dress over the sofa in the living room and slipped into the bathroom, pulled back the shower curtain, and, catching her first sight of her date's skeletal profile, screamed and ran back into the living room. By the time Barr, wearing a towel, caught up with her, the dress was back on. It took about an hour for him to overcome her reservations, but despite its inauspicious beginning, the assignation concluded on terms favorable to both parties. Still, the incident led Barr to subscribe to a Charles Atlas bodybuilding correspondence course and spend weekends hiking and boating in a partially successful effort to put some meat on his bones.[5]

Barr met another interesting woman through the local party organization, Mary Jane Gold. Gold was a wealthy socialite who, according to Barr, slipped money to the party to support its work in Washington, such as mimeographing FAECT recruitment flyers. Gold traveled to Europe in 1940, donating her personal airplane to the French Army shortly before the Nazi invasion. During the occupation, she helped an American journalist, Varian Fry, establish the Emergency Rescue Committee, which created escape routes for thousands of Jewish intellectuals, including the painter Marc Chagall and the philosopher Hannah Arendt. Fry's reputation has been tainted by allegations that he was sponsored by Moscow, that he gave precedence to furthering the KGB's aims over humanitarian tasks, and that he may have been directly or indirectly responsible for the deaths of refugees who were deemed threats to the USSR. Barr's assertion that Gold was a secret Communist lends weight to allegations that Fry's rescue mission had a darker side.[6]

Like Barr, Gold was circumspect about her connections to the Communist Party. Some of the other alumni of the Steinmetz Club living in Washington were not as discreet. Soon after Barr arrived in town, the names of his CCNY comrades began appearing in FBI files.

"On May 25, 1940, an anonymous telephone call was received from a woman who stated that she was a distant relative of one ETHEL ROSENBERG nee GREENGLASS who resides in Brooklyn, N.Y., street unknown," John B. Little, a special agent in the FBI's New York field office, reported in a memo to Bureau headquarters in Washington. "The informant stated that Miss ROSENBERG is extremely Communistic and has recently received an appointment to go to Washington, D.C. as an employee in the Census Bureau. The informant could furnish no additional information and no action is being taken by the New York City Office at this time in view of the non-specific nature of the complaint," Little stated. The memo, which today lies on top of tens of thousands of pages in the Bureau's file on Julius and Ethel Rosenberg, was diligently filed and promptly forgotten. In May 1940, chasing down bank robbers and busting gangsters was a far higher priority for G-men than scrutinizing the political proclivities of a Census Bureau typist. At the time, no one could have predicted that similar sentiments, expressed to the FBI by another relative, Ethel's brother David, would a decade later set in motion a chain of events that led to her execution.[7]

The unknown Greenglass relative's call came at a time when many Americans had begun to view the Soviet Union as at least as great a threat as Nazi

Germany, and thousands were contacting law enforcement agencies to report on suspected Communists. The Nazi-Soviet alliance turned public opinion against the USSR, while reports from CPUSA defectors made it clear that the party was controlled from Red Square, not Union Square. Newspaper articles in 1939 and 1940 frequently discussed Nazi and Soviet espionage as two sides of the same coin, warning that members of the CPUSA would emulate the "fifth column" of fighters camouflaged as government loyalists that General Franco famously claimed were hidden among the citizens of Madrid, waiting for a signal to assist the Fascists.[8]

Presaging McCarthyism, some Republican politicians who thought that President Roosevelt was using the New Deal to impose socialism resorted to exaggerated anticommunist demagogy to attack their political opponents. As happened in the 1950s, congressional investigations smeared innocent people, undermining legitimate attempts to uncover real spies in the process.[9] Many of the Americans serving as covert operatives for the Soviet Union were detected by loyalty screens or were the subject of FBI investigations before and during their espionage careers. Remarkably, government suspicions often proved little more than speed bumps, as agents for the Soviet Union managed to stay in positions of responsibility and to continue spying even after the U.S. government knew they were security risks.[10]

The government's failure to prevent individuals from spying even after learning that they were Communists and that they had access to classified information was largely the result of a lack of imagination. Red hunts were motivated by an unrealistic fear that Communists could subvert the government by converting their colleagues to the cause; there was little or no appreciation of the real threat of Soviet espionage. Anticommunists felt that the threat was Marxist ideology, not Soviet spying; the effort to purge government of Reds was also tainted by anti-Semitism. Thus, identifying and firing Communists, even if they held innocuous positions, took precedence over investigating espionage.

The FBI had only a vague picture of the KGB's espionage operations in the United States in the late 1930s and early 1940s and was completely unaware of their scope. In addition, the Bureau couldn't have followed up on every tip it received about possible Communist infiltration, even if it had wanted to do so. It simply didn't have the manpower. In 1940 the local Boy Scout troop in Washington, D.C. could muster a larger force than J. Edgar Hoover: He had fewer than 900 FBI agents spread out over the entire country, and they were charged with investigating a broad range of federal crimes.[11] More important, in the 1930s and 1940s, from his base in the Lubyanka building near Red Square, Lieutenant General Pavel Fitin, the head of Soviet foreign intelligence, commanded a covert force in the United States that outnumbered the FBI's counterintelligence corps.[12]

In the late spring of 1940, when the Rosenbergs moved to Washington, neither they nor the FBI knew that scores of government workers were secretly reporting to the KGB or the Soviet military intelligence agency, the GRU (Main Intelligence Administration). The idea that Communists might be spies, however, wasn't entirely novel to party members like the Rosenbergs. Whether it was targeted against Trotskyites or the U.S. government, spying came easily to the imaginations of Communists, who romanticized the Bolshevik movement's covert origins. Treason and espionage were constant themes in the Moscow show trials of former Communist leaders that American Communists read about in detail. Barr, the Rosenbergs, and other American Communists felt that they, like the prerevolutionary Bolsheviks, were in the vanguard of an underground movement fighting against a repressive state. Under such circumstances, Barr and many other CPUSA members considered that conventional notions of patriotism and morality were not applicable.[13]

Soon after arriving in Washington, Julius Rosenberg renewed contact with his old Steinmetz Club associates who were starting careers that would place some of the nation's most important military technology secrets in their hands. According to Sobell, the reunion occurred serendipitously, when Julius and Ethel ran into him and Elitcher at the public swimming pool on Haines Point, a narrow strip of land jutting into the Potomac River where the wind blows reliably, providing relief from Washington's stifling summer heat.

Sobell and Elitcher told their old friend that they and Danziger, who was living in Washington with his wife, Helene, were employed as civilian draftsmen for the Navy Bureau of Ordnance, working in "temporary" buildings that had been hastily tossed together on the Mall, along Constitution Avenue, during World War I. They reported every morning to large drafting rooms with views of the Washington Monument or the Lincoln Memorial, where more than a hundred men labored over drawings of turrets and mountings for guns. The trio from CCNY were in close contact with Perl, who was living three hours' drive from Washington in Hampton, Virginia, where he was working at the National Advisory Committee for Aeronautics (NACA) Langley Laboratory.

It was the first time any of the Steinmetz Club members had traveled outside the cultural orbit of New York City. Any other American city would have seemed strange to them, but Washington was particularly disconcerting. In those days it was a small southern town where the sons of immigrants stuck out like sore thumbs. Crude bigotry and discrimination, particularly against blacks, was much more evident than in New York. Only three days before Barr arrived in Washington, the world-famous contralto Marian Anderson had performed at the Lincoln Memorial after the Daughters of the American Revolution denied permission for her to sing at Constitution Hall because she was black. Jim Crow was alive and well in Washington. Blacks attended separate schools and were not permitted in "white" theaters, restaurants, hospitals, or churches. Thousands of blacks still lived in "alley dwellings," shacks built shortly after the Civil War that lacked running water.

Sobell and Elitcher settled into an apartment at 2225 N Street, N.W., a building that later attracted the FBI's attention because a high proportion of its residents were Communists. While the Bureau suspected that an unseen Red finger pointed radicals to the building, according to Sobell there was a more mundane explanation: It was a "white" apartment house in a "black" neighborhood, a rarity in polarized Washington. Progressives enjoyed both the lower rent and the opportunity to feel that they were striking a blow against segregation.[14]

For the CCNY engineers, the political environment in Washington was even more distressing than the racism. To blunt criticism that it was soft on Communism, the Roosevelt administration had ratcheted up its hunt for Reds. Although they knew that it would be grounds for dismissal from their positions with the Navy—a serious concern during the Depression, when jobs were hard to come by—Sobell, Elitcher, and Danziger all joined a Young Communist League chapter in January 1939, soon after they arrived in town. The group of about twenty people operated as a cell, purposely maintaining little or no contact with other, similar cells in the nation's capital.[15]

After a few months, Sobell, Elitcher, and the Danzigers learned that there was a Communist Party unit at the Navy Department, and they made the transition from YCL to full party membership. Sobell joined because "it was the only organization that got down to fundamentals and called for the overthrow of capitalism and its inherent evils," he remembered in his memoir; in contrast, the liberal reform groups "concentrated on individual obnoxious facets of the system rather than its essence."[16]

Unlike Barr and Rosenberg, who had joined in New York, Sobell, Elitcher, and the Danzigers were not "card-carrying" CPUSA members. To preclude the possibility of accidental disclosure through the loss of a card, and to eliminate physical evidence that defectors could retain, the Washington, D.C., branch of the CPUSA did not issue membership cards. This was only one of many peculiarities of life in the Communist underground in Washington. Unlike at CCNY's alcove 2, "the Kremlin," or its YCL meetings, which were open to all comers, Communists in Washington met in secret and took care to conceal their political ideals and affiliations. Elitcher later described the special precautions that were taken to prevent the government from learning the identities of CPUSA members in Washington. "The fact that all of the members of the secret cells of the Communist Party were either government employees, or had a close connection with government employees, made it necessary that a strict set of security regulations be adhered to to prevent disclosures in regard to the existence of the cell system and the identities of Communist Party members." A party member knew only the identities of the other members of his or her particular cell and was "urged never to divulge that such cells existed in government agencies in Washington. If a member was leaving Washington, D.C., he was instructed not to divulge that such an organization existed, inside or outside of government employment." As a result, few Communist Party members other than those who had lived in Washington were aware of the secret party organization there.[17]

Elitcher also provided some insight into the adamant refusal of many government employees to admit CPUSA membership, even in the face of strong evidence or testimony from other members. He said that "members of the Navy Department cell were instructed that in the event they were questioned by government investigators during the investigation either of themselves or other members of the cell regarding membership in the Communist Party, they should deny that they were members of the Communist Party and should state that they had no knowledge that the other individual was a member of the Communist Party. It was impressed upon them that this procedure should be strictly followed, since no record existed which could ever be utilized by a government agency to prove membership in the party. They were similarly instructed that all members of the party working for the government were also issued the same instructions, and that each member should feel secure in this knowledge."

Particular care was taken to avoid drawing attention to the regular meetings that were the center of party life. The biweekly assemblies were rotated among the homes of members of a cell. Strict instructions were given never "to mention, in the presence of anyone who was not a member of [their] cell, that any meeting was taking place at a designated time or place," Elitcher recalled. "In addition, at each meeting of the cell, the date and place of the next meeting was set, and sometimes the date and place of the meeting after the next one was set, so that in case anything prevented the next meeting from being held, the members would know when and where a subsequent meeting was to take place."

From six to eight individuals attended the meetings, staggering their entrances and departures to avoid attracting the attention of neighbors. Dues were collected at every meeting — as in the Soviet Union, they were assessed as a percentage of a comrade's salary — and were turned over the chairman, who in turn gave them to an individual from outside the cell who was in contact with the national Communist Party.[18] Party members felt that making a financial contribution was such an essential aspect of their lives, such a tangible expression of their faith, that even some individuals who severed all visible ties to the party in order to engage in espionage continued to pay dues secretly, much as a strict Catholic might feel bound to tithe regardless of the other contributions he or she made to the church.[19]

The party warned government workers to be very discreet over the telephone and to avoid being seen with Communist literature. Afraid to subscribe at home, Sobell bought the *Daily Worker* at a newsstand next to the *Washington Post* building on Pennsylvania Avenue, and even there he was afraid that the police might be watching.[20]

Both party meetings and the pages of the *Daily Worker* were dominated in those days by the CPUSA's effort to prevent America from joining or aiding the fight against Germany or Japan. Sobell, Elitcher, and the Danzigers joined a Communist front organization, American Peace Mobilization, that was dedicated to keeping America out of the war. Just as Popular Front groups attracted noncommunists who shared their antifascist goals, American Peace Mobilization and other organizations created or infiltrated by the CPUSA in the wake of the Nazi-Soviet Pact bolstered their enrollment and attempted to obscure their connections to the CPUSA by recruiting individuals from outside the party's ranks. Now, however, the CPUSA shared goals, and slogans, with the German-American Bund, a profascist organization.

Throughout his covert career, Sobell was an inept conspirator. Like other government employees who supported American Peace Mobilization, Sobell avoided the numerous antiwar rallies and demonstrations held in Washington, but he and Elitcher aided the cause by allowing their apartment to become a way station for people who traveled to Washington for the events. The FBI learned of Sobell's membership in the group almost as soon as he joined. An FBI memo dated February 17, 1940, stated that "a highly confidential and reliable source" — Bureau-speak for an informer, or possibly a purloined membership list — reported that "Morton Sobell . . . an engineer for the Navy Department, was a member of American Peace Mobilization." Possibly because it wanted to find out more about his activities, or possibly to avoid disrupting other investigations, the FBI decided to keep an eye on Sobell but did not immediately notify the Navy about its employee's extracurricular activities.[21]

Unenthusiastic about life in Washington and the mundane work at the CAA, Barr started looking for another job. Following the outbreak of war in Europe,

President Roosevelt had in September 1939 cajoled Congress into passing a law declaring a "limited emergency" that gave the administration authority to modestly increase the size and strength of the armed services. Preparing for war, the Roosevelt administration slashed spending across the board for social programs and applied the surplus funds to expanding defense programs. As a result of the realignment, there were few jobs available in the civilian sector, but the military was hiring.

Barr applied for an engineering job at the Coast Guard, the least militaristic branch of the armed services. When he was turned down, he sent his résumé to the Army, which was actively recruiting civilian scientists and engineers. The Signal Corps, the Army unit responsible for procuring and operating communications systems, desperately needed people who understood radio electronics to help transform the military, which had withered in the years after World War I, into a modern fighting force. The organization offered Barr a position as an electrical engineer at its R&D facility, the Signal Corps Laboratories, in Fort Monmouth, New Jersey. The job provided a salary of $2,600—far more than Barr or any of his family members had ever earned—and a chance to return to the New York area.

3

Fort Monmouth, 1940–1942

The summer of 1940 was a hard time to be an American Communist. Party discipline required Communists to oppose all assistance to the enemies of fascism even as German bombs were leveling British cities in preparation for an invasion that, if successful, would put all of Western Europe under Nazi domination. The Soviet Union, acting in concert with Germany, had swallowed eastern Poland, absorbed the tiny Baltic states, and bitten a bloody chunk out of Finland. In New York, Jewish Communists were taunted with "Heil Hitler" greetings, and liberal organizations throughout the country mobilized to expel "CommuNazis."[1]

Stalin's actions didn't keep Barr awake at night. A true believer, Barr uncritically accepted the party's justifications for the USSR's behavior, just as he naively cited the new Soviet constitution as evidence that there was more personal freedom in Russia than in the United States. Barr never seriously doubted the party's wisdom, and clung tightly to the "line," even as it pulled him into direct conflict with the national security interests of the United States. If the party had asked Barr to commit sabotage against the Army, he would certainly have given the proposal serious consideration and might have complied. He was not put in that position, but others who shared Barr's political beliefs responded with alacrity when called upon to derail the U.S. military buildup.[2]

Communists precipitated a series of strikes against defense factories in the spring and summer of 1940, earning the enmity of the White House, national union leaders, and the public. In July 1940 national union leaders denounced attempts by Communists to block a settlement at five aluminum plants in western Pennsylvania, charging that it was a subversive attempt to disrupt the national defense program. That fall, the FBI and Justice Department said that Communists seeking to cripple America's ability to arm Great Britain were behind a strike at the Vultee Aircraft Corporation. The most publicized anti-war strike occurred in late May and early June 1941, at North American Aviation, in Inglewood, California. The Confederation of Industrial Organi-zations (CIO) and national media attributed the strike to Communists who refused to settle when terms acceptable to the union's national leadership were offered. Their goal was disruption of America's ability to wage war, not an-other nickel an hour in wages, the union leadership charged. The Communist strikers managed to idle a fifth of the nation's aircraft production capacity and to turn a prolabor president into a strikebreaker. Roosevelt sent thousands of soldiers to reopen the plant, while members of his administration accused the Communists of attempting to subvert democracy. Later that year the CIO accused the Communist Party of making a "subversive attempt" to disrupt national defense by pushing for a wildcat strike at a Pennsylvania aluminum factory.[3]

In case there remained any doubt about the Communist Party's antiwar position, the YCL made it crystal clear on June 15, 1940. The 500 delegates to its annual meeting passed — as always, the vote was unanimous — a Father's Day resolution calling upon America's fathers to unite with their sons to prevent the country from becoming involved in "imperialist" wars. They then cheered a speaker who vilified Roosevelt as a "warmonger."[4]

As Britain's situation became desperate, American public opinion shifted to favor more active assistance. The Roosevelt administration pressed ahead with as much military modernization as Congress would fund in preparation for joining the war in Europe or defending North America if the Nazis de-feated Britain. The Signal Corps Laboratory's workforce expanded as budget increases started reinvigorating the Army.

Fort Monmouth was close enough to New York to allow Barr to visit family and friends. He came home for the Labor Day weekend in 1940 and stayed a couple of extra days in response to a call for the party faithful to assemble in Union Square on September 4 for what was supposed to be a massive antiwar rally. Despite the bright blue sky and unseasonably balmy temperatures, turn-out was meager, nothing like the tens of thousands who had jammed the square during the Popular Front days. Instead of the optimistic oratory from nationally known figures blasted over enthusiastic crowds by a powerful public address system that Barr remembered from the late 1930s, a handful of speakers stood on soapboxes. The unamplified rhetoric was bitter, focusing on denunciations of European politicians who were defying Hitler. President Roosevelt "was one of the day's star boo-ees," in large part because of his decision to ship four decrepit destroyers to Great Britain in exchange for leased military bases, the *New York Times* reported. Such events were commonplace in New York, and Barr correctly calculated that it was unlikely that his presence would be noted by the police or reported to the Army.[5]

Barr's former classmates who were living in Washington, where law enforcement kept a much closer eye on dissent, were more cautious. When right-wing isolationists and Communist-dominated peace groups joined forces to organize an anticonscription rally in the nation's capital on September 13, the event attracted a great deal more attention than the Union Square demonstration.

Afraid that word of their presence might get back to the Navy, Sobell and Elitcher decided not to attend, but they opened their apartment to comrades who had traveled to Washington to add their voices to others demanding that Congress reject pending conscription legislation. Sobell drove them to the rally in his 1936 Dodge sedan, dropping the protestors at 14th and W Streets, N.W., directly in front of Turner's Arena — and in clear sight of FBI agents who were noting down license plate numbers. A few days later, the agents learned from the D.C. police that the car was registered to Sobell.[6]

The Navy engineer's file got a bit thicker in November when his name turned up on a list of those attending a meeting of the American Youth Congress, a Communist-infiltrated organization that campaigned aggressively to keep the United States out of the war in Europe. Sobell was unaware of the FBI's interest in his activities, but, disturbed by the dissonance between his political beliefs and his work, he started looking for a job unconnected with the military.

Sobell, Danziger, Elitcher, Perl, and Barr all found themselves in the same unhappy boat in 1940. They were working for the military, helping America to arm Great Britain, and readying the country to fight in a war that they adamantly opposed. Given the paucity of jobs, they had little choice other than to continue working for a cause that was at odds with the party's goals. Their old friend, Julius Rosenberg, would come up with a way out of the dilemma, a solution that allowed them to work for the imperialist warmongers and remain true to their Communist ideals.

From the point of view of a foreign intelligence service seeking to acquire military technology, there were few better places in the United States to have agents than in mid-level jobs at the Signal Corps and its contractors. With the exception of the atom bomb — which didn't alter the course of the war in Europe — many of America's most important World War II weapons systems were developed or refined at Fort Monmouth and manufactured according to Signal Corps specifications. The "SCR" (Signal Corps Radio) designation was stamped on the walkie-talkies that G.I.'s on battlefields in Europe, Asia, and Africa shouted into when they needed reinforcements; on the machines that allowed airplane pilots to peer miles ahead, thereby turning Hitler's submarines from terrible predators to terrified prey; on the contraptions that transformed the V1 "buzz bombs" launched against Britain from lethal weapons into sitting ducks; and on the high-tech artillery shells that turned the tide against the Nazis' last offensive at the Battle of the Bulge. These weapons or their precursors, along with numerous more mundane but still vital components, were under development during the period when Barr, Rosenberg, and their collaborators had access to classified Signal Corps information.

The critical role that Fort Monmouth would play in the coming war was, however, far from obvious when Barr accepted a Signal Corps job. Fort Monmouth reflected the overall state of the U.S. Army: one boot was firmly planted in World War I, and another was tentatively aimed at the future. In the spirit of generals who prepare for the last war, the Signal Corps looked to the past for tools to cope with the Blitzkrieg tactics that had allowed the Nazi Army to sweep through France and occupy Paris in a month.

To address the need for rapid communications, the corps hired veterans of the Great War to help breed and train homing pigeons at Fort Monmouth. Hawks killed thirteen of forty-three pigeons that participated in an Army exercise in August 1939. Undaunted, a year and a half later, Major John Shawvan of the Signal Corps boasted to reporters that Fort Monmouth had achieved major advances in pigeon communications, including two-way and nocturnal capabilities. He ascribed the collapse of France's defenses to its failure to properly deploy pigeons. Shawvan even told the *New York Times* that America's trained birds were strategic weapons that must be registered with the government. "Homing pigeons are considered a menace to national safety if they are used for communication by fifth columnists. It is for that reason that every homing pigeon fancier will be asked to register his loft with the United States Army," Shawvan reported.[7]

The labs at Fort Monmouth were quietly working on a shoestring budget on far more promising innovations than pigeons, including one that arguably became World War II's single most important technology: the use of radio waves to detect and track aircraft, ships, and submarines. The scientific basis for radar had been independently discovered in the 1920s in England, the

United States, France, Germany, and Japan. From its inception military leaders understood radar's potential and took every step possible to keep it under wraps. "The secret was to be protected at every point of contact—against possible enemies, against possible allies, against commercial enterprises, particularly those with extranational interests, and even against other services of the inner defense force of the nation," according to an official history of the Army Signal Corps. The first American radar trainees were not permitted to speak about the technology to anyone who lacked specific clearance; they were not allowed to keep diaries, and to cloak their activities they were given chemistry books to carry home from classes.[8]

At the start of World War II, the technology was less than four years old; neither the Soviet Union, Italy, nor Japan had working radar systems. Even the word "radar" was classified throughout the war. When Pentagon security officials learned that signs to a "Radar Laboratory" had been posted at Fort Monmouth, they ordered them removed. The signs were destroyed in a bonfire. This security consciousness did not, however, permeate to lower levels.[9]

The United States was not at war when Barr arrived at Fort Monmouth, and despite evidence that German spies were active on American soil, the military officers in charge had not been entirely successful in instilling a culture of security in the base's large and growing workforce. Like the other 200 civilians working at the labs, Barr was issued a bright orange pass that granted entry to the base. The security guards who manned the gates, mostly retired soldiers, were so inattentive that some of the engineers repeatedly gained entrance to the base by pulling oranges from their lunchboxes and flashing them at the guards. A Nazi spy was able to wander around the base in early 1939 and collect information about radar and other experimental equipment from loquacious army officers and civilian scientists. The briefcases of men leaving the base were not searched, and as Barr and his colleagues were expected to work at home, there would have been no negative repercussions if he had been observed departing with classified documents.[10]

In the fall of 1940, Barr met up with Julius Rosenberg again, this time at Fort Monmouth. Unlike his friends who had aced the Civil Service exam, Rosenberg hadn't been quickly offered a government job; it took a year and a half for his application to rise to the top of the federal hiring bureaucracy's mound. When a job offer finally came, he jumped at the opportunity, dashing off to New Jersey to receive training as a Signal Corps inspector, leaving Ethel behind to serve out the required two months at the Census Bureau. On September 3, the day before the Communist Party's New York peace rally fizzled like a damp squib, Rosenberg reported for work.

The Signal Corps was in desperate need of engineers who could help manufacturers that were comfortable producing goods for civilian markets learn to meet more exacting military specifications. It wasn't a big deal if Aunt Lucy needed to bang on her Philco radio occasionally to get it to work, or if one of her electric appliances broke down unexpectedly. Similar unreliability on the battlefield, however, could have tragic consequences, so the Signal Corps trained men like Julius Rosenberg to inspect the factories that were turning America into the "arsenal of democracy." Ensuring quality didn't require a high level of engineering skill, just an ability to understand blueprints and technical manuals.

After two months of training at Fort Monmouth, Rosenberg was posted to the corps procurement headquarters in Brooklyn. Ethel joined him, and they moved into a large apartment in the Williamsburg neighborhood of Brooklyn with Marcus Pogarsky, an old friend of Julius's from high school and CCNY. Marcus and his wife, Stella, were open, active Communists. The boyhood friends were often joined by comrades from their days at the Steinmetz Club for evening bull sessions during which they chewed on the latest analysis of the world situation from the *Daily Worker*. Ethel and Stella sat in, asking questions and admiring their husbands, but, true to 1940s gender roles, they rarely interjected their own opinions.

While he was learning the ropes as a junior engineer in the Signal Corps procurement operation, Julius resumed his affiliation with the Federation of Architects, Engineers, Chemists, and Technicians, which was energetically recruiting members at the Signal Corps.

Rosenberg also took on the challenge of aligning service to the American military with loyalty to the CPUSA. The solution was staring him and the other Steinmetz Club alumni in the face every day when they reported to work. The blueprints, contract documents, and technical manuals they handled could be of great value to the Soviet Union. Security was lax, so there was no problem obtaining and "borrowing" classified documents, but finding a secure way to communicate information to Moscow was more difficult.

Rosenberg approached a succession of party members to ask for help making contact with someone who could pass secret military information to the Russians. One of the men he turned to in his quest for an intermediary was Abraham Osheroff, a wounded veteran of the Abraham Lincoln Brigade who ran for the New York Assembly as a Communist in 1940. Rosenberg told Osheroff that he had "specifications that would permit fighter planes to fire machine guns without damaging their propellers" and asked if he knew anyone who could send the information to Moscow. When he learned that Osheroff couldn't help, Rosenberg took the proposal to other party officials.[11]

The timing of Rosenberg's approach to Osheroff is noteworthy. It was before June 1941 — at a time when the Nazi-Soviet Pact was in force. Rosenberg didn't start on the path to becoming a spy with the goal of helping an American ally, or necessarily of fighting fascism. *Before* either the USSR or the United States was at war with Germany, he considered himself a partisan fighting behind enemy lines — that is, in the United States — on behalf of Soviet Communism. For Rosenberg, therefore, as for Barr, Stalin's alliance with the United States during World War II was a matter of convenience, a temporary expedient, much as Russia's prior alliance with Germany had been. They were eager to do anything they could to help the Soviet cause — before, during, and after the war against Hitler.

The Nazi-Soviet Pact didn't trouble Barr as much as it did some Communists, in part because he viewed it as a Machiavellian stratagem, but even more because his opposition to fascism hadn't been rooted in sympathy for European Jews. Unlike Rosenberg, who identified with and was tormented by the Jews' fate, Barr opposed the fascists primarily because of their threat to the Soviet Union. Barr described Stalin's deal with Hitler as "a blow," but it wasn't strong enough to knock him out of the party. He was happy to hew to Moscow's instructions to direct mock fury against Chamberlain, Churchill, and Roosevelt. While he never came close to supporting fascism, Barr didn't have the visceral hatred for Nazis that many of his peers felt; it is difficult for anyone who knew him to imagine Barr hating or wanting to hurt anyone. He abhorred all religion and was embarrassed by his parents' Old World mentality, as well as by his mother's illiteracy.

It isn't clear when Rosenberg first discussed the idea of espionage with Barr, but by early 1941 Barr was filling his little notebooks with everything he came across that could be useful to the Soviets. When he started providing classified information to Rosenberg for delivery to the KGB, Barr knew that Moscow's policies were in conflict with Washington's, just as he knew in later years that his contributions to Soviet military technology could put the lives of U.S. soldiers in jeopardy in Korea, Vietnam, and elsewhere. This knowledge never caused a moment's hesitation. Barr would take tremendous personal risks and do everything possible for the Soviet Union, not out of animosity to the United States, but driven by the belief that Communism represented the best hope for humanity. The only sovereign socialist country must be preserved at all costs, he believed.[12]

For about the first half-year that he worked at Fort Monmouth, Barr lived with Elaine Goldfarb, who had quit her job in Washington and moved north with him. The couple presented themselves to acquaintances as newlyweds, although they had never been legally married. Affordable housing was in short supply, so Goldfarb teamed up with another engineer's wife to look for an apartment. She had been introduced to Samuel Sack's wife through a party member in Washington. Sack was also just starting an engineering job at Fort Hancock, the Signal Corps radar research facility located near Fort Monmouth. The two couples' apartment in Long Branch, New Jersey, was 500 yards from the shore and about three miles from Fort Monmouth. Politics alone doesn't necessarily create personal compatibility. Goldfarb quickly found that she disliked Sack intensely, and even Barr, an outgoing person who could get along with almost anyone, was from their first meeting barely on speaking terms with him. Barr and Goldfarb moved out after two acrimonious months. Soon after leaving the Sacks' apartment, Barr and Goldfarb also parted company.

After breaking up with Goldfarb, Barr met the only person he would ever love unconditionally and faithfully, Alfred Epamenondas Sarant, a newly hired Signal Corps junior electrical engineer. Sarant, a short, wiry athlete with an intense sense of personal discipline that occasionally spilled over into bouts of depression, and Barr, tall, thin, perpetually cheerful, and extroverted, made an odd couple. They were as different as a cat and a dog, but starting from the time they met in September 1941, Sarant and Barr stuck together, shaping each other's path through life for the next three decades.

The son of Greek immigrants — his father, Epamenonda George Sarantopoulos, had been born in Sparta and changed his name to Nonda George Sarant after emigrating to America — Sarant was Barr's first Gentile close friend. Barr soon learned that Al had been raised in a completely different milieu from the self-contained Jewish ghettos he and all of his other friends experienced as children.

Sarant was an all-American boy from Hempstead, Long Island, a middle-class suburb of New York. As a kid he had had a newspaper route, played the flute in the high school orchestra, and spent a summer dangling high over the streets of Manhattan, cleaning skyscraper windows. At age seventeen he had won a regional fencing championship. Sarant had also excelled academically, scoring third out of 1,000 New York high school seniors who applied for entrance to Cooper Union, a private college where students who met the rigorous entry criteria — Julius Rosenberg tried to get in, but didn't make the cut — received a free, first-rate education in the sciences, engineering, and art. In 1937, he was elected vice-president both of his class at Cooper Union's Institute of Technology and of its newly created dramatics club.[13]

Cooper Union was less radical than CCNY, but the various shades of Red were well represented in the student body. Like Barr, Sarant joined the Young

Communist League as a college student and openly supported the Soviet Union. His first job after graduating with a degree in electrical engineering was at Western Electric, an enormous company that served as the Bell Telephone System's manufacturing subsidiary. Sarant left the company after six months to join the Signal Corps, hoping it would provide opportunities to work with more advanced technologies.[14]

Soon after they met, Barr introduced Sarant to Rosenberg. Sarant respected Rosenberg's dedication to the Communist cause, but the two were never close. As Barr's ambitions and interests expanded, he also came to view Julius less as a friend and more as a commissar. By Barr's standards, Rosenberg was too serious, even prudish. Julius considered Barr's enthusiasm for music frivolous, and he and Ethel rebuked him for fooling around with women.[15]

Barr avoided discussing politics at work, hiding his admiration for Stalin and Browder. He wasn't bashful about trying to convert colleagues or his party comrades to worship another of his idols, J. S. Bach. Ironically for an atheist, Barr maintained that Bach's *St. Matthew's Passion,* a three-hour oratorio that recounts Christ's Last Supper, crucifixion, and resurrection, was the greatest piece of music ever written.

In addition to his party work and his duties at the Signal Corps, Barr was hard at work on an invention — a system for transmitting voice over infrared light waves — that he hoped could bring him fame and fortune. He was confident enough of the idea's value and novelty that he filed a patent application.

Unlike Barr, Rosenberg wasn't intellectually engaged in his job, but the secure paycheck that it provided meant a great deal to him. He and Ethel had grown up in more dire poverty than Barr, so the $2,100 salary made it possible for the couple to greatly improve their lifestyle. They rode an elevator and for the first time in their lives had hot running water, luxuries that Ethel's mother still lacked a decade later.

The new job took Julius away from home a lot, traveling throughout New York and surrounding states to inspect electronics factories. He had to acquire a detailed understanding of the practical details of manufacturing — just the kind of information that would be useful to someone trying to tool-up factories to make copies. The quiet, mild-mannered young man showed no signs that he was destined to rise very high in the engineering profession. Still, he was hard working, and his job appeared to be completely secure.

It came as a complete surprise when the Civil Service informed Rosenberg in the spring of 1941 that he would soon be fired because the government had evidence indicating that he was a Communist. It looked as though Rosenberg's newfound economic success was coming to an abrupt end — and that his career as an espionage agent would be grounded before it even took off.

Rosenberg had been identified by an FBI screening program that attempted to cross-reference rosters of Reds with lists of government workers, especially individuals in positions that gave them access to sensitive military or political information. The Communist Party didn't publish membership lists, so the FBI used the next-best thing: lists of individuals who had linked their names to the party on public documents. Investigators came across Ethel Rosenberg's name on one of the nominating petitions circulated in 1939 to put Peter Cacchione on the ballot for the New York City Council as a CPUSA candidate.

From the perspective of law enforcement officials, the Cacchione petitions were excellent surrogates for a registry of CPUSA members living in Brooklyn in 1939. Individuals were self-identified, so the potential for malicious or unintentional mistaken identity that often occurs when tips come from informers was absent. The inclusion of home addresses and signatures helped track down the signers.

The FBI found that Ethel was no longer working for the government, but that her husband was employed by the Army. What's more, the investigators discovered that the Pogarskys (Marcus Pogarsky later changed his name to Mark Page), the couple the Rosenbergs shared an apartment with before moving to their own apartment in the Knickerbocker Village low-rent complex near Brooklyn Bridge, were open party members. All of this was sufficient evidence under the rules in force at the time to permit the government to dismiss Julius Rosenberg; many people were terminated on the basis of much less substantial and, as it turned out, less accurate suspicions. But as an experienced union organizer who had helped FAECT members fight firings, Rosenberg knew that things weren't as bleak as they seemed.

Refusing to accept his fate quietly, Rosenberg launched a strenuous defense. Appealing to his interrogators' sense of fairness, he argued at a Civil Service hearing that even if Ethel "did sign a petition, I don't see how that would affect me. After all, she is a different person and has rights." He supplemented this quite reasonable argument with lies designed to convince the authorities that he was loyal both to the United States and to the Signal Corps. First, Julius suggested that Ethel's political views were a mystery to him, although in fact their relationship centered on their shared passion for Communism. People who knew her said that Ethel would not "buy from a butcher or grocer unless he were an open sympathizer toward Soviet Russia. She considered everyone who was against Communism her personal enemy." Despite the countless nights Ethel spent listening to Julie, Marcus Pogarsky, and other comrades endlessly pick apart the latest missives from Moscow, he reported: "We never discuss politics, but I am quite sure her views are similar to my own." He flatly stated that his wife, a Communist Party member and former member of the

Young Communist League, "is no Communist." Ethel had signed the Cacchione petition only as a favor to a stranger who came to her door collecting signatures, Julius said.

Turning from Ethel's political views to his own, the man who had organized and led a YCL chapter at CCNY and edited a Communist newsletter said that as far as he knew "none of my friends at college were interested in the Communist Party . . . At no time in my life have I ever had anything to do with distribution of Communist literature." Then, as evidence of his devotion to the Signal Corps, Rosenberg claimed to have recently turned down an offer of a better job at NACA's Langley Laboratory in Hampton, Virginia. He didn't present any evidence that NACA had actually offered him a job, but it is possible that Perl had found him a position there.[16]

The arguments must have been convincing, because the Army reversed its decision to fire Rosenberg. Neither the FBI nor Army counterintelligence checked up on the references Rosenberg had provided to get the Signal Corps job. If they had, they would probably have asked Perl, whom Rosenberg listed as a reference, to vouch for his friend's reliability. Even if Perl had hidden his and Rosenberg's active involvement with the Communist Party, the aeronautical engineer's responses might have been recorded and remembered when Barr or others who listed him as a reference became the subject of investigations.

Barr's former roommate, Samuel Sack, wasn't as deft as Rosenberg at avoiding the consequences of association with the Cacchione campaign. Not only was his name on one of the nominating petitions, but Sack had been indiscreet enough to register his affiliation as a Communist in the 1935, 1936, and 1937 elections. He was fired on June 16, 1941. Apparently it didn't occur to the FBI or the Army to investigate Sack's roommates.[17]

Four days later, on June 20, the Communist-dominated peace movement announced a milestone. American Peace Mobilization had completed 1,000 hours of continuous parading in front of the White House and issued a statement claiming "brilliant" attainment of its objective of "dramatically presenting to the Administration the people's loathing of war." Frederick V. Field, American Peace Mobilization's executive secretary, announced that he would soon reveal "new forms of action in the attack on warmongers." Two days later, the *New York Times* reported on APM's vow to hold similar vigils in front of the Capitol and throughout the country.[18]

Just as the Popular Front crumbled in a single day in August 1939 after the world learned of Stalin's deal with Hitler, the CPUSA's opposition to America's joining the war in Europe exploded in the early hours of June 22, 1941, when German shells destroyed border outposts in Byelorussia and bombs landed on

Kiev and other Soviet cities. Notwithstanding the embarrassing timing of reports of a new round of antiwar activism, the CPUSA and its members turned on a dime when they learned of the Nazi invasion.

For Barr, horror at the attack on the land of his dreams was mixed with relief that he was free to throw himself enthusiastically into his work for the Army. Barr knew, however, that the CPUSA's support for war didn't make it safe to reveal his political views. The Smith Act, which essentially criminalized the Communist Party, was in force. Sack's fate was fresh in his mind, as was the deep antipathy to the Soviet Union among some American politicians. Barr noticed that there was no outcry when a senator from Missouri told his colleagues just days after the Nazis crossed into Russia: "If we see that Germany is winning, we should aid Russia, and if we see that Russia is winning, we should aid Germany, and that way let them kill as many as possible, although I don't want to see Hitler victorious under any circumstances." During the same debate, another Democrat said that the German attack on the Soviet Union was "a case of dog eat dog." The views of the future president, Harry Truman, did not prevail, but Barr and his comrades felt throughout the war that the United States and its allies were at a minimum holding out on Russia, and more likely were secretly plotting its destruction. In contrast to Truman's response to the Nazi invasion of Russia, the American Communist movement's attention was focused on getting the United States into the war as quickly as possible and on convincing Congress to rush tanks, airplanes, and other assistance to the Red Army.[19]

With Nazi troops on Russian soil, Rosenberg's efforts to transmit information to the Soviet Union acquired new urgency. Sometime before the end of 1941, the Signal Corps inspector's inquiries about Soviet intelligence contacts brought him to the attention of Bernard Schuster, a senior CPUSA official who acted as an intermediary between Soviet intelligence (which assigned him the cover name "Chester") and party members, including Earl Browder. Given Browder's personal role in espionage and his oversight of the party's "secret work," it is likely that he approved or directed Schuster's recruitment of Rosenberg.[20]

Schuster put Rosenberg in touch with Jacob Raisen, who was known to his party comrades as Jacob Golos. Golos, which means "voice" in Russian, was one of several pseudonyms Raisen adopted during a lifetime of conspiracy. A naturalized American citizen who retained his Russian accent, Golos persuaded the engineer that he had the appropriate connections to ensure that information would be sent on securely to Moscow. As one of the CPUSA's most experienced, trusted intelligence operatives, he took orders from and delivered information directly to Russian KGB officers, as well as from senior

U.S. officials, especially Earl Browder. Short, stocky, poorly dressed, and with the labored breathing of a man with a serious heart condition, Golos didn't match Hollywood's image of a macho spymaster. Neither did the thin, sickly Rosenberg, who complained bitterly of boils and had bad table manners, conform to the public's picture of a suave spy.[21]

Like Rosenberg, Golos had substituted fanatic devotion to Communism for the Jewish faith of his parents. He picked up the traits that made him a successful KGB agent early in life, in tsarist Russia. One of these attributes, street smarts, was acquired as an eight- year-old, when he learned to avoid detection while distributing Marxist literature. His survival instincts were honed in a Russian prison after being arrested as a teenager by the Okhrana, the secret police. Another helpful feature, visceral hatred of the tsarist government, was reinforced by jail, particularly an episode in which Golos was among a group of revolutionaries who were dragged into a prison courtyard to be shot. As his associates were crumpling to the ground, Golos fell and feigned death for two days. He was found and released when relatives of the victims stormed the prison to claim the bodies.[22]

Golos was further toughened by exile to Siberia in 1907, imposed for operating a secret Bolshevik printing shop. He escaped to Japan two years later and traveled via China to New York. A founding member in 1919 of the American Communist Party, Golos was unswervingly loyal to the Bolshevik cause. After the revolution, he traveled to the Soviet Union several times, where the KGB recruited him.

In 1927, the KGB set up Golos with a cover as the head of World Tourists, Inc., a travel agency located in New York at 60 Fifth Avenue specializing in arranging tours of the USSR. Golos publicized the travel agency's services in Communist as well as mainstream publications. A typical advertisement for World Tourists placed in the *New York Times* on May 24, 1931, offered Americans a twenty-six-day "social study tour" of the Soviet Union under the auspices of "the first American travel organization to conduct tours to the Soviet Union." Ironically, the $389 price included round-trip transportation on a German liner, the S.S. *Bremen,* the ship that had provoked the rage of American Communists in 1935. A few years later, a World Tourists advertisement ("Inflation Does Not Affect Your Trip to the USSR, Full Value for Your Dollar") was placed on the back pages of *Soviet Russia Today* just above an ad for Camp Unity touting a "Newly Built Tennis Court" and "Believe it or not, a workers' school in the camp."[23]

In addition to his official job at World Tourists, Golos had two overlapping covert posts: he was chairman of the CPUSA's "Control Commission," a secretive body charged with investigating and rooting out ideological deviation, and the head of a network of American espionage agents. In his former role, Golos inspired terror among American party officials. He was also surprisingly successful as a recruiter and case officer. In addition to ideologically motivated recruits, such as Communist merchant seamen who served as KGB couriers, Golos managed to weave a network of corrupt government officials in the United States and Canada with whom he exchanged cash for the currency that was essential for KGB operatives to cross borders and create new identities: passports, naturalization papers, birth certificates, and other official documentation.[24]

In terms of his work on behalf of Soviet intelligence, Golos had one major fault: little patience for the intricacies and discipline of the dance the Russians call *konspiratsia* and Americans refer to as "tradecraft." In both lexicons, the term refers to the ingenious, and often tedious, techniques and precautions taken by intelligence operatives to keep their actions secret from hostile forces. Golos knew that the rules of *konspiratsia* did not allow case officers to fall in love with their agents, so in 1938, when he started a romance with Elizabeth Bentley, a young American who had infiltrated an Italian Fascist organization's New York office, he hid the affair from KGB superiors. By the time they learned of the relationship, Bentley had become an integral link in a chain conveying intelligence from agents in government and industry to the KGB. She knew and met with Communists and Communist sympathizers in Washington and New York, passing on their information to her lover.[25]

The FBI came close to putting Golos out of the espionage business on several occasions, but each time it backed off. In October 1939, federal agents raided World Tourists seeking evidence to prove that senior members of the Communist Party had committed passport fraud. In part because Golos had neglected to destroy evidence that World Tourists had helped Browder travel under assumed identities — documentation that a more careful intelligence operative would have destroyed — the CPUSA leader was convicted of passport fraud in January 1940. Browder was sentenced to four years in prison, an unusually harsh sentence compared with punishments meted out to others for the same crime.[26]

The FBI determined that the Soviet state-owned travel agency Intourist subsidized World Tourists, and that its activities included distributing propaganda in the United States. In March 1940, the Justice Department indicted "Jacob Raisen, also known as Jacob Golos," for failure to register as a foreign agent. As part of an agreement with the government that spared other Communist agents from prosecution, Golos pleaded guilty and received a slap on the wrist: a four-month suspended sentence and a $500 fine. Attorney General Frank Murphy publicly accused Golos of being a spy, and the FBI put him under surveillance for a while, but he managed to continue running an extensive espionage network by establishing a new front company and leaving much of the actual contact with agents to Bentley. After public disclosure of his connection to Soviet espionage, Golos played a key role in recruiting agents for and planning the logistics of one of the KGB's highest priorities, the brutal assassination of Trotsky—a pickaxe blow to the head—which was accomplished in Mexico in August 1940.[27]

During the time Rosenberg was providing information to him, Golos was reporting to a veteran KGB officer named Iskhak Akhmerov. Akhmerov was married to Earl Browder's niece, Helen Lowry. Akhmerov headed the KGB's "illegal" organization, called a *rezidentura* (Soviet intelligence made a distinction between "legal" operations, which were conducted under cover of diplomatic immunity, and "illegal" operations that lacked such cover). Operating without the protection of diplomatic immunity, he set up and ran a fur and clothing shop in Baltimore. In 1942, Akhmerov forwarded fifty-nine rolls of microfilm, presumably including some of the material Rosenberg had given to Golos, to Moscow via the KGB office at the New York consulate.[28]

A KGB document indicates that from the start of his relationship with Golos, Rosenberg was collecting information and party dues from four other engineers. Rosenberg and his team understood that their information was going directly to the Soviet Union, unlike many other Americans recruited by the CPUSA for espionage who were told various fairy tales, most commonly that the ultimate recipient of intelligence was the Comintern, the international Communist movement's coordinating body. Although Rosenberg's quartet of informants isn't named in the KGB memo, there can be little doubt that Barr was one of them.[29]

Eventually Rosenberg's ring expanded to include eight informants. With the exception of Sarant, the known members of the circle shared a number of characteristics. Each had been born in New York into families where Yiddish was spoken more fluently than English. Every one of them had at least one parent who was born in Russia, and in most cases both parents had grown up as subjects of the tsar. They had been raised in poverty, on the margins of American society, the children of immigrants who hadn't fully assimilated, and as a result they lacked roots in American society as well as any expectation of attaining material prosperity. Their early lives had presented little reason to reject the Communist story line. It seemed self-evident that the capitalist economic system, which was unable to provide many Americans with decent lives, was teetering on the edge of collapse. The notion that democracy was a complete sham, and that in reality the United States was run by and for a tiny group of greedy men who owned and manipulated the newspapers, oppressed workers, and rigged elections, also seemed quite reasonable to the men Rosenberg recruited.

In fact, the term "recruited," which suggests persuasion or enticement, is too strong. Barr and the others enlisted eagerly. Since their teenage years, they had romanticized rebellion against the capitalist oppressors. For Barr, a devotee of revolution, there was little or no mental boundary between dissent and subversion, and when the USSR was fighting for its very existence, distinctions between helping an ally and espionage seemed irrelevant.

Covert organizing for the Federation of Architects, Engineers, Chemists, and Technicians, sheltering and chauffeuring comrades who were attending antiwar rallies, and shaking their fists at Nazi ships had seemed adventurous ways to strike blows against the enemies of Communism. Faced with the opportunity to provide information that they believed could help turn the tide of war against the Nazis, Barr and his comrades realized that these had been child's play. When Rosenberg's friends learned that he was in touch with Soviet intelligence and that they could be of service also, it must have seemed as if Stalin himself had singled them out, humble cogs in the revolutionary machine, for special roles in defending the revolution. There was as much chance of a dedicated Communist's turning down the offer as of a devout Catholic's declining to come to the pope's aid in his hour of need.

The knowledge that he faced serious consequences if caught heightened the allure to Barr, not because he was a thrill seeker, but because the risks made the venture, and his role in it, seem more important. He retained this idealistic motivation, but the habits of concealment and the pleasure at having a secret purpose changed his character. Leading a dual life, pretending to be an ordinary engineer just like his peers, while at the same time thinking secret thoughts and plotting adventures unknown and unimaginable to his colleagues, was exhilarating. As part of a secret conspiracy, Barr wasn't bound by the rules that constrained other men. Like an addict's first fix, the pleasure and pain, the sense of superiority and the fear of detection associated with secrecy and deception were permanently seared into Barr's personality.

Americans who were Communists in the 1930s have noted that the intense loyalty and insularity of party life led them to contemplate and even seek out extreme behaviors. "Anyone who has never been associated with a movement for a cause he has judged to be great will perhaps not be able to understand . . . his own potential for crime," Lionel Abel, a dedicated follower of Trotsky during the Depression, noted. "For the prospect of committing a crime to further a cause in which you deeply believe is a very exciting one. Here is a test not only of what you believe, but also of what you are."[30]

For the rest of his days, in one way or another, Barr led parallel lives, keeping even individuals with whom he was on the closest and most intimate terms completely unaware of his secret activities, thoughts, and feelings. Unlike many people who, finding themselves in circumstances that require concealment, become withdrawn and avoid human contact, Barr was outgoing to an extreme, charming, and seemingly absolutely guileless. Perhaps he was so confident because he so thoroughly enjoyed the game, or more likely it was because he simply immersed himself in each moment. Like an experienced tightrope walker, Barr always looked ahead, rarely glancing down.

Although he wasn't aware of it, just as Rosenberg's intelligence enterprise was getting started, events unfolded in Washington that could have curtailed or shut it down. On September 14, 1941, the FBI finally got around to sending an official memo to the Office of Naval Intelligence (ONI) reporting that Sobell was "listed on the mailing or membership lists of American Peace Mobilization [and the] American Youth Congress." The Bureau knew this because it had illegally broken into APM's Washington office and copied the membership list. The Navy conducted an investigation of Sobell, but dropped it when he resigned to go back to school. ONI replied to the FBI in December, stating that "due to fact that Morton Sobell resigned on Oct. 1, 41 . . . Navy interest does not exist at this time." The FBI checked up on Sobell, found that he'd gone to the University of Michigan to study for a master's degree in electrical engineering, and lost interest in him.[31]

A few months later, ONI informed the FBI that it had investigated Elitcher because he shared Sobell's apartment on N Street. Sobell "was allegedly conducting subversive activities" while he was employed by the Navy, the ONI stated, but it "advised that this report contained nothing of a derogatory nature relative to Elitcher other than his association with Sobell." Neither the FBI nor ONI contacted Elitcher to ask if he was involved with or aware of Sobell's "subversive activities."

The only other piece of information ONI turned up about Elitcher was that "in addition to the fact that they lived together [during the time Sobell was in Washington], they had previously attended City College of New York together." If ONI or the FBI, which maintained an extraordinarily efficient cross-referenced filing system, had pursued the lead, in addition to uncovering the fact that Elitcher and his wife were active CPUSA members, they might have discovered that a third CCNY classmate with similar loyalties, Bill Danziger, was also working for the Navy. The Navy learned of Danziger's Communist affiliation and fired him, but it didn't investigate his associates. A vigorous investigation into other government employees from the CCNY electrical engineering class of 1939 might have turned up some other interesting conjunctions, including the fact that two other classmates, Rosenberg and Barr, were working for the military, and that Perl had tried to get Sobell and Rosenberg jobs at NACA.[32]

Another potentially devastating blow to the Rosenberg ring came on December 16, 1941, when FBI investigators finally turned their attention to page 2,133, dated August 9, 1939, of a petition to place Peter Cacchione on the ballot for the New York City Council. That page contained the names Arthur and Joel Barr. An agent cross-checked the Civil Service files and found that someone named Joel Barr was listed as a government employee. He placed a piece of onionskin paper over the photostat duplicate of the petition and traced the signature. Ten days later — the day after Christmas and two weeks after the Japanese attack on Pearl Harbor — another agent was dispatched to 641 Washington Street, New York City, where he plucked the final page of Barr's Civil Service employment application from a file folder and traced the signature. When the two scraps of translucent paper were placed on top of each other "a conclusion was made that the identity of the two signatures was unmistakable," according to an FBI memo.[33]

The Bureau quickly determined that Barr was working at Fort Monmouth. On January 16, 1942, it sent G-2, the Army's counterintelligence division, copies of the signature tracings along with a report noting that Barr had attended CCNY and that he had shared an apartment with Sack, who had been discharged the previous June because of his Communist affiliation. The report contained another piece of information: Barr had listed a NACA engineer, William Perl, as a reference when applying for the Signal Corps position; but this lead wasn't pursued.

On February 23, 1942, newspapers printed a map of the world and instructed readers to "clip and save" it for use during a speech that President Roosevelt would deliver in the evening, his first major address to the American people since two days after the Pearl Harbor attack. Barr had just arrived at his desk and was discussing the upcoming speech with a couple of the other engineers when two sergeants approached, told him to remove any personal belongings from his workplace, and requested that he accompany them. They led him to an office where an Army officer said that he was being terminated as a security risk. The sergeants searched Barr's briefcase to ensure that it didn't contain any Army property — the first time it had been examined — confiscated the orange base pass, and escorted him to the civilian side of the entrance gate.[34]

That afternoon the Fort Monmouth Intelligence Office placed Barr's name on a list of undesirable employees who were ineligible for employment by the Army. If the FBI or the Army had implemented efficient vetting procedures, this could have been the end of Barr's career both in military electronics and as a spy for the Soviet Union.[35]

In the evening, Barr and Sarant listened together as FDR explained to the American people the unique nature of the conflict. He asked them to "take out and spread before you a map of the whole Earth, and to follow with me the references which I shall make to the world-encircling battle lines of this war." Roosevelt also saluted the "superb Russian Army as it celebrates the twenty-fourth anniversary of its first assembly." He warned Americans to prepare for a long war of attrition, and stressed the importance of increasing armaments production.[36]

Barr and Sarant found themselves in a tightly knit movement, certain that they were in the vanguard of a revolution that would sweep capitalism from America. They were impervious to, and largely unaware of, criticism of the Soviet model or of Stalinism. On the one hand, the fatal flaws of capitalism were evident, part of their everyday lives, and on the other hand reports critical of the Soviet line were perceived as vile propaganda. The knowledge that their beliefs put their careers at risk only intensified their religious belief in Communism: after all, the capitalists must really have something to fear if they would go to such lengths to root out Communists.

4

Western Electric, 1942–1945

News of Barr's firing reverberated through the Signal Corps Labs, prompting more than a hundred people, including many who barely knew him, to sign petitions expressing concern and requesting that the officer in command "very carefully consider whether he had done the right thing." Such an outpouring of support would have been unusual under any circumstances, but coming as it did during wartime, when the expression of grievances to military authorities could be considered unpatriotic, it was extraordinary.

"He was one of those people that everybody in the section liked," Ralph Iannarone, an engineer who worked in the same branch as Barr at Fort Monmouth, and whose signature appeared at the top of one of the petitions, told Senator Joseph McCarthy's subcommittee in 1953. "It was the first incident which ever came to my knowledge and most everybody else's of somebody being picked out of the place and suspended. Everybody's sympathy went to the fellow. We couldn't understand on what basis the man was suspended." When word got around the lab that Barr had been fired because he was a Communist, however, views quickly changed. Many of the engineers removed their names or tore up the petitions.[1]

Barr, confident that he'd be able to find another job, didn't waste time moping. He turned to Sarant, who had resigned from Western Electric to join the Signal Corps, for help. Sarant gave Barr introductions to executives at his old firm who were glad to hear from an engineer with hands-on radar experience.

In his employment application, Barr stated that he had voluntarily resigned from the Signal Corps to seek a position with greater prospects for professional advancement. Outlining his qualifications to work at Western Electric, he reported that he had "done quite a bit of radio designing, construction and repair on my own. I possess radio amateur license WXKEN (W2KEN), and I was very active on ultra high frequency bands. I have applied for a patent on the method of frequency modulation [on] a beam of light."[2]

If executives at Western Electric had placed a single telephone call to the personnel office at Fort Monmouth, or to one of Barr's former supervisors or co-workers, or if procedures had been in place to ask the FBI to vet employees slated to handle classified information, Barr wouldn't have been hired. In addition to being noted in Barr's personnel file, the reason for his termination was widely known at Fort Monmouth. As there was a great deal of formal and informal communication between the Signal Corps Labs and Western Electric, gossip from any of the hundreds of people who knew that Barr had been fired as a security risk could have reached Western Electric's security office. But there were no calls, no gossip, and no FBI vetting procedures. It wasn't the last time Barr navigated through a virtual minefield, seemingly oblivious to danger. In this regard, he was a bit like Mr. Magoo, the nearsighted comic character who careened through life barely avoiding pitfalls that he couldn't see.

If Western Electric or the U.S. government had been sufficiently vigilant to ascertain that Barr's first step after being fired from Fort Monmouth was to seek another job involving classified information, the Rosenberg spy ring might have been shut down long before it obtained much information of value. No spy acts in isolation — at a minimum, there must be someone to pass information to — and the essence of effective counterintelligence is aggressive investigation of a suspected individual's connections. An investigation of Barr would probably have been focused on identifying his friends and collaborators. The natural follow-up would have included a close examination of his employment application, where (like Rosenberg) he had listed Perl as a reference. Close scrutiny of Perl could easily have led to Rosenberg. At a minimum, an aggressive investigation would almost certainly have spooked the Russians into shutting down a network that up to this time hadn't yielded many secrets.

There was no investigation, so Barr was hired as an assistant engineer on March 16, 1942, and assigned to work at Western Electric's Bayonne plant in Kearny, New Jersey, on airborne radar systems that incorporated some of the most highly classified, sensitive technologies in the American arsenal. He was quickly promoted to manufacturing engineer, a position that made him privy to the fruits of an extraordinary collaboration between the Signal Corps and MIT's Radiation Laboratory. Some of the world's leading scientists, operating in extraordinary haste and under strict security restrictions, made break-throughs at MIT during World War II that laid the foundations for many of the technologies that transformed twentieth-century warfare and civilian life, from radar to computers and the science of cybernetics.

The Army's role in the partnership wasn't as sexy as MIT's, but it was no less important or demanding. The Rad Lab turned rough prototypes — often flimsy creations assembled from spare parts and even recycled kitchen appliances — over to the Signal Corps, which had to translate them into detailed specifications, recipes that could be reproduced on an industrial scale. Then a handful of companies, including Western Electric, faced the difficult task of manufacturing the equipment at breakneck speed, under a heavy blanket of secrecy.

While security officials could compartmentalize much of the R&D, for example by assigning the design of the various components in a weapons system to teams at different institutions, at some point all the pieces had to be assembled and tested by people who understood how they fitted together and what they were supposed to do. As a manufacturing engineer, Barr was placed at exactly that point. In order to help design the manufacturing process and iron out any problems that developed, he had to comprehend the basic principles underlying a particular weapon and to have a detailed knowledge of all the components. Because practical "how-to" experience from related weapons might be relevant, manufacturing engineers were given free access to the entire factory and were encouraged to study projects that they were not specifically assigned to work on. Men assigned to figure out how to build advanced technologies were in an excellent position to teach the Soviets how to do the same.

Barr, "along with the other engineers working in [his] department, had complete freedom of the plant and were permitted to go into any other sections, and to constantly check to find out if there were any errors in the use of the computer or the Norden bombsight in order that they might correct any of these errors," one of his former supervisors at Western Electric later told the FBI. The Norden bombsight, which used radar to help target and time bomb releases, was so secret that the U.S. government refused to grant the British access to patents describing it, or a manufacturing license. He also said that engineers like Barr "were in the habit of taking papers and plans out of the plant with the idea that they might or would work on them at home. Under these conditions, he stated that BARR, along with the other engineers, could have carried briefcases out of the plant at any time without question."[3]

As America's involvement in the war intensified, the wheels of the FBI's counterintelligence machinery were calibrated to grind more finely, but with regard to Barr, the output consisted entirely of anodyne papers that gave the misleading impression of diligent follow-up. During the summer of 1942, FBI agents spent far more time typing reports about Barr and batting memos about him back and forth between Washington and New York than they did investigating him.

On July 3, 1942, FBI headquarters sent a memo to its New York field office describing the investigation that had led to Barr's dismissal from the Signal Corps. The New York office was instructed to investigate Barr to determine if he should be placed on a list of individuals targeted for "custodial detention" as security risks. Putting Barr's name on the list would have committed the FBI to keep track of where he lived and worked so that the Bureau could arrest him on short notice. Doing so would also have alerted the authorities that a man who had been fired as a security risk was again handling classified documents.[4]

On July 14, Percy Foxworth, the assistant director of the New York field office, sent headquarters a memo stating that the "case after due consideration has been placed in a deferred status. It will receive appropriate attention immediately when personnel is available." The Bureau had no idea that Barr was again employed in a position that gave him access to secret documents.[5]

Barr and his comrades were fortunate that the U.S. government wasn't taking the threat of Soviet espionage seriously. Just as the engineers casually carried classified documents through the security checkpoints at their workplaces, they took few security precautions in their off-duty hours, retaining membership in the CPUSA, meeting at each other's apartments to discuss their espionage activities as well as current politics, and subscribing to Communist publications at home. Their sole precaution was to avoid discussing politics at work. Despite Golos's exposure as a Soviet intelligence operative, he met personally with Rosenberg, taking only cursory measures to evade detection.[6]

Elizabeth Bentley described these measures three years later. One evening in the summer of 1942—at about the time the FBI's Foxworth was giving the Barr investigation "due consideration"—Golos was driving Bentley to a dinner engagement when he stopped the car near Knickerbocker Village. "I remained in the car and saw Golos meet an individual on the street corner. I managed to get only a fleeting glimpse of this individual and recall that he was tall, thin, and wore horn-rimmed eyeglasses," Bentley remembered. "Golos told me that this person was one of a group of engineers and that he had given this person my residence telephone number so that he would be able to reach Golos whenever he desired." Golos "did not elaborate on the activities of this person and his associates nor did he ever identify any of them except that this one man to whom he gave my telephone number was referred to as 'Julius.'" Bentley added that she didn't think Julius was his real name—probably she found it hard to believe that an experienced conspirator would be that careless —and that she thought he lived in Knickerbocker Village.[7]

Bentley's physical description of "Julius," his address, and his occupation are consistent with Rosenberg's particulars. Bentley's credibility is enhanced by the fact that she provided these details in 1945, five years before the FBI arrested him. Data from Soviet archives as well as Rosenberg's statements reported by individuals who knew him confirm that he was the person who called Bentley to arrange meetings with Golos.[8]

Communications with the spectacled engineer followed a pattern, Bentley remembered. She would be awakened "in the wee hours," well after midnight, by the telephone ringing in her apartment at 58 Barrow Street, in Greenwich Village. The voice on the other end of the line, calling from a pay phone, always started off in the same way, announcing "This is Julius." Except for one occasion when Golos was in bed next to her when Rosenberg called, she would get up, dress, and call her lover from a pay phone. The calls started in the fall of 1942, and there were only about a half-dozen of them, she recalled.[9]

In declining health, overwhelmed by the work required to run a far-flung network of agents, and lacking the technical education needed to direct the engineers' efforts, Golos did a poor job of managing Rosenberg's espionage. Nonetheless, he wasn't eager to pass an agent on to interlopers from Moscow. Golos didn't initially identify the leader of the cell of engineer spies to his KGB superiors, referring to him only by the code name "Antenna," an elegant moniker for a radio engineer, but a clear breach of the rules of *konspiratsia*, which dictate the use of code names that, if discovered by the opposition, will not help identify an asset.

The New York *rezidentura* first heard Rosenberg's name in June 1942, but it didn't know at the time that he was Antenna. He came to the New York branch's attention when the Center, as the KGB referred to its Moscow headquarters, sent a note cautioning that someone named Julius Rosenberg, whom the cable simply identified as "a stranger" to the KGB, had alerted Golos that another agent was being indiscreet. Rosenberg didn't remain a "stranger" for long.[10]

Bentley heard from Rosenberg only a few times because he was one of the first of many agents taken away from Golos. In the wake of the exposure of World Tourists as a front for Soviet espionage, the KGB became increasingly anxious that Golos was a liability. It was worried both that his cover had been blown and that his lack of professionalism might lead to the exposure of espionage operations. His independence, especially the proprietary way in which he and Bentley treated assets, was also troubling. Golos bitterly fought the KGB's demands to turn over any contacts to officers appointed by the Lubyanka. KGB agents posted to America were clumsy bears, lacking the language skills and sophisticated understanding of American culture required to run American agents, Golos and Bentley argued. Both appealed unsuccessfully to Earl Browder (who had been released from jail in May 1942 in a goodwill gesture to Moscow and the CPUSA), complaining that the hamhanded Russians would destroy the networks Browder and Golos had recruited and run for years. The cagey operative also flatly refused to comply with requests to return to Russia, a decision that, given the executions of other repatriated spies during this period, probably extended his life.[11]

Despite Golos's strong objections to relinquishing control to the new generation of professionals, KGB officers working out of the third floor of the Soviet consulate in New York began reviewing his reports in 1942, looking for assets that could be peeled away. In the spring of 1942, one of these officers, Semyon Semyonov (code name "Tvain," as in Mark Twain), came across communications indicating that Golos "was working with a group of local compatriots [Communist Party members] in the field of technical intelligence," as he stated in a subsequent report to superiors in Moscow. Golos had provided only sketchy information about the group, but it was sufficient to attract Semyonov's interest. Semyonov argued that although the group was producing "desultory materials rated low in importance," it could provide more useful information under better leadership. He asked his boss, Vassily Zarubin (known in the United States as Vassily Zubilin), to give him control of Antenna. Zarubin, nominally a third secretary in the consulate, but actually the highest-ranking KGB official posted to the United States at the time, agreed "despite a certain resistance on [Golos's] part," Semyonov noted laconically.[12]

Office politics may have played a part in Zarubin's decision to give the Rosenberg account to Semyonov. Zarubin, a blunt, tough-talking agent who had earned the trust of top intelligence officers in prior postings to Berlin — and as one of the agents involved with the KGB's massacre of 15,000 Polish Army officers in the Katyn forest — was a polarizing figure. KGB agents who served under Zarubin in the United States either adored or detested him. Golos's KGB contact, Akhmerov, made no secret of his contempt for Zarubin. At first, the professional KGB staff was able to keep a lid on the personal tensions provoked by Zarubin's abrasive personality, but later they erupted in a manner that had dire consequences for the Soviet Union.[13]

Although many of the KGB men posted to the United States fitted Golos's stereotype, Semyonov was an exception, and he was an excellent choice to run Antenna. Both his Russian colleagues and American agents said that Semyonov could easily pass as an American businessman. They praised him as a warmhearted, erudite, and compassionate man equally comfortable discussing in unaccented American English the finer points of romantic novels or chemical engineering. He preferred the poet Robert Frost to Carl Sandburg, whom he considered a "mediocrity" and "a bit of a faker." Semyonov, who worked a cover job as an engineer at Amtorg, a Soviet trading company, seemed to his American agents too nice to be a spy. In conversations with one of his American couriers, Semyonov bemoaned the drudgery and deception that were part and parcel of a case officer's life. Semyonov "spoke of the inherent troubles in attempting to get individuals to supply technical information and of the many disappointments; of the necessary cajoling and flattering; of the importuning and of the deceit; of the promises never meant to be kept; of the outright threats — when required; of the dreary, but apprehensive waiting on street corners for appointments never kept; of the whole discouraging business. It was deadeningly dull, dirty, sullying work."[14]

Rosenberg would probably have been amazed to learn that Semyonov, whose real name was Alexander Taubman, launched his espionage career in a pool of blood. His first KGB assignment was to travel to Paris to befriend and betray Rudolf Klement, the head of Trotsky's European organization, the Fourth International. In July 1938, after cultivating him for a year and a half, Taubman lured Klement to an apartment in the French capital where, according to a senior KGB official, KGB thugs stabbed Klement to death, "cut off his head, and put his body into a suitcase and threw it into the Seine." French police fished the torso out of the river two weeks after the murder; Klement's severed legs were discovered a couple of days later. By the time the police deduced Taubman's role in the grisly business, he was back in Moscow, where he was renamed and sent to a technical school.[15]

Alexander Feklisov, then a young KGB officer starting his first overseas assignment, described in his memoir how Rosenberg was transferred to Semyonov. The Russians, unsure of Rosenberg's motivation and level of commitment, apparently treated it as a *de novo* recruitment. While Golos apparently had a free hand to recruit and run agents, Semyonov and the other career KBG men posted to the United States were required to send detailed information to Moscow supporting every proposed recruitment and to wait for approval before making a pitch to a potential agent. After KBG headquarters finally signed off on Rosenberg in the summer of 1942, the New York *rezidentura* began planning the most sensitive step in agent recruitment, approaching the target and asking him or her to spy.[16]

The Communists didn't hold their traditional Labor Day demonstration in Union Square in 1942. Instead, the CPUSA participated in a rally in Central Park, where representatives from the Soviet Union shared the stage with mainstream American celebrities and dignitaries. In New York, as in other parts of the country, men and women employed at defense plants spent the holiday on the job. Still, about 50,000 people, including masses of soldiers in uniform, streamed into the park to hear Mayor Fiorello La Guardia and union leaders urge Americans to pull together and sacrifice for the war effort.

Following the principle that the easiest place to hide is in a crowd, the KGB selected the Labor Day rally as the venue for transferring control over Antenna to Semyonov. Bernard Schuster, the CPUSA operative who had introduced Rosenberg to Golos, brought the engineer to the park. Schuster's case officer, Konstantin Chugunov, one of the KGB's top political espionage operatives, introduced the two Americans to his friend "Henry" (Semyonov). Once they ascertained that Henry had established rapport with his new agent, Chugunov and Schuster melted into the crowd.

"Julius invited [Semyonov] to have lunch at a restaurant and through the meal he fired away questions about life in the USSR, the attitude towards Jews, their extermination by the Nazis, and the harshness of the fighting on a front that was several thousand miles long," Feklisov reported on the basis of Semyonov's account of the meeting. Rosenberg was shocked to learn that Semyonov's father was trapped in Nazi-occupied Odessa.

The fight against anti-Semitism and Nazism was a powerful appeal for Soviet recruiters. Harry Gold, an American Jew, devoted his life to the KGB, even though he had little interest in Communism, largely because he wanted to fight the Nazis. Gold, who reported to Semyonov at the same time as Rosenberg, later recounted the KGB's lines to the FBI: "If the Nazis triumph, the Jews are done. Extermination. The Soviet Union is the one unyielding opponent of Hitler's fascism. Therefore, anything that strengthens the Soviet Union helps save the Jews." Gold said that this "was in reality the big drive that kept me so resolutely working in espionage."[17]

Semyonov, according Feklisov's account, met with Rosenberg several times, gradually getting around to complaining that "America, in spite of its commitments, was hiding its latest technological innovations from its ally who needed them very badly," and then propositioning him to pass secrets. He was pushing on an open door. "I find it unfair that you should be fighting the common enemy alone. If I can do anything to help, you can count on me," Rosenberg said.[18]

Semyonov's assertion that the United States was withholding weapons technology was quite accurate. Although the United States gave massive amounts of materiel to the Soviet Union, decisions were made in Washington and London early in the war to keep sensitive technologies out of Russian hands. In December 1941 the British military decided that "nothing under development" was to be disclosed to the Russians, nor were they to receive any item that the British or American armed forces did not already have in service. The Americans had a similar policy.[19]

As a highly trained, dedicated intelligence officer, Semyonov must have been horrified when Julius told him how he and his colleagues had been operating. The KGB's fears about Golos had been fully justified; the old conspirator was breaking almost every rule of covert communications. Even in the KGB's inner sanctum in New York, the third floor of the Soviet consulate, at 7 East 61st Street, agents adhered to almost comically stringent security rules. Not only was it strictly forbidden to utter the real or cover names of agents — when discussing them, KGB officers paused to write their names on a pad — but KGB officers had to assume pseudonyms when they climbed the stairs from the first two floors, where they engaged in their official cover jobs, to the third floor. Foreign Ministry employees were not supposed to know which of their colleagues were working for the KGB, although they often found out. To complicate matters further, KGB officers lived in the United States under false names — for example, Feklisov gave his name as Alexander Fomin, while Zarubin was known in the United States as Zubilin — and they employed several different names with their agents. Inevitably, even experienced officers sometimes got mixed up about who they were supposed to be in a particular situation.[20]

Because the KGB correctly assumed that the FBI made extensive use of wiretaps, its officers assigned to the consulate were forbidden to contact their agents by telephone. As an added security measure, KGB officers rarely gave their informants any way to contact them. Instead, the Russians either summoned an agent for a meeting by using a signal, such as a postcard of the Empire State Building, or predesignated times and places, with fallbacks in case either party was unable to meet. KGB officers employed elaborate techniques to detect and evade surveillance and to conduct routine exchanges of information virtually invisibly.

While the KGB officers stationed at the consulate were going to great lengths to cloak their activities, how did Golos set up meetings with Rosenberg? When the engineer wanted to transfer information, he called Bentley on the telephone in the middle of the night (when a call would be sure to arouse the interest of anyone tapping the line) and identified himself as "Julius." This was all at a time when Golos and Bentley knew that the FBI was aware of his connections with Soviet espionage and, because she was working at his front company, had reason to suspect her as well. To make matters worse, Golos had allowed Rosenberg and his wife, Ethel, to continue openly displaying their party affiliation.

Semyonov gave Rosenberg a crash course in *konspiratsia,* especially the art of the "brush pass," a technique in which two agents exchange documents while passing each other. The Russians' preferred procedure was for the American agent to place his or her materials in a folded newspaper. The receiving agent would carry an identically folded newspaper. With a bit of training, it is possible to make the switch in a flash, and when the maneuver is conducted in a crowded place, such as on a subway platform or in the crowds milling outside Madison Square Garden before the Friday night fights, it is virtually undetectable. There were instances when Soviet case officers received documents from American agents and FBI men who were watching at close range didn't spot the exchange.[21]

Semyonov would generally receive documents from Rosenberg in the early evening, after both of them finished work. The Russian would first spend an hour or two "dry cleaning," wandering the city to spot and throw off surveillance. Then exactly at an agreed time, he would approach Rosenberg, usually in a location where they could look over each other's shoulders. If either spotted someone who he thought could be FBI or police, he would give a signal, perhaps shifting the newspaper from one hand to another, or adjusting his tie, to abort the transfer. If the coast was clear, Rosenberg would silently pass his cache of secrets to the man he knew as Henry, taking care not to look at him or to give any sign of recognition. Semyonov quickly handed off the material in a similar manner to Feklisov. Relieved of the incriminating papers, Semyonov would meet Rosenberg at a restaurant to discuss their enterprise, boost his agent's morale, and relay any special requests from the Center.

The KGB, convinced that the FBI followed its own long-standing practice of recruiting waiters and waitresses to spy on foreigners in Russia, preferred to meet in automats, where customers purchased food by putting coins into a slot and sliding back a glass window, or in cafeterias. Their next choice was a diner, the cheaper the better. This was partly because the high turnover made it easy to spot surveillance by individuals who were lingering, because the noise made it difficult to eavesdrop, and also in large part because protocol required that the case officer always pay the bill. The KGB was tight with money, and during the war the New York *rezidentura* reimbursed only for the agent's portion of a meal. Given their modest salaries, entertaining agents in expensive restaurants could quickly bankrupt a case officer. Semyonov and Rosenberg would sometimes meet at the Childs restaurant on 34th Street, a block from Madison Square Garden, where fifty-five cents bought a full dinner of kidney and fresh mushroom casserole, string beans and butter, soup, dessert, and a drink.[22]

While Semyonov and Rosenberg were chewing their food, Feklisov hightailed it back to the consulate, madly microfilmed documents and rushed to return them to Semyonov, who would slip outside, collect them before the pie was finished, and pass them to Rosenberg during coffee. If the documents were from Fort Monmouth, Rosenberg would return them to Barr early the next morning. While Barr was returning the documents to their secure homes inside a well-guarded military base, Feklisov was developing the film at the consulate. He studied the contents and wrote a detailed report for his boss, Semyonov. If the material was particularly important, Semyonov would write a summary report for immediate transmission to the Center.

All urgent reports to and from Moscow were sent via a system that, if used properly, was 100 percent secure, albeit labor intensive. First, the intelligence officer wrote a report, substituting cover names for the names of people and places, and submitted it to the *rezident,* who officially signed all outgoing messages. Agents and KGB staff were assigned cover names, as were some individuals with no involvement in espionage who were frequently mentioned in reports, such as President Roosevelt (cover name "Captain"). The FBI's cover name was "KhATA," which means "Hut." The selection of cover names for places revealed a fondness for classical history: New York was Tyre; Washington, D.C., was Carthage; while San Francisco, appropriately, was Babylon.

Outgoing reports were given to a code clerk, who converted the text into four-digit numbers based on a codebook. The coded text was passed on to a cipher clerk, who transformed the four-digit codes into encrypted five-digit sequences by performing mathematical calculations, based in part on numbers from a special table that he tore off a pad filled with similar tables and discarded after one use. Because the tables were used only once and then destroyed, they were called "one-time pads." Soviet experts were confident that it was impossible for the Americans or anyone else to make any sense of the numbers, so the KGB was comfortable sending its most sensitive reports via Western Union telegrams. As the KGB suspected, its counterparts at the Hut retained copies of the messages, but, lacking the appropriate conversion tables, they found them to be complete gibberish.[23]

The person who received one of the Western Union cables simply reversed the process that was used to encipher and encode the text, using the corresponding one-time pad and codebook. The main limitation of the system was the long time required to convert text manually into and out of the four- and five-digit sequences. As a result, the messages were generally limited to bare-bones summary reports, topics of great urgency, and administrative details that couldn't wait for slower or less secure forms of communication.

As far as scientific and technical intelligence was concerned, the cables represented the gravy; the microfilm copies of secret documents that constituted the meat and potatoes were sent to Russia via diplomatic pouches carried by KGB men who had been deemed unsuitable for covert work. "Pouch" was, and still is, a term of art referring to any baggage that is designated as diplomatic and is therefore granted immunity from inspection. The most sensitive materials, such as microfilms of classified documents provided by the Rosenberg group, were transported in special bags. If the diplomatic courier who was entrusted with the bag thought there was a danger that it would be inspected or confiscated, he could press a button that released acid, quickly destroying the contents. Upon arriving in Moscow, the intelligence catch was sorted, then distributed to those who could put it to use. Barr's radar secrets, for example, were routed to Admiral Axel Berg, who was in charge of the USSR's nascent radar program.[24]

Semyonov, having gained Rosenberg's trust, convinced him to break all visible ties to the party. Unwilling to go completely underground, Julius became chairman of his own secret party cell, Branch 16B of the Industrial Division of the CPUSA, in the latter half of 1942. Ethel took an active part in the discussions and acted as a secretary at the meetings, which were held in their Knickerbocker Village apartment, Barr remembered. In addition to Barr and Sarant, Julius Rosenberg recruited seven people to join Branch 16B, including two longtime friends and former members of the Steinmetz Club: Nathan Sussman, who had received a master's degree in electrical engineering from CCNY in 1939; and Morris Savitsky, who had received a bachelor's degree in electrical engineering the same year. Like Rosenberg, Sussman and Savitsky worked for the military as inspectors in factories producing weapons.[25]

Although they never left the physical safety of the United States, American engineers and scientists were locked in a fierce and lethal competition with their counterparts in Germany. Every time the Allies or the Axis introduced a new technology, the opposition attempted to find a way to neutralize it. Many of the technologies that Barr and his comrades passed to the Soviet Union were useful only as long as knowledge about them was kept out of German hands. This was particularly true of radar. The Allies knew that the day a new type of radar was introduced, the Germans would immediately begin to search for ways to detect or jam it. To develop effective countermeasures, the enemy needed detailed information about the radar, particularly its frequency.[26]

The Nazis also had to contend with successful electronic countermeasures. For example, although the Germans developed early-warning radar and deployed it around Berlin and other cities, jamming by the United States and United Kingdom effectively blinded it. After the war, Reichsmarshall Hermann Goering told the U.S. general in charge of strategic bombing that Allied jamming had often reduced German radar and communications to uselessness.[27]

The first technology Barr worked on at Western Electric, an airborne radar system, was part of this stealthy game of technological attack and counterattack that was played out far behind the front lines. The Allies had deployed an airborne radar in the spring of 1942 capable of pinpointing a surfaced submarine five miles away. This airborne sub-detecting radar had an unfortunate characteristic: as soon as the plane approached to within one mile, the sub disappeared from the screen. To overcome this handicap, bright lights were mounted on the bellies of planes so that their crews could spot and kill the subs, which dived frantically when the planes approached. The radar-equipped planes forced U-boats to spend much more time traveling underwater, which was much slower than cruising on the surface. As a result, pressure on the Atlantic sea routes, essential to keeping Britain fed and supplied, was substantially reduced.[28]

The Germans learned the Allied sub hunters' secrets and in the winter of 1942 began to deploy receivers, including one of French design, that could detect the long-wave radar emanating from Allied planes. Soon Nazi submarines were able to dive to safety at the first sign of radar, well before the planes were in bombing range. The journey across the Atlantic became more perilous, and losses of men and materiel mounted to record levels.[29]

One of Barr's first assignments at Western Electric involved the SCR-517, a new airborne radar system that was designed to reinvigorate the war against Hitler's submarine wolf packs. The SCR-517 used much shorter wavelengths than conventional radar. The use of microwaves improved overall performance while rendering the signal undetectable by the equipment deployed on German submarines. The new microwave radar's ability to hunt submarines depended entirely on keeping the enemy ignorant; if they had known how it worked, the Germans could easily have built detectors. They didn't even come close for the simple reason that their top scientists were completely confident that microwave radar was impossible. German engineers were shocked and dismayed when, in the last days of the war, they got their hands on a descendent of the SCR-517 salvaged from a downed plane and learned that the Americans had developed microwave radar.[30]

Secrecy was so vital that the Americans refused to provide many of their most advanced weapons, especially innovative radars, to other nations, including their closest ally, Great Britain, for fear they would fall into German hands. Especially at a time when Soviet territory was being overrun by rapidly advancing Axis armies, there was no way that the American or British military would supply such weapons to the Soviet Union. Even when the Soviets had the Germans on the run, Russian requests for information on airborne radar to support night operations — precisely the type of data that Barr was providing the KGB — were routinely denied.[31]

Barr was unaware of the risks to which he was unwittingly subjecting the entire war effort when he gave Rosenberg details of the SCR-517. Questioned about it fifty years later, Barr said that it had never occurred to him that by taking decisions about which technologies should be transferred to the USSR out of the hands of the American government, individuals passing secrets to the KGB might have significantly undermined the safety of all Allied forces. His primary interest was helping the Soviets win the war, and this pushed all other considerations out of his consciousness.[32]

The detailed information about radar that Barr provided was valuable to the Soviet Union, which started the war with virtually no capacity to build or operate radar. It would take some time, however, to build a high-tech industry from scratch. The kind of data Bill Perl was collecting, however, could be used immediately to turbocharge the Soviet aircraft industry, which was working at a furious pace to replace the fleet that had been destroyed in the early days of the war with modern planes.[33]

Perl's work at the National Advisory Committee for Aeronautics, or NACA (NACA was incorporated into the National Aeronautics and Space Administration, or NASA, in 1958), which served as the government's primary aircraft R&D lab, gave him access to detailed data about aircraft design that could be invaluable to Soviet engineers, who had been hastily evacuated to the Asian side of the Caucasus, where they designed and supervised the construction of new planes under primitive conditions. Around the time Rosenberg started transmitting his agents' information to Semyonov, Perl's research gave him routine access to data from the world's largest high-speed wind tunnel. He also received results of tests conducted in a wind tunnel created specifically to study techniques for making air flow smoothly over a plane's surface, an important consideration as flight speeds increased. Perl's data must have saved Soviet aircraft designers a great deal of time, especially as they were unlikely to have been able to generate it themselves. In 1940 and 1941, Perl conducted advanced research on the aerodynamic characteristics of tail surfaces that would also have been directly applicable to the Soviet aeronautics industry. By the end of the war, he was turning over detailed information about jet engines.[34]

Perl traveled to New York on weekends to visit family and friends. The trips served as an excellent cover for transporting documents to Rosenberg, but the timing presented a problem for the New York *rezidentura,* which worried that bringing Perl's documents to the consulate on weekends, when most staff didn't work, would attract the FBI's attention. To avoid this, KGB officers copied the documents in their apartments.[35]

The *rezidentura* had good reasons to be concerned about operational security. In February 1943, around the time of the Soviet victory over the Nazis at the epic battle of Stalingrad, the FBI finally began to wake up to the Soviet espionage threat, and dramatically increased surveillance of Russian diplomats and Amtorg employees. The Bureau also began to take some interest in American Communists. In April 1943, an FBI bug in the Berkeley, California, home of Steve Nelson, a Communist organizer suspected of involvement in espionage, captured a conversation with a man who had a Russian accent, who clearly was Nelson's superior. The conversation intrigued the Bureau from the start, when Nelson was overheard saying: "Jesus, you count money like a banker," and the Russian replied: "Vell, you know I used to do it in Moskva." The nimble-fingered paymaster was quickly identified as the diplomat Vassily Zubilin (Zarubin's cover name).[36]

Zarubin's behavior in California suggests that he was completely confident that the FBI was making no effort to track the movements of diplomats. He made no attempt to hide his visit, ordering the KGB's top West Coast spy to chauffeur him to and from Nelson's house in a car registered to the Soviet consulate. In addition to his incautious statements about money, Zarubin emphasized his stature to Nelson, boasting that he was "about five heads up over people you know nothing about." They discussed the establishment of a formal liaison system between the KGB and local CPUSA operatives around the country. The meeting left the FBI with little doubt that the party and Soviet intelligence were closely intertwined, and that the KGB was pursuing an aggressive campaign to obtain political and technical information from the United States. The information was the impetus for a major counterintelligence investigation of Soviet espionage.[37]

The FBI's consciousness of Soviet espionage was intensified dramatically in the summer of 1943 after the Bureau received one of the most extraordinary letters in the history of American counterintelligence. The anonymous letter, typed in Russian with corrections inserted in a cramped handwriting, was sent on August 7, 1943. Addressed to "Mr. Hoover" at the FBI, it accurately identified Zubilin, who had been transferred to the Soviet embassy in Washington, as the "director of Soviet intelligence" in the United States. Several other KGB officers, including Feklisov's boss, Leonid Kvasnikov, the head of scientific and technological intelligence in the United States, and Semyonov were also fingered. The letter stated that Semyonov "has his agents in all the industrial cities of the U.S.A., in all aviation and chemical war factories and in big institutes. He works very brazenly and roughly, it would be very easy to follow him and catch him red handed. He would be glad to be arrested as he has long been seeking a reason to remain in the U.S.A., hates the [KGB] but is a frightful coward and loves money. He will give all his agents away with pleasure if he is promised an American passport." The letter, composed and mailed by a mid-level KGB agent working in the embassy who hated Zarubin, also named Earl Browder as a KBG source of "very important information" about the Soviet Union.[38]

The KGB didn't know about the letter, but it was clear to agents on the ground that the Hut was shining a searchlight on Soviet activities in an effort to illuminate espionage. FBI agents started following Semyonov day and night, making little effort to disguise themselves. It was a signal that the game was over; the Bureau knew he was a spy and wanted him to clear out. The FBI never observed Semyonov meeting with an agent, because its conspicuous surveillance prompted him to drop all contact with Rosenberg and other sources.[39]

Scores of G-men were assigned to follow Soviet citizens mentioned in the letter, a tactic that left little manpower to root out their American collaborators.[40] In their eagerness to obtain intelligence, the FBI agents conducted illegal burglaries and took other short cuts, contaminating possible prosecutions. In contrast to the frenzy over suspicions that Soviet citizens were spying on the U.S. government, when it came to domestic Communists, for the most part paper shuffling was substituted for gumshoe detective work.

The FBI investigation of Barr exemplified the Bureau's posture. On August 30, 1943, the special agent in charge of the Bureau's New York field office informed headquarters that Barr's "case has been carefully reviewed by this office and it is my belief that the information available to this office does not justify any further investigative effort at the present time. The case is therefore being placed in a closed status subject to being opened upon receipt of additional information which would appear to justify further investigation." When this memo was written, Barr had taken a hiatus from espionage because Rosenberg had lost contact with the KGB. The FBI missed an opportunity to make his vacation permanent.[41]

As a security precaution, Semyonov hadn't given his agents any idea of how to make contact with him or anyone else connected with the KGB. After Henry missed meeting after meeting, Rosenberg grew desperate. Finally, he called Elizabeth Bentley late one night in November 1943 and asked her to tell Golos that he wanted to get back in touch with the Russians.[42]

Zarubin assigned Feklisov to take over responsibility for Rosenberg. Feklisov started by studying the *rezidentura*'s file on the young engineer. Like most people recruited to provide information to the KGB, Rosenberg had written an autobiography, which was in the file, as were his photograph, address, and telephone number. The KGB, overestimating the FBI's vigilance, determined that it was too dangerous to telephone him because the line of an individual with access to classified information was likely to be bugged.[43]

The Russians decided to use a direct approach to reestablishing contact with agent Antenna. On a Sunday in late 1943, Feklisov set out from his apartment at 12:30 P.M., strolled casually through Central Park, darted across the street a few times — a maneuver that provided an opportunity to look over both shoulders — took the subway to Little Italy, walked around, and hopped on an uptown bus to Grand Central Station, where he ate a hot dog. Satisfied that he wasn't being followed, he boarded a bus heading downtown, alighting near the Brooklyn Bridge. At 2:00 P.M., a time selected because Rosenberg was most likely to be at home, Feklisov pushed the intercom button in front of Building G at 10 Monroe Street.

"Hello, I'm looking for Julius Rosenberg," Feklisov said in Russian-accented English. "That's me," the voice emanating from the intercom box replied. "I am a friend of Henry's," said Feklisov. "May I come up for a minute?" Rosenberg intercepted his visitor as he stepped off the elevator on the eighth floor and explained that he couldn't invite him in because there was a visitor in the apartment. Walking down the steps, Feklisov told Rosenberg why Henry had disappeared and arranged a meeting for the next Tuesday at the Childs diner near Madison Square Garden.

Two evenings later, Feklisov was standing across the street at 7:30, pretending to be window-shopping, when he saw Rosenberg walk into Childs. After satisfying himself that Antenna wasn't being tailed, Feklisov crossed the street and found Rosenberg's table. Convinced that "many waiters and bartenders were police or FBI informants," and fearing that his accent would attract attention, Feklisov asked Rosenberg to order. Taking care to avoid speaking when the waitress approached, the Russian described his family and their tribulations in war-torn Russia and asked about Rosenberg's family. Then, in order to demonstrate that he really was a Soviet intelligence officer, he asked questions "to find out if there was anything amiss around him and his friends Joel Barr and William Perl, who were also working for us. I made sure I used their real names and showed that I knew many details about both of them," Feklisov recalled. Rosenberg told his new contact that Barr and Perl had stopped bringing secret military information after Semyonov had broken off contact, "but they're ready to start again."[44]

Soon Rosenberg was bringing hundreds of pages of technical drawings, manuals, and specifications about new planes, radar, analog computers, artillery, and other weapons to his weekly meetings with Feklisov. Barr's workplace, Western Electric, was an intelligence goldmine; the process of transferring nuggets from the company's filing cabinets to the Soviet Union was smooth and could be quite rapid. It started with Barr removing some documents, for example a hundred pages of technical specifications for a new radar system, from a filing cabinet and placing them in his briefcase shortly before quitting time. He would drive into New York with the briefcase on the passenger seat and deliver it to Rosenberg. At about the same time, Feklisov would start his dry-cleaning routine.

While Feklisov was running errands, perhaps shopping for a present for his new wife, Zina, Rosenberg was slipping Barr's documents into a newspaper and stepping onto a subway platform. Information transfers often took place in movie theaters, where the Russian would sit in the back, watching as his agent entered and settled into an empty seat. After a few minutes, Feklisov would get up and find a new seat in the same row. During the moment when Rosenberg stood up to allow him to squeeze past, the two men exchanged newspapers. It is unlikely that even someone sitting right next to them could have spotted the exchange. Because movies were shown continuously in those days, it wasn't unusual for people to come and go at any hour. After half an hour or so, Feklisov would exit and, carefully checking to make sure he wasn't being followed, head to the consulate to copy the papers.

The next morning, Rosenberg and Feklisov would wake early and exchange newspapers, this time on a subway platform or maybe while standing next to each other on a bus. Rosenberg had to get the documents back to Barr in time for him to bring them to work, but there was no need for the longtime friends to meet clandestinely. Back at Western Electric, Barr removed the papers from his briefcase, casually returning them to the filing cabinet.

Among the documents that Barr took on a round trip to Manhattan was technical documentation for an Identification-Friend-or-Foe (IFF) technology that was under development at Fort Monmouth. The need for such systems became immediately obvious to every country soon after it deployed radar and inadvertently fired on its own planes. Just as the British had learned in the Battle of Britain, and the Americans at Pearl Harbor, the Russians soon realized they needed ways to distinguish their own planes from the enemy's. America gave the USSR a variety of radar sets during the war, but just as it didn't include instructions on how to build radar, Lend-Lease aid did not help with the IFF problem.[45]

Feklisov was not mentioned in the 1943 anonymous letter, the FBI followed him only sporadically, and during his five years in New York it never identified him as an intelligence agent. Rosenberg and Feklisov's weekly brush passes were supplemented about every six weeks with meetings, usually in cafeterias or automats, during which they took care not to carry any compromising materials. In addition to building rapport with his agent, Feklisov used the sessions to instill a greater appreciation for the need to conform to the dictates of *konspiratsia*.

Worried that Rosenberg was taking unnecessary risks, Feklisov convinced him to cancel subscriptions to the *Daily Worker* and other Communist publications, to avoid attending public events associated with the party such as Red Army rallies, and to disband Branch 16B. Ethel, who had abandoned her teenage dream of a career on the stage to dedicate herself to the Communist cause after she met Julius, sang at a farewell party in February 1944 marking the last time Branch 16B met as a group. Rosenberg was officially transferred to the East Side Club of the First Assembly District of the Manhattan branch of the CPUSA, although he never attended its meetings and appeared to drop out of the party. Even after he went underground, Rosenberg met Bernard Schuster, the party's primary liaison to Soviet intelligence, monthly to pay dues. It wasn't enough for him to risk his life to give the USSR priceless military secrets; Rosenberg also felt compelled to contribute financially.[46]

The Communist Party paid a great deal of attention to bureaucratic formalities. Thus, when Barr was transferred to the Ninth Assembly District, the Industrial Division assigned a transfer number, 12185, and the change was noted in a file at the headquarters of the New York County Committee of the Communist Party, as was Sarant's transfer to the Greenwich Village Club, which was headed by Bill Browder. Bill was quite a contrast from his strait-laced brother, Earl, a family man who rarely invited people connected with his work to his home and scrupulously avoided being seen in public with Soviet intelligence operatives. Bill and his wife, Rose, heavy drinkers and late-night partiers, entertained a virtual who's who of KGB agents, including Zarubin, Golos, and Gold, at their Greenwich Village apartment.[47]

The FBI, which had ballooned to 4,380 agents during the war, finally started to take a close look at the Communist Party, especially in New York, the city where it was most active. The ostentatious surveillance of Soviet nationals undertaken in 1943 was very irritating to the KGB, but it didn't put the espionage service out of business. In the spring of 1944, however, agents at the Bureau and in military counterintelligence began to take steps that would have far more chilling effects on Soviet intelligence. These included bugging the Soviet consulate in New York. When the KGB learned about this step, probably from Judith Coplon, an agent who worked for the Department of Justice in Washington, D.C., it assigned new cover names to most of its agents. Rosenberg, formerly identified as Antenna, became "Liberal"; from this period on, Barr was referred to in KGB cables by the cover name "Meter" instead of the previously used "Scout"; and the six-foot three-inch Perl, originally given the ironic moniker "Gnome," was henceforth referred to as "Yakov" (Jacob).[48]

The FBI didn't realize they were Soviet agents, but it had already documented the fact that many members of the Rosenberg ring were Communists who had access to classified military technology. A March 14, 1944, FBI memo noted that "records maintained at the Headquarters of the New York County Committee of the Communist Party, 147 Fourth Avenue, New York City . . . were made available to Special Agents A. Robert Swanson, R. Campbell Carden and Jerome M. Garland." Although the memo didn't state how the records were "made available," the method used was almost certainly an FBI burglary. Among the documents were records of the transfer of Branch 16B members, including Rosenberg, Barr, and Sarant, to other CPUSA units.[49]

Failing to take advantage of its home-court advantage, the FBI allowed the KGB to run circles around it and to continue scoring major intelligence victories long after it had amassed sufficient evidence to shut down the Rosenberg ring. Soviet intelligence was aware of the FBI's surveillance activities and took seriously the need to cloak its activities. The Bureau moved at a far more leisurely pace than Rosenberg and his comrades. While counterintelligence agents slowly started refining raw intelligence such as Communist Party membership lists into actionable information, the radio engineers were becoming more productive than ever.[50]

The KGB's U.S. operations weren't set up to handle the volume of information that Rosenberg and his colleagues provided. Processing this embarrassment of riches placed a tremendous burden on harried KGB operatives, who had to cope with their cover jobs and handle a stream of data from other agent networks. In addition to overwhelming its officers and threatening to eat up its reserves of film, receiving, copying, and returning documents exposed both the KGB officers and their sources to danger. Concerns about security became particularly acute in the spring of 1944, when the New York *rezidentura* complained to Moscow that "unceasing surveillance" made it difficult to bring materials to the consulate for filming. At first the apartments of two KGB officers were used as copying centers, but this arrangement only slightly reduced the risks and did little to relieve the workload.[51]

Moscow agreed in the summer of 1944 to New York's request to have Rosenberg microfilm his group's documents. As its operations expanded, the New York *rezidentura* ran into another logistics problem: it was running out of cameras, and there were no suitable replacements for sale in Tyre (the KGB's cover name for New York). On July 11, 1944, the New York *resident* sent a message to Moscow explaining the situation and requesting that instructions be sent to the "Countryside" (the cover name for Mexico) "to buy two cameras and send them to Tyre by the first post." He noted that Moscow had allowed one camera for Antenna. The second was needed for the work of the New York *rezidentura*. The message added that Leica cameras "find their way to the Countryside from Germany and cost 200 dollars." Incredibly, the New York branch of the KGB was procuring cameras from Nazi Germany. The Leicas were fitted with a special lens that was suitable for microfilming. Although Rosenberg apparently wasn't very good at it, the procedure was quite simple: the camera had to be placed on a tripod, face down, 15–20 inches above the documents, which were lit by two side lamps.[52]

By mid-1944, the Rosenberg group was operating smoothly enough for the KGB to consider expanding it. In May, the New York *rezidentura* sent a coded and encrypted Western Union cable asking the Center to "please carry out a check and sanction the recruitment of Alfred Sarant, a lead of ANTENNA's. He is 25 years old, a Greek, an American citizen and lives in Tyre. He completed the engineering course at Cooper Union in 1940. He worked for two years in the Signal Corps Laboratory at Fort MONMOUTH. He was discharged for union activity. He has been working for two years at Western Electric." The cable, which later figured prominently in the FBI's investigation of wartime Soviet espionage, concluded with a plea: "Answer without delay."[53]

As the cable noted, the Army had fired Sarant in September 1942 over his attempts to recruit civilian engineers to join the FAECT. The day after the Army terminated his employment "with prejudice," Sarant sent a petulant five-page resignation letter. The "you can't fire me, I quit" missive concluded with an assertion that "as a patriotic citizen of the United States and one who is interested in all-out war effort, I cannot, in clear conscience, remain at the laboratories under existing conditions. I feel that with my engineering training and ability I can be of more value to my country and to the war effort else-where. This is especially important to me since I have a brother serving in the U.S. forces in England now, a second brother who is entering the Naval Air Corps and a third brother who is entering the Coast Guard services."[54]

Sarant was fired on September 6, 1942; he reported for work at Western Electric on September 30. He didn't discuss politics at work, but made little effort to hide his affinity for the Soviet Union, taping Margaret Bourke-White's photos of Moscow from *Life* magazine to the wall of his bedroom, where visitors who came to listen to his record collection saw them. One of Sarant's friends from Western Electric remembered him as "an exceptionally brilliant, sharp, very capable, quick witted individual who was very attractive to members of the opposite sex."[55]

The KGB wasn't the only intelligence agency evaluating Sarant's loyalty in the summer of 1944. Less than a month after the New York *rezidentura* requested authorization to recruit Sarant, he came to the attention of the FBI, when the Bureau gained access to the files that Viola Brothers Shore, membership director of the Sacco-Vanzetti Club of the Communist Political Association

Figure 1. Joel Barr on the roof of 65 Morton Street, Greenwich Village, New York, in 1944. (Source: Joel Barr's personal papers; photographer unknown.)

(as the CPUSA was renamed in 1944), First and Second Assembly Districts, kept in her office at One Sheridan Square, New York City. The FBI started a file on each of the listed members, including Al Sarant. Among the additional Communist Political Association records obtained by the Bureau in August was a photograph of a file card on member number 5451, an individual who went by the party name "Raymond Cooper." The card also revealed his real name and address: Alfred Sarant, 65 Morton Street. There was absolutely no FBI follow-up on the information about Sarant.[56]

Six months passed before the New York field office issued a memorandum for the file on the case labeled "Alfred Sarant, Security Matter — C" (for Communist). Although there is no evidence that any investigation was conducted, the memo stated that "further investigation is not justified at this time and this case is being placed in a closed status." By this time Sarant had begun to spy for the Soviet Union.[57]

Figure 2. Joel Barr (left) and Alfred Sarant in front of 65 Morton Street, Greenwich Village, New York, in 1944. (Source: Joel Barr's personal papers; photographer unknown.)

Feklisov was eager to recruit another agent, especially one who could work closely with Barr, but KGB rules compelled him to proceed cautiously. Before exposing himself as a spy, Barr was instructed to test Sarant's willingness to put friendship ahead of his sworn oath to abide by the government's security classification procedures. Barr asked his friend to lend him some secret documents for his personal use, without any mention of the Soviet Union. Sarant readily complied, and, after Moscow gave the go-ahead, Barr was told to close the deal. Barr balked at first—it isn't easy to ask someone to become a spy—but when he popped the question, Sarant agreed readily.[58]

The Center was informed on November 11, 1944, that "Liberal has safely carried through the contracting of Hughes [Sarant]. Hughes is a good pal of METER's. We propose to pair them off and get them to photograph their own materials having given a camera for this purpose. Hughes is a good photographer, has a large darkroom and all the equipment but he does not have a Leica. LIBERAL will receive the films from METER for passing on. Direction of the probationers [the KGB term for its agents] will be continued through LIBERAL, this will ease the load on him." A December 5 cable from the New York *rezidentura* requested that the Center "expedite consent to the joint filming of their materials by both METER and HUGHES . . . LIBERAL has on hand eight people plus the filming of materials. The state of LIBERAL's health is nothing splendid. We are afraid of putting LIBERAL out of action with overwork."[59]

Feklisov received authorization from the Center to meet personally with Barr, instituting a bi-weekly routine. "Once a month, early in the morning, he would slip me a roll of about twenty films representing 400–500 pages of documents," Feklisov remembered. Instructional meetings were also held about once a month, always in the evenings, after both finished their work.[60]

Barr moved in with Sarant at apartment 6I at 65 Morton Street. Feklisov visited the apartment at least once when Sarant wasn't home to help Barr create two hiding places under the floorboards, one for camera equipment and the other for film. Barr also had a room at his parents' apartment where he could hide film. The Barr family's fortunes had taken a turn for the better in the early 1940s after Joel and his brothers started bringing home substantial paychecks, allowing them to move to a penthouse apartment at 241 West 97th Street, Manhattan.[61]

America's unprecedented pace of technological progress during the war, much of it flowing through the Signal Corps to Western Electric, provided Barr and Sarant with plenty of espionage targets to choose from. The U.S. military invested massive resources to create countless technological innovations during World War II.

Hitler, under intense pressure to orient a much smaller pool of technical manpower to high-impact projects, pushed aside requests to fund many of the same technologies. Instead of pursuing microwave radar or proximity fuses, the Nazis improved one of the oldest high-tech weapons, the rocket. The first results of the Nazi rocket program, V-1s, each carrying a ton of explosives, crashed into southern England a few hours before dawn on June 13, 1944.

Once it became clear that the Germans intended a sustained campaign, the British organized defenses against the rockets, which they dubbed "doodle-bugs" and "buzz bombs." Fighters could shoot down a few, but antiaircraft guns were pathetically ineffective against them. The V-1 was a weapon of terror, or, as Hitler called it, a *Vergeltungswaffen*, a revenge weapon. Soon more than 100 were hitting Britain every night, with scores landing in London, denting morale by driving the population to sleep in bomb shelters or even to flee the city.

To cope with the V-1 menace, American and British engineers merged three innovative weapons systems. The first component was the SCR-584, a microwave radar system designed at MIT's Radiation Lab, which the U.S. Army hailed as one of the most important technological breakthroughs of the war (and to which radar engineers today still pay homage). The second was the M-9 gun director, also called a "predictor," an analog computer capable of estimating a moving object's future position on the basis of radar input, and controlling the aiming and firing of an artillery shell. Proximity fuses, which destroyed the buzz bombs by detonating warheads that splattered them with metal balls, were the icing on the cake.

The kill rate against the V-1s soared with the deployment of the new weapons system, transforming them from a menace into a nuisance. Using the technology pioneered on the English beaches, the U.S. Army later managed to destroy 92 percent of the V-1s fired at Antwerp in November 1944.[62]

The troika of computer fire-control, microwave radar, and proximity fuses continued to serve as the backbone of antiaircraft defenses as recently as the 2003 Iraq war. The Rosenberg group gave details of each element to the Soviet Union.

In general, the Russians provided vague guidance about acquisition targets to officers handling the Rosenberg ring — for example, expressing interest in radar — and were pleased with whatever material they were given. Moscow put in a special request, however, for information about the SCR-584 and the M-9 predictor, which the British had recently demonstrated to Russian military observers. Feklisov communicated the request to Barr at a breakfast meeting in a cafeteria, passing him a note under the table asking for detailed information about the technologies that were being used at a facility near London to track and shoot down German rockets. "That's funny! We must have a crystal ball!" Barr replied. "Five days ago we read your minds and got the technical manual of this facility. We just finished photographing it last night at 2am."[63]

The films were rushed to Moscow and landed on Pavel Fitin's desk at the Lubyanka barely a week after the head of Soviet foreign intelligence signed the order requesting the information. The Center quickly dashed off a cable congratulating its officers in New York and providing for a special $1,000 bonus for Barr and Sarant. This was a huge amount of money, nearly half a year's salary. When Feklisov tried to give it to Barr, he immediately refused to accept it, but said he'd have to ask Sarant if he wanted his share. The next day, Barr reported that Sarant had also declined the money. Other ideologically motivated agents also refused to accept large amounts of money from the KGB. During the war, Rosenberg took only small sums, $25 or so at a time, to cover a portion of his expenses for running espionage agents, and Barr also received some modest payments.[64]

Their putting a few KGB dollars in their pockets does not alter the fact that

Rosenberg, Barr, Sarant, and the other members of their circle were motivated by deeply felt beliefs in Communism and admiration for the Soviet Union. They were volunteers who had little in common with the post–World War II mercenary spies.

In the summer of 1944, Rosenberg recruited Morton Sobell to participate in his espionage collective. Sobell was working for General Electric in Schenectady, New York, on servo-mechanisms, the electromechanical devices that physically react to the inputs from radar and fire-control computers to move artillery pieces. It must have been easy to convince the lifelong, second-generation Communist to come to the aid of the Soviet Union.[65]

Sobell felt alienated from his peers at GE. "The overthrow of capitalism was a basic premise of my existence," he recalled, while the other engineers "never questioned our system." He felt that revolution was such an integral part of Communism that the American Communist Party's decision to throw its support behind Roosevelt during the war made it seem "superfluous." Sobell remembered that he "couldn't conceive of a meaningful Communist Party except in opposition to the capitalist system."

Sobell often relieved the isolation by taking a Saturday evening train to Manhattan and returning to Schenectady on Monday morning "just in time to go home, shave, and go to work." The trips were long enough to take a girl to a show and have a chat with the Rosenbergs about the progress of the war, Sobell wrote. He didn't mention that they also provided just enough time for his documents to be copied.[66]

At first Sobell brought documents to Rosenberg, who passed them to Feklisov for copying. After two deliveries of documents, Feklisov took over. The Russian quickly ascertained that Sobell was capable of microfilming—like Barr, he had his own darkroom and was a talented photographer—and arranged to allocate one of the New York *rezidentura*'s scarce Leicas—one formerly used by another agent, Joseph "Jack" Katz—to Sobell. Feklisov received film from Sobell about once a month. Sobell showed off his Leica, equipped with a special close-up lens, to colleagues and friends.[67]

With Sobell on board, Rosenberg decided to expand his network by adding a friend and old comrade from the Steinmetz Club. In July 1944 Rosenberg used a routine business trip to Washington as an opportunity to visit Max Elitcher, who had been Sobell's roommate in Washington and the best man at his wedding. Elitcher had remained in the Communist Party and was working on fire-control systems for large-caliber ship-mounted guns. Rosenberg telephoned from Washington, and Elitcher invited his old classmate to visit his apartment that evening. Soon after Rosenberg arrived, he asked Mrs. Helene

Elitcher to leave the room so he and Max could discuss some business privately. With Helene in the bedroom, Rosenberg started his pitch, beginning with the fact that the United States was withholding valuable military technology from its Soviet ally and ending with a request that Elitcher turn over secrets from his workplace.[68]

Elitcher later remembered that Rosenberg "said there were many people who were implementing aid to the Soviet Union by providing classified information about military equipment, and so forth, and asked whether in my capacity at the Bureau of Ordnance working on antiaircraft devices, and computer control of firing missiles, would I turn information over to him?" Rosenberg added that "any information [Elitcher] gave him would be taken to New York, processed photographically and would be returned overnight — so it would not be missed. The process would be safe as far as I was concerned."[69]

Elitcher, unlike Sobell, Perl, and Barr, didn't agree right away. He didn't refuse outright either, however, instead making excuses about how risky it would be to take material to New York, and promising to consider Rosenberg's proposal. Elitcher later told FBI investigators that Rosenberg repeated the request six or eight times. Elitcher contended that he had never wavered and never turned over any information to Rosenberg. Possibly because his collaboration was essential to their cases against Rosenberg and Sobell, the FBI didn't push very hard to find out if he was telling the truth.

Elitcher wasn't Rosenberg's only comrade to brush off his requests to spy on the United States. His old friend Mark Page (formerly Marcus Pogarsky) refused a similar request.[70]

The Rosenbergs had better luck with Ethel's baby brother, David Greenglass, who had been posted as a machinist to a top-secret facility in the New Mexico desert. In December 1944 Greenglass agreed to Julius's request to pass along information on the project that the Soviets code-named "Enormous" and the American government called the Manhattan Engineering District, or the Manhattan Project.

While Rosenberg's most vital tasks were recruiting and managing Barr, Perl, Sobell, and other agents, he also pulled off an operation on his own initiative that gave the Soviet Union access to one of the most important and most closely guarded secret technologies developed during the war. The proximity fuse, which Rosenberg literally wrapped up and delivered to the KGB as a Christmas present, rivaled the atomic bomb in its impact on World War II and subsequent conflicts, as well as in the expense and logistical difficulties of producing it and in the strength of the security wall erected around its development, manufacturing, and deployment.

The proximity fuse was created to solve the problem of shooting down ever-faster airplanes, but it was adapted to a variety of uses. At the start of World War II, there were two basic systems for using artillery to shoot down airplanes: either shells detonated on impact with the target, or timers were set to make them explode at a moment when they were likely to be within killing range. For planes flying slowly along a predictable path, a simple calculation could be made, taking into account factors such as wind direction and velocity, to aim a shell so that it was reasonably likely to intersect with its intended target. The kill rates for conventional antiaircraft batteries declined precipitously as airplanes became faster and more maneuverable, adopting tactics such as dive-bombing. Winston Churchill noted the problem, writing that "an aeroplane end-on is a very small target and a contact fuze will work only in the rare event of a direct hit. To set a time fuze so that the shell explodes at the exact moment when it is passing the aircraft is almost impossible. An error in timing of one-tenth of a second causes a miss of many hundreds of feet."[71]

Starting in the 1920s, a number of designs were proposed for fuses that would detonate a shell when it got close to an airplane. Some were based on photosensitive elements that triggered an explosion as soon as an airplane blocked out the sun, while others were cued by the sound of an engine. None of them worked in practice, however. One of the most difficult challenges was devising a mechanism that could withstand the pressure, up to 20,000 times the gravitational force of the Earth, and the 30,000 revolutions-per-minute spin, imparted by an artillery gun.

During the war, the United States perfected an ingenious design, based on a British idea. The Anglo-American proximity fuse contained a miniature radio transmitter that sent a continuous signal, a receiver to listen for an echo of the signal bouncing back from the target, and an amplifier to boost the strength of that echo. Outgoing and incoming signals collided with each other, creating a distinct interference pattern that varied according to the distance from the target. When the alignment of the radio waves indicated that a target was in range, the shell exploded. It was not necessary to hit a plane; a near-miss was good enough to knock the enemy out of the sky.

A collaboration between academic researchers and industry managed to solve a myriad of seemingly intractable technical problems, and succeeded in turning the design into a robust device. Security around the project was so tight that when researchers were overheard discussing their work at a Hot Shoppes diner in Washington, D.C., they were informed that "any discussion of the fuze project inside the restaurant would result in the arrest of all the members of a conversational group." Such measures were not unwarranted.[72]

The FBI caught three Nazi spies who had instructions, written on a tiny piece of microfilm hidden in the back of a watch, to gather information about "an antiaircraft shell with a so-called electric eye." In addition to preventing the Nazis from penetrating the proximity fuse program, the American and British military tried to hide the proximity fuse from their Soviet ally.[73]

The American armed forces were extremely worried about the prospect that the Germans or Japanese might get their hands on a proximity fuse, or detailed information about the device. The thought that the Germans might be able to produce proximity fuses sent shivers down the spine of Allied bomber command. General Omar Bradley recalled that "each month that dragged by caused Tooey Spaatz [commander of the U.S. Strategic Air Force in Europe during World War II] greater anxiety over . . . German discovery of the proximity fuse. For Tooey had long ago estimated that [equipped with proximity fuses, the Germans] might blast our bombers out of the skies." There was an even greater concern that the enemy could implement countermeasures, such as broadcasting a signal that would cause premature detonation. In fact, in at least one instance, the American Navy inadvertently did this. During the U.S. invasion of Okinawa, Japan, artillery shells equipped with proximity fuses "burst all along the trajectory," triggered by signals from radar on Allied destroyers.[74]

The extremely tight security surrounding the proximity fuse extended from the design labs and manufacturing plant to deployment. Initially the fuses were used only over water, where unexploded ordnance could not fall into enemy hands. The proximity fuse was first used in anger on January 5, 1943, by gunners on the U.S.S. *Helena* to shoot down a Japanese dive-bomber near Guadalcanal. Its success in the Pacific theater led the Japanese to adopt desperate tactics, such as massing Kamikaze suicide bombers. The fuses were gradually diffused more broadly; fortuitously, just days before a massive surprise German counteroffensive, the Army received approval to use a version that had been adapted to explode over foxholes. U.S. General George Patton said that the "funny fuze won the Battle of the Bulge for us. I think that when all armies get this shell we will have to devise some new method of warfare."[75]

The basic idea for the proximity fuse was simple, but mass-producing the tiny radios was devilishly difficult. The United States mounted a program to produce millions of custom-made batteries and very small, extremely rugged vacuum tubes. Few of the 80,000 people, 80 percent of them women — preferred because they had smaller, more nimble fingers — who were employed manufacturing components for the fuses had any idea of the ultimate use made of their work.[76]

In his work as a Signal Corps inspector at Emerson Radio and Phonograph

Corporation, which produced a million proximity fuses during the war, Rosenberg was one of the few individuals who knew not only what the strange devices were intended for, but also the details of how they were constructed and the technical characteristics of the constituent parts.[77]

The U.S. Army developed new statistical testing methods to assure the quality of proximity fuses. In addition to describing how the proximity fuse was built, Rosenberg was in a position to communicate essential information about these statistical quality-control procedures.

First Rosenberg gave Feklisov written materials about the proximity fuse. Then, just before Christmas in 1944, he astounded Soviet intelligence. At 7:30 on the evening of December 24, 1944, Feklisov walked up to a booth at the Horn and Hardart automat on West 38th Street near Broadway, where Liberal was waiting. The KGB officer set a box on the windowsill next to one his agent had placed there. "Don't forget to take the box I brought you. Those are your Christmas presents," Feklisov almost whispered. The box contained a teddy bear for Rosenberg's son Michael, an Omega stainless steel watch for Julius, and crocodile handbag for Ethel, all purchased at Gimbel's department store. Rosenberg thanked him and said he'd brought Feklisov a present, warning him that it was heavy. They left the automat through different doors.[78]

The Russian lugged the fifteen-pound box to the consulate, opened it, and, on the basis of technical information that Rosenberg had previously supplied, immediately recognized that it was a proximity fuse: "The complete device, in working order, brand new, smelling of metal and oil, with an additional supply of miniaturized replacement metal tubes fastened on top." Joy turned to apprehension when Feklisov's boss learned of the heist and demanded to know how Liberal had evaded the tight security at the Emerson plant. Rosenberg allayed the *rezidentura*'s suspicions at his next meeting with Feklisov, explaining that he'd set aside a defective fuse at the factory and, over the course of three months, replaced it bit by bit with working parts. On December 23, the day before he'd given the present to Feklisov, Rosenberg had been assigned to accompany a van load of defective fuses to a secure location for supervised destruction. He placed his functioning fuse in the back of the van, hopped in front with the driver, and, once they were on the road, asked him to wait while he dashed into a grocery store. Rosenberg put the groceries in the back of the van, next to the box holding his treasure, and asked the driver for one more favor. The driver detoured a couple of blocks and stopped for a few minutes outside 10 Monroe Street while Rosenberg delivered the groceries — and the parcel containing the fuse.

Feklisov admonished Rosenberg to be more cautious in the future, but the engineer shrugged him off. At a time when millions of Russians were risking their lives every day, smuggling a box out of a factory didn't seem like a big sacrifice to Rosenberg. Apparently, the thought that he was also risking his life never occurred to him, or if it did, the cost didn't seem too high.

The FBI's counterintelligence machine finally started to click into gear in the fall of 1944 — at least with regard to Rosenberg — correlating the information it had received seven months previously regarding his CPUSA membership with his position as a Signal Corps inspector. "My dear Colonel Constant," the special agent in charge (SAC) of the FBI's New York field office wrote to the director of the Security and Intelligence Division of the Army's Second Service Command, "During the course of an official investigation, it was determined from a reliable and confidential source that JULIUS ROSENBERG of 10 Monroe Street, Manhattan, New York City, is a member of the Communist Party and transferred from Branch 16B of the Industrial Division of the Communist Party to the East Side Club of the First A.D. under transfer number 12179, February 1944." The letter noted that the FBI had confirmed Julius Rosenberg's address and the fact that he had listed his employment as an inspector for the Signal Corps when he signed a lease for the apartment.

The FBI letter also revealed that Mrs. Florence McLaughlin, secretary to the vice-president of Knickerbocker Village, was a good deal more diligent about checking out the bona fides of her tenants than the management of Western Electric had been when it hired Barr, or than the FBI had been in investigating Rosenberg, Barr, or Sarant. Mrs. McLaughlin had verified Rosenberg's employment both before he moved in and again in January 1944, when he renewed the lease. Responding to an FBI inquiry about Rosenberg, she was able to report that the Army had confirmed in writing in 1944 that "Mr. Rosenberg had been with the Signal Corps approximately three years," the SAC noted. He concluded by telling Constant that the "information is being submitted to your office for whatever action you deem advisable."[79]

The Army deemed that another loyalty investigation was advisable. This time there were no hearings; in the face of documentary evidence of his Communist Party membership as recently as February 1944, no one was interested in listening to Rosenberg's explanations.

On February 9, 1945, the Army notified Rosenberg of his indefinite suspension.

The KGB was concerned, but not panicked, by the news. "The latest events with [Julius Rosenberg], his having been fired, are highly serious and demand on our part, first, a correct assessment of what happened, and second, a decision about [his] role in the future. Deciding the latter, we should proceed from the fact that, in him, we have a man devoted to us, whom we can trust completely, a man who by his practical activities for several years has shown how strong is his desire to help our country," the Center cabled to Feklisov's boss, Leonid Kvasnikov, on February 23, 1945. The message added that although "we don't have any documentary data saying the [FBI is] aware to an extent of his connection with us, we, nevertheless, must take into account the circumstances preceding [Rosenberg's] sacking—his extremely active work, especially in the first period of working with us, and his certain haste in the work. We consider it necessary to take immediate measures to secure both [Rosenberg] and the agents with whom he was connected."

Those measures included immediately isolating Rosenberg from Barr, Sarant, and all his other agents to prevent him from infecting them. Concerned that contagion could spread into its own ranks, the KGB also ordered Feklisov to break off direct contact with Rosenberg. He was instructed to communicate with Liberal through a cutout—a trusted intermediary who communicates between two intelligence operatives so that they can avoid being observed together. Moscow suggested using an American, Lona Cohen (code name "Leslie"), for the task.[80]

As with Barr, being fired by the U.S. Army as a security risk didn't have a detrimental effect on Rosenberg's career. Putting out the word that the dismissal was motivated by anti-Semitism, Rosenberg was almost immediately hired by one of the companies where he had been stationed as a Signal Corps inspector. Emerson Radio and Phonograph Corporation—the firm he'd stolen the proximity fuse from—gave him a similar job. The KGB, worried that the FBI might have Rosenberg under surveillance, had to restrain him from resuming his technology transfer activities. They needn't have worried: neither the Army nor the FBI made any effort to track Rosenberg's activities after he was fired.

While Rosenberg was out of commission, his troops continued to soldier on for the Soviet Union. Perl was poised to make a dramatic contribution. A gifted engineer, he had advanced rapidly at NACA to a position that provided access to information of particular interest to Russia. The Soviet aircraft industry had started the war at technological parity with the rest of the world but couldn't keep up with its allies or enemies. Soviet designers, as well as their customers in the Red Army, looked on with envy as Germany and the United States raced to build bigger, better, and much faster planes. In the winter of 1944, the U.S. Army Air Corps deflected an official Soviet request for intelligence about German jet aircraft. Ironically, thanks to Perl, Russia was having more luck obtaining information about the U.S. jet program.[81]

In mid-1944, Mutterperl was transferred to NACA's engine design facility in Cleveland. The New York *rezidentura* was so excited about information obtained from its agent Gnome in May that it telegraphed a summary to Moscow. The object of its enthusiasm was a description of the Westinghouse 19A, the first practical jet engine wholly American in design, a breakthrough that was the precursor of a series of engines that propelled the United States into the jet age. In addition to keeping up with jet engine designs, Perl had access to data from supersonic wind tunnels, which he almost certainly passed on to the KGB.[82]

Feklisov traveled to Cleveland in February 1945 to check up on a couple, friends recruited by Julius Rosenberg, whom the KGB had sent there to service Perl by microfilming his material and bringing it to New York once a month. He told the courier to install a deadbolt on his front door at least half an inch thick so that "if the cops are trying to break the door down, you'll have enough time to destroy or expose all the film."[83]

After Feklisov visited him in Cleveland, Perl gave the New York *rezidentura* a document that rivaled in importance, and bulk, anything Barr or Rosenberg provided to the USSR. It was the complete 12,000-page blueprint of the Lockheed P-80 Shooting Star, the plane that marked the U.S. military's entry into the jet age. Designed, built, and flown in 143 days, the P-80 was the first American jet aircraft to be manufactured in large quantities. Completed too late to see combat during World War II, it was widely used in the Korean War.

In addition to the P-80 blueprints, Perl provided about 5,000 pages of documents in 1945. According to Feklisov, the KGB classified half of these as "very valuable," 40 percent as "valuable," and 10 percent as "of informational interest."[84]

The Shooting Star blueprints may have been the last blockbuster piece of intelligence the Rosenberg ring sent to Russia. The group's production to this point was impressive by any measure. In addition to the proximity fuse, M-9 predictor, SCR-517 airborne and SCR-584 land-based radar, and Perl's aviation information, it provided details on many other weapons. A comprehensive inventory of the materials they gave to the Soviet Union will be possible only when the archives of the institutions that inherited the KGB's files are opened to public scrutiny. Those files will reveal specifics about the over 9,165 pages of secret documents relating to more than 100 weapons programs that Barr and Sarant alone turned over to the KGB.[85]

Barr and the other members of the Rosenberg ring weren't the only agents informing the KGB about radar and other technologies under development at Western Electric and the Signal Corps. As with political information, whenever possible Soviet intelligence services used multiple sources. This strategy ensured complete coverage and made it possible to check the veracity of information. The KGB and GRU (Soviet military intelligence), which referred to each other as "neighbors" and operated independently, sometimes overlapped or inadvertently tried to recruit each other's agents.

A Naval GRU agent, Eugene Coleman, worked at RCA in Princeton, New Jersey, where he ran a network similar to Rosenberg's. According to an August 1943 GRU memo, Coleman, whose cover name was "Carter," was "entrusted with drawing up instructions and a manual for" two radar projects involving navigation and blind bombing that were incorporated into the B17 Flying Fortress, the mainstay of the American bomber fleet throughout World War II. In addition to his own spying, Coleman received information from four agents, including one described in a GRU memo as an "engineer-physicist" who worked at Western Electric; a rubber chemist at Bell Telephone's labs; a radio engineer at the Signal Corps's Sandy Hook radar lab; and an engineer-physicist at Sperry Gyroscope working on "secret systems for electro-mechanical gun sights and ship and aircraft control."[86]

It is reasonable to assume that, at a minimum, Barr and Sarant gave the KGB information about every project they worked on. Barr's assignments included helping design manufacturing processes for two related airborne radars designed for nighttime navigation and bombing, the SCR-520 and SCR-720, that gave American pilots an advantage over the Lüftwaffe, which was blind at night and myopic in cloudy weather. The 720 incorporated newly developed technologies that made it more powerful and less susceptible to jamming than other radars. "If an individual knew the Model 720, he knew practically every other set that was built by Western Electric," an engineer who worked with Barr told the FBI. One measure of the value of the radar is the fact that the U.S. Army commissioned a new type of airplane, the P-61 Black Widow, specifically to incorporate it.[87]

The United States sent forty-nine copies of the SCR-584 radar set to Russia during the war, but they didn't come with manufacturing instructions. The detailed specifications that Barr provided to Feklisov must have been extremely useful to the Soviet engineers who produced an almost exact copy, the SON-4 radar, which was deployed during the Korean and Vietnam conflicts to direct artillery fire against American planes.[88]

Barr also worked on an analog computer that was linked to the APQ-13 radar, the radar-assisted Norden bombsight that the U.S. Army took great pains to keep secret, and a ground radar used by the U.S. Marine Corps. Both Barr and Sarant worked on the AN/APQ-7 and APQ-13, search-and-bombing radar sets that were used on a wide range of American combat aircraft. A December 1944 KGB cable from New York reported to Moscow that Sarant had "handed over 17 authentic drawings related to the APQ-7." The B-29s that dropped atomic bombs on Hiroshima and Nagasaki in August 1945 were equipped with either the AN/APQ-7 or the closely related AN/APQ-13 radar.[89]

In 1945 Sobell provided 2,000 pages of technical data, including information about servomechanisms, sonar and missile guidance systems, and "secret reports on the meetings of the Coordinating Committee for Radio Technology, which were priceless documents allowing [Soviet] specialists to follow all the studies undertaken in the United States in that area, revealing the direction research would be taking in the years to come."[90]

The KGB probably never told Sobell, Rosenberg, or Barr exactly how the technology they transferred was put to use. Even when no secret intelligence was involved, the USSR went to great lengths to claim credit for many inventions that it had adopted or appropriated from the capitalist world. In some instances, however, it was impossible to hide the foreign paternity of the children of Soviet industry. This was the case with the USSR's first long-range bomber.

The Soviet government made a special point of inviting American and European military observers to Tushino airfield on August 3, 1947, for the annual Aviation Day celebrations. The Westerners were mildly surprised when they saw what appeared to be a U.S. B-29 bomber with Soviet markings fly overhead. They knew that the Soviet government had impounded three of the "Superfortresses" after they crash-landed in the Russian Far East during the war, so they initially assumed that the Soviets had managed to patch them up and were putting on a show. Surprise turned to astonishment when a *fourth* B-29 clone lumbered past, incontrovertibly demonstrating that the Russians had managed to reproduce the plane. By the time the news was forwarded to the Pentagon, astonishment was distilled into fear. The capability to produce B-29s gave the Soviet Union the ability to reach targets in North America, at least on one-way missions.

The secret of how Stalin ordered a massive program to clone the B-29 didn't come to light until the end of the Cold War, and the role that Barr, Sobell, and other members of the Rosenberg ring played in facilitating that program has never been told. Tens of thousands of Russians were mobilized to accomplish the task, which involved taking one of the impounded planes apart, analyzing and photographing over 100,000 individual parts, then attempting to precisely reproduce them. The end result was a dead ringer for the Superfortresses that dropped atomic bombs on Hiroshima and Nagasaki.

Coupled with the atom bomb, the TU-4 put the fear of Armageddon into the Pentagon. A top-secret Defense Department planning document circulated in 1951 warned: "Because of its resemblance to the US B-29, the Soviet TU-4 could be disguised with US markings and employed for clandestine delivery of atomic bombs. Flying a one-way mission, the TU-4 has sufficient range to reach every important target in the US and the USSR has an adequate number of TU-4s and trained crews to perform such missions." The report also stated that "a small number of disguised TU-4s, by taking advantage of the gaps in our radar screen, might escape detection. This would greatly increase the probability of a successful attack on high priority targets, such as the Washington area, for the purpose of paralyzing the top military and civil command a few hours prior to the initiation of hostilities elsewhere."[91]

It is possible to physically copy mechanical devices, but reproducing inert electronics is similar to, and only slightly easier than, breathing life into a dead organism. The B-29 incorporated sophisticated avionics and electromechanical control systems that couldn't be reproduced without a detailed understanding of how they worked and specific manufacturing know-how. When the Soviet Union's leading aircraft designer, Andrei Tupolev, examined one of the B-29s at a Moscow airfield, he quickly determined that building the fuselage, wings, and tail was difficult but feasible. Coming to the remote-controlled machine guns, radar sights, range-finders, computers, and automated plotters, "the Old Man began to get irritated," one of his close aides recalled. Tugging on a wire, Tupelov began shouting. There were tens of thousands, maybe millions, of wires, and his team would need to trace the pathways for each of them. The information provided by the Rosenberg ring must have made it immensely easier to make sense of the spaghetti, and to make facsimiles of the complex equipment connected to it.[92]

American observers were shocked to discover that the Soviets had managed to copy the B-29's central station fire-control system, which allowed any gunner in the plane to maneuver and fire any of the plane's numerous guns. The Soviet engineer assigned to copy the fire-control system "succeeded, to the amazement of Tupolev and the consternation of observers in the West, who believed this advanced system was beyond the capacity of the Soviets."[93]

Russian technological genius was aided considerably by the clandestine contributions from Barr and company. The B-29's fire-control system was designed at the General Electric facility where Sobell worked. Detailed "information was available to [Sobell] on practically all of the General Electric Company's work on fire control radar," according to a colleague; it is very likely that the diplomatic pouches Feklisov sent to Moscow during the war included instructions for their manufacture and use. Similarly, Tupelov's engineers almost certainly had printouts of microfilmed copies of specifications of the Norden bombsight, navigation instruments, and other equipment used on the B-29 that Barr had slipped to Feklisov. Technical documentation on other weapons systems would have given the Soviets valuable background information about American electronics.[94]

With a few exceptions, such as the atomic bomb and the B-29 bomber, the Soviet Union did not generally make exact copies of weapons based on information obtained by the KGB, so it is not possible to trace the path from a specific piece of stolen information to a particular weapon. But the fact that the exact impact of the thousands of pages of secret documents that the Rosenberg group sent to Russia is difficult to discern does not diminish their value. The documents contained insights into completed and ongoing high-tech projects that allowed the Soviets to avoid some of the dead ends and false starts that characterize any R&D endeavor. The very practical manufacturing details were also valuable. For example, given the primitive level of the Soviet vacuum tube industry, Rosenberg's information was probably of incalculable assistance in its successful production of the small, shock-resistant tubes used in proximity fuses.[95]

The American military was surprised by the rapid development of the Soviet radar industry after the war. To some extent Russia's rapid progress could be attributed to the massive transfer of German engineers to the Soviet Union, but it is very likely that the data which Barr, Sarant, and other American agents sent to Russia made substantial contributions. Soviet radar designs were modeled on American, not German, equipment.[96]

Knowledge of the technical specifications of American weapons systems also helped the Soviet Union prepare for armed conflict with the United States, which seemed a real possibility in the immediate postwar period. In this regard, Perl's P-80 blueprints provided valuable insights into the capabilities of potential rivals. The U.S. Air Force was shocked to discover in the skies over Korea that the Soviet MIG-15s could fly faster and at higher altitudes than the American F-80Cs.[97] Although the MIG-15 wasn't based on designs that Perl provided — it leaned very heavily on German designs and was powered by an unauthorized copy of a Rolls-Royce engine — its designers had sufficient detail about the F-80C to know that their machine would be superior. Detailed knowledge of the characteristics of opposing weapons systems is critically important. Information that Barr provided may have helped the MIG-15 designers incorporate computerized gunsights that were more advanced than the optical gunsights on which F-80C pilots relied.[98]

Perl's information was probably incorporated in the next generation of Soviet jet, the MIG-19, the first Soviet supersonic fighter, launched in 1953, which was superior to its contemporaneous U.S. counterpart, the F-100.[99]

Somehow, while working six-day weeks at Western Electric and putting in long nights microfilming documents, Barr and Sarant found time for an active social life. Barr built a cabinet in his parents' apartment to store hundreds of classical music records, purchased in part with pocket money from the KGB, and Sarant kept a more eclectic collection, leaning heavily to folk music, at Morton Street. They often held "musicales," inviting bohemians and Communist Party friends over to listen to records and sing, accompanied by Sarant on the guitar, late into the night. Sarant, Barr, and his girlfriend also went on canoeing and camping trips together.

Both Sarant and Barr burned with an intense intellectual curiosity that led them to debate each other constantly about anything and everything: politics, evolution, music, astronomy. They developed the habit of making competing predictions: When would the United States become a Communist country? In what year would men first reach the moon? (They were sure that both would occur in their lifetimes.) Which of them would be a millionaire first?

As much as they shared interests and dreams, they had very different personalities. Barr was outgoing, displaying his *joie de vivre* with a perpetual smile. Sarant was witty, charming, and brilliant, but a dark side of his character emerged whenever he felt slighted or betrayed. He was prone to spells of depression, during which he retreated from the world.

The two friends constantly tinkered with electronic and mechanical gadgets. Barr came up with innovative, sometimes whimsical solutions to engineering problems that he would turn into functioning but sloppy prototypes. Having seen that something worked, he moved on to the next project; the details weren't important. Not content to produce a prototype, Sarant wouldn't stop until he'd built a perfectly crafted, elegant specimen. Their different characters were also on display when they went camping. Sarant would argue passionately that they should build the smallest, most efficient fire possible, while Barr wanted a big blaze. The conflict was resolved by Barr's reluctantly waiting for the food to cook on a carefully constructed fire, then throwing on piles of wood to fuel a bonfire, the bigger the better, while Al played the guitar and sang.[100]

As the war news grew more positive in 1945, Barr realized that any scientific or technical information given to the USSR would play little if any part in its war against Germany. He knew that Russia wouldn't have time to put new weapons into production before the inevitable fall of Berlin. This knowledge didn't cause Barr, Sarant, or their comrades to pull back from their relationship with the KGB or to stop mining their employers' filing cabinets for state-of-the-art weapons technology data.

With the war winding down, the two friends started to think about their economic prospects in peacetime. They decided to try going into business, first of all by finding a patron to support the development of Barr's idea for a new telecommunications technology. Almost all of their work experience involved military contracting, so it was natural to turn to the War Department for funding. The would-be entrepreneurs saw no conflict between stealing military secrets from the U.S. military and offering to help the Navy create a new weapon; nor did they find it inconsistent to solicit startup capital for a new company while ardently believing in Communism.

Initially, Barr and Sarant planned to call their new enterprise Ideas, Incorporated, but they settled on Sarant Laboratories, because it sounded like the famous television pioneer's Sarnoff Laboratories. They sent requests for funding on expensive paper with an embossed letterhead bearing enigmatic, high-tech slogans: "Electron-Beam Recording, Optical Communication, Projection In Depth." "For the past few years we have been attempting to develop a method for voice communication over a beam of light. As a result of this work, we have recently devised a new and practical method for accomplishing this purpose. We feel this system would be a valuable war weapon," Sarant wrote in a March 19, 1945, letter to the Navy Department's Bureau of Ships. The letter described the concept and asked for sponsorship to procure "certain laboratory equipment" that would be required to "complete the first working model of this device."

Sarant received a response in June expressing skepticism about the practicality of the invention, indicating that the Navy would be interested only if Sarant Laboratories could come up with a working model. Sarant responded by explaining that if the Navy Department provided the necessary sponsorship "we will be able to proceed at once with the development of this model." The letter had the initials AS/vg on the bottom, indicating that Barr's girlfriend, Vivian Glassman, typed it. It finished by stating: "In conclusion, we wish to emphasize our sincere desire as citizens and experienced, graduate engineers, to devote our energy to the successful completion of this project, which we are sure will give our country a valuable war weapon."

In a July 13 reply the Bureau of Ships raised additional technical points that, it said, established that "the fundamental character of the investigations conducted to date do not warrant the undertaking of this project by the Bureau. Should you decide to exploit this development to the extent of building an operating model, it is desired to witness and discuss the operation of this device when completed." That letter was as far as Barr and Sarant's invention got, and it was also the high point for Sarant Laboratories. Later they bought some secondhand equipment and set it up in a basement workshop, but never seriously tried to do any business.[101]

This was the first but far from the last time that Barr and Sarant failed to convince a government agency to fund one of their ideas. As with many other proposals that were killed off by risk-averse bureaucrats, this one had some merit and was realized decades later by another inventor. In April 1964,

NASA announced that one of its scientists, working at the Langley Research Center — Perl's former workplace — had invented "a new system of voice communications transmitted on a beam of light" that closely resembled the Sarant Laboratories proposal.[102]

Sources like Barr and Sarant were a challenge for the KGB to manage. As true volunteers, they had much more freedom of action than professional agents. Russian case officers could make suggestions to them, but the KGB couldn't compel them to do anything. Barr's meetings with Feklisov were always brief, and after Rosenberg's firing, meetings between KGB officers and their American agents were reduced to the bare minimum. It is possible that the KGB never sanctioned or even knew about Barr and Sarant's idea to solicit military contracts.

Barr didn't share in the unbridled joy expressed by most Americans when victory was declared over Germany and Japan. Convinced that the economy would implode again as it had during the Depression, he and Sarant worried that the United States, emboldened by its monopoly over the atom bomb, would turn on the Soviet Union. In their fantasy, capitalists, desperate to retain world supremacy and terrified of the economic threat posed by socialism, would nuke Moscow and Leningrad. "At that time, we saw America practically surrounding Russia and invading," Barr recalled. He cited the precedent of the Anglo-American expeditionary force that intervened in Siberia and the Russian Far East, attempting to nip the revolution in the bud.

"We basically felt that the American system was full of contradictions, that it was a system that had no future, that it led to war. Not particularly the American system, but the whole capitalist structure, of dividing the world into spheres of influence, into markets, and then fighting for these markets," Barr recalled in 1992. "We were reading a lot of Communist literature, and it seemed to us that there was an answer. That answer was a world in which the rules were not the rules of the society in which we lived, but they were rules based on helping one another, on more international cooperation, and I would say the elimination — that was the most important factor — the complete elimination of the struggle or the battle for markets. That was what we visualized. It was a dream that the world was united and cooperating with one another, all countries, for the benefit of each country."

Their experiences at the Signal Corps and Western Electric reinforced Barr's and Sarant's faith in technology. "I felt, and my friend [Sarant] did also, that the ultimate answer to making a society that would work was progress in technology. The real secret, the real answer to the problem of getting society to a state where there were no poor people, where food, clothing and shelter was in abundance, hinged upon the use of technology, high technology, to the maximum." Although they weren't blind to the evidence that technologically the United States was ahead of the Soviet Union, they still were certain that everything would be better in a planned, Communist state. "There was no denying that the Industrial Revolution under the capitalist system brought the world to a new state of development in spite of the many contradictions that were existent. But the ultimate solution, we felt, was some form of a socialist society where the factories and the means of production were not owned by individuals."[103]

5

Sperry Gyroscope, 1946–1948

Barr was a faithful, dedicated Marxist who voluntarily risked his career, liberty, and perhaps his life to help arm the Soviet Union during World War II. But he was far from the doctrinaire, dry automaton that so many men who dedicated themselves to Communism resembled. He was a splash of Technicolor compared to the serious, gray affect of Julius Rosenberg. Barr respected him as a dedicated revolutionary but considered him a nudnik and a prude. People who knew them both were surprised to learn that Barr — who seemed more intelligent and successful — reported to Julius, both in the party hierarchy and in their espionage enterprises.[1]

Especially after the demise of the Popular Front in the wake of the Nazi-Soviet Pact, many people with imagination and independence left or were ejected from the party in the early 1940s. It took a particular personality type to give the 100 percent dedication the party required: willingly submitting to its discipline and following its wild policy gyrations without question. The daily life of a rank-and-file Communist in the 1940s could be "summed up in the word RUSH," Louis Budenz, a high party official until he defected in 1948, wrote. "It is a whirlwind of hurry from party conference to party conference, from the ringing of one's neighbor's doorbell to the ringing of another's, from peddling of papers and the handing out of leaflets to attendance night after night at classes and committees — always to the accompaniment of slogans and arguments taken from the *Daily Worker,* which must be read faithfully every day, and from the 'theoretical' publications which few of the rank and file really grasp in full. These little people in the party accept the discipline of the party, do what they are told, think what they are told; and if these things seem contrary to reason, patriotic duty or common sense, they do them because the party says that is the correct thing to do 'at this time.' "[2]

Although he was fiercely loyal to the party, Barr's life was a stark contrast to that depicted by Budenz. Neither Communism nor espionage dominated his thoughts, partly because he had a habit that he described as "mentally switching channels," of abruptly and completely immersing himself in the moment. He might be terrified one moment while passing a roll of microfilm to a Russian agent — Feklisov described Barr as being extremely anxious during such encounters, reporting that when handing over film "he would look around with an anguished expression on his face seeing an FBI agent in anyone walking by" — but an hour later could be calmly immersed in a Beethoven symphony.[3]

His love of music and intense enthusiasm for engineering differentiated Barr from the typical, one-dimensional Communist. These interests also bound him to Sarant. While the KGB, and later the FBI, were interested in the Morton Street apartment because it was used as a studio to covertly microfilm secret documents, Barr and Sarant appreciated it mainly as a bachelor's paradise. For most of the time they lived in Greenwich Village, the furnishing consisted of a couple of homemade beds and a few chairs. The other contents of the apartment, in addition to camera equipment secreted under the floorboards, were Sarant's guitar, an ever-growing collection of phonograph records, a record player, a single table covered by Barr's ham radio equipment, a powerful light clamped to the wall (for photography), and a few piles of newspapers, which included, of course, the *Daily Worker.*

Barr and Sarant stayed up late several nights a month copying documents they had "borrowed" from the U.S. government. Once the film was surreptitiously stashed at Barr's parents' apartment or with the Leica under the floor at Morton Street, they turned to other pursuits, literally dancing on top of their espionage apparatus.

About once a week, Barr and Sarant hosted "musicales," with live music provided by Sarant or one of his folksinger friends, supplemented with records. The bare living room served as a dance floor into the early hours. In the morning it was common to see up to a dozen people snoozing on it in sleeping bags, waking up to the smell of pancakes that Barr, an avid cook, was flipping on the stove. The superintendent of the building next door sometimes climbed with his wife onto their roof to watch these parties, which they later described as "wild." They may have been spirited, but there were no spirits: both Sarant and Barr were teetotalers. It was the presence of single girls and, as the superintendent put it, "Negroes," at the gatherings, not raucous behavior, that scandalized him.[4]

The building superintendent and his wife weren't the only people troubled by Barr and Sarant's lifestyle. Rosenberg urged his comrade to settle down. Barr described his social life to Feklisov, who "found it all quite alarming, because since the dawn of history the pillow has always been the best way to break a secret." The worry proved groundless, as Vivian Glassman, the woman Barr preferred to share his pillow with, was a dedicated Communist who, with a single exception, proved herself to be discreet.[5]

Glassman, a petite, intellectual woman who was two years younger than Barr, had found a job at the Signal Corps at Fort Monmouth in May 1942 after graduating from college. In September the corps sent her to Philadelphia for training as an inspector, where she met Rosenberg. He introduced Glassman to Barr after she returned to Fort Monmouth in October. Soon she was describing him as her fiancé, although Barr never proposed marriage. Barr was strongly attached to both Sarant and Glassman, and the trio became inseparable comrades, going camping together, attending concerts, and organizing musicales.

Like Barr's, Glassman's parents were Russian-born Jews, and like him, she was active in the late 1930s in the Young Communist League. The extent of her knowledge of or involvement in her boyfriend's illegal extracurricular activities is unclear. Glassman is the only person alive who knows, and she isn't willing to discuss the topic. The location of Glassman's apartment fits the general description of the one David Greenglass told the FBI the Rosenberg network used for microfilming documents, but despite strong suspicions on the FBI's part, no solid evidence linking her to espionage activities emerged. Glassman acknowledged to the FBI that Julius Rosenberg had visited the apartment late at night, but she said he was accompanying her home, a plausible explanation because she frequently babysat the Rosenberg children. She admitted to accepting money from a Russian agent and carrying it, along with instructions for fleeing to Czechoslovakia via Mexico, to Perl, but claimed to the FBI it was her first and only contact with the KGB. As he clearly demonstrated later in his life, Barr was very capable of hiding thoughts and actions from the people he was most intimate with, so it is possible that Glassman was unaware of her lover's espionage activities.[6]

Barr and Sarant believed passionately in Communism, and they were spies for the Soviet Union, but for both espionage was a temporary avocation, not a vocation. They didn't do a great job of hiding their Communist allegiance (Barr had been fired because of links to Communism, and Sarant subscribed to the *Daily Worker*). The fact that they operated freely for years cannot be attributed to Barr's or Sarant's mastery of *konspiratsia*. Rather, they weren't caught because the FBI and the Army weren't serious about rooting out Communist espionage. Government investigations of Communists were motivated more by antipathy to radical political beliefs and by anti-Semitism than by counterintelligence.[7]

Recruiting American spies from the ranks of the Communist Party was a brazen, high-risk practice that went undetected largely because of the counterintelligence community's preoccupation with German and Japanese threats. The tactic worked brilliantly for years, providing dedicated agents like Barr, the other members of the Rosenberg group, and many others. Rosenberg's band of amateur spies turned over detailed information on a wide range of technologies and weapons systems that hastened the Red Army's march to Berlin, jump-started its postwar development of nuclear weapons and delivery systems, and later helped Communist troops in North Korea fight the American military to a standoff.

But Soviet espionage in North America was built on a house of cards, which collapsed soon after American counterintelligence shifted focus from its World War II enemies to its erstwhile ally. Ironically, it wasn't primarily the amateurs' mistakes that unmasked Barr and destroyed some of the USSR's most productive espionage networks. Rather, the most egregious errors, those that ended the golden age of Soviet espionage in the United States, were committed by seasoned professionals who violated basic rules of tradecraft, thereby turning what could have been relatively minor setbacks into major disasters.

One of the most consequential instances of corner-cutting created a crack in the armor shielding some of the Soviet espionage establishment's most carefully guarded secrets. In 1942 — during the darkest days of the war in Russia, when everything, including manpower, was in short supply — Soviet code clerks produced and distributed to agents around the globe thousands of duplicate copies of "one-time" pads used to encrypt communications. The name itself makes it plain that the code tables were to be used only once, but with the Germans at the gates of Stalingrad, punctilious adherence to the rules must have seemed an unaffordable luxury. The individuals responsible for generating the unique pairs of code sheets would have been correct if they'd thought the chances that their shortcut would be detected were vanishingly small. In the era before digital computers, it was the kind of mistake that could easily have been overlooked. The replication was detected and exploited only years later through a combination of extraordinary luck and the tremendous talent of a handful of American and British cryptographers.[8]

While pencil pushers far removed from undercover operations created the KGB's encryption vulnerability, KGB officers on the ground in New York and their superiors in Moscow were responsible for another type of blunder: allowing the separate strands that made up their networks to become entangled. Jacob Golos set the pattern, permitting agents to engage simultaneously in espionage and overt radical politics, and to intermingle their covert activities with their social lives. Properly set up, if one thread in an espionage network snaps, only a few agents fall into the enemy's hands. As would become clear later, Golos's threads were interconnected, so when the FBI pulled on one, the fabric unraveled.

The KGB eventually realized that Golos had created an untenable situation; the transfer of the Rosenberg group to Semyonov was part of the Center's effort to disentangle Golos's networks. Soviet intelligence even considered killing Golos to ensure that he took its secrets to his grave. Toward the end of World War II, however, even the career KGB officers who had been sent to the United States to professionalize agent handling got sloppy, allowing couriers to communicate with multiple espionage networks. Cells that should have been hermetically sealed were linked, so that leakage in one compartment spread into the others, eventually sinking the whole enterprise.[9]

The most serious leak, the one that compromised the Rosenberg group, was created over the objections of its unwitting perpetrator, Harry Gold. Gold was a loser, an impotent fantasist whose sole distinguishing accomplishment in life was serving as an unpaid courier for Soviet intelligence. But even he knew that there was something wrong with the mission that a veteran KGB officer, Anatoly Yatskov (known in the United States as Yakovlev), outlined at a meeting at Volk's Restaurant on Third Avenue in New York on the last Saturday of May 1945. The first part of the job was not problematic: Gold was to travel to Santa Fe for a rendezvous with Klaus Fuchs, a physicist he had met previously, who was feeding the Soviets extremely valuable information about the Manhattan Project. It was the second part of the job, continuing on to Albuquerque to pick up atomic secrets from David Greenglass, that disturbed Gold, who was aware that contacting two separate agent networks violated a cardinal rule of *konspiratsia*. Gold balked at the assignment, but he was overruled by KGB officers who were short on manpower and under intense pressure to deliver information about the atom bomb as quickly as possible.[10]

At Volk's, Yatskov gave Gold a piece of onionskin paper with an address in Albuquerque and the name Greenglass written on it. He also handed him a scrap of cardboard, torn from the side of a Jell-O box, to use as a recognition key. Gold didn't know it, but six months earlier the intact box had been resting in Julius and Ethel Rosenberg's kitchen. Using a technique he must have learned from the Russians, during a visit in January from David and Ruth Greenglass, Julius Rosenberg had emptied the powder from the box, ripped off part, cut it in two at a jagged angle with a pair of scissors, and given it to Ruth Greenglass. The courier who would meet her and David in New Mexico would produce the matching piece, Rosenberg said.[11]

The two pieces of the Jell-O box were united one day in June 1945. "There was a knock on the door," according to Greenglass. "We had just completed eating breakfast, and there was a man standing in the hallway who asked if I was Mr. Greenglass and I said, yes. He stepped through the door and said, 'Julius sent me.' " David and Ruth saw at a glance that the jagged edges of the piece of cardboard Gold produced, which was destined to become the world's most famous dessert container, would mesh with the piece Ruth then fetched from her purse. Gold later said he suspected the Greenglasses were Jewish because the first words out of David's mouth were an invitation to have something to eat; later he complained about how difficult it was to find a kosher deli in Albuquerque. David gave Gold drawings of a lens mold used in implosion experiments and the names of potential Communist spies at Los Alamos. Following Yatskov's instructions, Gold gave the couple $500 to fortify their commitment to socialism.[12]

In the weeks and months after his June trip to New Mexico, Gold's premonitions of disaster seemed unjustified, but ultimately he was proved correct. The decision to service Fuchs and Julius Rosenberg's brother-in-law with the same courier had fatal consequences.

Gold's ill-fated trip wasn't the only instance in which the KGB acted as its own worst enemy. And the KGB's mistakes weren't all caused by haste or sloppiness; some of its most serious self-inflicted wounds were a result of its culture and the influence of the society that nurtured it. Even more than other intelligence services, the KGB under Stalin was a psychological pressure cooker filled with mistrust and deceit; the stress was intensified by periodic purges that decimated its ranks, crushing the spirit of some of the employees who were spared. In addition to tactical errors made by individual KGB operatives, a rash of defections, provoked in part by the climate of fear, endangered Barr and his colleagues. The anonymous letter of August 1943 was only one in a series of treasonous acts by Russian officers and their American agents that alerted the FBI to Soviet penetration of U.S. institutions. Like that letter, many of the revelations and confessions were provoked by personal fears and tensions, not by philosophical opposition to Communism.

In September 1945, Igor Gouzenko, a GRU code clerk at the Soviet embassy in Ottawa, was recalled to Moscow after committing a minor error. Terrified by thoughts of the fate awaiting him, Gouzenko stuffed a pile of highly sensitive telegrams and pages from his superior's diary under his shirt and walked out of the embassy, hoping to trade the information for safety and freedom. Canadian government officials, finding Gouzenko's story incredible, initially refused his pleas for protective custody. In a scene reminiscent of a bad spy movie, when the Royal Canadian Mounted Police finally arrived at Gouzenko's apartment to pick him up twenty-four hours later, they found a clutch of his colleagues from the embassy desperately trying to bash in the door, intent on bringing Gouzenko, and his knowledge of GRU and KGB operations, back to Soviet territory. Rescued by the Mounties, the code clerk was thereafter taken very seriously by counterintelligence officials in Canada, the United States, and the United Kingdom.[13]

Gouzenko's information led Canadian authorities to break up several GRU networks, imprison five spies, and fire numerous government employees. More significantly, it alerted the FBI that the USSR was operating large-scale espionage operations against its allies. Gouzenko disclosed that Russian recruiters had specifically targeted Jewish members of the Communist Party, telling them that a Soviet victory was the world's only hope for destroying Hitler. Although Gouzenko didn't name specific agents working in the United States, it was reasonable for the Americans who debriefed him to believe his assertions that Soviet intelligence had a similar modus operandi south of the border.

Gouzenko said that Moscow was intensely interested in precisely the targets Barr and his comrades were attacking: the atomic bomb, radar, and the proximity fuse. Gouzenko also described Soviet techniques for transmitting secret information securely via Western Union, but he did not turn over codebooks or cipher tables that could directly help his debriefers to read the cables.[14]

The Ottawa defection was a body blow to the KGB, but the punch that sent its North American operations to the mat came two months later, on November 6, when Elizabeth Bentley walked into the FBI field office in New York intent on inflicting the greatest damage possible on Soviet intelligence.

Bentley's defection wasn't inevitable. If the KGB had handled her more compassionately, it might have retained her loyalty, or at least her silence. Bentley's resentment against the KGB dated back to 1942, when it began stripping agents like Julius Rosenberg from Golos, and it turned to hatred after the latter's death in 1943, when the Center insisted that Russians control all her remaining agents. A bad situation was made worse by KGB officers who treated Bentley far less tenderly than Golos had. Perhaps because they were dealing with many agents like Barr who were motivated by an intense commitment to Communism, the Russians assigned to deal with Bentley failed to realize that she had been drawn to espionage primarily through an emotional attachment to Golos, not through ideological conviction.[15]

Before turning herself in to the FBI in New York, Bentley had been convinced, incorrectly, that the Bureau had been shadowing her for months, if not years. Overinterpreting a chance encounter with a man whom she wrongly took for an undercover FBI agent, Bentley became afraid that she was on the verge of being arrested.

Bentley turned to the FBI because she was even more afraid of the Russians — especially after she'd worked herself into a drunken rage in September 1945 and told a KGB officer exactly what she thought of him and his colleagues, hinting about plans to become an FBI informant. These fears were justified: after her outburst, the KGB cooked up several plans to silence the agent whom they'd once dubbed *"umnitsa"* (clever girl) — permanently — but didn't follow through with them.[16] Anatoly Gorsky, the KGB's Washington *rezident,* considered and rejected shooting Bentley, arranging a car accident, pushing her in front of a subway train, or faking a suicide. The fake suicide was rejected because Bentley was "a very strong, tall and healthy woman," in contrast to Joseph Katz, the KGB operative assigned to liquidate her. Gorsky tentatively decided on a slow-acting poison to be delivered in food or on a handkerchief, but was told not to implement the plan because Lavrenty Beria, Stalin's intelligence chief, had his own plans for the turncoat.[17]

Unlike Gouzenko, Bentley didn't arrive at law enforcement's door with documents stuffed under her shirt, but her head was a veritable filing cabinet, filled with operational details of Soviet espionage. By the time she finished talking to the FBI, Bentley had identified more than eighty men and women who had spied or were still spying for the Soviet Union.[18]

Hoping to deploy Bentley as a double agent against the KGB, FBI Director J. Edgar Hoover admonished his staff to take great care to keep her defection secret. She was even given a male cover name, Gregory, to throw the Soviets off the track. Ironically, Hoover's own indiscretion propelled the information to the Lubyanka. Unable to contain himself, the FBI chief bragged about the counterintelligence coup to Sir William Stephenson, the head of British intelligence in the United States, the day after Bentley stepped into the Bureau's Manhattan office.[19]

Hoover's news traveled quickly from Stephenson to Kim Philby, a Soviet agent who had penetrated to the top echelons of MI6, the U.K. external intelligence agency. On November 20, 1945, a cable arrived in Moscow communicating Philby's warning that in "early November 1945, Elizabeth Terrill Bentley came to the FBI and reported about her work at Global Tourist corporation in New York," and that on the basis of Bentley's leads the FBI had "succeeded in spotting 30 Soviet agents."[20]

Barr was not among those agents, although the information Bentley gave the FBI could have indirectly exposed him. She described her encounter in the summer of 1942 with an engineer-spy who lived in Knickerbocker Village and the subsequent telephone calls from an agent who identified himself as Julius. Fortunately for the KGB, the FBI responded sluggishly to Bentley's disclosures. A telephone call to Mrs. McLaughlin in the Knickerbocker Village management office asking if there were any government engineers living there named Julius would have quickly led the Bureau to Rosenberg's doorstep.

Bentley's damage to the Soviet Union's interests was attenuated by the fact that the KGB rapidly learned of her treachery and froze activities that she might compromise. Nevertheless, the twin blows of Gouzenko's and Bentley's defections prompted the Soviet Union in November 1945 to temporarily suspend its North American espionage activities and to shut down all but its most important and best-hidden operations. The move was prudent: because the KGB was on guard, the FBI found it impossible to catch its agents red-handed, and not one person was successfully prosecuted as a result of Bentley's information, despite the hundreds of agents assigned to tracking down her leads (Bentley testified at the Rosenberg trial, but her comments were not decisive factors in the prosecution's case). At this time, Rosenberg was sidelined while the KGB tried to figure out why he'd been fired, and Barr had recently put himself temporarily out of commission.

With the war over, military contractors were planning massive layoffs. Feklisov suggested that it would be better for Barr's career if he quit rather than wait for a pink slip, and that he continue his education. In October 1945, a month before Bentley defected, Barr suddenly quit his job at Western Electric and enrolled in an electrical engineering master's degree program at Columbia University, joining his class two weeks into the semester. In a KGB version of the G.I. Bill, Soviet intelligence paid Barr's tuition and provided a monthly stipend of about fifty dollars. The KGB encouraged several other American agents during this period, including David Greenglass, to continue their education, offering to pay their tuition.[21]

As with all the New York *rezidentura*'s other agents, the KGB put Barr on ice for at least six months starting in November 1945. Since there was no reason to believe he was under suspicion, however, Feklisov remained in contact with Barr during this period of forced inactivity. In December, Feklisov requested that Barr set up an urgent meeting with Rosenberg, whom the Russians had up to that point avoided contacting directly. Spooked by a false alarm about FBI surveillance of Rosenberg, Feklisov choreographed a dance that was intended to enhance the security of the visit.

Three inches of snow had fallen the night before, and the sidewalks were still slippery on the afternoon of December 15 when Feklisov started a dry-cleaning routine, first visiting his wife, Zina, in a Brooklyn maternity hospital, and later warming up at a Turkish bath. Light snow was falling at 11:00 P.M. as he walked into a drugstore on Monroe Street, near the Rosenbergs' apartment building. Following the instructions Barr had relayed, Ethel Rosenberg walked into the store a few minutes later, ignored Feklisov, bought something, and returned home. This was the signal that the coast was clear. Ethel's tracks were still fresh as Feklisov followed a few minutes later, buzzing the intercom button he'd pressed two years before at his first meeting with Antenna.[22]

The drugstore maneuver and Feklisov's subsequent late-night meeting with Julius in the kitchen of the Rosenbergs' small apartment raise questions about the extent of Ethel's participation in her husband's espionage activities. At a minimum, Feklisov must have known what Ethel looked like in order to recognize her in the store. According to Feklisov's report to the KGB, Ethel was instructed to avoid approaching him, a detail that suggests that she had an idea of what he looked like as well. One explanation is that Julius had given the KGB photos of his wife and had described his Russian friend to Ethel; another is that Ethel and Feklisov had previously met each other. Feklisov didn't mention Ethel in his report to Moscow about his conversation with Julius, but even if she didn't overhear the two men speaking in the small apartment, it strains credulity to believe that Julius didn't tell his wife the substance of the Russian's remarks.[23]

Feklisov questioned Julius closely to determine if he knew any of the individuals, particularly any women, connected with his first KGB contact, Jacob Golos. At first Rosenberg drew a blank, but then he remembered the "secretary" whom he would call to contact Golos. "To that secretary, he always gave only his first name, Julius. He never met her personally," Feklisov noted in a report to the Center describing their conversation. The report, which is preserved in the KGB's archives, corroborates Bentley's version of events. Rosenberg also told Feklisov that he'd given Golos personal data on himself, Perl, Barr, and an agent with the cover name "Nil" who hasn't been identified, but that he didn't know whether the secretary would have seen this material. Feklisov requested that Moscow search its files to determine if documents describing Barr or the other agents had been typed on Bentley's typewriter.[24]

Before leaving Rosenberg, Feklisov told him that Golos's secretary, whom he didn't name, "had betrayed us and that in this connection we worried very much about him. I instructed him on how to behave if summoned to the Hut

[FBI]." Rosenberg must deny having been a CPUSA member, because he'd done so in 1941 and 1945 when questioned by the Civil Service and the Army; he should also disavow any knowledge of Bernard Schuster, the party functionary who had introduced him to Golos and Semyonov. "In case he is asked to name his friends, he will name [Joel Barr] and 'Nil,' who are his old friends," Feklisov reported.

After instructing Rosenberg to cease all espionage activities and to burn any materials that could link him to the Communist Party — another activity Ethel is likely to have been at least aware of — Feklisov arranged a followup meeting for 8:00 P.M. on Sunday, March 17, 1946, at the Colony Theater at 79th Street and Second Avenue. Warning him that the KGB might send someone else to the meeting, Feklisov told Rosenberg to carry a copy of the *New York Post*. The KGB man would approach Rosenberg carrying a *Reader's Digest* in his left hand and ask, "Aren't you waiting for Al?," to which Rosenberg would reply, "No, I'm waiting for Helen." The KGB man would respond that he was "Helen's brother. She asked me to tell you something."

The KGB kept Rosenberg sidelined, aware that the FBI had more than enough leads to track him down and, through him, to roll up Barr, Perl, Sarant, Sobell, and others. Despite Moscow's instructions to communicate with Rosenberg only through a cutout, Feklisov, who hadn't seen Liberal for over six months, got permission to meet with him in September 1946. The ostensible purpose was to tell his favorite agent how the KGB would contact him in the future if and when the time was ripe to renew clandestine work. The real purpose was for Feklisov to personally break the news that he was going home. Departing from precedent, he picked a posh Hungarian restaurant with gypsy violinists, the Golden Fiddle, which was off the lobby of the Hotel Belleclaire at 77th and Broadway. After Feklisov gave Rosenberg details, including a password, for meeting another KGB officer in six months, they fell into nostalgic reminiscences about the highlights of their collaboration, including the purloined proximity fuse and recruiting Sarant and Sobell. Julius told Feklisov that he "was dreaming about a trip to the Soviet Union someday to see for himself the society he thought represented the future of humanity." After dinner they walked along Riverside Drive and sat on a bench, where Feklisov handed Rosenberg $1,000 to deal with any unforeseen emergencies. The Russian portrayed his posting to Moscow as a routine rotation. He didn't reveal that as a result of the deteriorating security situation, the KGB had pulled back virtually all experienced agent handlers from the United States. Nor did he reveal his fear that their replacements were incompetent.[25]

Shortly after returning to Moscow, Feklisov wrote a report summarizing his achievements in the United States. The top five agents in the Rosenberg network (Rosenberg, Barr, Sarant, Perl, and Sobell) had given Feklisov "over 20,000 pages of technical documents plus another 12,000 pages of the complete design manual for the first U.S. jet fighter, the P-80 Shooting Star."[26]

The Center's sense of dread about its U.S. operations intensified the day after Christmas 1946 as a result of a disturbing encounter between Gold and his KGB handler, Yatskov. It started routinely enough, in the men's room of the Earle Theater in Manhattan, where Gold had gone in accord with a previous arrangement. An unknown Russian approached him brandishing a scrap of paper that Gold recognized as half of a bill that he'd given to Yatskov as a recognition device. "You Harry, you have material from the doctor," the Russian said in broken English, and instructed Gold to meet Yatskov in the Third Avenue Bar in an hour.

Gold denied that he had anything for "the doctor," but he complied with the instruction. Yatskov told Gold that he would soon be sent to Paris, and briefed him on the procedure for a clandestine meeting. Gold would go to a specific stop of the Paris Metro and wait; after a specified number of trains had passed, his contact would approach him. Excited by the prospect of visiting France, Gold mentioned that he could come up with a legitimate business reason for the trip, prompting Yatskov to ask where he was working. It turned out that Gold was working for Abe Brothman, a chemist from whom he had purchased low-grade intelligence in the 1930s. At that time Gold had used a pseudonym with Brothman, but now he was using his real name. This was a serious violation of *konspiratsia*. An informant like Brothman should never learn the real identity of an agent who is in direct contact with officers of a foreign intelligence service.

Brothman had come under suspicion from the FBI, and he was the last person to whom the KGB would have wanted Gold to reveal his identity. Instantly recognizing the danger posed by Gold's relationship with Brothman, Yatskov grabbed his head with both hands and moaned. "Look, don't you know that this man is suspect" by the FBI, the Russian asked. "You fool," he spit out, "you have spoiled eleven years of preparation!" Throwing a twenty-dollar bill on the table, Yatskov stormed out of the bar, telling Gold that he would never see him again. Yatskov sailed to France the next day aboard the S.S. *America*. His fears were justified: when the FBI finally tracked down Gold, it was through Brothman.[27]

Released from the heavy workload imposed by Western Electric, as well as the late nights microfilming secret documents and the tension surrounding meetings with Feklisov, Barr dove into his studies, writing a dissertation, "Solving

Transcendental Equations by Means of Lissajou Figures." He also concentrated seriously on music, returning to the piano, which he'd learned to play as
a child. Barr rebelled against traditional teaching methods, boycotting scales
and études, instead devising his own system, mimicking the masters whose
techniques were etched on his extensive record collection.

Barr also studied classical composition with Elie Siegmeister, a prominent
figure in American music at the time. A Communist, in the 1930s Siegmeister
had written classical music reviews under a pseudonym for the *Daily Worker,*
traveled to Russia to learn about "proletarian music," and got to know folk
and blues musicians such as Woody Guthrie and Huddie Ledbetter (Lead-
belly), integrating their work into his operas and symphonic works. Siegmeister was at the height of his career when Barr knew him. In November 1945
Siegmeister's *Western Suite* was debuted by Arturo Toscanini leading the NBC
Symphony Orchestra, and in December 1946 his *Prairie Legend* was pre-
miered at Carnegie Hall by the New York Philharmonic under the guest baton
of Leopold Stokowski.

Siegmeister and Barr had a lot in common beyond their shared passions for
music and Communism. The sons of Russian Jews, both were outgoing, warm
men with extraordinarily active minds that never stopped whirling. They became close friends, and under Siegmeister's influence Barr seriously considered
a career in music.

Struggling trying to decide whether his future path was to be a composer or
an engineer, Barr graduated from Columbia and settled temporarily on the
more practical path. In the fall of 1946 he applied for a position at Sperry
Gyroscope Company. The application form asked if he had "ever been fired,
asked to resign, furloughed or put on an inactive status for cause while serving
in the Army, Navy, Marine Corps or Coast Guard of the United States or in
any position of private or Government employment? If so, state circumstances." Barr falsely answered "no" and listed his employment at the Signal
Corps from 1940 to 1942, stating that he had left to accept a better offer.[28]

Sperry was helping the military both exploit and defend against the advances in missiles the Germans had pioneered during the war and were reconstructing for the Soviet Union. When Barr reported for work at Sperry on
October 28, 1946, he was assigned to a top-secret Air Force research program
related to long-range radar. He quickly impressed co-workers and supervisors
as a brilliant engineer. Barr was living in the Morton Street apartment, which
he'd vacated, moving back into his parents' apartment, a year and a half
earlier, just before Sarant married his girlfriend, Louise Ross.[29]

Ross, known to her friends as "Puss," lived a few doors down Morton Street
from Sarant's apartment when they met. A member of the Greenwich Village

Figure 3. Joel Barr, Vivian Glassman, and Louise and Alfred Sarant in front of 65 Morton Street, Greenwich Village, New York, probably 1945. (Source: Exhibits from the Julius and Ethel Rosenberg Case File, 03/13/1951–03/27/1951, Record Group 118, National Archives and Records Administration, New York City.)

Branch of the CPUSA, from an upper-crust family, she had worked as a secretary during the war for the Soviet Purchasing Commission in Washington, D.C., an organization engaged in both legal acquisition of military supplies and illegal espionage. She and Al shared a love of folk music and a curiosity about science that are reflected in the card file they used to store names and addresses. One card, filed under "B" for bets and signed by "Puss and Alfred," recorded that at 10:25 P.M. on Tuesday, November 27, 1945, "Alfred bets Puss 1000 (one thousand) dollars that someone will reach the moon or any other heavenly body by the time Puss is 55 (fifty-five) years old." Other neatly typed cards contained the lyrics for folk songs, some bawdy, some political, and the names and addresses of folksinger friends, including Betty Sanders, who was a cofounder with Pete Seeger of People's Artists, and Oscar Brand, who was just starting "Folk-song Festival," which was destined to become the longest continuously running radio program in American history. He was still hosting it fifty-eight years later.[30]

The Morton Street apartment was available for Barr in October 1946 because Sarant had resigned his job at Bell Labs a month earlier. Dejected about rejections from the graduate schools of physics at MIT, Princeton, and Cornell, Sarant moved to Ithaca and took a job helping to build Cornell University's cyclotron, hoping it would help him gain admittance to its graduate school. Sarant befriended several world-class physicists in Ithaca, including his neighbor, Philip Morrison. Morrison had worked at Los Alamos on the atom bomb; when Sarant knew Morrison, he was a vocal opponent of nuclear weapons. The Sarants shared a house with another physicist, Bruce Dayton, and later the two families built adjacent homes. Dayton introduced Sarant to the Nobel laureate Hans Bethe. Bethe refused to help get him into Cornell because Sarant lacked the necessary academic qualifications. Bethe later said he felt that Sarant was of average abilities but was frustrated, bitter that the world didn't appreciate his talents. Another friend of Sarant's, Richard Feynman, a physicist who was later awarded a Nobel Prize, shared Bethe's view that he didn't have what it took to realize his dream to become a physicist. Sarant remembered these slights and in later years seemed to be driven by the need to prove men like Bethe and Feynman wrong.[31]

The Sarants' card file also recorded Louise's appointments at a birth control clinic, as well as details of her unsuccessful attempts to avoid pregnancy. On December 5, 1946, the day after Jeremy Sarant was born, she received a telegram from Barr and Perl: "MISS PUSS SARANT, THE THOMPKINS COUNTY MEMORIAL HOSPITAL. THE AMALGAMATED ASSOCIATION OF GODFATHERS CIO GREETS WITH OVERWHELMING JOY ITS FIRST AND MOST AUSPICIOUS GODSON. ALL HAIL MOTHER PUSS THOU DELIVERETH AND CREATOR PAR EXCELLENCE HURRAH LOVE. JOEL AND BILL."

Sarant was out of the espionage business when Jeremy was born, and it is unlikely that he had any intention of getting back into it. He was busy pursuing bourgeois goals: building a home construction business, investing in a paint store. It is probable that Barr, however, reverted to habit at Sperry, resuming his extracurricular copying of secret documents. Rosenberg boasted to David Greenglass in 1947 that "one of the boys" had "obtained and furnished to him the whole theory of guided missile control and that he, Rosenberg, had furnished the same to Russia." Rosenberg didn't tell Greenglass which of his "boys" had picked up this information, but he was almost certainly referring to Barr.[32]

The dust settled after the stir caused by Bentley's defection with no sign that Rosenberg had been compromised. Acting on his own initiative and against the KGB's instructions, Rosenberg reassembled his network, putting himself at its center. He longed to regain the sense of purpose that spying had given his life, and, having survived two loyalty investigations and Bentley's defection unscathed, he probably believed that the FBI would never catch him.[33]

Files on Barr, Julius and Ethel Rosenberg, Sobell, and Sarant rested in the FBI's cabinets undisturbed for most of 1946. On October 18 an FBI agent pulled

Sarant's file and placed a piece of paper inside noting that there was an entry in the directory of the Communist-infiltrated Federation of Architects, Engineers, Chemists, and Technicians (FAECT) for a Raymond Cooper at 65 Morton Street. The memo also observed that this matched the party name for Alfred Sarant, who lived at that address and had transferred into the Greenwich Village Club on February 14, 1944, from Branch 16B of the industrial division of the CPUSA. After filing the memo, the agent closed the drawer, and Sarant's file was not disturbed again for almost four years.[34]

Other hands reached for Barr's file the next summer. In June 1947, Sperry Gyroscope's security office contacted the FBI asking for information about Barr. He'd been entrusted with countless classified documents and worked on scores of secret military research projects during the war, but this was the first time since Barr had left the Signal Corps in 1942 that anyone had checked on him. A quick glance at Barr's file revealed that the Bureau had informed the Army of his CPUSA membership in 1942, so a request was made for his Army records. The FBI knew that it could take months for the Army to sift through its millions of personnel files to locate a specific record. In the meantime, the Bureau snooped into Barr's bank accounts and contacted Western Electric, which reported that upon resigning his performance had been rated "very good."

In July the FBI interviewed two of the references Barr had provided to Sperry. One didn't know him well enough to provide any useful information, while the other "considered Barr of good reputation, and believed he was entirely loyal to the United States." The FBI's memos on the investigation report two facts about the third reference: his name was Julius Rosenberg, and he wasn't contacted.

On September 3, 1947, the Army file arrived at the FBI's New York field office. It indicated that Barr had been discharged in 1942 on the basis of the FBI's disclosure that he was an active Communist. Two weeks later, on September 14, 1947, a confidential informant, apparently a former neighbor, told the FBI that she knew the entire Barr family and that they "were all Communists and very active in Communist activity; that [Joel] Barr and his family often participated in Communist rallies; that the neighborhood was full of Communist sympathizers, and that circulation of Communist pamphlets in the neighborhood was very common." Barr's FBI file included a photo, which the Bureau had obtained more than two years previously, of a document recording his membership in Branch 16B of the CPUSA. It also listed several other members, including Julius Rosenberg, but the FBI investigators did not notice the coincidence that someone with the same rather unusual name was also one of Barr's professional references.[35]

The FBI sent a summary of its background investigation of Barr to Sperry during the first week of October. His employment was unceremoniously terminated on October 16, 1947. The company told him it had learned about his 1942 firing from the Signal Corps, and that as a result both of that incident and of his failure to mention it on his employment application and on a security questionnaire, he'd been denied the clearance needed to work on classified defense projects. There was no mention of his more recent affiliation with the Communist Party, so neither Barr nor the KGB learned that the FBI possessed detailed membership records.

Barr correctly surmised that, at least for the foreseeable future, his career in military electronics was over. There was little prospect that any firm with defense contracts would hire someone who had been denied a security clearance after being labeled a Communist, and civilian electrical engineering jobs were scarce, especially for someone whose specialized knowledge was confined to radar and fire-control computing.

The newspapers were filled with reports about the emerging Cold War. Politicians were competing with each other over the strength of their anticommunist convictions. "It was a tremendous shock that the world was turning into this period which became known as the Cold War. We were convinced that this was artificially stimulated by certain circles who were convinced that if the Soviet experiment were to succeed" it would be a threat to the United States and capitalism, Barr remembered. His firing made perfect sense in the context of shrill party propaganda characterizing the U.S. government as an equivalent to Nazi Germany. "We had been under the influence of socialist psychology. We knew that there were fascist elements in the American government, in the FBI," Barr said in 1992, looking back at this period.[36]

Seeking to leave the United States and his troubles behind, Barr applied to the Kungl Technical University in Stockholm. The KGB agreed to help pay his tuition. His plans were firm enough by December 1 to state on a passport application that he planned to study in Sweden for one year and then to attend the University of Delft in Holland for a year. A week later, the State Department issued him U.S. passport number 133825.[37]

Barr's response to the situation sets him apart from the other members of the Rosenberg spy ring. All spoke and dreamed vaguely about international travel, especially a pilgrimage to Moscow, but none of the others had the curiosity or the nerve to leap into the unknown or to immerse themselves voluntarily in a foreign culture.

Preparing to leave and with no commitments in New York, Barr took Vivian Glassman on a car trip to Florida in mid-December. Soon after they returned, he sold the car to his brother Arthur, who agreed to wire installment payments to Europe. Barr also sold his precious record collection. According to David

Greenglass, Julius Rosenberg contributed some money for the trip — presumably part of the emergency funds Feklisov had left in his care. Feklisov was long gone, but Barr had stayed in touch with the KGB's New York *rezidentura,* and he made arrangements to contact Soviet intelligence while traveling.[38]

Barr told Glassman, Rosenberg, and other close friends that he might travel to the Soviet Union, and he visited the Czechoslovakian consulate to find out the requirements for obtaining a visa. The Communists hadn't yet consolidated power in Prague, but Czechoslovakia was clearly moving into the Soviet camp, so it was a way to travel to the USSR.

"The situation we were living through at that time led me to the conclusion that even as a scientist, I would certainly like to see with my own eyes how the [Soviet] system worked. This was in the back of my mind. I discussed it with all of my friends. The conversation often turned to working in the Soviet Union. I made the decision to go to Europe using whatever savings I had and try to perhaps get into the Soviet Union and see what it was like there," Barr remembered in 1992.[39]

With his departure imminent, Glassman told Barr that she too was planning to go to Europe and suggested that they sail together. On January 6, 1948, Glassman applied for a passport, telling the State Department that she expected to leave on January 21 aboard the S.S. *America* for a six-month trip to France as a tourist, and enclosed a letter from a steamship agent confirming her purchase of a roundtrip ticket. Barr cashed in his ticket and bought a new one matching Glassman's.

The State Department sent Glassman's passport by registered mail a week after she applied, but no one accepted the package, and she didn't respond to the mailman's note indicating that it could be collected at a nearby post office. At almost the last moment, she changed her mind about the trip. Asked about it a couple of years later by FBI agents, Glassman said that Barr had promised to marry her, and that when he didn't follow through, she decided not to accompany him.[40]

In 2003 Glassman denied that the lack of a marriage certificate had had anything to do with her decision to remain in New York. Rather, it was prompted by a premonition that Barr wasn't coming back, and that she might not either. "I was planning to go to France with Joel because I cared for him a lot," she said. "I had some reservations about how things might turn out. It was very vague, but I thought we might not be coming back. I was fearful in a sense. I had obligations here and a family." She probably had more than a premonition; she knew he was considering traveling to the Soviet Union, a place it was hard for most Americans at the time to imagine visiting, and harder to conceive of someone returning from.

Vivian and Joel spent the night of January 20 together, and the next morning, a frigid, snowy day, she drove him to the pier in his car, which now belonged to Arthur. They embraced on the quay, and he walked up the gangplank of the largest and most luxurious U.S.-flagged liner.[41]

As Barr and the three other men in his tourist-class room settled in for the voyage, another group of young men was sitting in Arlington Hall, a former girls' school in suburban Washington that served as headquarters for America's decoding efforts, struggling with a sea of seemingly random numbers. Their success in plotting a course through those digits would shape Barr's future as well as the lives of his closest friends, and have lasting effects on the course of the Cold War.

Throughout 1947, an Army Security Agency (ASA) team was slogging through coded messages that various Soviet agencies had sent to and received from Moscow via Western Union, putting in long hours at the mind-numbing work. At the end of August 1947, Meredith Gardner, the quiet genius responsible for much of the success of the decryption program, produced an eleven-page report summarizing progress in deciphering diplomatic cables. It contained tantalizing clues, including the news that an agent with the cover name "LIB . . . or possibly LIBERAL," who was also called "ANTENKO" (Antenna) until September 1944, was mentioned six times in messages sent from October 22 to December 20, 1944. A November 27 message "speaks of his wife ETHEL, 29 years old married (?) 5 years . . . husband's work and the role of METR(O) and NIL." Regarding "metr" (Meter), the report stated that in addition to the November 27 cable, a December 5 cable mentioned him and "HYUSON."

Given the difficulties the ASA team had overcome, the results were impressive. Nonetheless, their output consisted mostly of fragments, and as Gardner's report concluded: "In its present state the [decrypted cable] traffic tends to arouse curiosity more than it does to satisfy it. This unsatisfactory state of affairs makes it imperative that this report be supplemented at intervals."[42]

The ASA team kept working on the cables. At first they got only a word here and there; later phrases and eventually whole sentences emerged, and in some cases paragraphs. Trying to make sense of data shards sometimes sent investigators onto false trails, but even when it was chasing illusions, the fact that the FBI finally had a grasp of its adversary's methods and goals put it many steps closer to success.

By mid-1948 Gardner had produced translations or summaries of dozens of cables. On April 28 he completed a revised report that seemed to provide the key to unmasking the agent referred to as Antenna and Liberal, described in the cables as the central figure in an espionage operation that had penetrated the Los Alamos nuclear weapons laboratory.

Robert Lamphere, one of a handful of FBI employees who learned of the ASA's work, was particularly excited about a May 5, 1944, message from the New York *rezidentura* to Moscow. There were a few blocks of text missing, but it seemed that the cable indicated that Antenna had "completed the engineering course at Cooper Union" and had worked for Western Electric. It would take two years for Gardner to decrypt a few more critical words, which dramatically modified the message's meaning.

Lamphere sent FBI agents around the country scrambling to establish Antenna's identity. They uncovered a number of fascinating pieces of information, but Lamphere couldn't put them together in a way that was entirely consistent with the picture painted by Gardner's decryption. Eventually Lamphere learned that it was impossible to fit the pieces together because he was trying to fit them into the wrong frame.

In addition to Cooper Union and Western Electric, the memo that appeared to describe Antenna also mentioned "the Signal Corps LABORATORY at Fort MONMOUTH." Searching FBI files for security cases involving Fort Monmouth, Lamphere came up with two names: Emanuel Mittleman and Joel Barr. Mittleman had been dismissed from the Signal Corps in 1942 because of "moral charges brought against him by his wife," according to the Army, and had also been accused by an informant of subversive activities. Mittleman didn't match the other known facts about Antenna, so attention quickly focused on Barr.[43]

Lamphere sent a letter to several FBI field offices in June 1948 requesting help with an investigation into the identity of an "unknown subject" who, as a subsequent FBI memo noted, "was believed to have acted as an intermediary between person or persons who were working on wartime nuclear fission research and MGB [the Soviet Ministry for State Security, later called the KGB] agents." Lamphere's letter carefully masked the source of the original leads. Instead of indicating that the information came from decrypted cables, Lamphere attributed it to a "confidential informant." The information about Barr that flowed into FBI headquarters convinced Lamphere that he was on Antenna's trail. Scotty Miller, an agent in the New York field office, summarized the status of the investigation in an October 1948 memo, concluding that information obtained about Barr to that point "establishes him as possibly being identical with [the unknown] subject."[44]

Describing the FBI's 1942 investigation, Miller noted that none of the three references Barr provided to the Signal Corps had been interviewed or investigated. He didn't, however, suggest that the FBI correct the oversight. The Bureau later became well acquainted with one of Barr's references, Bill Perl, eventually learning that he had been among the most productive sources of technical intelligence for the Soviet Union during World War II.

Miller also described Barr's subsequent employment at Western Electric — a detail that fitted with the known facts about Antenna — and provided reports about Barr's bank accounts, comments made by his neighbors to FBI investigators, his Communist Party membership, and his hiring and firing by Sperry Gyroscope.

Frustratingly, one element of Barr's life story didn't match the description provided by Lamphere's "confidential informant." Miller reported that he "had checked the records of Cooper Union, Astor Place and 4th Avenue, New York City, but they did not reflect that anyone under the name of JOEL BARR was ever in attendance at that institution."[45]

Miller went to 241 West 97th Street, the home address for Joel Barr provided by a security officer at Sperry. He "ascertained it to be a rather large apartment house with an elevator. There were no mail boxes in the lobby of the building, but it was noted that the combination elevator operator-doorman presumably handles the mail at this establishment." Miller got the telephone company to hand over records of all toll calls from the Barr apartment, but there was nothing out of the ordinary.

Miller's report stated that on "August 25, 1948, the writer made a pretext telephone call to the above-mentioned BARR, telephone Monument 2–5602. Mrs. REBECCA BARR (JOEL's mother) advised the writer that JOEL has been in Europe for about six months. She stated he was working towards getting his doctor's degree in engineering (electrical), continuing that he had been in Paris, Sweden and presently in Finland, where he would be for about another two weeks. She said she does not know when he expects to return to the United States." Next Miller placed a "mail cover" on Barr's relatives; that is, the post office wrote down or made photostats of information from all envelopes and packages addressed to them, including particulars of the sender, as well as the place and date of the postmark. The FBI also sent urgent messages to customs-houses at every possible port of entry into the United States requesting that it be immediately notified if Barr reentered the country.

The FBI's reach didn't extend much beyond the borders of the United States in 1948, so the Barr investigation was turned over to the CIA. "Information has been recently received to the effect that Joel Barr may have acted as a Soviet espionage agent in the United States prior to leaving the United States for Sweden in January, 1948," Hoover stated in a November 19, 1948, letter to the CIA director. Hoover didn't mention the source of the information; the FBI took great care to prevent the CIA from learning about its success in reading Soviet messages. Stalin was better informed of Arlington Hall's progress than President Truman, and far more was known about the decryption project in the Lubyanka than at the CIA.[46]

While its investigation of Barr was suspended, the FBI continued to probe for information about his associates, especially the women in his life. This interest was prompted by a tantalizing clue that Gardner had plucked from the November 1944 KGB cable from New York to Moscow. On the basis of the decryption, which Gardner had included in his summary report, Lamphere told the agents who were pounding the pavements that his "confidential informant" had revealed that someone connected to Antenna had the "Christian name, ETHEL, [and] used her husband's last name; had been married for five years [in 1944]; 29 years of age; member of the Communist Party, USA, possibly joining in 1938; probably knew about her husband's work with the Soviets." The FBI quickly identified the two women who conceivably could have been referred to as Barr's wife. The mystery thickened when it turned out that neither Glassman nor Goldfarb was named Ethel.[47]

The FBI was having better luck with another name that Gardner had fished from the sea of numbers. He told Lamphere that a July 26, 1944, message indicated that Antenna had tried to recruit an engineer in Washington, D.C. Unlike all the previous messages related to Antenna, this one provided a real name, not a cover name. The recruitment target's name, spelled out in Latin letters, was Max Elitcher.[48]

The FBI dove into its files for clues about Elitcher, placed a mail cover on his residence, and put him and his wife, Helene, under surveillance. The files revealed the Office of Naval Intelligence's brief interest in Elitcher in 1941, when it had come across his name in connection with an investigation of Morton Sobell, and the fact that the ONI had paid some attention to him in late 1947. When the FBI started looking into Elitcher's background, it found that he'd attended CCNY along with Sobell.[49]

Elitcher began acting strangely soon after the FBI started watching him, abruptly making plans to quit his job and move to New York — behavior suggesting to Lamphere that he might have become conscious of the surveillance. On July 30, 1948, the FBI was tailing the Elitchers as they headed north out of Washington in their seven-year-old Chevy. Just after they passed Baltimore, Elitcher thought he spotted a car following him and began driving erratically. When the car disappeared near Philadelphia, he thought he'd shaken the tail. In fact the FBI had merely turned over the surveillance to another car, which had no problem following the Elitchers to Max's mother's apartment on Lexington Avenue in Manhattan, and later to Sobell's house in Queens. The Elitchers were clearly "tail conscious," as the FBI team reported later, so the surveillance was discontinued.[50]

If the G-men had stayed on the job that night, they would have witnessed a very interesting scene. An hour or two after arriving at Sobell's, Sobell and Elitcher walked out of the house, got into Elitcher's car, and took a drive.

According to Elitcher's version of events, the two drove to Catherine Slip, a short street in Manhattan one block off the East River, midway between the Brooklyn and Manhattan bridges — and exactly half a mile from Julius Rosenberg's apartment. Elitcher parked the car, and Sobell disappeared into the rain, returning a half-hour later, when they drove back to Sobell's house.

Accounts by Sobell and Elitcher agree that early that evening, after putting his daughter to sleep at the Sobells' home, Max told Morty about the FBI tail. Sobell, a mercurial character in the best of circumstances, was infuriated that the Elitchers had brought the FBI to his doorstep. He shouted at Elitcher, telling him to hit the road and hide out in the Catskills, or go anywhere, just get the hell out. After cooling down, according to Sobell, he decided to go for a drive, and the two men just drove around, trying to determine if Sobell's house was under surveillance.[51]

In statements to the FBI, a grand jury, a Senate subcommittee, and in open court, Elitcher presented a rather different narrative: When Sobell had recovered his equilibrium after learning that Elitcher had drawn the FBI to his house, he said that he had some valuable, presumably compromising, information that he'd been meaning for some time to give to Rosenberg. The information was "too valuable to destroy and too dangerous to keep around the house." Complaining that he was too tired to drive safely, Sobell insisted that Elitcher chauffeur him. Sobell pocketed a metal film can as they left the house, put it in the glove compartment in the car, and took it with him when they parked at Catherine Slip. Sobell then met with Rosenberg.

On the drive back to Queens, Elitcher told the Senate subcommittee, he asked Sobell: "What does Julie think about my being followed?" Rosenberg was calm, Sobell said. Rosenberg told Sobell he "had spoken to Elizabeth Bentley on the phone at one time, but . . . she didn't know who he was, and everything was all right, and not to worry about it . . . Don't be concerned about it. It is ok."[52]

As Sobell and Rosenberg would learn, there was plenty to be concerned about. For the time being, however, it looked as if they had ridden out the storm. The FBI kept an eye on Elitcher, but it didn't have enough information to accuse him of a crime and, afraid that he'd tip off Sobell or other Soviet agents, decided not to question him.

At the end of the summer of 1948, the investigations of Barr, Elitcher, and Sobell were stalled, but Lamphere was confident that the efforts of the codebreakers at Arlington Hall, combined with old-fashioned police work, would lead to Antenna and other KGB agents. Looking back on the second half of 1948, he remembered it as "a golden time. We were inside the enemy's house; men were coursing down the corridors, following the leads to which our keys had opened the doors. Already I had begun investigations of Max Elitcher, Joel Barr, Morton Sobell, the unknown 'Ethel,' White Russians and odd recruits. It was easy to envision that soon, very soon, there would be more keys available, more corridors to explore."[53]

Lamphere and the ASA didn't know it at the time, but the enemy had already learned that its locks were being picked and was taking steps to move as many valuables as possible beyond the FBI's reach.

The KGB had hints in March 1946, and perhaps earlier, that the U.S. Army was making progress in decrypting wartime cable traffic between Soviet intelligence operatives in North America and their superiors in Moscow. It acquired detailed, and alarming, information about the project from an agent named William Weisband, an American citizen born in Egypt to Russian parents. Weisband was working at Arlington Hall as a language consultant and was literally looking over Gardner's shoulder in late 1946 as he deciphered a 1944 message about "Enormous," the KGB's codename for America's atomic bomb program. All contact with Weisband had been cut off as part of the general suspension of its American intelligence operations in the winter of 1945, so the KGB probably didn't learn about the ASA's breakthroughs until February 1948, when it reactivated him.[54]

The FBI's ability to read some of the KGB's most secret communications, and more aggressive surveillance of Soviet diplomats instituted as result, put the men in the Lubyanka on edge. In December 1948 the Center warned the New York station that it had "special concern provoked by the fact that possibly [Julius Rosenberg] is still engaged in conversations with athletes [agents] on the issues of our work at his apartment. We have exact information that the competitors [the FBI] use technical means to listen into apartments of people whom they [then] take into cultivation. Therefore, it is necessary once more to warn [Rosenberg] categorically about the inadmissibility of [continuing] such conversations at his apartment or at some of the athletes' [apartments]."[55]

FBI headquarters reprimanded the New York field office in May 1949 when an audit revealed that it had dropped the ball on the Barr case. Under the heading "delinquency," an official inspection report on the search for the "unknown subject" identified in the Venona decrypts stated that it "appears that the subject is now believed to be identical with JOEL BARR, presently studying in Europe. No report has ever been submitted by this office which should be done immediately, after a thorough review of all files has been made."[56]

The FBI didn't hear anything specific about Barr's whereabouts until July 1949, when the CIA sent a memo stating that Barr was in Sweden and intended to return to the United States "in the near future." The FBI sent another round of notices to customs officers reminding them to alert it immediately if and when Barr reentered the country.[57]

In October the mail cover on Barr's relatives finally paid off. Joel had sent his mother a letter with a return address in a suburb of Paris clearly written on the envelope. The October 27, 1949, memo from the New York field office reporting this bit of news to headquarters ended with the statement: "A report in this case will be submitted" soon. The report from the special agent in charge of the New York field office did not contemplate contacting or attempting to arrest Barr while he was in France. It stated that the FBI and Army had conducted thorough background investigations of Barr, and therefore further investigation "would not be sufficiently productive to warrant the possible jeopardy which might result to this case by any repetition of background investigation." The SAC added: "This case is, accordingly, being placed in a pending inactive status until such time as BARR returns to the United States. Upon BARR's return, this case will be given preferred attention and all investigative techniques will be utilized in monitoring his activities." No effort was made to contact or observe Barr; the CIA wasn't alerted, nor was the American embassy in Paris informed of the Bureau's interest in him.[58]

When Barr walked into the U.S. embassy in Paris on November 10, 1949, no one in the building had ever heard of him. The staff renewed his passport for a year, probably without a second thought, and certainly without asking any of the questions the FBI was curious about. If they had been primed to question him, consular officials could have learned that after traveling to Delft on January 29, 1948, Barr had slowly made his way to Stockholm, first stopping in Paris.[59]

Barr would probably have said he was visiting the City of Light as a curious tourist. He certainly wouldn't have mentioned that Anatoly Yatskov, the KGB officer who had handled Harry Gold and Julius Rosenberg — and probably Barr — and had debriefed David Greenglass about his knowledge of the atomic bomb, was posted to Paris at the time. It is likely that Barr either met directly with Yatskov or communicated with him through a cutout.[60]

Arriving in the Swedish capital on March 27, Barr immediately took off for Helsinki. Before leaving the United States, Barr had told friends about plans to study with the Finnish composer Jean Sibelius, whose work he loved. Sibelius, like Barr's teacher Siegmeister, used classical forms in innovative ways, filling his music with melodies drawn from folk music. Barr stayed in Finland for four months, picking up some money by playing the piano in clubs, but he didn't connect with Sibelius. When he traveled back to Stockholm in late

August, just in time for the school year, Barr was again torn between dreams of becoming a world famous inventor and expressing himself as a composer. He paid minimal attention to his studies and barely avoided being expelled. He did, however, learn to speak Swedish fluently.

At the end of the semester, Barr took off, reaching Paris on July 4, 1949. He plunged into the avant-garde music scene, taking up the viola and gaining acceptance as a student by Olivier Messiaen. At the time, Messiaen was best known for the *Quatuor pour la fin du temps* (Quartet for the End of Time), a piece that was written and first performed in a German prisoner-of-war camp. Messiaen had a strong influence on contemporary music, primarily as a composer, but also as a teacher of theory and composition. At the time Barr began studying composition with him, Messiaen was the center of a vibrant group of young avant-garde musicians who believed they were writing and creating the future of music; several of his students became prominent avant-garde composers. Barr remembered for the rest of his life listening to Messiaen take apart and explain Beethoven's symphonies.[61]

Barr bought a motorcycle and traveled with a viola strapped to his back from the Conservatoire de Music in downtown Paris to rooms he rented in a large house in the suburb of Neuilly-Plaisance. The landlady, Mme. Gazeilles, schemed for the young American boarder to marry her daughter. This was the address on the letter Barr sent his mother in October 1949.

Throughout his travels, Barr periodically received car payments from his brother Art, which he recorded in a brown leather-covered shirt-pocket-sized address book. He also recorded somewhat more mysterious payments, such as one from an individual identified only as "girl" and others from "Jack" and "Vic," which could have been KGB stipends. "The [KGB] paid for [Barr's] studies in Paris just as it had done at Columbia University, in New York," according to Feklisov, who also noted that "naturally, Barr was in contact with an officer at the Paris rezidentura."[62]

The book contains addresses from New York, Delft, Stockholm, Helsinki, Paris, and later travels. It also includes numerous notes for what could only be clandestine meetings, presumably with KGB operatives. The details of meeting logistics mirror those used by Harry Gold and other American KGB agents. There can be little doubt that Barr was supposed to keep these details in his head — Gold said he was strictly forbidden to record similar instructions — but perhaps out of fear of losing his lifeline to the KGB, he jotted down reminders about times, places, and procedures for meetings. For example, one page contains a recognition sequence that is reminiscent of the dialogue that Feklisov instructed Julius Rosenberg to use in March 1946 to identify a new KGB contact: someone would approach Barr and ask if he was waiting for Ida, to which Barr was to reply, "No, for Al." His interlocutor was to then ask if he had change for a dollar, and Barr would respond "twice." This recognition sequence appears just above a note describing meeting places, including what seems to be a reference to the statue of Henry IV at the middle of the Pont Neuf, near Notre-Dame Cathedral.

Barr also scribbled notes about a scheme the KGB used to inform him of upcoming meetings. One note indicates that he would receive some kind of news item with a date — perhaps a newspaper with the date in an article under-lined — and would add three to discover the date for his meeting. A similar note specifies that a message would be connected with an ad, with again a number used as a key. Other notes indicate that something, perhaps meetings or pickups or deliveries of some sort, were scheduled for the "1st & 3rd M @3," which probably meant the first and third Monday at 3:00 P.M.

Barr's notes are quite similar to a procedure Gold described to the FBI. Gold "advised [that Yatskov] had a plan for emergency meetings, which was that he would send GOLD two tickets to some event to be held in New York City, and that the date printed on the tickets would indicate that the meeting was to be held two or three days after that date. GOLD advised that a place and hour for these meets were always set" in advance.[63]

Given the intelligence they were receiving from Washington and New York, the Russians were probably preparing Barr to flee and making sure they could contact him on short notice.

From their chairs in the Lubyanka building, the news for Soviet spymasters from the United States was consistently grim. The elation Lamphere felt as new Venona messages were decrypted and holes in earlier decrypts were filled in was matched by apprehension in Moscow. The KGB knew even better than Lamphere how close he was to reaching pay dirt.

Starting in October 1949 Kim Philby, who had been posted to Washington as MI6's liaison to the American intelligence community, received regular briefings from Lamphere on the FBI's progress in matching codenames in the decrypted messages to the real identities of Soviet spies. The British traitor was treated to a visit to Arlington Hall, where he was introduced to the Venona team. The FBI swore Philby to secrecy, to ensure that their competitors across the Potomac River didn't learn about Venona, so the KGB was briefed about the program a decade before the CIA.[64]

Philby may have passed on progress reports about Venona even before he arrived in Washington. British intelligence had a codebreaker working full-time with Gardner at Arlington Hall from the summer of 1949, whose reports may have been routed to Philby. In any case, during the most critical phase of

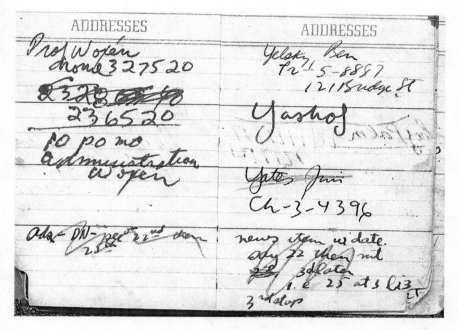

Figure 4. Two pages from Joel Barr's address book with instructions for a covert meeting with a KGB officer. Left page, bottom: "Ads — DN [down]—second 22nd then 25th." Right page, bottom: "news item w[ith] date. Say 22 then m[ee]t 3 d[ays] later, i.e. 25 at 3 liz (?) 3rd stop." (Source: Joel Barr's personal papers; photo by author.)

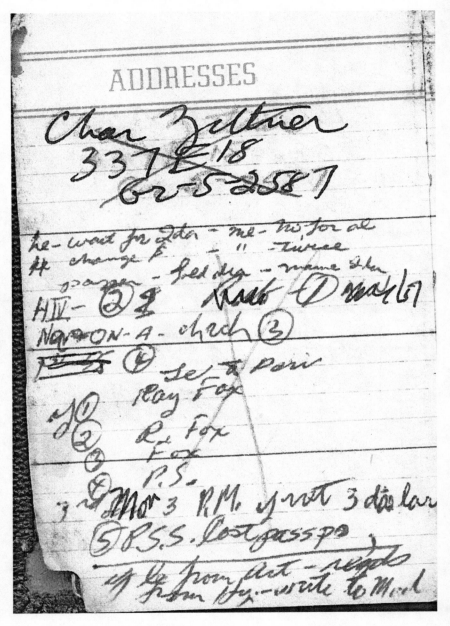

Figure 5. Page from Joel Barr's address book with notes on a recognition dialogue for a covert meeting. "He — wait for Ida — me — no, for al; He — change $ — me twice." Other notes on the same page seem to be notes regarding a meeting: "Mon[day] 3 P.M. if not 3 days [later]." (Source: Joel Barr's personal papers; photo by author.)

the Venona project, when its revelations were fueling active espionage investigations, the Soviet Union was well informed about its status by Philby and Weisband.

For intelligence officers in Moscow, comparing Philby's reports about the FBI's exploitation of Venona with the text of cables the ASA was gradually decrypting was like watching two trains approaching each other on the same track: the impending catastrophe was clear, but there wasn't much they could do to avert it. The Center tried to get some of its agents to move off the tracks, but they either didn't appreciate the danger or were paralyzed, stunned like animals caught in a car's headlights.

Barr was the only member of the Rosenberg group out of harm's way. While the others were terribly vulnerable, none of those warned by the Russians, including Rosenberg, his brother-in-law David Greenglass, and Perl, took bold actions to save themselves, partly because they couldn't imagine voluntarily spending the rest of their lives abroad.

By the early winter of 1949, the Russians were worried enough about their American agents to start making plans for getting Rosenberg, members of his network, and other agents to safer ground. In October the Center sent word to New York to prepare Gold for the possibility that he'd have to leave the United States for Europe, this time for good, and at the same time Rosenberg and Greenglass were instructed to make preparations to travel to Czechoslovakia via Paris. Greenglass was told that a member of Rosenberg's espionage ring would meet him and his wife in Paris. This could have been a reference to Barr, who was in Paris at the time. Both Gold and Greenglass balked; neither could conceive of spending the rest his life away from his family in a country he had long stopped believing was a workers' paradise. Julius Rosenberg also hesitated, probably feeling that he couldn't abandon David, and especially Ruth, who was pregnant and in poor health.[65]

The Russians were worried, but not nearly as worried as they would have been if they'd known that British counterintelligence had started interrogating Fuchs in December. At first the Brits were skeptical about the FBI's assertions that Fuchs was a Soviet agent, but they assigned a first-rate interrogator to gain his trust and worm the truth out of the Communist who had escaped Germany in the early 1930s a few steps ahead of the Gestapo. Ironically, the Nazis helped seal Fuchs's fate. The presence of his name on a captured list of Reds wanted by the Gestapo played a role in the decision by British counterintelligence to investigate him.

Back in the United States, the FBI's counterintelligence investigations picked up speed in the new year. On January 4, 1950, headquarters sent a memo over Hoover's name to New York requesting a list of all June 1938 City College electrical engineering graduates. Three weeks later, the New York office reported an interesting lead in the Barr investigation. "Employment records at Bell Telephone Labs West Street, NYC, reflect Alfred Sarant born September twenty six, nineteen eighteen, NYC, attended Cooper Union from October thirty six to May forty one and received bachelor of electrical engineering degree," the memo stated. It added that he had been employed at Western Electric, the Signal Corps Labs, and then again at Western Electric and Bell Labs. The memo didn't set off alarm bells in Washington, but it should have: the details about Sarant dovetailed perfectly with what the FBI knew about the KGB agent codenamed Liberal and Antenna.[66]

By coincidence, a separate investigation into theft of government property, not espionage, brought the FBI to one of the Rosenberg ring's door three weeks later. On January 27, 1950, an FBI agent telephoned David Greenglass and insisted that he needed to speak with him that afternoon. Having braced himself for the worst, Greenglass was relieved when it appeared that the visit was not connected with Soviet espionage, but was part of an effort to track down uranium hemispheres that soldiers had stolen from Los Alamos. Greenglass lied, denying that he had taken any samples of uranium as souvenirs home from New Mexico. In fact he had helped himself to two chunks of the radioactive material. The KGB had sent one to Moscow in a diplomatic pouch, and as the G-men were interviewing Greenglass, the second golf-ball-sized piece of uranium was slowly decaying in a closet a few yards away.[67]

Greenglass and Rosenberg had just about convinced themselves that the FBI visit was a fluke when Julius received more troubling news. Fuchs had been arrested in England on February 2, and he had cracked, confessing to espionage on behalf of the Soviet Union. Neither Rosenberg nor the KGB knew it at the time, but the Venona decryptions had helped identify the physicist as a Soviet spy. Rosenberg and the KGB did know, however, that although Rosenberg had never met Fuchs, the two men were connected. The link was Harry Gold.

The sound of insistent pounding rousted Greenglass out of bed on February 4. It was Julius at the front door, demanding that his brother-in-law accompany him for a walk. Once they were out on the street, away from the listening devices he feared the FBI might have installed in the apartment, Rosenberg explained that the courier who had brought the Jell-O box in June 1944 had also been Fuchs's courier. Rosenberg said that the Russians were convinced that the FBI would put the pieces together, arrest Gold, and come after Greenglass. "Now, you will have to leave," Julius insisted. Time was of the essence: the FBI would nab Greenglass by early summer if he didn't flee first, Rosenberg predicted. David and Ruth must immediately get passports; they would sail to France and travel from there to Czechoslovakia. David protested that if he was under suspicion, the State Department wouldn't give him a passport.

"Oh, they let other people out who are more important than you are . . . they let Barr out, Joel Barr, and he was a member of our espionage ring," Julius replied.[68]

Stalin learned of Fuchs's arrest the day after Rosenberg warned Greenglass. Like Rosenberg, the KGB focused on Gold, but it had reached a slightly different conclusion. The Soviet leader was informed, incorrectly, that Fuchs had probably been betrayed by Gold. Rather optimistically, the KGB also told the Great Helmsman that it was taking steps to exfiltrate four other agents from the United States, who clearly included Rosenberg and Greenglass.[69]

Two days later, on February 7, FBI headquarters sent an urgent teletype to the Bureau's Albuquerque office requesting that it "immediately check records for Los Alamos, for individual employed in 44 and 45 by name of Shmel." There was no Shmel—Shmel, "bumblebee" in Russian, was the KGB's cover name for Greenglass used in cables the ASA had decrypted, while Ruth was Osa, or "wasp"—but the FBI was getting close.[70]

Moscow pushed hard to get the Greenglasses and Rosenbergs to flee but was continually frustrated. On February 14, Ruth Greenglass, who was pregnant, stepped too close to a gas heater, her bathrobe ignited, and she was rushed to the hospital in critical condition. When David's appeal for donations of her rare blood type was broadcast on the radio, the KGB worried that somehow the publicity could put the FBI on his trail.

In April, about the time Ruth returned home from the hospital eight months pregnant, the Center sent a cable to New York insisting again that the Greenglasses get out of the country. The cable was remarkably prescient: "In the case of [the Greenglasses] the competitors [FBI] have not only a clear and (for them) unquestionable association with our work but the fact of [their] having passed to us secret materials on the atomic bomb. On these grounds, the competitors will exert strong pressure on [the Greenglasses], threatening and using other measures right up to their arrest, and in the end will force them to testify with all the consequences proceeding from this for [Julius Rosenberg], his group, and all of our work in the country."[71]

David Greenglass was the subject of another urgent electronic communication in April. On the eighteenth, the FBI's Albuquerque office sent a teletype to headquarters listing six individuals who matched some criteria attributed to Shmel, which it realized by then was a cover name. One of them was David Greenglass. While the FBI worked through the list of possible bumblebees, it didn't forget completely about Barr. An agent went around to his mother's apartment building on April 24 to speak with the elevator man, who reported that Joel was still in France "studying to be a doctor."[72]

On May 12 the agent in charge of the New York field office sent a memo to

Hoover stating that his report about the Barr investigation "will be delayed inasmuch as the agent to whom this case is assigned has been for the past few weeks engaged in the interview of HARRY GOLD in Philadelphia." Clues from Venona had revived the FBI's interest in Gold, who had previously come to the Bureau's attention in connection with an aborted investigation of Soviet industrial espionage.[73]

Ruth brought her new baby home from the hospital on May 23, but when Julius Rosenberg showed up on the Greenglasses' doorstep the next day, it wasn't to congratulate the mother or to kiss the baby. He came with a copy of the *New York Herald Tribune* and pointed excitedly to a headline on the front page: "U.S. Arrests Go-Between for Soviets in Fuchs Case." There was also a picture of the KGB courier. He'd lost some weight, but there could be no mistake: it was the man whom Ruth and David had met in Albuquerque in 1944, Harry Gold.[74]

Suddenly all the cracks in the KGB's American espionage edifice merged into a deadly fissure, exactly as the Soviets had feared. Fuchs told Lamphere, who traveled to England to visit him in the Wormwood Scrubs maximum-security prison, about a courier named Raymond, a Jewish chemical engineer who lived in Philadelphia. On the basis of clues provided by Venona decryptions and hunches of experienced investigators, the FBI had already visited Brothman's offices, where a detail in a secretary's description of Harry Gold clicked in an agent's mind. He remembered that Fuchs's landlady had made a similar remark about a man who had once stopped by looking for Fuchs.[75]

The FBI's next stop was Gold's apartment and a series of interrogations and a search. Gold was defiant until an agent found a map with the words "Land of Enchantment" printed on the cover in his bookshelf. The chemist, who had told the FBI that he'd never been west of the Mississippi River, was unable to explain the street map of Santa Fe or the red circle around Alameda Street, where Fuchs lived. He collapsed, confessing: "I am the man to whom Klaus Fuchs gave information about atomic energy."[76]

The KGB's reaction to Gold's arrest was frantic. The Greenglasses must escape at once; if they remained their arrest was "inevitable," a May 24 cable from Moscow to the New York *rezident* declared. Rosenberg's escape was also imperative. The New York office was to give Julius $10,000 for expenses and instruct him to get photos of his family and the Greenglasses that could be used to create false passports. The plan for a leisurely cruise to Europe was jettisoned, replaced by a scheme involving a dash to Mexico. Julius and David were to leave with whichever family members were ready to go, to leave their wives and children behind if necessary, and perhaps to go underground in the United States for a time if they couldn't get across the border safely. "If I get word that it is too hot, we'll just have to take off and leave the children and the women behind," Rosenberg told Greenglass, who was stunned by the thought.[77]

Whatever they were going to do, it had to be done quickly. Rosenberg told Greenglass they had to leave by June 11 or 12 at the very latest to avoid arrest.

The Center fired off cables to the Mexico City KGB office instructing it to prepare a place to hide two families with children, and to Stockholm requesting information on ships between Mexico and Sweden.

Greenglass played along with Rosenberg's demands, never intending to leave but hoping to squeeze some money out of his brother-in-law. The little scam worked: Julius delivered $4,000 to David on Friday, June 2, more than a year's salary and certainly more money than he'd ever had at one time.

That same afternoon, Barr ran into Bill Perl's brother, Sam, on a Paris street in front of the Students Cité Club, at the corner of Boulevard Malesherbes and Boulevard Courcelles. Barr said that he was leaving Paris soon. When Perl asked where he was going, Barr said, "It would be better if you don't know." He added: "Don't worry, I just won't be around."[78]

On Monday, June 5, Greenglass arrived at his job in Brooklyn early to request a six-week leave of absence to take care of Ruth. By this time, Gold had been spilling his guts for over a week. Psychologically fragile, he was as eager to please his new masters as he'd been to work for the KGB. To his dismay, Gold simply couldn't remember the names of the couple he'd met in Albuquerque six years before. After a few days, Gold dredged up sufficient information from his memory to put the FBI on the track of the Greenglasses.

As Gold had predicted to Yatskov years before, it had been a terrible mistake to send him to meet with David Greenglass. If Gold's atomic espionage contact had been limited to Fuchs, it is possible that the Rosenbergs would have had time to escape before the FBI found them, or that in the absence of Gold's identification, Greenglass might not have cooperated with the Bureau.[79]

Because of the KGB's mistake, as David Greenglass left for his job in Brooklyn on the morning of June 5, the FBI knew exactly who Shmel was and where he lived. When he returned home, agents were watching from a van parked across the street from the front door. David spotted the watchers almost right away and took Ruth up to the roof to get her opinion about the suspicious van. It had "Acme Construction Company" and an address and telephone number written on the side. Ruth consulted the investigator's best friend, the telephone directory. There was no listing in New York for Acme Construction.

Two days later, Julius spotted the same van in front of the Greenglasses' building, and in the evening he saw a carload of men parked behind it, and also noticed that there were four men positioned on nearby street corners. Rosenberg consulted with a KGB operative on June 9 who said that he shouldn't visit Greenglass again, that Ethel should transmit any necessary messages to her brother.

On June 10 David Greenglass took a bus to Phoenicia, New York, a small town in the Catskills, with the pathetic idea of finding a hideout in the hills where his family could ride out the storm, as if the FBI could be ducked like a debt collector. Getting off, he saw that a car with two men who were obviously plainclothes police of some sort had followed the bus. Dejected, Greenglass gave up and took the next bus back to Manhattan's 50th Street bus station. A couple of days later Ruth was hospitalized again because the burn wounds on her legs had become badly infected. Taking care of two young children took David's mind off his troubles, and when he noticed that the June 11 deadline had passed with no knock on the door from the FBI, he began to cheer up. Maybe Julius had been wrong; maybe he'd exaggerated the threat.[80]

Julius had miscalculated, but not by much. The FBI didn't knock on Greenglass's door on June 12, or the next day, or the day after. At 1:46 P.M. on June 15, David was mixing baby formula when he heard the firm, insistent rapping that signals the arrival of law enforcement. The agents didn't have warrants to search the apartment or to arrest Greenglass, but he let them in, answered questions, signed a waiver allowing them to search the place, and agreed to go to downtown to answer more questions. At that time the FBI lacked sufficient information to charge Greenglass or any of his relatives with a crime, especially because much of its evidence was derived from secret documents that the government would not make public and that would not have held up in court. If Greenglass had kept his promise to Rosenberg to remain silent, it is very likely that neither he nor his relatives ever would have been indicted or convicted.

Greenglass, who had promised Julius Rosenberg that he would never crack, confessed to atomic espionage at 9:25 P.M. on June 15. Before bedding down for the night under the watchful eyes of federal agents, he volunteered the information that his brother-in-law was the ringleader of a spy network.

6

Prague, 1950–1955

Reports in the evening papers on June 16, 1950, of the arrest of David Greenglass resounded around the world like the crack of a starting pistol, launching former members of Industrial Branch 16B of the Communist Party of the United States and their closest comrades on a race for their lives. The swiftest beat the FBI, crossing into the Soviet bloc ahead of their pursuers, while those with luck and good nerves managed to hide on the sidelines and live relatively unmolested. The fates of those who refused to flee or were caught — death for the Rosenbergs and years in prison for Morton Sobell and Bill Perl — proved that the race was for the most serious stakes.

Joel Barr was the first out of the starting blocks. On the morning of Saturday, June 17, a few hours after American newspapers reported that yet another Red spy had been nabbed, Barr told Mme. Gazeilles to expect him as usual for dinner and calmly walked out of the Villa Regine in Neuilly-Plaisance with a viola slung over his shoulder and a briefcase in his hand. Barr left behind forever Messiaen and his own dreams of becoming a composer. He was stepping into a new life carrying only a few slender traces of his identity: a passport and an address book with a picture of his sister Iris tucked into it.

Barr had been preparing a clean break with his past for two years, never once writing to old friends like Vivian Glassman, Al Sarant, or Julius Rosenberg, and contacting relatives infrequently. He did stay in touch with KGB operatives, and it is likely that Barr's uncharacteristic silence stemmed from the advice of men who had known for years that the Americans were closing in on the KGB's wartime espionage operations. The Russians' warnings would have started to look very realistic to Barr in February 1950, when Fuchs was arrested in London, and even more compelling in May, when Gold was arrested in Philadelphia. The news that the FBI had its hands on Greenglass was particularly alarming to Barr because, unlike Fuchs and Gold, he knew David personally—and didn't trust him. Barr recalled decades later that his first thought was that Greenglass would "spill his guts, do anything to save his skin," even if it meant lying or ratting on his friends and family.[1]

As far as could be determined by FBI and CIA investigators who were to spend decades trying to track him, Barr vanished the moment he stepped out of the Villa Regine. In fact, following a contingency plan conceived by the KGB weeks or months earlier, Barr went to the Gare de l'Est station in central Paris, where he purchased a newspaper and a train ticket.

A front-page *Herald Tribune* article confirmed and amplified Barr's initial fears. "More Arrested by FBI on Charges They Divulged Secrets to Soviet Union," the banner headline screamed. The story explained that Greenglass— whom Barr knew as Ethel Rosenberg's pudgy, somewhat dimwitted kid brother—was being accused of spying while he worked as a machinist for the Manhattan Project at Los Alamos, New Mexico.[2]

"The FBI said that Greenglass's explanation [for his espionage] was that Russia was an ally entitled to the information," the Associated Press dispatch reported. In words that Barr echoed decades later to justify his own actions, Edward Scheidt, the agent in charge of the FBI's New York office, quoted Greenglass as saying: "I felt it was gross negligence on the part of the United States not to give Russia the information about the atom bomb because she was an ally." Another line in the story prompted Barr to look over his shoulder to doublecheck for signs that someone was following him: because their espionage activities had occurred during a time of war, Greenglass and other recently arrested spies faced the death penalty.

He had the advantage of a month's head start before the FBI began hunting for him in earnest, but Barr's trail was cold within hours. The first step in the disappearing act was a train from Paris to Zurich, where Soviet agents instructed the American to lie low while they watched for any signs of pursuit. He spent a few nerve-wracking days waiting, reading newspaper articles about the unfolding atomic espionage investigations, worrying about his friends in New York, and trying to imagine what life would be like in the socialist world he'd been dreaming and fantasizing about for years. The thirty-four-year-old amateur spy was afraid, but not terrified: meetings with Feklisov back in New

York, when he was sure that every suit in the cafeteria was a G-man, had been far scarier, and any trepidation about being caught was tempered by excitement and tremendous curiosity about life under socialism. He would finally get to meet men and women who, like himself, had devoted their lives to building a new, just, Communist society![3]

Barr had a hyperactive imagination, which, coupled with a sharp mind, allowed him to conceive a goal and devise a method for attaining it quickly. Whether the aim was playing the piano, speaking a foreign language, or solving an engineering problem, the results may have been a bit rough, but generally they were impressive. Although he had mastered the art of compartmentalizing, leading separate, parallel lives — for example, working as an engineer on American military projects without revealing a hint of his simultaneous life as a Soviet agent — he wasn't fully in control of his imagination. Sometimes, especially under stress, streams of thought that he could usually keep in separate channels collided, and his mind conjured vivid images of detection, arrest, and persecution. As the train pulled out of Zurich and passed through Austria, the tension and fear returned; he imagined that police would be waiting for him at the border to block his exit from the capitalist world.

After he had successfully cleared passport control and entered Czechoslovakia, anxieties that had built up over years of secret service to Communism gradually fell away, along with Barr's grip on his emotions. When the train pulled into Hlavni Nadrazi station in downtown Prague on June 22, he was crying, and he cried and laughed as he exchanged bear hugs with the serious young men who met him on the platform. The Russian KGB officers greeted Barr like a relative returning from an extended absence. They took him to the Regina, a mid-level hotel near the center of Prague, two tram stops from the main railroad station.

The Russians warned Barr that contacting family or friends in the United States would endanger both his safety and theirs. Barr realized from the start that there was no turning back, but — unlike most other American and British agents who escaped to the east side of the Iron Curtain, leaving family, friends, and a familiar culture behind — he looked forward with enthusiasm to living the rest of his life under Communism. From the first day he was bubbling with enthusiasm, peppering his bemused minders with questions about life in a workers' paradise and offering nonstop ideas for improving it through technology and American-style marketing.

The Russians quickly set to work crafting and documenting a new identity for their protégé. First they asked him to come up with an easily remembered birthday. He picked October 7, 1917, the day his younger brother Arthur had been born; the date also resonated because of its association with the October

1917 Bolshevik revolution. Next they briefed him on his new biography, warning that spies for the United States were ubiquitous, so it wouldn't be safe to reveal his true identity to anyone, regardless of the person's seniority in the party or how trustworthy he seemed. Although it was behind the Iron Curtain and dominated by the Soviet Union, for the KGB Czechoslovakia was a foreign country.

The KGB continued to run Barr as an agent while he was in Prague, communicating with him covertly. Notes in Barr's address book from his early days there document classic tradecraft. To arrange a meeting, he was to telephone someone who spoke only Czech and Russian and to say in German, "Mein Name Joe." This indicated that the meeting would be the next day at number 6 "Staro," short for Staromestske namesti, Old Town Square, in the medieval city center; number 6 was the District National Committee office, a local government administrative office. If either he or his contact missed the meeting, they would try again at the same time on the next day. Barr also noted the signal the KGB would use to initiate a meeting: "When paper under door next day Staro 6." A bit lower on the page he wrote: "New — if no meeting — one week later Staro 6." One note refers to a meeting at 19 Staromestske, which at that time was a restaurant. Another mentions a meeting slated for three days after the receipt of a "letter from H" at 7:00 P.M. at the Old Clock, today a famous tourist attraction in the Old Town, but in the 1950s a neglected and nearly deserted neighborhood.[4]

Barr rehearsed his legend over and over, keeping in his pocket a scrap of paper with vital details and studying it in spare moments. For the next five decades, Barr asserted that he was the son of Jews from the Bohemia region of the Austro-Hungarian empire who had emigrated in 1908 to Johannesburg, South Africa, where they acquired British citizenship. He was supposed to have graduated from the University of the Witwatersrand (Johannesburg) in 1939 with a bachelor of science degree in electronics. According to his legend,

---

Figure 6. Notebook page stuck into Joel Barr's address book with description of the KGB's procedures for arranging covert meetings in Prague. The notes appear to indicate that he is to telephone someone who speaks Czech and Russian after 9:00 and say, "Mein Name Joe." The day after the call, he could meet someone at "6 Staro," a reference to 6 Staromestske in the Old Town Square, the location of a local government office. If he or the other person missed the meeting, he was to report to the same location on the next day. If the KGB wanted to summon Barr to a meeting, someone would place a newspaper under his door. Later Barr noted a new instruction: if the meeting didn't come off as planned, he was to go one week later to 6 Staromestske. The notes on the bottom of the page refer to his cover story, including a reminder that he was supposed to say that he received a Czech visa in Brussels. (Source: Joel Barr's personal papers; photo by author.)

~~Dividustatdatan datan~~
75-81 2 (4-5)

Other pad by Capt Kal

1. Language - Czech & Russ
73 5-94 2
~~Dipiguid~~ Mein Name
give call after 9

every @ 6 Staro next
day after call

When miss - next day
Staro 6
When paper under door
next day Staro 6
from 1 ty
—————————————
new —
if no meet - one
week later Staro 6
—————————————
Journey - Johann - Lozolive
Kano - Puzzle - Rawedo
Sabena - syl Czech
russ or Russ
~~u—~~

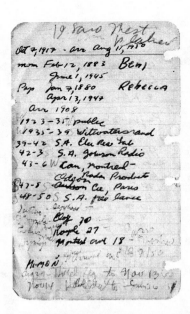

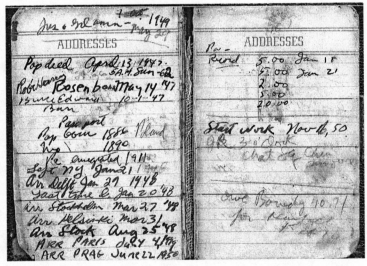

Figure 7. (top) Notebook page stuck into Joel Barr's address book outlining his legend, or cover story. It specifies that in his new identity as Joseph Berg, he was to report that his birthday was October 7, 1917, and that he had arrived in Prague on August 11, 1950; putative dates for the birth and death of his parents, Benjamin and Rebecca; the date his parents allegedly arrived in South Africa; and the dates of Berg's education and work. A Czechoslovakian secret police report notes that when Berg was questioned about his past, he pulled a scrap of paper exactly like this one out of his pocket and read off dates and places. (bottom) Joel Barr's notes on his father's actual time of death; the birth of Julius and Ethel Rosenberg's son Robert; his parents' real birthdays; and his actual itinerary. (Source: Joel Barr's personal papers; photos by author.)

Barr had lived in British-ruled South Africa until 1943, when he left for Canada, where he lived until 1946. Then he had moved to France for a year and, unable to find work, returned to South Africa for a year. The details of this new identity would be difficult to verify, especially for anyone Barr might encounter in the Soviet bloc, where placing even a domestic long-distance telephone call was a time-consuming process requiring advance booking, and it was virtually impossible to communicate with a registrar's office in South Africa.

Perhaps because it was so implausible, Barr rarely told anyone the next part of his life story, but he wrote it on job applications that have been preserved in the Czech archives. He was instructed to say that he traveled to Czechoslovakia in 1950, two years after the Communist coup—at a time when the economy was imploding and the Western news media were reporting on the penetration of totalitarian repression into Czech society—"to find the place where his ancestors were buried and to look for work."[5]

Soon after arriving in Prague, Barr gave the Russians his American passport, driver's license, and all other documentation of his previous life, and received in their place a South African birth certificate, British passport, and other documents that appeared authentic enough to withstand scrutiny by Czechoslovakian police and intelligence services. Improbably, the KGB demonstrated a sense of humor in its choice of a new name: for the rest of his life, Joel Barr was known as Joseph Berg, or Joe Berg, from Jo'burg.

In addition to its comical aspect, the name suggested—and Joe's features verified—his Jewish heritage. Despite the focus on "class struggle," a few years of Communism had not erased centuries of prejudice in Central Europe. The facts that he felt no allegiance to Jewish culture and abhorred religion as superstitious mumbo jumbo were irrelevant. Czechs and Russians immediately identified Berg as a Jew, and this perception, conscious or not, shaped the way people treated him.

The passport bore stamps indicating that Berg had obtained a three-month tourist visa from the Czechoslovakian consulate in Brussels, a city he had never visited, during the second week of June 1950 and had traveled from there to Prague. There was nothing linking Berg's travel to Prague with Barr's disappearance from Paris.

While Soviet intelligence agents were quite capable of constructing an airtight set of documents to support a plausible legend, there were a few rough edges around Joe Berg's story that even Felix Dzerzinsky, the founder of the Soviet Union's first intelligence service, couldn't have smoothed. For example, no matter how convincingly he described his childhood in South Africa, he did so with what anyone who had lived in the United States or watched American movies would instantly recognize as a classic Brooklyn accent. Barr learned to speak Swedish, Czech, and Russian fluently just as he learned the piano, by ear, rejecting all formal training or repetitive exercises, and in each language he sounded like a grown-up Bugs Bunny. He was sometimes asked how he'd acquired distinctively American inflection and expressions — not many Englishmen said they were "in like Flynn" — while growing up in South Africa. Berg would look the questioner straight in the eye, say with a smile that he came from a neighborhood with a lot of New Yorkers, tell a joke, and quickly change the subject. When foreigners inquired about his ability to speak English like a native, Berg sometimes replied: "We have excellent schools here."

While Berg was settling into his new identity, some of his comrades in New York were struggling to shed their old lives.

Just as the members of Julius Rosenberg's espionage apparatus and their Soviet handlers had feared, David Greenglass quickly struck a bargain with the FBI. To save his wife Ruth and, he thought, buy himself a light sentence, Greenglass was more than willing to implicate others, including his own sister and brother-in-law. David's strategy hinged on his ability to convince the FBI that he had valuable information and could be a credible witness in court. Ironically, although his testimony was directly responsible for his sister's execution, the U.S. government didn't think it greatly mitigated the gravity of his crimes. Prosecutors recommended, and a federal judge imposed, a sentence of fifteen years.

On July 17, 1950, in an effort to substantiate his assertions that Julius Rosenberg was the head of an espionage ring, Greenglass recalled a conversation in which his brother-in-law urged him to flee with Ruth and their children to Mexico, where the Russians would arrange their safe transport to Czechoslovakia. Greenglass said that when he expressed incredulity that anyone under FBI investigation could get out of the United States, Julius replied: "Oh, they let other people out who are more important than you are . . . they let Barr out, Joel Barr, and he was a member of our espionage ring."[6]

Greenglass's statement lit a fire under the FBI's dormant investigation of Barr, prompting it to attempt to determine whether the U.S. government could lay its hands on him. Within days of David's arrest, the Bureau updated its security index card for Barr, adding his Paris address. Under "method of verification," the updated card cited "Joseph Gruber, Supt, 241 West 97th St, NYC."[7]

On July 25, a week after Julius Rosenberg was taken into custody, Hoover sent an urgent request to the U.S. legal attaché in Paris requesting that he track down Barr. The attaché visited Villa Regine and quickly learned he was a month too late. Mme. Gazeilles and her lonely daughter had no idea where their boarder had gone. Most of his clothing and his beloved motorcycle were still at the house. A thorough search of his belongings yielded no clues about the dual life Barr had led during World War II or any hints about his future plans. The timing and suddenness of Barr's disappearance added to the FBI's suspicions that he had been a major actor in the Rosenberg ring.

Since Barr had not been formally charged with a crime, if the attaché had found Barr at home, he could have done little more than ask him to voluntarily answer a few questions, and could have done nothing to stop Barr from leaving Paris. At the FBI's request, the Justice Department quickly drafted paperwork that would support a demand that a foreign government arrest and extradite Barr. The criminal complaint form, dated July 27, two days after the visit to Villa Regine, was succinct: "Character of case: Espionage — R [Russian]. Facts of Complaint: Investigation reflects subject engaged in espionage activity."

The same day, FBI Special Agent Richard B. Hood sent a confidential memorandum to customs offices at all ports of entry into the United States alerting them to look out for Barr and requesting his delay "insofar as possible without arrest in order that he may be placed under physical surveillance by Special Agents of the Federal Bureau of investigation." Barr was described as:

Sex: male
Color: white
Age: 34 years
Born: January 1, 1916, Brooklyn, New York
Height: 5′11″ to 6′
Weight: 150 pounds
Eyes: brown, nearsighted, may wear glasses
Hair: brown
Complexion: light
Occupation: Engineering Student
Marital Status: Unknown
Home Address: 241 West 97th Street, New York City

The confidential lookout request concluded: "Under no circumstances should he be made aware of the Federal Bureau of Investigation's interest in him."[8]

Lamphere coordinated an international manhunt for Barr, calling on legal attachés and CIA contacts abroad, while continuing to monitor friends and relatives in the United States. Throughout the summer and into the fall, the Bureau chased false leads in Sweden, Brazil, Mexico, and Wales, but it never came close to finding Barr. His mother, Rebecca, told the FBI she hadn't heard from Joel in a year, and "as she cannot write, she has never written him and is able to read very little."[9]

Despite Feklisov's view that Barr "didn't have the makings of a good spy, lacking courage at critical moments and having trouble controlling himself," he was the only member of Rosenberg's group to make a disciplined escape. In fact Barr, a volunteer with little training in tradecraft, is one of the few Americans ever to slip away from the FBI while under KGB control.[10]

Lona Cohen, the agent tapped to carry messages between Julius Rosenberg and his KGB handlers after he was fired from the Signal Corps, escaped along with her husband, Morris. The Cohens were fulltime KGB agents, but unlike Barr, they were not under investigation or suspicion by any American law enforcement or counterintelligence agencies. A few years later the couple resurfaced in London under a new identity, resumed their espionage activities, and eventually were caught, imprisoned, and freed in a prisoner exchange.

The fate of Rosenberg's other recruits highlighted the perils for the KGB of relying on amateur spies. Though willing to take risks unacceptable to less dedicated agents, the Communist engineers had far too little discipline and too many personal entanglements to avoid detection or to melt into the shadows when their covers were blown. Family ties kept the Rosenbergs from acting on the KGB's offer to arrange an escape; Bill Perl refused to accept money and escape instructions from Vivian Glassman; Greenglass took Julius Rosenberg's money but didn't seriously consider complying with his plea to flee; and Morton Sobell botched a half-baked flight attempt. Barr was different: when he smelled danger years earlier, he severed ties with family and friends and left the United States.

The Bureau's files on Barr are packed with information detailing his education from Public School 156 through Columbia University, work history, and Communist Party membership; with reports on interviews of family, friends, and lovers; and with glimpses of his activities in Scandinavia and France. But the rich stew of biographical detail abruptly turns to water in June 1950. Month after month FBI clerks stuffed the files with requests for the post office to maintain "covers" on all mail received by Barr's relatives, renewals of the customs look-out requests, and reports from agents sent every year to interview his brothers, Arthur and Bernard Barr. Joel's sister Iris's husband approached the FBI voluntarily to offer to spy on the family and report any news about him, but he never learned anything. Within a few months of his vanishing, the family acted as if Joel were dead, but the FBI didn't, and the complete failure to pierce the mystery surrounding Barr's disappearance fueled Hoover's and Lamphere's interest.[11]

In many cases the Soviets made little or no effort to hide agents once they were safely in Moscow, often trumpeting their accomplishments to the Western media and allowing them to meet with relatives and former colleagues.

The novelist Graham Greene, a former British intelligence agent, corresponded with Philby, who had done so much to alert the Soviets that the FBI was closing in on Rosenberg and company, and was allowed to visit him in Moscow. The KGB permitted Philby to publish his memoirs, which were published in the United Kingdom with a foreword by Greene.[12]

Even the activities of scientific defectors were widely known in the West. Three months after Barr disappeared, Bruno Pontecorvo, a nuclear scientist who had worked with Klaus Fuchs at the Harwell Atomic Research Center in England, took a vacation with his family and never returned. In 1955 Pontecorvo held a press conference in Moscow and in later years the Soviets made no effort to hide the fact that he was working in Dubna, the Soviet counterpart of the Lawrence Livermore nuclear weapons design laboratory.[13]

The Soviet government never uttered a word about Barr. The complete lack of information about the defector fed the FBI's suspicions that he was working undercover in Europe or the United States. For decades Hoover rejected requests from field agents, tired of filling out forms about a case that was clearly going nowhere, for permission to RUC (a frequently used FBI abbreviation for "Referred upon completion to office of origin") the case. As late as 1972, the FBI renewed requests for the post office to maintain mail covers on Bernard and Arthur Barr, whom it still interviewed annually. The Bureau finally quit looking for Joel Barr in 1977, more than a quarter of a century after he had left Paris.[14]

When Berg was comfortable with his new identity and had learned enough Czech to communicate, Russian intelligence officials introduced him to their counterparts at the Statni Bezpecnost, the Czech secret police, universally referred to as the StB. In those days, the StB, part of the Ministry of Interior, was firmly under the control of Russians seconded from the KGB as "liaison" officers. The StB was not informed of Berg's real name or of his association with the Rosenbergs, and even the most senior officials of the Czechoslovakian Communist Party were kept in the dark. Though not revealing why, the KGB made it clear to the Czechs that their new guest was valued and trusted and should be treated accordingly.

When Berg's three-month visa expired in mid-August, he needed new documents to function and to avoid arrest if he was stopped in the street by police checking documents—a real hazard, particularly for someone who was clearly a foreigner. On August 25, 1950, a senior Czechoslovakian Interior Ministry official telephoned a subordinate and ordered him to prepare an identity card for Berg. Berg's photo was sent by messenger, and the card, conferring residency status, was returned the same day. The informal request and the quick response underscore Berg's importance to the StB.

Berg was eager to get to work helping build socialism. It isn't clear why Berg's pleas to move on to the Soviet Union were denied, but it was common for the Soviets to settle defectors in Prague. Perhaps they thought Westerners would be more at home in Czechoslovakia, which was more economically advanced and closer culturally to Europe and the United States than was Russia.

Berg began work on November 1, 1950, in central Prague as an engineer at Tesla, a state-owned electronics and telecommunications conglomerate. As part of the Communist nationalization of industry, Tesla had taken over the assets of foreign companies, including Philips and Siemens, which had manufactured radios, vacuum tubes, and other electronic components in Czechoslovakia before and during the war. The work wasn't interesting, but Tesla provided a safe environment for Berg to integrate into Czech life and for the authorities to evaluate the foreigner who expressed such enthusiasm for Communism. Berg attended the frequent compulsory political meetings at Tesla, which, like those held in all Czechoslovakian enterprises, served to disseminate the latest government and party news, and he focused on improving his command of the language. He kept his past carefully hidden. In some ways it was like his days at Western Electric: leading a dual existence, hiding a secret life from co-workers and reporting in secret to Russian intelligence officers.

Berg moved into the Hotel Ostas, which catered to budget travelers (as it does today), and explored Prague on a moped he'd cobbled together from an old bicycle, an electric motor, and a battery. Unlike the millions of tourists who are drawn today to Prague's medieval and baroque splendor, he had no reverence for the city. Like many Marxists, Joe was almost completely fixated on the future; the past was primarily of interest as a reservoir of negative examples of injustice or irrationality that could be contrasted with Communist ideals. Central Prague was simply a pile of old, crumbling buildings with bad plumbing and churches that were nothing more than reminders of a superstitious past. The only structures in the city that held special meaning for Berg were the Hapsburg-era opera house and theaters, where even under the Communist regime he could hear classical masterpieces.

Berg was struck by the lack of commercial activity in Prague, in sharp contrast to New York, as well as to Paris and other European cities. The Communist government had closed most stores and restaurants, converting them into offices or warehouses, and the few that remained were grim and largely barren. This wasn't anything like the material and cultural prosperity the denizens of CCNY's Kremlin had imagined under Communism. Berg justified the situation by noting that Czechoslovakia had abandoned capitalism only two years previously and was still recovering from the war.

Any lingering ideas Berg may have had about returning to America were extinguished in August by the news that Morton Sobell had been kidnapped in Mexico and turned over to the FBI. Sobell was indicted along with the Rosenbergs on January 31, 1951. Czech newspapers reported their conviction in March 1951, followed by the Rosenbergs' death sentence in April. Berg had little doubt that he would have suffered the same fate if the FBI had been able to get its hands on him, and he worried a great deal about comrades who had shared his secret life, especially his closest friend and collaborator, Al Sarant.[15]

By the summer of 1951, the novelty of living in a socialist country was starting to fade, and the realities of life in Prague were looking a bit less attractive to Berg. The work at Tesla was monotonous, and it was difficult even for an inveterate optimist to imagine a heroic future that in any way approached his ambitions. While his work at Western Electric and for the Signal Corps hadn't always been stimulating, it had been fulfilling to know that he was helping the American and, more important, the Soviet war effort.

The routine was broken suddenly on June 15 by an unexpected visit to Tesla from an StB agent. Berg was informed that his employment at Tesla was over and that he was to go home immediately to wait for further instructions. Berg had learned that it was better not to ask many questions, so he hurried to his room at the Ostas, where a Russian delivered a three-month Soviet visa and a one-way air ticket to Moscow for the next day. The Russian, a stranger to Berg, provided no details about the purpose or duration of the trip beyond stating that he would be working with a Russian engineer on a "special task."[16]

Just as he'd left Paris, Berg departed Prague with a single bag — a habit he retained for the rest of his life — and without telling anyone where he was going. The KGB man who met Berg at the airport didn't speak much English, or pretended not to, and as they drove silently in a black ZIM limousine, Berg pressed his eyes close to the window, excited at his first glimpses of the capital of world Communism. They traveled first on two-lane roads through open fields and dilapidated villages with traditional Russian wooden houses and *zhuravl,* old-fashioned wells with buckets tied to cantilevered wooden beams, and then into the bustling streets of central Moscow.[17]

The limo pulled up at the Moskva Hotel, just outside Red Square and within sight of the Kremlin walls, behind which, Berg imagined, Comrade Stalin was hard at work right that minute. Even in the rain, the golden troika sparkled atop the Bolshoi Theater across the busy Prospect Marxa where dancers were rehearsing a performance of Tchaikovsky's *Eugene Onegin*. Berg was unaware that only blocks away, in the basement of a once-grand building on Lubyanka Square that had housed an insurance company before the revolution, a darker performance was under way: round-the-clock torture and execution of Stalin's innocent victims. A few flights above, KGB officers were debating the best way to make use of the American engineer.

Berg was instructed to hand over his Czechoslovakian identity document at the front desk and was given a room key. He may have shared an elevator during this visit or on subsequent sojourns at the Moskva with Guy Burgess, who, along with Philby, Donald MacLean, and Anthony Blunt, was a member of the Cambridge spy ring that penetrated the top echelons of British government and society. Burgess, like Berg and many other Soviet operatives, had taken a path to Moscow that ran through Prague, where he and MacLean paused briefly after fleeing London and before arriving at the Moskva Hotel in June 1951. Burgess never moved out, living in the hotel until he drank himself to death in 1963. If Barr and Burgess met, they would have introduced themselves as Joe Berg and Jim Elliott, their KGB-supplied aliases, and Joe at least would probably not have had a clue that the other man was a spy.

Since its completion in 1938, the Moskva, located a short walk from Red Square as well from as the most elegant theaters and stores in the Soviet Union, had been home to top party officials and foreign journalists and dignitaries visiting the capital. Care was taken to ensure that its guests benefited from all the luxuries available in a city that was still recovering from the ravages of war. An even greater level of attention was lavished on unseen amenities. The rooms were equipped with the USSR's best listening and recording devices, which were monitored by teams of multilingual transcriptionists.

Buried somewhere in the KGB archives, there may still be a transcript of the emotional scene that exploded seconds after Berg turned the key and pushed open the heavy door to his room. For an instant he couldn't make out the identity of the man standing by the window or the pregnant woman sitting on the bed with astonished expressions on their faces. But Al Sarant recognized his old comrade immediately. When the screaming and hugging and laughing died down a bit, they compared notes on the improbable series of events that led up to the dramatic reunion, which of course had been set up by their KGB handlers.

Reconstructing the events of the past half-year, Sarant pinpointed with unusual specificity the day and time when his life began hurtling down the track that led him and Carol to the Moskva Hotel: 2:00 P.M. on July 19, 1950, when FBI Special Agents John D. Mahoney and Bill F. Maxson knocked on the door of his house on Cayuga Heights Road in Ithaca, asking him to come with them to "answer a few questions." They drove him to the town's main post office, where they'd arranged to borrow the postmaster's office.[18]

The interview started at 2:30 with questions about his relationship with

Julius Rosenberg. Sarant said he wasn't sure, but probably he had first met Rosenberg in 1942 through Barr when Rosenberg's father was in the hospital and Barr took Sarant along to donate blood. Mahoney and Maxson quickly made it clear that they knew a great deal about Sarant, asking detailed questions about his work history and about Barr, Bill Perl, Betty Sanders, and other close friends. Sarant admitted being a member of the Communist Political Association in New York City for eighteen months starting in 1944, but denied knowing Rosenberg was a party member or that he'd been a member of Branch 16B, Industrial Division during the war. Asked about Barr's girlfriend, Sarant claimed he could remember only her first name, "Vivie."[19]

Sarant didn't ask for an attorney, and after an hour he agreed to sign a waiver voluntarily granting Mahoney and Maxson the right to search and "take from my residence any letters, papers, materials or other property which they may desire." The agents drove Sarant back to Cayuga Heights Road and started a methodical search of the house at 5:55. At 8:20 they drove Sarant to the College Spa restaurant for a quick roast beef dinner, then returned and resumed the search, piling up papers and objects in cardboard boxes. Around 1:00 A.M. Sarant signed a receipt for twenty-six items the agents decided to take away, starting with "one small address book" and ending with "4 letters from William Sarant." Other items included a camera; a "Microwave Transmission Design Data book marked confidential"; a "five-page letter dated 10-4-49 signed Butch (Betty Sanders)" — a fascinating firsthand account of the two anticommunist Peekskill riots; six letters from Bill Perl; and "one ribbon 'Open Western Front Now,' on reverse side in pen 'Salud to Comrade Puss — CB.'" Just before Mahoney and Maxson finally left, at 2:05 A.M., another FBI agent parked his car directly across the street from the house. The Sarants could see him sitting there all night, watching.

Mahoney and Maxson returned the next morning at about 9:30 and brought Sarant back to the post office. As on the day before, the first questions were about the Rosenbergs. Sarant told them that Louise "spoke with Ethel on the telephone sometimes about babies." When Mahoney challenged him, saying the FBI knew Rosenberg had spied for the Russians during the war, Sarant acknowledged that he had some inkling of his friend's activities. One evening, Sarant told Mahoney, he took a walk alone with Julius; he didn't remember exactly where or when, but maybe it was after a union meeting. Rosenberg "may have been sounding me out politically. I'm quite sure that we discussed political issues." Recording Sarant's comments quickly on a lined yellow pad, the FBI agent scribbled: "In conclusion, he was sounding me out politically — (for purpose of getting info.)." "But I didn't bite," Sarant hastened to add.[20]

The agents questioned Sarant closely about the Morton Street apartment,

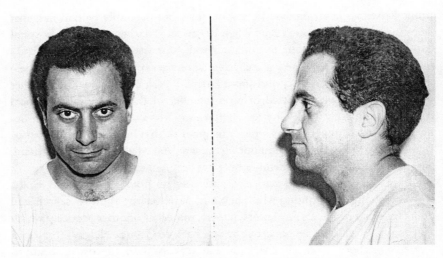

Figure 8. FBI mug shot of Alfred Sarant, July, 1950. (Source: Exhibits from the Julius and Ethel Rosenberg Case File, 03/13/1951–03/27/1951, Record Group 118, National Archives and Records Administration, New York City.)

going over and over details of who sublet it and the payment arrangements. They also asked about Barr and Perl. The interview lasted until 5:25 P.M. Mahoney and Maxson returned again the next day at 1:00 P.M., spent an hour searching the house, and drove Sarant to the now-familiar postmaster's office, where they grilled him until 11:15, with a break from 7:00 to 8:00 for a roast beef dinner at the College Spa. They recycled questions asked in previous days, probing for more details and chipping away at inconsistencies. If he barely knew Barr's girlfriend, how did he explain the photos of her they'd found in his house? Sarant acknowledged meeting Vivian at one of the Morton Street musicales and that the three of them later took a canoe trip, but still said he couldn't recall her last name or address. Yes, his wife had had some contacts with the USSR — she had worked as a secretary for the Soviet Purchasing Commission in Washington, D.C., during the war. Sarant also remembered that Ethel Rosenberg shared his interest in folk songs and that she "wanted to try to sing [but] had a shrill voice." Sarant wrote and signed a statement swearing that he'd never met or heard of Max Elitcher and didn't recall ever seeing anyone resembling the photograph of Elitcher that the FBI agents showed him.[21]

The interrogation continued on the evening of July 22, but it shifted to a more alarming venue, the Tompkins County sheriff's office. The agents asked about Sarant Labs. Sarant said it had been Barr's idea to rent the workshop and register the company, and that it was "just a hobby shop." He couldn't understand why Barr had gone to the extravagance of printing embossed stationary or putting gold letters on the door. The FBI agents asked Sarant about every person listed in his address book, took him for a chicken pie dinner at Tompkins House from 5:30 to 7:00, and returned to the sheriff's office, where Sarant wrote and signed a statement asserting that he'd never met Morton or Helen Sobell. They wrapped up the session at 9:10 and drove Sarant home. When they pulled up at his house, Sarant saw the FBI surveillance car parked in its customary spot, across the street from his front door.

The surveillance was unrelenting, but there was no interrogation the next day, and the interview on July 24 lasted only forty-five minutes. During a two-hour discussion the following day, Sarant provided a few more details on his interactions with the Rosenbergs and about activities at Morton Street. The FBI was particularly interested in photography. He said he couldn't recall Barr's ever owning a Leica camera, then later admitted that Barr did have a Leica. At first Sarant said that he and Barr only did "portrait work" in the Morton Street apartment and that the two friends developed film and printed together. Then, in contrast to his earlier statement, he said they might have copied some documents, but only sheet music. He denied any acquaintance with Klaus Fuchs. Mahoney drove Sarant to his house, where he obtained permission to remove four books, including an English-Russian/Russian-English dictionary.

Although he did his best to appear calm and unconcerned to the FBI, and to hide his fear from Louise and their sons, Jeremy, three, and Stephen, five, after a week of interrogation and surveillance Sarant was in a panic, and Louise, shaken by two FBI interrogations, wasn't much better. Unlike Julius Rosenberg, who had remained in touch with KGB agents until shortly before his arrest, or Bill Perl, who was offered and rejected an opportunity to escape, Sarant was on his own. He'd never communicated directly with Golos, Feklisov, or any other KGB officer, and had no idea how to get word about his predicament to someone who could help. Even if Feklisov's replacements in New York were aware of the FBI's interest in Sarant, they were not about to risk their necks attempting to extricate him. Events were clearly spinning out of control, and the New York KGB *rezidentia* was doing its best to keep a low profile.[22]

Cayuga Heights Road was becoming intolerable for Sarant. His relations with Louise, which hadn't been good for some time, were at an all-time low. Fears that the Rosenbergs might crack any minute, or that someone familiar with their operation would implicate Sarant, added to the tension.

Afraid that arrest was imminent, Sarant went to his next door neighbor, Carol Dayton, for help. Sarant's marriage had been on the rocks for some time, exacerbated by Louise's frustration over the failure of birth-control techniques, and several months previously he'd turned for solace to Carol, a woman described in the usually laconic FBI reports as "28, five feet four, one hundred twenty pounds, blond hair, very attractive." He shared her outrage at the social injustices they felt marked capitalist society, from racism to exploitation of workers, and had dreamy notions of the Soviet Union as a paradise. Sarant was a dedicated Communist, but unlike the typical party activist he had an encyclopedic range of interests — physics, linguistics, history, science, engineering, and music — and his intense intellectual focus was leavened by a talent for playing the guitar and singing folk songs. Although Carol's marriage to Bruce Dayton, a brilliant physicist, was happy, like many women she found it impossible to resist Sarant. Deciding that it was better to confess than to be caught, Carol and Al told their spouses about the affair in the spring of 1950. Louise's feelings for Al had cooled to the point that she didn't care, and Bruce was so preoccupied with the final stages of his Ph.D. dissertation that he pushed the subject out of his mind.[23]

Al and Louise Sarant sat down at the Daytons' house with Bruce and Carol. Al said he had to escape. His only chance was a dash for the Mexican border, but he'd never make it alone; someone would have to help with the driving. Louise didn't drive, and in any case she had children to take care of. Bruce's parents were visiting Ithaca, so they could help look after the kids. Bruce said that he couldn't take time away from his dissertation. To Carol and Al's astonishment, he agreed to let her go.[24]

Putting the first element of the plan into effect, Sarant told the FBI that he wanted to visit his father, Nonda Sarant, in Baldwin, on Long Island, for a few days. Until it was ready to make an arrest, the Bureau had no legal basis for stopping Sarant from traveling. The FBI decided that for the time being it would be sufficient to keep an eye on him. It seemed unlikely that a man living in a house he'd built from the ground up with a wife and two young children would flee. The FBI's confidence was reinforced by the fact that Sarant had voluntarily undergone days of intense interrogation and allowed agents free access to his home.[25]

The FBI's decision to allow Sarant to remain at liberty is not a reflection of its uncertainty regarding his guilt. All doubt that Sarant was a Soviet agent had been erased on June 27, 1950, when the code-crackers at the ASA gave the FBI's liaison, Robert Lamphere, a revised version of the May 5, 1944, KGB cable that had fueled his search for Antenna/Liberal. The new, more complete version made it clear why Lamphere had been unable to find an individual who matched all the known facts about Antenna/Liberal as well as the description provided in the cable. It turned out that the cable was a request for permission to recruit a lead of Rosenberg's; the description applied not to Rosenberg, but to the potential recruit, who was named in clear text: Alfred Sarant. Now Lamphere knew that the cable stated: "Please carry out a check and sanction the recruitment of Alfred SARANT, a lead of ANTENNA's. He is 25 years old, a Greek, an American citizen and lives in TYRE [New York]. He completed the engineering course at Cooper Union in 1940. He worked for two years in the Signal Corps Laboratory at Fort MONMOUTH. He was discharged for past union activity. He has been working for two years at Western Electric."[26]

The ASA had also decrypted subsequent cables indicating that Sarant had been recruited and paired up with Barr.

Although Lamphere was convinced that Sarant was the person identified in the Venona decryptions as Barr's partner, he needed to build a legal case based on other sources because the FBI had determined that the existence of the Venona program couldn't be disclosed. This decision was made in part because the government didn't want to reveal to the Soviets the extent of its progress in breaking the KGB's codes, but also because senior FBI officials were skeptical that Venona documents would hold up in court.[27]

On Wednesday, July 26, 1950, Special Agents Mahoney and Maxson, driving a black Pontiac, tailed Sarant as he drove south from Ithaca in a 1936 gray Dodge sedan, New York license number 7x-4997.[28] They followed him to Nonda Sarant's house and requested that the New York City field office conduct spot checks to confirm that Sarant remained at the house at 160 West Merrick Road, and to inform the Albany field office when he departed. The Albany SAC "stated that it would not be necessary to surveil him back to Ithaca," according to an FBI report written on the night of the twenty-sixth. A few minutes before 9:00 P.M., after turning over surveillance duties to agents from the New York office, Mahoney called the Albany FBI office and, according to a memo typed by Charles H. Sheldon, a night clerk in the FBI's Albany office, reported that he "was advised by agents of the New York office that all relatives of Sarant on Long Island had been interviewed and furnished no pertinent info with the exception that they were all aware of the fact that subject was acquainted with Joel Barr."[29]

Two days later, agents from the FBI's New York field office brought Sarant into their Manhattan office for questioning "principally so that he could be discreetly observed by superintendents from 65 Morton Street and from another apartment building in which [the FBI] suspected Rosenberg had an apartment," Lamphere recalled. The superintendent from Morton Street recognized Sarant, but the other didn't.[30]

On Thursday, August 3, Edward Scheidt, special agent in charge of the FBI's New York office, wrote a memo outlining "discrepancies" between answers Sarant had provided agents during interviews conducted in Ithaca and facts known from Venona and other sources. The memo noted that Sarant "denies knowing Julius Rosenberg as a member of the CP and ever having membership at Branch 16B, Industrial Division, CP." The FBI knew this was a lie: it had thoroughly penetrated the party and had photocopies of records for most New York party members. The Bureau was aware that in July 1944 Sarant had transferred from Branch 16B to the Sacco-Vanzetti Club of the Communist Political Association. The memo didn't mention that the Bureau also knew, from the Venona decryptions available at the time, that Sarant had been recruited by Barr as a spy; it is possible that Lamphere kept this information to himself.

Scheidt noted that Sarant

> admitted that Rosenberg might have told him that Russians or the Soviets were our allies during the war period and that every effort possible should be extended to them to furnish as much info as possible and as fellow communists that he should be one of those who should assist. However, he stated that he does not recall Rosenberg having stated this. He admitted that he could have furnished vital info pertaining to airborne radar when employed by the Western Electric Co., and at the same time stated that Joel Barr could have supplied the same info because he too was employed by the Western Electric Co. during the same period. However he says that he never furnished any info and that to the best of his knowledge that Joel Barr has never furnished any info to Julius Rosenberg or any other agent of a foreign power.

The memo concluded: "Sarant's sister, Mrs. [Elektra] Jayson, advised August two, last, that the subject would probably be in the NY area for approximately two additional days and then he would return to Ithaca, NY. William Sarant, subject's brother, advised August three, instant, that the subject did not stay at father's home last evening and that possibly he was on his way back to Ithaca."[31]

While Al was driving to Long Island, Carol took a bus to Rochester to visit Bernard Peters, a close friend of Bruce's who had fled Nazi Germany just ahead of the Gestapo, which had targeted him for arrest as a Communist. Carol confided her plans, asked Peters for advice — he didn't have much to offer — and returned the same day to Ithaca.

On August 4, Carol packed a small suitcase, enough for a week or so, and tucked pictures of her two young children, Derry and Eric, into her wallet. She told friends that she was going to Boston to stay with a friend, Judy Bregman, and hunt for a house where the family could live when Bruce started a postdoctoral assignment at MIT. Bruce gave her a $100 bill and dropped her at the Ithaca bus station. "I want you to know that I'll be waiting for you to come back," he said. "Don't worry, I will," she replied.[32]

Al was waiting for Carol at the bus station in Manhattan. He'd told Elektra about his marital problems and explained that the FBI was hounding him, trying to extract false testimony against Julius Rosenberg. In those days, it was easy for Elektra to believe that Al had done nothing wrong but was nonetheless in danger. The front pages of newspapers were spattered with anticommunist hysteria, reports of arrests of accused spies and of ordinary people fired from their jobs as teachers or librarians because of alleged Communist connections. There was a sense among progressives that the government was getting ready to round up people who were guilty of nothing more than expressing radical ideas or being associated with the Communist Party. There was also a strong feeling that the arrests and blacklists were a prelude to a harsher crackdown.

Decades later, Sobell remembered the "apprehensions which pervaded the American Left in 1950, and which I shared. The belief was widespread that World War III was in the offing. It seemed to us that America was veering toward fascism, a fascism that would be much the same as that of Nazi Germany. We saw mass roundups, concentration camps, and death ovens, à la Hitler."[33]

On the evening of August 4, Elektra, her husband, Joe, Al, and Carol piled into a car and drove to Roosevelt Raceway, where the Jaysons kept horses. It was a sweltering Friday night, and Roosevelt, one of the largest venues for harness racing in America, was packed. While FBI agents watched the main exits and the crowds cheered a horse named Scottish Pence upset Jerry the First for the $50,000 purse, Al and Carol slipped out through the paddock and found Al's car, which his brother-in-law had prepositioned earlier in the day. The FBI agents must have assumed that they had missed Sarant and Dayton in the thick crowds, because they did not raise an alarm.[34]

The couple were pretty sure the car wasn't being followed, but nonetheless they watched nervously for signs of pursuit as Al maneuvered the Dodge off Long Island and headed south. They drove in shifts night and day, Carol going as fast as she dared, her lifelong passion for speed barely restrained by the fear that there might be an all-points bulletin out for Al and that a police stop for speeding could land them both in jail. In fact, the FBI, believing that more information could be squeezed out of Sarant if he wasn't facing criminal charges, hadn't requested an arrest warrant, and no one was looking for him.

The FBI's New York City field office assumed that Sarant was on the way back to Ithaca, and it hadn't occurred to the Albany field office yet that it should check to see if he'd returned to upstate New York. The FBI screwup created a narrow gap in the net that had quickly been closing in on Sarant, and he and Carol literally drove right through it.

On August 8, the gray Dodge pulled up in front of 2805 East Drachman Street in Tucson, Arizona, the home of Donald Haines, Carol's cousin. Carol felt that her role in the adventure was almost complete. Much as she loved Al, she had never wanted to leave her children or to hurt Bruce. She would see Al across the Mexican border, make sure that he had a route to safety, and use the $100 bill to buy a ticket back to her husband and children.

That day, Carol wrote a letter to her friend Judy Bregman and slipped it into her purse.

> Dear Judy, you probably know by now that I'm supposed to be in Boston looking for a house for us. That I am not is the result of many strange circumstances. In any case, it will look better to certain people in Ithaca if this letter to Bruce (enclosed) comes with a Boston postmark. So will you send it there for me, please? And you would be a most wonderful help if you could manage to turn up a house or apartment. Have you heard of anything? I had a paper with names to contact but now I can't locate it. Weiskopt is going on sabbatical — that's a possibility. Oh woe. Bruce's parents are visiting Ithaca. I hope he has finished his thesis — in which case he would have more visiting time. My kids are there, and boy, do I miss them. Thanks, Judy, and please find us a house. Bye now, Carol.[35]

The letter to Bruce, which Bregman read before mailing, stated that Carol could not communicate directly with him, that she planned to be back home by the time they were ready to move to Boston, and that her return had been delayed by circumstances beyond her control. The letter concluded with kind words for the children and instructions on how to care for them in her absence.[36]

Al sold the car to Donald's son, Warren, and the couple rested for a day. On August 10, Donald and his wife drove Carol and Al 125 miles south of the border to Hermosillo, Mexico. Al used Bruce's name on the tourist card at the border. As Donald was getting back into the car, he urged Carol to return with him. She refused — how could she leave Al alone, facing an uncertain future? — and handed her cousin the letter to Bregman, with instructions to mail it the next day from Tucson.[37]

As Carol and Al were getting their bearings — it was the first time either had been outside the United States — alarm bells were finally starting to go off at the FBI. A file memo written by Charles Sheldon, night clerk at the Albany field office, noted:

Night supervisor, A. T. Healey of the New York Office called at about 11:15 this evening to advise that Agents of the New York office had interviewed Mrs. Elektra Jayson, sister of Sarant and she advised them that Sarant had left Baldwin, L.I. Saturday morning with his "girlfriend" Carol, who is a neighbor of his in Ithaca, NY. Mrs. Jayson denied knowing where Sarant and Carol were going, but that she did state that Sarant was to arrive back in Ithaca sometime today (8/10/50) probably late in the day. Contact was made with SA [Special Agent] Maxson at Ithaca who stated that he would advise SA Mahoney, who would in turn check to verify the fact that Sarant did return to Ithaca and a call would be placed in the morning to the SAC to advise him of their findings.[38]

The next day, R. W. Wall Jr., special agent in charge of the Albany FBI field office, memorialized his version of events:

At 5:35 pm August 10, I received a telephone call from Robert Granville, Supervisor in the New York Office. Granville stated that Alfred Sarant had departed New York sometime either Friday or Saturday and that his destination was unknown. In view of the fact that Sarant has been observed in the company of a girl believed to be Carol Dayton, Granville suggested that I call Boston and have them check with the individuals whom Carol Dayton was supposed to be visiting, to determine if Sarant might be in Boston. At 8:45 am on August 11, 1950, in view of the fact that Sarant had not returned to Ithaca, I telephonically contacted ASA Ed McCabe of the Boston Office and advised him that Carol Dayton was visiting Judy Bregman at 72 Frances Street, Cambridge, Mass. I requested McCabe to have an agent contact Bregman in an effort to locate Dayton for an interview. I told McCabe in the event Dayton was located, she should be asked if she had seen or heard of Alfred Sarant. I further told him that if through this contact Sarant was located, the Boston Office should have no compunction in contacting him and asking him when he plans to return to Ithaca.[39]

Bregman rebuffed the FBI, refusing to talk to its agents on the telephone or in person. Finally, on August 22, she changed her mind and agreed to visit the Bureau's Boston office. She insisted on bringing an attorney, and, according to a cable marked "most urgent," "advised she had received a letter from Carol Dayton, postmarked at Tucson, Arizona, August twelfth, last with no return address. Bregman states the letter did not mention Alfred Sarant and she declined to discuss the contents of the letter further unless advised of the purpose of the Bureau investigation. Bregman and attorney [were] advised that the only purpose of contacting her was to obtain current addresses of Sarant and Dayton." The cable added that "Bregman will be recontacted periodically by Boston [FBI office] and mail cover being placed. States, how-ever, she does not expect to receive other correspondence from Mrs. Dayton." A handwritten note on the bottom of the cable records that it was read to Maxson over the telephone.[40]

Bregman had provided a critical lead — the Tucson postmark — and the next morning, August 23, FBI agents were knocking on the door at 2805 East Drachman Street. Warren Haines told them that his parents had dropped Al and Carol in Hermosillo thirteen days before, and that his parents had then gone on to visit his grandmother in Sacramento, California. "Warren advised [that] his father, Donald Haines, told him Carol Dayton had been 'very radical during her college days' and in his opinion, she may be a communist. He also advised Warren that in his opinion Alfred Sarant may be a communist."[41]

Judy Bregman's father, fearing serious consequences from withholding in-formation from the government, convinced her to call the FBI on August 25. Bregman read the letter from Carol and summarized the letter to Bruce Day-ton. However, she refused to comply with the FBI's requests for a copy of the letter or a more detailed description of its contents.[42]

Sarant wasn't the only member of the Rosenberg ring south of the border. News of the arrest of Greenglass had so shocked Sobell that he immediately requested a leave of absence from his job and within days flew with his wife and two young children to Mexico City. Sobell had neither the KGB's assis-tance, which had made Barr's escape possible, nor the tenacity and intelligence that Sarant displayed. While Sarant and Dayton stayed on the move, making good use of Carol's fluent Spanish, constantly looking out for the FBI, and never staying in the same cheap hotel two nights in a row, Sobell took few measures to avoid detection.

Sarant and Dayton were quite right to be afraid. While they were slowly making their way to Mexico City, an official in the American embassy coordi-nated a successful manhunt for Sobell and arranged for Mexican police to kidnap and drive him, along with his wife and two children, to the U.S. border. Sobell's deportation was conducted in an informal, and probably illegal, man-ner. Although a sealed complaint charging Sobell with espionage had been filed in a New York federal court, under Mexican law it would not have supported an extradition request, Assistant Attorney General James McIner-ney notified FBI Director Hoover in August 1950. The FBI was concerned that it might not be able to rely on similar cooperation in the case of Sarant and Dayton, especially if they were caught outside Mexico.[43]

The FBI consulted with Justice Department lawyers to come up with a plan of action in case the Mexicans caught up with Sarant or he reentered the

United States. The Bureau considered asking a U.S. attorney to issue a warrant for his detention as a material witness in the Rosenberg case, but rejected this because it would not be grounds for extradition. In a memo to the assistant U.S. attorney in Phoenix, the FBI laid out its case against Sarant — omitting data from the Venona decryptions — and suggested a course of action. It stated that the circumstances "strongly indicate that Sarant was a member of the Rosenberg espionage group. However, it appears that insufficient information is available for prosecution of Sarant for espionage. However, serious consideration should be given to immediately obtaining evidence of intimacy between Sarant and Carol Dorothy Dayton and then obtaining warrant for Sarant based on his interstate transportation of Carol Dayton for immoral purposes. This case could appear to warrant prosecution under WSTA [White Slave Traffic Act] based on aggravating circumstances of married persons deserting young children. Both Sarants and Daytons have two children. Carol Dayton might then be held as material witness." FBI officials later discussed the possibility that the Mexican authorities would deport Sarant without legal niceties, a service they had provided American law enforcement in the past, most recently with regard to Sobell.[44]

The FBI and the Mexican authorities were unable to track Sarant and Dayton. After two months of wandering, the couple arrived in Mexico City nearly out of money. They located the Soviet embassy and screwed up their courage to walk in and request help, but were spooked at the last minute by a circling black car that they imagined carried FBI agents.

At wit's end, Al thumbed through a telephone book looking for an East bloc contact that might be safer. When the couple found their way to the shabby offices of the Polish trade mission on a quiet back street, Al felt that he could trust the man behind the cluttered desk. In any case, they had few if any alternatives. He announced to the bemused Pole: "We want to build socialism," explained that they were on the run from the FBI, and requested help getting to Russia. The Pole warned the Americans never to return to the office because it was under surveillance by the Americans and instructed them to go in five days at 3:00 P.M. to a bench in a small park on Montero Street to wait for instructions. If no one came, they were to return at the same time every day.

They waited an hour on the appointed day, but nothing happened. Day after day they returned, their hopes melting like the ice cream cones they ate in an effort to look like tourists on holiday. Carol started to lose her nerve, one minute crying in their dingy hotel room over the thought that she might never see her children again, and the next arguing with Al that they should risk approaching the Soviets directly. By the seventh day they had just about given up hope and were glumly eating *helado* when an elegantly dressed blond man sat on the bench next to them, unfolded a newspaper, and, after a few moments, asked in accented English, "Are you Alfred Sarant?" He introduced himself as Mr. Winter and said he was a Polish diplomat.

It turned out that Sarant's intuition had been excellent. The Polish trade official was actually an intelligence officer. The cable he sent to Warsaw about Sarant and Dayton's visit was quickly forwarded to Yatskov and Kvasnikov at the Lubyanka.[45]

Ironically, a couple of months before, Sobell had wandered into exactly the same Polish trade mission office but, rather than asking for help, had merely requested information about ships traveling between Mexico and Poland. Instead of finding a route to a new life, like Sarant and Dayton, all he got was a handful of shipping schedules that the Mexican police later found in his apartment. "When I visited the Polish mission in June and asked whether there was a Polish ship harbored in one of the Mexican ports by which I could leave the country, they told me I could not expect anything sooner than in two months. And they were so cold and noncommittal that I gave up on them right away," Sobell remembered.[46]

The KGB replied to the cable from Warsaw with a request to smuggle the Americans to the Soviet Union. It wasn't an easy task for the Poles or for Al and Carol. She was torn between a desperate desire to return to her children and a growing attachment to Al. One day she and Al bought four little sombreros, imagining that they'd give them to their kids. Another day, Carol announced that she'd finally made up her mind: she wasn't going to continue with Al; she was going to get use the $100 Bruce had given her for a bus ticket back to her children and husband. Sarant sunk into a depression and lay in bed all day, refusing to get up or to respond to Carol. The next day, the couple's new Polish friends convinced Carol that if she returned she would end up not with her children, but in a jail cell facing the death penalty, like Ethel Rosenberg. Meanwhile, Bruce still looked forward to being reunited with his wife. He wrote to Donald Haines in September, reporting that he expected Carol to return soon, the FBI learned.[47]

Sarant and Dayton didn't have passports, and even if they had it would have been too dangerous to use them. Polish intelligence kept the couple hidden in Mexico for six months while documents and an escape plan were prepared. Al grew a beard; Carol dyed her hair black. Eventually they were driven to southern Mexico, where they had to wait three days for a moonless night to wade across the Usumacinta River into a remote area of Guatemala, carrying little but the clothes they were wearing. Carol managed to bring her wallet with photos of her children and an old California driver's license — a document that played a critical role in her family's life more than four decades later. In Puerto

Barrios, on the Caribbean coast, they boarded a cargo ship to Casablanca, Morocco, transferred to another ship that took them to Spain, and finally traveled by plane to Warsaw.

Sarant and Dayton spent six months in Warsaw, living in a furnished apartment with a cook and a maid, before getting permission to move on to Moscow, where they landed a few days before Barr stumbled into them in the Moskva Hotel.

After Berg told his tale — from that point on, even in private conversations, he was called Joe, never Joel — the trio took to the streets to get an up-close look at the center of world Communism, which they'd fantasized about for years. They strolled up Gorky Street — a beautiful boulevard rivaling Fifth Avenue, lined on both sides with elegant shop windows displaying furs and jewelry — up to Yeliseev's delicatessen, a grandiose establishment, little changed from the days of the tsars, with gold-encrusted columns and mounds of caviar. The Americans were unaware that admission was restricted to a tiny elite and that for most Muscovites this was a time of hunger and gloom. They marveled at the Metro, with its elaborately decorated, marble-clad stations, Joe saying that in comparison the New York subway looked like a public toilet. The threesome strolled past the exotic onion domes of St. Basil's Cathedral and stood in line at the mausoleum in Red Square to pay homage to Lenin's mummified corpse. They excused the gangs of shabbily dressed children and poor old women on the streets, and other evidence of poverty, blaming the immense toll the war had taken on the Soviet Union. Lacking any contact with ordinary people, the Americans had no way of knowing about the fear that permeated Russians' lives at that time, which started with their arrival at work — Stalin had decreed jail sentences for tardiness — and followed them home, where casual remarks overheard by friends or neighbors would be reported to the KGB.

While they toured Moscow, Berg and Sarant discussed their future. Back in the United States, Barr had been the dominant figure in the relationship. He had recruited Sarant into espionage activities and was their point of contact with Feklisov and other KGB officers; at Fort Monmouth, and later at Western Electric, he had held more senior positions. When they had decided to go into business together, Al had convinced Joel that "Sarant Laboratories" sounded more reputable than "Ideas, Inc." but they were equal partners financially and personally.

By the time they met in Moscow, however, something had changed in Sarant's mind. "Let's get one thing straight: From now on, I'm the boss," Sarant announced on one of their walks around the hotel, speaking in the blunt way that the two old friends used with each other. Berg felt it was an unimportant formality, so he agreed, and from that day on Sarant took the lead in the pair's interactions with the outside world. The two were inseparable companions for decades, but in every endeavor Sarant was the superior, sometimes emphasizing his position by publicly humiliating Berg. He seemed to derive strength from Berg's subservience, and Berg came to love him with a passion and loyalty that was never even approached in his relations with anyone else, man or woman. "I know I'm not gay, but if I was, I would have married him," Berg said in later years. "I really loved Al like a woman loves her husband."[48]

Sarant's changed attitude toward Berg was part of a larger transformation in his character. Despite his dreams of pioneering new fields of electronics or becoming a nuclear physicist, Sarant hadn't left lasting impressions about his intellect on his employers or colleagues the way Barr had. The most responsible position he had ever held was a low-level engineering job, and when he left Ithaca he was running a small home construction and repair business. His friends were struck by Sarant's mechanical abilities; Bethe and Feynman thought he was a congenial companion, but not suitable material for Cornell's graduate school.[49] In Moscow, however, a new confidence led Sarant to present himself as a genius prevented by anticommunist persecution from realizing his potential; his intensity led senior Soviet officials, especially those responsible for defense electronics, to believe and trust him.

The KGB created less elaborate identities for Al and Carol than Berg's. Sarant became Philip Staros, born in Greece on February 24, 1917, who had emigrated to Canada with his parents as a child. According to his official biography, having graduated from the University of Toronto with a degree in electrical engineering, Staros had worked in Canada at a facility that produced radar systems from 1940 to 1943, then left for the United States, where he had worked for Western Electric and Bell Laboratories until 1947. Starting in 1948 he had worked as a builder/contractor. In 1950 he had traveled to Mexico and in 1951 to Poland. Staros was instructed to explain that he had been fired from Bell Laboratories because of his progressive political views and decided to seek employment in a socialist country to help build Communism. Carol became Anna Staros, a Canadian, and retained her real birthday.

The Soviet authorities decided to send the trio to Prague, where Staros and Berg could put experience gained on defense projects at Western Electric and Bell Laboratories to use for the socialist bloc. The move almost certainly saved their lives. It is very unlikely that the Americans would have survived the paranoid purges that marked Stalin's last years, in which even unproved allegations of contacts with foreigners often led to fatal encounters with the KGB and its prison camps. Many American Communists who had the misfortune to travel to Russia seeking to put their skills in the service of socialism were executed or suffered horribly in the Gulag. Even in Prague, Berg and Staros only narrowly avoided the maelstrom that decimated the top ranks of science and technology throughout the Soviet bloc.[50]

Berg flew back to Prague in the second week of October, a week or two after Staros. He was driven straight from the airport to the VTU (Army Technical Institute), a high-security military R&D center, where he met Staros and General Lastovicka, Colonel Kukal, and Major Halek from the Czechoslovakian Army. The group proceeded to the office of Dr. Bedrich Goldschmied, the institute's director, who, acting on instructions from Lastovicka and the Czechoslovakian Communist Party Central Committee, signed papers officially hiring Berg. Goldschmied had little choice: Berg's personnel file included a personal recommendation signed by Party Chairman Rudolph Slansky, and Lastovicka had previously ordered him to hire Staros. A Ministry of Interior internal memo about Berg and Staros also mentioned that "both were in the MNB," the Ministry of Interior's security department, and that they had been sent to the VTU by the MNB head, in addition to General Lastovicka.[51]

Goldschmied became a close friend and mentor to Berg and Staros. Communism did nothing to erase the hypersensitivity of Czechs and other East Europeans to ethnicity, and Goldschmied and Berg, both aggressive atheists, shared the burden of being identified as Jews.

Soon after Berg and Staros began working at the VTU, a Soviet advisor to the StB identified in the Ministry of Interior records only as "Aleksejev" arranged to meet them at a quiet table in a restaurant in a Prague park. Aleksejev introduced the pair to Major Bedrich Radon of the StB, who took charge of their interactions with the security services and made sure that they were provided with salaries and accommodations befitting their status as foreign experts.

Berg and Staros were assigned the task of designing and building a prototype of a special-purpose analog computer system to control antiaircraft missile batteries. At the time, the Soviet bloc was bracing for an expected assault from the United States, so the assignment was of critical significance to the Czechs and their Soviet patrons. Tensions were especially high because the United States, desperate to learn as much as it could about Soviet defenses, was engaging in dangerous aerial cat-and-mouse games, intentionally violating the airspace of the Soviets and their allies and monitoring the responses. The game turned ugly on several occasions, including an incident on March 10, 1953, when a Czechoslovakian MIG-15 shot down a U.S. Air Force fighter plane over the West German border.

The computer proposed by Staros and Berg was inspired by the M9 Predictor fire-control computer developed during World War II that, coupled with the SCR-584 radar system and artillery, had proved tremendously successful at shooting down German V-1 rockets and airplanes. Although the M9 Predictor provided a point of departure for the analog computer that Staros and Berg designed, their computer was not a copy of the Bell Laboratories machine, and to succeed they would have to master skills far beyond those taught to them by their U.S. employers. For example, in addition to building the hardware, their project could succeed only if they worked out the complex mathematics required to predict an airplane's future position accurately and embedded the necessary algorithms in the hardware. It was also necessary to interface the computer with antiaircraft weapons and make the device sufficiently robust to work in the field.

Berg and Staros were familiar with the M9; they'd once stayed up until 2:00 A.M. copying the M9 manual for Feklisov. Both had also worked on analog fire-control computers in the United States. Moreover, they had a valuable resource at hand. Antonin Svoboda, a Czech who during World War II had been a senior computer scientist at MIT's Radiation Laboratory, where he designed computerized antiaircraft systems, was living in Prague.

Svoboda's life is almost a mirror image of Berg's and Staros's. A Czech, as a young man he had developed a design for an analog computer-based antiaircraft weapon. He had escaped to Paris in 1939 soon after the Nazis occupied Prague, was hired by the French government to perfect his antiaircraft system, but was forced to flee in advance of the German invasion of France. After a series of harrowing adventures, including fleeing German troops on a bicycle and the loss of much of his work when a French customs official threw the bike in which his plans were hidden into the Mediterranean, Svoboda had managed to escape to the United States in 1941. During World War II he had worked at MIT's Radiation Laboratory designing the servomechanical systems that linked analog computers to antiaircraft guns—creating designs that General Electric turned into manufacturing specifications and Morton Sobell turned over to Russia. Svoboda had been granted over 100 U.S. patents, received the Naval Ordnance Development Award, and been one of two dozen computer scientists from the Radiation Laboratory selected to write books about their pathbreaking wartime research. His book, *Computing Mechanisms and Linkages,* is still considered a classic in the history of computers.

After the war, Svoboda had returned to Czechoslovakia, then a democracy, with the idea of turning his native country into the world's leading computer manufacturer. Czechoslovakia could, he dreamed, become to computers what Switzerland was to watches. Trapped in Prague after the Communist takeover in 1948, he managed to build some pioneering computers in the 1950s and 1960s. An avid musician like Berg, Svoboda played percussion in the Czech symphony orchestra. In 1964 Svoboda managed to escape with his family and some colleagues. He settled in the United States and became a leading computing theoretician.[52]

Even with their knowledge of the M9 and assistance from Svoboda, Staros and Berg faced a daunting challenge. Between the world wars, Czechoslovakian industry and technology, especially its weapons production, had been on a par with Germany's and Austria's, but by the 1950s Czechoslovakia had fallen far behind the West. Even before the German invasion, the Czech government had started seizing Jewish-owned businesses and turning them over to ethnic Slavs, including many who were incapable of running them efficiently. During the Nazi occupation and immediate postwar years, Czechoslovakian industry had remained untouched by the leaps in technology made elsewhere.

Undeterred by the lack of even basic components, Staros and Berg set out to build a sophisticated computer from the ground up. Their most difficult technical hurdle was a lack of precision potentiometers, instruments that can vary the magnitude of voltage or be used to compare an unknown voltage to a standard voltage. Potentiometers were the basic computing element in the M9, and in Staros and Berg's updated version of the machine.

A request to Goldschmied for purchases of American-made potentiometers and other basic components was turned down because they were considered far too expensive, so Staros and Berg decided to make the necessary components themselves. In order to manufacture the potentiometers, the team designed and built an ingenious machine that precisely wound fine wire onto a thin shaft, creating the guts of a potentiometer, and crafted the bushings, terminals, and housings. Their potentiometer winding design was put into production and was widely used in Czechoslovakia and later the Soviet Union.

The team's progress came to the attention of the Soviet defense establishment, which had become aware during the war of the significance of electronics and was desperately trying to catch up with the West. In mid-1952 a delegation from Moscow visited Staros and Berg in Prague to offer them leading positions in a planned Soviet R&D institute. In later years, both Staros and Berg said that the Central Committee of the Communist Party of the Soviet Union had issued a *postanovlenie* (decree) signed by Stalin that awarded them the status of full members of the Soviet Academy of Sciences and put them at the head of an organization that was to have 50,000 employees.[53]

The American engineers demurred, citing a need to finish the antiaircraft project and a preference for hands-on research to administration. "We were naive. Why do we need fancy titles and thousands of workers? We thought it was enough to have a small lab," Berg remembered. Berg also had another reason for remaining in Prague, though it is unlikely that he mentioned it to the Russian military officials.[54]

Philip and Anna Staros never legally married, but they lived as a couple from the day they slipped out of Ithaca until his death. When their first child, Kolya, was born in Prague in 1952 — the third child for each of them — Joe's joy was tinged with loneliness. He hadn't had a close relationship with a woman since breaking up with Vivian Glassman just before his departure for Europe.

A few weeks before rebuffing the Soviet offer, Joe decided to take a weekend trip to a spa in the mountains, and, uncharacteristically, he went alone. He shared the train compartment with a farmer named Anton Krcmarov, his wife, and their strikingly attractive daughter, Vera, who was nine years younger than Joe. Joe and Vera spent three days together, lying on the grass and strolling around the resort town, Joe bubbling all the time in ungrammatical Czech. By the end of the weekend, the dashing foreigner and the farmer's daughter were inseparable.[55]

The powerful electricity between Joe and Vera was more than matched by the sparks that flew between the suitor and the father. Krcmarov was a strong-willed man who had been driven almost to fanaticism by the Communist revolution, which had taken away the land in and around the village of Mnichovice that his ancestors had acquired through decades of toil. Despite strong pressure from Communist officials, he had refused to sign papers formally transferring the family's eleven hectares to the state and had rejected demands to work in the local collective farm. Agricultural collectivization was less brutal in 1950s Czechoslovakia than it had been in the 1930s in the Soviet Union, where "kulaks" like Krcmarov were often exiled and/or killed. Although the Krcmarovs' land was seized, ties with his neighbors going back generations led local party bosses to soften their responses to the counter-revolutionary intransigence. The family was permitted to remain in the farmhouse that Krcmarov had built in 1929 to replace one that had burned down. Vera, his only child, helped support the family with her meager earnings as a nurse in the village kindergarten.

Krcmarov hated the Communists for taking his land, and he detested them for closing the churches and advocating atheism. A staunch fundamentalist Catholic and Czech nationalist, Krcmarov disliked only one group more passionately than Communists: Jews. In fact his anti-Semitism predated the Communist accession to power. Berg, a fervent Communist with a stereotypical Jewish face, represented the epitome of evil to Krcmarov.

For Joe, who had always lived in cities, Vera's living conditions — the family drew water from a hand pump in the yard, their toilet was an outhouse, and cows and pigs lived in the barn adjacent to the house — were as appalling and primitive as her father's opinions. During their first meeting at the family home in Mnichovice, Joe infuriated the old man by trying to convince him to sign over his land to the state and to embrace Communism.

The authorities in Mnichovice and Prague, who took a dim view of the romance, reinforced the mutual hostility. The village police told Krcmarov that his daughter's fiancé was "a mysterious foreigner" who would bring trouble to the family. Joe's contacts in the Communist Party were equally unenthusiastic about his liaison with the daughter of an unrepentant rich peasant, a paradigm of the class that the party was struggling to eliminate.[56]

Joe, however, was determined to overcome all obstacles to marriage. When he discovered that it was against the law for a foreigner to marry a Czechoslovakian citizen, he launched a campaign with Goldshmied's backing to obtain Czech citizenship. Both Berg and Staros applied for citizenship on October 24, 1952, and Berg pestered the authorities daily for weeks until they issued the papers.[57]

Krcmarov became increasingly distraught at the prospect of losing his only daughter to a Jewish Communist. On the night before the wedding, the tension became unbearable. Feeling that she was better off dead than in Joe's arms, Krcmarov tried to strangle Vera. His wife heard the commotion and rushed to help Vera pry her father's hands loose from her neck. Vera was certain that without her mother's intervention, her father would have squeezed the life out of her. Krcmarov took to his bed and refused to get out of it to attend the wedding.[58]

Joe and his father-in-law met in person a few months later at the funeral for Vera's mother. Standing at the family's plot on the edge of the village cemetery, shrouded in mist, Berg heard Krcmarov declare to the assembled villagers that his wife's death was God's retribution for allowing Vera to marry a Jew. Although over the decades they overcame their differences enough to be able to speak, Krcmarov and Berg never reconciled.

Joe and Vera moved into a comfortable apartment at 7 Bubenska Street, in a prestigious Prague neighborhood a few blocks north of the Vltava River and not far from the medieval city center. They strolled in the evenings and weekends in nearby Letna Park and watched as workers built the largest of the many statues of Stalin erected throughout the Soviet world. A fifteen-meter-tall granite monstrosity, it portrayed the Soviet dictator gazing down across the Vltava River into Prague, behind him a line of men representing the solidarity of the

Czechoslovakian and Soviet armies. The official commemorative brochure distributed at the dedication said: "In the forefront [is] the figure of J. V. Stalin, behind him marching on one side representatives of the Soviet people and on the other side representatives of the Czechoslovak people. By this means the unity of Stalin's person with the people and the eternal brotherhood of the Czechoslovak people with the Soviet people in the struggle for the realization of the great ideas of peace and socialism are expressively conveyed."[59]

The ensemble, which rested on a huge mound, was popularly known as the "bread line" or the "meat line," depending on which commodity was in short supply at the time. Standing in Old Town Square in the heart of ancient Prague, residents and visitors who glanced up Parizska Trida (Paris Boulevard) couldn't miss the Soviet leader's visage. To Berg, the monument was a fitting, if somewhat garish, tribute to the Man of Steel. For many Czechs, it was emblematic of the Soviet Union: overbearing, oversized, and primitive in comparison to the jewel-like medieval city it loomed over.

The news of Stalin's death in March 1953 was devastating to Berg, as to millions of Russians and Communists around the world. Joe had idealized Stalin from childhood, and it was difficult, and more than a little frightening, to think of a world without "the great architect of Communism," as he was frequently called. Berg was completely ignorant of the atrocities undertaken on Stalin's orders, and, like many idealistic Communists, he readily believed the fantastic charges of espionage publicized in the show trials. Even after Stalin was repudiated by the Soviet leadership, Berg clung to his faith in the man who had transformed Russia from a peasant society into an industrial power, and he frequently commented on the contrast between Stalin's annual May Day decrees lowering the prices of staple foods and inflation in capitalist societies.

Given his own experiences, it didn't take a tremendous leap of imagination to believe that people who pretended to be loyal Soviets or Czech Communists might be leading double lives, secretly plotting the downfall of the state.

Joe and Vera joined a million Czechs on December 21, 1955, the seventy-sixth anniversary of Stalin's birth, for the dedication of the statue in Letna Park. In contrast to the throngs who braved the cold to hear long speeches praising the Georgian dictator, few people were on hand to witness its destruction in a series of explosions in 1962.[60]

It is remarkable that Berg emerged unscathed from the political and social turmoil that swept Prague in the 1950s. His survival depended on the patronage of powerful men at the top of the Czech government who were acting on orders from Moscow, and on surreptitious interventions by Russian "liaison" officers who effectively controlled the StB. The most senior officials in the

Czech power structure were aware of Berg. He became acquainted with at least one top government official, the deputy interior minister, Antonin Prchal. Although there is no evidence that Berg met Rudolf Slansky, the leader of the Czechoslovakian Communist Party personally signed documents recommending that Berg be granted security clearances and hired for defense work. The recommendation was almost certainly made at the request of officials in Moscow.

Berg encountered a country in turmoil. A year before his arrival, Czech authorities bowed to demands from Moscow and launched an overhaul of the economy that was intended to orient it toward the needs of the Soviet Union and other socialist countries. As trade ties with Western Europe were cut, living standards deteriorated sharply. From 1949 to 1953, anticommunist demonstrations and strikes convulsed Czechoslovakia. Fearing that they were losing control, the Czech leaders launched a series of purges and show trials that paralyzed the country for years, arresting and torturing thousands and executing hundreds of loyal senior party officials. By the end of January 1951, 169,000 members of the Czechoslovakian Communist Party — 10 percent of the membership — had been arrested. From 1948 to 1954, more than 50,000 Czechoslovakians were sentenced to jail terms of at least ten years for resistance, real or imagined, to the regime.

During the time he was in touch with Berg, Prchal played a central role in some of the darker episodes of Czech history. The deputy interior minister was in charge of the investigations, especially the fabrication of evidence, that formed the backbone of the show trials of the 1950s, including perhaps the most odious, that of Slansky. Slansky, a dedicated Communist of Jewish descent, was arrested in November 1951 and tortured for a year. By the time he was put on trial, Stalin had ordered the arrest of a group of Jewish doctors and launched a fierce purge of Jews in the USSR. The purge spread to Prague, and when Slansky's trial started in November 1952, all but one of his eleven codefendants were Jews. Berg readily believed the incredible lies propagated about Slansky's betrayal of his country. After all, he'd seen for himself how outwardly loyal Americans had created a secret underground and served the USSR while working in responsible positions in the United States during World War II.[61]

Slansky's execution in December marked the beginning of decades of semi-official anti-Semitism throughout the Soviet bloc. In Czechoslovakia, anyone with a connection to Slansky, or Jewish heritage, or Jewish friends was suspect. Berg, whose file noted Slansky's personal endorsement, his own Jewish background, and his close working relationship with Goldschmied, was guilty on all three counts; had it not been for the intervention of the KGB, he would probably have ended his days in a Czech prison. Like a cat with nine lives, Berg landed on his feet after several serious brushes with Czech internal security investigators, though he was only dimly aware of them and at the time had no idea of the danger he was in.[62]

He was acutely aware, however, of the danger he'd left behind. On the morning of Sunday, June 21, 1953, Berg picked up a copy of *Rude Pravo,* gasped, and slumped in his chair as if he'd been struck with a bat. His hands trembled as he saw photos of his old comrades and friends, Julius and Ethel Rosenberg, under a headline announcing their execution. The article mentioned that they left two young sons behind. The paper didn't mention Robert and Michael Rosenberg's birthdays, but Berg knew them—they were written on a page at the back of his address book, along with those of his own brothers and sister.

It is hard to overestimate the effect the killing had on Berg, tingeing his intellectual rejection of capitalism with grief, outrage, and sorrow. For the first time in his life, Berg sank into despondency. Like many others who had been closely connected with the Rosenbergs, he felt a deep sense of guilt. Berg and Staros were alive and safe, while their comrades had made the highest sacrifice with such dignity, and so senselessly, that even hardened FBI agents felt regret and anger. For the rest of his life, Berg was convinced that he should and could have done something to save the Rosenbergs. If he'd stayed he would at least have hired a better lawyer, Berg said.[63]

The Soviets orchestrated public outrage over the Rosenberg case into a tremendous propaganda weapon, mobilizing millions of people worldwide to demonstrate against the execution, persuading world leaders to plead for clemency, and convincing a generation of American liberals that the U.S. government had intentionally murdered two innocent people. The case came at a convenient time for the Soviet Union, distracting attention from the execution of Slansky and allowing the Russians to hold a mirror to American accusations of anti-Semitism.

Although the senior leadership and many in the KGB knew the Rosenbergs were guilty, their angry response was not entirely cynical. There was a genuine sense of outrage and shock at the execution of agents whose activities, though important, were minor compared with those of others, such as the atom spies Theodore Hall, who was never prosecuted, and Klaus Fuchs, who received a jail sentence and was ultimately released in a prisoner exchange. The extraordinary treatment accorded Berg and Staros by the Soviet government may have been motivated at least in part by guilt over the Rosenbergs' execution.[64]

One of Julius Rosenberg's case officers, Alexander Feklisov, expressed regret about their fate for the rest of his life, writing to Berg when they were both in their eighties suggesting that they cooperate to rehabilitate the reputations of their old comrades. Even the hard-hearted master spy Kim Philby, who expressed no remorse that his betrayals caused the deaths of many British and American agents, felt guilty that he had failed to take any steps to save the Rosenbergs. Philby and other members of the Soviet intelligence establishment were struck by the fact that others who were far more culpable either confessed or escaped to Moscow, while the Rosenbergs stoically made the ultimate sacrifice.[65]

Berg knew that, had he remained in the United States, he would probably have suffered the Rosenbergs' fate or, at a minimum, been sentenced like Sobell to spend the most productive years of his life alone in a cell on Alcatraz Island. The pain of his loss, and of the certainty that he'd never be able to return, was tempered by appreciation toward the Soviet Union. Perhaps because he felt this sense of gratitude, and was blinded by outrage at the United States for killing the Rosenbergs, Berg never fully recognized the evils of the Soviet Union. Even when he learned about Stalin's crimes, Berg remembered that the man who in those years embodied the Soviet Union had saved him from the electric chair, and that America had killed and imprisoned his close friends. The injustices that were too obvious to ignore, such as anti-Semitism, corruption, and suppression of expression, Berg attributed to the character flaws of individuals in power and the rough, rapid transformation of Russia into an industrialized country, not to the Soviet system.

Stalin's death and the execution on December 23, 1953, of his secret police chief, Lavrenty Pavlovich Beria, gradually slowed the pace of the downward spiral of terror in Soviet-dominated countries. The train of terror didn't brake immediately and never halted completely, however. The inertia created by years of denunciations and torture-induced confessions of fantastic crimes kept it going at a rapid pace for months, and habitual paranoia, manifested in the denunciation of co-workers and even family members, corroded "socialist" life for generations.

Unlike most foreigners who visited or lived in Czechoslovakia during the Communist regime, Berg and Staros were not followed by the StB department that was responsible for keeping tabs on the numerous political émigrés who moved to Prague in the 1950s. They avoided attracting the attention of the StB's counterintelligence corps until July 1953, when the secret police received a report from VTU employees about suspicious foreigners. Records in the Czech Republic's Ministry of Interior Archives shed some light on these investigations, illuminate the partners' relationships with colleagues, and hint at the shadowy role of the KGB in quashing the investigations.

Soon after arriving at the VTU, Staros was put in charge of a thirty-person group and Berg was appointed as his deputy. Before their arrival, the team had puttered away, making little progress on designing a practical antiaircraft computer. Part of the problem, Staros and Berg decided, was the "socialist" work environment, in which individuals were discouraged from taking initiative, there were few incentives to take risks, and it was impossible to assign responsibility for failure to any individual. In September 1952 Staros, who had a burning desire to prove himself, decided to shake things up. According to a complaint filed with the StB by his own employees, one day he summoned all the members of the team individually to his office and assigned each specific tasks and deadlines. Staros "required that everyone work on their own problems by themselves and come to him if they didn't understand something. He made it clear that he would not put up with colleagues helping each other, and forbade us to speak among ourselves about our tasks. He insisted on taking a strict stand against those who did not follow his orders." When one of the engineers said that Staros's management techniques clashed with "socialist collective cooperation," Staros "laughed cynically" and said he had Goldschmied's full support.[66]

Staros and Berg were certain that their success in Czechoslovakia and subsequent achievements in the Soviet Union were the result of their insistence on individual responsibility and their policy of recruiting and promoting personnel solely on the basis of merit — policies that went against the grain in Soviet-dominated economies. While his employees were confident that Staros's insistence on compartmentalizing their assignments was a security measure intended to prevent any individual from knowing how the device they were building worked, it is likely that he was actually trying to instill discipline and to counteract pessimism.[67]

Suppressing collaboration among employees wasn't the only way the two foreigners aroused the enmity and suspicion of their employees. They "displayed tremendous curiosity about our national industrial production and planned production for the future, especially about electronics," a member of their team reported to the StB. Although at work they usually spoke to each other in Czech, sometimes they were overheard speaking in English, a habit that, given the Communist regime's xenophobic propaganda, was bound to arouse distrust. The men and women who reported to Staros noted his technical expertise, but they were more impressed by his confident demeanor and insistence on using Western management techniques.

Most of the anonymous reports to the StB about Berg and Staros were negative, but some portrayed them in a favorable light. One informant noted approvingly that in November 1952 Staros donated 300 crowns to a fund for soldiers fighting in North Korea and that he had tears in his eyes when he expressed solidarity with Korea's war against the capitalist nations. Staros had no way of knowing that his own brother, Richard, was serving in Korea in a U.S. Army airborne unit.[68]

The Korean war, perceived behind the Iron Curtain as a warm-up for the inevitable American invasion of Eastern Europe and the USSR, added to the spy mania that was rife in Prague and every other Communist-bloc capital. The United States fueled the paranoia, infiltrating agents by air, sea, and land into the Soviet Union, Czechoslovakia, and other Communist countries — men who were invariably exposed in advance by KGB moles in U.S. and British intelligence and rapidly executed. In Czechoslovakia, the fear of traitors was stimulated by émigré provocateurs broadcasting over Radio Free Europe who attributed industrial accidents and train wrecks to a mythical fifth column of anticommunist partisans.

The constant threat of denunciation, humiliation, loss of employment, and even arrest and torture created intolerable tensions. One way of relieving the pressure and deflecting attention was to file reports on actual, exaggerated, or completely fictitious lapses from Communist orthodoxy by neighbors, friends, and colleagues. Sometimes these reports had tragic consequences. An StB report on Berg noted in passing that a VTU employee had reported seeing Goldschmied leaving the Swiss embassy in Prague in October 1952. A few days later, when Berg and Staros were on a business trip to Pilzen, Goldschmied jumped out of a window. The suicide came at the start of a campaign to drive ethnic Jews, even dedicated Communists with no religious convictions, out of positions of authority throughout Czechoslovakia.[69]

In the summer of 1953, several of Berg's colleagues at the VTU sent gossip about the two suspicious foreigners to the StB's department for internal political reporting, Section 312. The reports were unsigned, but the StB knew who had sent them. In internal StB memoranda attributing the reports to anonymous informants, the word "anonymous" was in quotation marks, and the informants, engineers who worked with Berg on the antiaircraft project, were identified. Although the reports were vague and innocuous, an StB officer named Burda took an interest in the case. Burda felt he'd hit pay dirt when he learned that Berg and Staros had obtained their jobs at the VTU on Slansky's personal orders. He referred the case to the Communist Party Central Committee, which was energetically rooting out and persecuting "Slanskyists." In the ordinary course of events, anyone tainted by association with Slansky in 1953 would at a minimum have been fired and barred from employment in a sensitive position.[70]

Three VTU engineers told the StB that they were "suspicious about [Staros's] confidence in making decisions and in dealing with other workers, and thus we suppose he is supported by high-ranked individuals. He also tried to get a position from which he could better monitor the antiaircraft defense program." The July 1953 report obliquely referred to Staros's frank discussion of the growing disillusionment among ordinary Czechs with plunging living standards, the decline in industrial production, and massive strikes in East Germany. "Staros is always interested in public opinion and tries to find out more about political ideas of the population. Lately he is focused on personnel turnover and personnel absences in other factories, financial reform, and the recent events in Germany," the informants stated.[71]

In every Czech workplace, management regularly convened "twenty-minute meetings," which often lasted much longer and were ostensibly open discussions but in practice served as forums for dissemination of the latest party line. Staros frequently told his employees that there was freedom of expression at the VTU, encouraged them to speak freely at the meetings, and was openly irritated when none of them was foolish enough to do so. Staros's comments about the Czechoslovakian constitution's guarantee of freedom of expression notwithstanding, all the Czechs knew that their conversations were reported to the secret police — at least three of the two dozen or so engineers who attended the sessions were themselves informers.

On several occasions, Staros and Berg spoke critically about a wildly unpopular currency reform that effectively wiped out all personal savings. As part of a Soviet-ordered campaign to eliminate inflation, without warning the Czech government overnight introduced a new pricing system, replaced the first 300 crowns in personal bank accounts with 60 crowns, divided any remaining funds by 50, and reduced salaries to a fifth of their previous levels. On June 1, 1953, a day after the reforms were announced, workers at an armaments factory in Pilzen rioted, sabotaging factory machinery and looting a government office. Although troops quickly suppressed the uprising, news of the events in Pilzen, including the fact that the protesters had carried British and American flags, spread quickly, and smaller demonstrations were held in other Czech cities. The military and armed Communist militias clamped down hard on the disgruntled workers, preventing demonstrations in Prague that the authorities feared could have spiraled out of control.

The VTU "anonymous" informants reported to the StB in July 1953 that Berg had criticized the currency reform in a twenty-minute meeting and, when he was unable to convince anyone to discuss the subject, spoke about recent strikes in Pilzen and Koblenz, as well as in Stalingrad. Staros "entered the discussion and said people must not be afraid to discuss this reform and put forth their opinion, because our institute guarantees freedom of expression," the StB was later informed. The Czech engineers greeted Staros's comments with frosty silence, the "anonymous" report on the meeting noted. They were, no doubt, acutely conscious that the ears of the StB were particularly tuned for discussions about such sensitive topics.[72]

Apparently Berg and Staros were completely oblivious of the suspicions of their colleagues. In late 1953 they wrote to the Czech deputy minister of defense proposing the creation of a new central antiaircraft defense research institute. The clear implication was that it should be headed by Staros and Berg. There was no response, and the foreigners, already socially isolated, began to feel that they would never realize their ambitions in Prague. Their frustration was particularly acute because it came just as they began to realize that electronics technology was at an inflexion point and they were in the running to be its pioneers.[73]

Through a close reading of American technical journals and remarkable intuition, starting in 1953 Staros and Berg became convinced that the future of electronics, and more broadly of technical progress in a wide range of endeavors, centered on the emerging field of microelectronics. They envisioned the transistor, which was invented in 1948, replacing vacuum tubes and ushering in a new era in which computers and communication equipment would be digital, compact, reliable, and ubiquitous. They briefed senior officials in Prague about these ideas and requested resources to conduct research, promising to make Czechoslovakia a world leader in technology, but were rebuffed by bureaucrats who had neither the financial resources nor the imagination to embark on expensive, highly speculative research projects. Their thinking was way ahead of the scientific and technical establishments in Czechoslovakia and the USSR — and of most of their former colleagues in the United States.

Staros and Berg also wrote in late 1953 to Nikita Khrushchev. They described their conviction that the invention of the transistor heralded the emergence of an entirely new field that would be the basis for a wide range of military and civilian technologies in the near future. The socialist countries had an opportunity to develop semiconductor technology ahead of the West. Frustrated by the lack of resources and interest in Czechoslovakia, Staros and Berg asked permission to come to the Soviet Union to pursue electronics R&D.[74]

While Staros and Berg didn't mention their intention to move to the Soviet Union, they also didn't hide their admiration for the USSR. "Joseph Berg said in front of Staros and [one of the informants] that our equipment which was finished in 1952 is outmoded and that both of them know how to and wish to work on new, better projects. Staros lately has been studying Russian very hard, and he seems to have a talent. We have the impression that he would like to go to the Soviet Union in the future as a scientist," their employees told the secret police.[75]

Meanwhile, in the winter of 1953 Burda pressed his superiors to take some action against Berg and Staros. Instead of giving him permission to arrest the foreigners, the chief of Section 312 told Burda to drop the case because it had been transferred to the Ministry of Interior's foreign political espionage group. Burda, however, was tenacious, and in 1954 he sent a request for an update on the investigation. The department replied that it had no information about Berg or Staros; it had never received a request to investigate them. Apparently, the claim that the case had been turned over to the foreign political espionage group was a ruse, intended to derail Burda's investigation. A separate investigation by military counterintelligence officers, acting independently of the StB and the Ministry of Interior, on suspicions that Berg and Staros were spying for foreign powers was also abruptly aborted.[76]

The attempt to throw him off the case apparently intrigued Burda, and he resumed the investigation. In March 1954, StB officers approached the VTU management directly, indicating that they were investigating Staros and Berg as possible "evildoers." The investigation was halted again, however, in May, by a memorandum signed by Minister of the Interior Rudolf Barak and by Slansky's successor as first secretary of the Central Committee of the Communist Party, Antonin Novotny, which stated that Berg and Staros were trustworthy and should be given clearance to conduct defense research. Given the sensitivity of the antiaircraft project and widespread paranoia about foreign spies, Barak and Novotny would not have interceded without instructions from Moscow.

A summary of the investigation, filed along with all the StB files on Staros and Berg in a section of the archives that was accessible during the Communist regime only with specific permission from the interior minister, mentions Berg's contact with Prchal and bears a handwritten notation indicating that Minister of Defense Alexej Cepicka had reviewed the case, as well as Berg's connection with "friends," a euphemism for Soviet advisors to the Czech government. None of the files even hints at Berg's or Staros's real identity, their connection with the Rosenbergs, or their American origins.[77]

By the time the StB investigations wrapped up, Berg and Staros had finished building the potentiometer winding machine, an elegant piece of equipment, and were making rapid progress on the analog computer. In mid-1955, a prototype of the computer-controlled antiaircraft battery, the first in the Soviet bloc capable of aiming missiles in real time against jet aircraft, was tested by the Czechoslovakian Army. The test was successful, prompting the Czechoslovakian government to award prizes to Staros and Berg in recognition of their achievements. The technology they developed formed the core of Czechoslovakia's antiaircraft defenses at least until the early 1990s, Czech scientists told Berg.[78]

In digital computers, the quality of the components determines the reliability, and perhaps the speed, of the equipment, but it rarely has an impact on the accuracy of the results. The precision of an analog computer, however, is directly related to the quality of the elements it is constructed from. Staros and Berg's computer was capable of shooting down airplanes because they designed it correctly, but also because they designed and controlled the components and procedures for manufacturing them.

The technical success that Staros and Berg achieved in creating the Soviet bloc's first automated antiaircraft weapon brought them recognition within the Soviet defense establishment. It demonstrated—to others and to themselves—that the two Americans, who had never before been entrusted with responsibility for anything of consequence, could creatively overcome technical and political impediments and could manage scientific and technical employees. It created a hunger for bigger achievements and fueled their conviction that Czechoslovakia was too small to support their ambitions.

In 1955, their credibility enhanced by successful completion of the antiaircraft project, Staros and Berg reiterated requests to be given facilities in the Soviet Union where their ideas could be tested. In the summer of 1955, Feklisov, who had been posted as one of Russia's "liaisons" to the StB, was ordered to meet with Berg and Staros. "I invited my former agents to a good restaurant [in Prague]. Barr came alone but Carol accompanied Sarant. It was the first time I was meeting the latter because in New York all his work came to me through Barr," Feklisov recalled almost a half-century later.

Although Feklisov's personal connection was with Barr, Staros did most of the talking, asserting himself as the senior partner. Both were gloomy to start with, and their moods weren't improved by Feklisov's toast to Julius and Ethel Rosenberg. They told Feklisov that they "liked their lives in Prague and had no material problems; their Czech colleagues were friendly but they felt professionally stifled. The objectives they had set for themselves—which they could reasonably achieve—were very promising but far beyond the capabilities of Czechoslovakia as a country. They wanted to build compact computers for military purposes but only the Soviet Union could provide the necessary funds to make headway in this area. Barr and Sarant wanted to work in the USSR." It was Feklisov's last meeting with Barr, although they were to correspond under very different circumstances many years later.[79]

Soon after the meeting with Feklisov, Staros and Berg were again contacted by representatives of the Soviet military-industrial establishment and offered positions in Russia. The head of the GKAT (State Committee on Aviation

Technology), Pyotr V. Dementyev, came to Prague to recruit them. Dementyev had a great ability for spotting talent and the authority to set up his protégés with autonomy. He championed the careers of men who became general designers — an elite status, comparable to chief operating officer and senior scientist combined at an American defense contractor — of the Sukhoi Design Bureau, which developed some of the USSR's most important fighter aircraft, and of the Kamov Design Bureau, which created many of its military and civilian helicopters.[80]

After Dementyev recruited the Americans, they in turn tried to convince a compatriot to join them in Russia. One day in late 1955, Staros and Berg arrived at Svoboda's computer institute to meet one of his Ph.D. students, an American named Morton Nadler. Like Berg, Nadler was a City College alumnus, a former member of the Young Communist League and the CPUSA, but he had graduated three years later than Berg, and their paths hadn't crossed in New York. When they met in Prague, Nadler had no idea that Berg had attended City College, or even that he was an American. "He was introduced as a South African, and I believed it," Nadler remembered. Nadler had the strong impression that both Berg and Staros, who introduced himself as a Canadian, were much better connected than he and other Communist expatriates in Prague. Staros and Berg had an easy manner, a sense of confidence that Nadler and the other Americans he knew at the time lacked. Nadler was afraid of being branded an enemy of the people or an American spy, and of a late-night knock on the door.[81]

He and Berg were going to Leningrad, where the Soviets would provide far better resources than were available in Czechoslovakia, Staros said. Nadler was tempted by their offer to work in Russia. He couldn't make up his mind on the spot, but he asked Staros to stay in touch. Maybe, he said, he would join them in Leningrad.[82]

Berg summed up his accomplishments in Czechoslovakia in a 1994 letter offering his services to the Chinese government:

> When we arrived in Czechoslovakia, we explained that we were electronic engineers and wanted to use our skills to help the building of socialism. We had had some experience in the new field of analog computers and so we made a proposal to try to design and build an electronic antiaircraft guidance analog computer for the defense of the Czechoslovakian Socialist Republic.
>
> This proposal was accepted, and we were given a small electronics laboratory with about 30 people. Due to the lack of an electronic analog computer component base in Czechoslovakia at that time, it was necessary to develop many of the required components. Chief among these were precision linear and functional potentiometers. In order to manufacture the high precision

potentiometers which were the heart of the computer, we designed and built an original programmed automatic potentiometer-winding machine.

The analog computer was built and tested and accepted by the Czechoslovakian government in 1955, and with some modifications is basically still part of the Czech air defense system today.

At this time the transistor had appeared, and we understood that the future of computers was to be digital using semiconductors as the active element. We therefore made a proposal to the Czechs to start a program for building semiconductor digital computers. Since this program would have required a very great financial support, which the Czechs were unable to do at that time, we wrote to the Soviet government. Our proposal to help organize a new industry in the Soviet Union, microelectronics, was accepted.[83]

In early January 1956, Berg and Staros left secretly for Russia, without informing colleagues at the VTU. They told Vera and Anna that the trip was temporary, that they would soon be returning to Prague, although they never had any intention to do so.

Special Laboratory 11, 1956–1962

The Soviet microelectronics industry was founded in the late 1950s in the unfinished attic of an old four-story gray-brick building on Volkovskaya Street in Leningrad, much as Silicon Valley was born in garages and store-fronts adjacent to the orange groves that stretched from Palo Alto to San Jose. Like innumerable high-tech startups that sprouted under the California sun, Special Laboratory Number 11 (SL-11) was staffed by eager young engineers voluntarily working long hours, fueled by caffeine, tobacco, and excitement over being present at the birth of a new era in technology.[1]

SL-11 also resembled the Skunk Works, a secret organization within Lockheed that designed the U-2 spy plane. Both were heavily guarded and closely connected to air force and intelligence organizations, and each succeeded because its leadership thought and acted outside the bureaucratic box.

The engineers in the Volkovskaya Street attic worked for two mysterious foreigners. Officially the bosses were Czechs, and although their accents and even more their mannerisms betrayed origins that weren't Slavic, none of the employees enquired about their true antecedents. Anyone smart enough to be hired by an organization like SL-11 was also sufficiently astute to know that prying into areas beyond their "need to know" could have unpleasant consequences. Moreover, it was obvious to anyone who had grown up in Stalinist Russia that two foreigners in charge of a secret high-technology R&D operation must have been cleared by the highest levels of the KGB. Even very senior government officials were too cautious to ask the "Czechs" about their backgrounds. The SL-11 employees addressed their bosses as Philip Georgeivich and Joseph Venyaminovich (in Russian, their names were Filipp Georgeivich Staros and Iosif Venjaminovich Berg, often abbreviated as F. G. Staros and I. V. Berg), using the patronymics that are an essential element of the polite form of address in Russian.

In addition to middle names, soon after they arrived in Leningrad Staros and Berg were given titles: chief designer and chief engineer, respectively, of SL-11. From the start, they aspired to reach the top ranks of Soviet industry. Their first step in charting that route was to understand clearly their starting place in the politico-industrial hierarchy.

SL-11 was formally a unit of the Experimental Design Bureau, P.O. Box 998 (OKB-998), which was part of a vast galaxy of secret, primarily military-oriented research facilities. These installations had no official names other than the number of the post office boxes where they received mail. Mailbox organizations, or *yashchiki*, were not listed in any telephone directory, and it was forbidden to write their physical location on correspondence. In order to work at a *yashchik*, a potential employee had to pass a KGB background investigation; those with questionable political credentials were excluded. Mailbox employees were not allowed to meet foreigners without prior approval, and any contacts with a foreigner (other than with one who was working for the mailbox) had to be reported in writing to the "first department" (*pervyi otdel*), the KGB-staffed security department attached to all Soviet enterprises.[2]

While they were organizing their own laboratory, the new arrivals were treated as employees of OKB-998, part of the GKAT (State Committee on Aviation Technology). Later OKB-998 provided security for SL-11 and acted as an interface with the Soviet bureaucracy for functions such as accounting, and purchasing.

The Americans quickly found the daily routines and rhythms of life in a Soviet enterprise shocking. "Our first contacts with Soviet political and social life showed us that it was in some respects completely different from American life," Berg recalled.

> Now, in American political life there was a very sharp demarcation between your work and your politics. You can work in a firm that is owned by Republicans or Democrats and never even know it. I'd never been subjected in America to propaganda from the higher-ups, although I know there are cases when the owners are very politically minded and try to get workers to vote in a certain way, but this is very rare. And to talk about [political] meetings

during working hours, I never remember a meeting during working hours in America. And this is one of the first things we came across.

Practically the first week, we were called in for a political meeting where we were lectured and then there was some kind of a vote. This was not a party meeting; this was a meeting of the workers of the plant where we were working. And what did I notice? For me it was amazing. I was trying my best to understand what the lecturer was saying. It was a politically oriented speech where he was showing the tremendous advantages of the socialist society in some respect, I don't remember what. And we had to vote for who was going to be our representative. I think it was in the union. All organizations in the Soviet Union were unionized, and you had to be members of a union. There were cases where people refused to pay their dues, but they were quickly shown the error of their ways.

At any rate, what astounded me was the indifference of the people to what the speaker was talking about. People absolutely were whispering and talking to one another, not paying any attention to what was being said. And when the voting came, who was for, who was against, and who abstained, well people just voted 100 percent for. And it took a long time for us to become inured to this. There were meetings of some sort at least once a week. You were called in during working hours, and if you were the head of some kind of a department you were asked to speak. On what topic it didn't matter. It could be to discuss some problem we had, like why was the plan not being fulfilled. Many of these meetings turned out to be criticisms of people who were not fulfilling the plan.[3]

While they were mapping out the terrain of the Soviet military-industrial complex, Staros and Berg were also finding places for themselves and their families in Russian daily life. At first each family was assigned a hotel room, where they stayed for months because Joe was trying to maintain the fiction to Vera that the visit to Russia was temporary. Eventually the families moved into apartments on the same floor of a prestigious building constructed in the weddingcake style favored by Stalin on Kuznetskaya Street, in central Leningrad. At a time when a tremendous housing shortage forced millions of Russians to crowd into communal apartments, squabbling endlessly over access to bathrooms and kitchens, and raising families with no privacy, many Russians would have been ecstatic at the prospect of a private apartment of any size. While the accommodations — two rooms plus kitchen and bath for the Bergs, an extra room for the larger Staros family — were luxurious by contemporary Soviet standards, to someone coming from the United States or Czechoslovakia, the conditions were barely tolerable, and they were especially difficult for Anna Staros.

Anna had three children in Prague and was pregnant with her fourth child when the family moved into the building on Kuznetskaya Street. A driver came for Phil early in the morning five days a week, leaving Anna to care for Kolya, Kristina, Mila, and, after a few months, the newborn Tonya. Her life was physically and psychologically harsh. Taking care of four children in a small apartment would be difficult in the United States, but it was far more challenging in Russia, especially for someone who was used to Western conveniences. She had to queue in the cold for potatoes "that weren't fit for pigs," Anna told her children later. The logistics of keeping herself, the children, and Phil fed and clothed in an alien environment were nearly overwhelming.[4]

The heavy workload didn't give Anna time to learn Russian — even after forty years in the Soviet Union, she spoke the language poorly — so her sense of isolation was intense. To make matters worse, she desperately missed Derry and Eric, the daughter and son she had left behind in Ithaca. Throughout her life in Russia, they were never far from her thoughts. She treasured their pictures and marked their birthdays, dreaming that it would be possible someday to see them again. On top of everything else, she discovered that Phil was having affairs with Russian women. Disappointment, weariness, and helplessness turned the vivacious, assertive Carol Dayton who had left Ithaca on a romantic adventure into Anna Petrovna Staros, a withdrawn, passive, submissive woman.

Like Anna, Vera never felt at home in Russia, but her Czech background made it far easier to adjust to life in Leningrad, although she never lost her disdain for the country or for Communism. Czech and Russian are close cousins, so she learned the language quite easily. Growing up in a village, Vera had never experienced the conveniences that Anna took for granted. Vera's life in Leningrad was also easier than Anna's to start with because she had only one child, Vivian — born in Prague in 1954 and named after the girlfriend Joe had left behind in New York, Vivian Glassman. She caught up quickly, however, bearing three more children, Robert, Alena, and Anton, in quick succession. Joe, who was much more easygoing and family-oriented than Phil, always had time for the children, especially his first son, Robert. He made motorized toys for them and shot home movies of their birthdays. Vera had another advantage over Anna, a pressure-relief valve: she traveled frequently to Czechoslovakia to visit family and friends, and to relax in familiar surroundings.

The Soviet Union was a socialist country, but that fact didn't mean that money didn't matter. With the exception of items in short supply, which required connections as well as cash to acquire, just as in the capitalist world a family's lifestyle was determined to a great extent by the size of its budget. More rubles meant higher-quality food, a nanny, bribes to get better medical care or entrance to an elite university, and maybe a car. Unlike in the capitalist world, salaries were not considered private information in Soviet Russia. The size of a co-worker's pay packet could often be found listed on documents posted on a bulletin board in an office or factory hallway, perhaps on a recruitment or promotion announcement.

Staros's and Berg's salaries were breathtaking by Soviet standards. Each was making over 800 rubles a month, about eight times the salary of most engineers, and more than the 550 rubles the deputy minister of electronic industry earned. High salaries cushioned their families from the privations that most Soviet citizens endured—the Bergs ate grapefruits and bananas year-round, a tremendous luxury at the time in Russia—but by American or Soviet standards, they did not live lavishly. They never had access to the special stores stocked with imported foods or the spacious vacation *dachas* and other perquisites reserved for the elite. Although they were devoted Communists, Staros and Berg never got along well with the party bosses who controlled the subterranean distribution of scarce booty.[5]

Within six weeks, the leaders of SL-11 were settled into the Volkovskaya Street building and, bolstered by their fluency in Czech, had sufficient command of Russian to dismiss their translator. Staros had started learning Russian in the United States from phonograph records. In Leningrad he studied intensely, memorizing tables of irregular verbs and spending hours with dictionaries, absorbing vocabulary. Within a few years, he was so proficient that most Russians didn't realize they were speaking with a foreigner, and native Russians brought manuscripts and correspondence to him to correct their grammar and spelling.

If Staros's Russian was like a well-oiled machine, Berg's could be compared to an old secondhand car: it usually got him where he wanted to go, even if it broke down a few times on the way. Berg's peculiar accent was immediately evident, but very few Russians realized that it originated in the streets of Brooklyn. Russians tend to be highly attuned to ethnicity; it was immediately obvious to most of the people whom Berg encountered that, wherever he came from, his forebears were more familiar with the Talmud than with the New Testament.

By March 1956, SL-11's chief designer and his deputy were ready to start recruiting and hiring staff. They preferred bright people straight out of school who hadn't been ruined by sustained exposure to Soviet workplaces where fulfilling a plan was paramount, risk-taking was avoided whenever possible, and employees conspired with their peers against the hated "big pinecones," or bosses. The SL-11 leaders strived to keep the spark of innovation, which was extinguished by the rigid, conservative management prevalent in most Russian labs, alive in their young engineers. Seeking to attract top-level talent, they ignored the unspoken but universally understood rules regarding the employment of Jews.

At exactly the time when Staros and Berg started recruiting the first staff for SL-11, the first secretary of the Communist Party of the Soviet Union was candidly enlightening Polish Communist leaders about these rules. In remarks that weren't supposed to be made public, Khrushchev counseled a small group of Polish Communist leaders on March 20, 1956, to emulate the USSR's practice, which was to limit the proportion of Jews in high positions to their proportion of the Soviet population. "In the Soviet Union, we have two percent, which means that ministries, universities — everything — is made up of two percent Jews," he said to the scandalized Poles, adding: "I'm not an anti-Semite, indeed we have this minister who's a Jew; he's a good minister, [Benjamin] Dimschitz is his name, and we respect him, but you have to know the limits."[6]

Staros and Berg were informed and repeatedly reminded of these limits but intentionally defied them, not out of outrage over anti-Semitism or to make a moral statement, but rather out of a pragmatic desire to build a talented, loyal team. Other organizations, particularly mailboxes, hired as few Jews as possible, so the pool of highly qualified engineers and scientists available for SL-11 included a very high proportion of persons who were classified as Jews.[7] Recruiting solely on the basis of merit ensured that SL-11 and its successor organizations were packed with Jews. The ability to flout convention was an indication of the deference the party and KGB afforded SL-11, or, put another way, of the power of its backers. It also meant that Staros and Berg began accumulating enemies during their earliest days in Leningrad.[8]

Staros quickly grasped that the essence of success in the Soviet state, despite official rhetoric about scientific central planning, was forging close personal relationships. Accordingly, he constantly sought to bind himself to powerful individuals. Through Dementyev, the GKAT head, who had traveled to Prague to invite them to Leningrad, Staros and Berg became acquainted with Dmitri Fedorovich Ustinov, a consummate networker who rose to the top and dominated Soviet defense policy for decades.

Dementyev was one of a large group of defense industry managers who ran what amounted to a state within the state. This group was headed by Ustinov, a shadowy figure little known at the time in either Russia or the West, who was one of the most powerful and enduring political figures in Soviet history. His ascent to at the top of the defense industry started in 1941 when Stalin made him the head of the Ministry for Armaments, the position he held when Staros and Berg first met him, and ran all the way through the middle of Brezhnev's rule, Ustinov retired in 1976 as minister of defense. Throughout this period,

Ustinov retained the personal loyalty of a group of military industry administrators who, like Dementyev, created similar networks. The system was remarkably stable: men loyal to Ustinov headed the nine powerful ministries
that controlled the Soviet defense industry for a quarter-century.[9]

In 1957 Ustinov created and became the first chairman of the VPK (Military-
Industrial Commission). A secretive organization virtually unknown outside
the Kremlin and the leadership of the largest military contractors, the VPK
wielded enormous power through its control of the defense industry. As the
body responsible for coordinating all military R&D and production, the VPK
had the highest priority in terms of the allocation of resources and manpower. It
was unusual for the leaders of a small lab like SL-11 to even know of the
existence of the VPK, and extraordinary that they were well acquainted with its
chairman. Their association with Ustinov and his "mafia" was to be crucial to
Staros and Berg's success.[10]

During their careers in the Soviet Union, Staros and Berg served each branch
of the armed forces, but none of the organizations they worked in was under
direct military control. Rather, they aggressively solicited military orders because defense projects were the best funded and had first call on scarce resources. Staros spent a great deal of time lecturing generals and admirals about
technology, promoting the potential applications of microelectronics for
weaponry, in an effort that was analogous to an American arms manufacturer's or military contractor's sales presentations.[11]

SL-11 was created to realize Staros and Berg's dream of leapfrogging the
West by developing a Soviet microelectronics industry. Its first assignment,
however, was an extension of the work on analog computing they had performed in Prague. They were asked by the GKAT to design miniature helical
potentiometers, or "helipots," as well as the equipment to manufacture them.

Invented in the United States by Arnold O. Beckman in 1940 and rugged-
ized for military applications in 1942, the helipot was far more reliable and
precise than conventional potentiometers. Helipots were an essential component of the radar systems developed during World War II, and are still used in a
myriad of applications ranging from the electromechanical systems controlling the flaps on aircraft to electronic games. Berg and Staros were familiar
with helipots, but they had had no exposure in the United States to techniques
for manufacturing them. SL-11's success in this instance, as in all its later
endeavors, stands on its own and cannot be directly attributed to information
its leaders appropriated from their American employers.[12]

The helipot contract was awarded to SL-11 on the orders of Vice Admiral
Aksel Berg, the deputy minister of defense who was responsible for radar. The
two Bergs shared more than a last name. During World War II Aksel Berg had

been deputy chairman of the Council on Radiolocation, a position that gave him access to a steady stream of valuable intelligence on American radar, electronics, and computing, including materials obtained from Western Electric by the Rosenberg ring. Detailed information about American R&D helped Admiral Berg take Soviet radar from zero in 1940 to a level in 1956 that was equal to or better than any produced in the United States.[13]

When the two Bergs and Staros met for the first time, the USSR's output of electronics equipment was second only to that of the United States. Although quantitatively the level of Soviet electronics production approached the Americans', it was, according to a then secret CIA report, grossly imbalanced: fully 40 percent of Soviet electronics production was oriented toward radar, a much higher proportion than in the United States, where the civilian sector dominated.[14]

Much of the Russian radar bore a striking resemblance to American technology, particularly the radar sets commissioned by the Army Signal Corps and manufactured at Western Electric. In 1949, the USSR started mass-producing replicas of the SCR-584 radar system, the V-1 killer for which Berg had provided Feklisov detailed manufacturing specifications. At that time, Russian plants also started cloning the AN/APQ-13, a close cousin of the AN/APQ-7, about which a KGB cable from New York to Moscow stated Staros had "handed over 17 authentic drawings."[15]

During the war, Admiral Berg would have had no reason to know the identities of the agents who risked their lives to pilfer the information that landed on his desk, and the KGB would certainly not have identified its agents to him. It is very likely, however, that when Admiral Berg met Joseph Berg and Philip Staros in 1956, he knew he was speaking with the men who a dozen years earlier had raided Western Electric's filing cabinets to provide the KGB with the reports he had found so useful in developing the USSR's radar capabilities. In later years, Admiral Berg sometimes jokingly told Joe's associates that he was the only "real" Berg, though he didn't explain what he meant.[16]

It must have been an extraordinary meeting, a rare chance for Admiral Berg to match faces and personalities to the anonymous reports that had reached him during the war, and for Berg and Staros to discuss the fruits of their exploits. Quite apart from old war stories, the three engineers had a lot to talk about. Admiral Berg had been put in charge of defending the Soviet Union from air attack. As part of this commission, he was responsible for military computing, as well as radar. Berg brought the two disciplines together while directing the development and construction of the Moscow air defense system, which was started during Stalin's rule and completed in 1958.[17] Already a well-respected scientist and military leader when the SL-11 leaders met him,

Berg went on to become one of the country's most prominent scientists, heading the Cybernetics Council of the USSR Academy of Sciences and developing critical components of the Soviet Union's most powerful intercontinental ballistic missile, the R-36.[18]

The recently arrived "Czech" engineers also met with one of Admiral Berg's protégés, Anatoly Kitov. Three years earlier, Berg had assigned Kitov the task of preparing a report on Western computing that prompted the Ministry of Defense to dramatically increase its investment in cybernetics and computing. When he met Staros and Berg, Kitov was head of the Defense Ministry's computer center and the author of the first Russian computer textbook.[19]

Soon after SL-11 was up and running, Staros wrote to Morton Nadler, the CCNY engineer he and Berg had met in Prague, offering him a job. Staros "boasted about the lab the Soviets gave them," indicating that the facilities were far superior to those in Prague, Nadler remembered. "He wrote me that they could get any parts, any journals from the West they need, that they had an unlimited hard currency budget. When I wrote back asking what I'd be working on, the answer was 'an eye in the sky.' At the time, the phrase didn't mean anything to me, but in hindsight, I realize it must have been the Sputnik." The helipots created by SL-11 were probably critical components of the radar that was used to track the Sputnik. It is possible that the lab played other, more direct roles in the program that allowed the Soviet Union to launch the world's first artificial satellite into orbit on October 4, 1957.[20]

The potentiometer program established SL-11's reputation as an organization that could actually deliver the goods, a feature that endeared it to men like Ustinov who were struggling to find ways of squeezing results from hidebound military contractors. It also laid the foundation for the loyalty, almost awe, that Staros and Berg inspired in their employees. "When I was a young kid, a year or so after joining SL-11, I was dealing with our mechanics who told me about our bosses," Henry Eric Firdman, an engineer who went on to become a senior manager at the laboratory, recalled. "Russian mechanics, who by definition are drunkards, are also known for having 'golden hands.' This is the Russian tradition, going back to the nineteenth century, when Nikolai Leskov wrote about a smith who put horseshoes on a tiny mechanical flea." Discussing SL-11's early work on helipots and subsequent projects, the mechanics "told me they were stunned by what Joe could do himself, with any tool, any lathe. They were absolutely stunned that these two guys who ran the lab could come to the prototype lab and they could say 'step aside' and they would do something with their own hands better than the highest-class mechanics in the Soviet Union."[21]

Especially during their first years in Leningrad, Berg did a great deal of hands-on work. Staros articulated the big ideas, sold them to higher authorities, and organized the lab. Typically, when a technical roadblock prevented the work from moving forward, Joe would disappear and reappear a week or so later with a solution. For example, when the first iteration of the miniature helipots wore out too quickly, Berg developed an alloy that extended their life span severalfold.[22]

For Russians, the sight of a chief engineer or a chief designer rolling up his sleeves and soldering a circuit or showing a technician how to use a machine tool was without precedent. It was impossible to imagine Igor Kurchatov, the genius behind the Soviet atom bomb, or the aircraft designer Andrei Tupolev doing anything with his hands except signing orders. These men were imperious rulers who terrified their subordinates, not hands-on inventors.

The Americans who had worked with Berg, and especially with Staros, at Western Electric would also have been astonished, but for a very different reason. Their skills with lathes and soldering irons wouldn't have been surprising, but it would have been impossible to predict that two men who had never had any significant management responsibility could organize highly complex projects, lead large groups, and navigate the treacherous Soviet bureaucracy. Staros started on the bottom step at Western Electric and Bell Labs and never climbed more than one or two higher; there was no evidence of a latent talent for management. In Russia, however, he was widely admired by his employees and by top government officials as a highly skilled manager. He also inspired fierce loyalty in his employees, who viewed him as a mentor and role model.[23]

Their love of engineering as a discipline, of seeing ideas elegantly transformed into practical objects, also set SL-11's leaders apart from the mainstream of Soviet tradition. "The Soviet Union was a society that valued scientists very highly, but didn't respect engineers. Engineering and technology were always second-class citizens, and that's why the Soviet Union was full of invention, full of great ideas, and nothing was implemented. For that reason, whatever Staros and Berg did in the Soviet Union was like a miracle, because we'd never seen that level of engineering and technology," Firdman recalled.

The Soviet Union acknowledged important accomplishments by awarding orders (medals) to individuals or occasionally to small groups who had collectively accomplished something of particular merit. In a country where there were scarcely any avenues for an individual to achieve recognition — the state-controlled media created few celebrities — the receipt of an award was a matter of great pride. On February 26, 1958, Staros and Berg were awarded the Order of the Red Banner, one of the Soviet Union's most prestigious medals.

The commendation accompanying the order bore the stamp of the Presidium of the Supreme Soviet and the signature of Mikhail Georgadze, the longtime secretary of the Presidium. As was often the case when orders were issued to members of secret organizations, there was no indication of why it had been awarded, and it was a mystery to the employees of SL-11, who felt that their accomplishments up to that time had not been sufficient to justify it.

The Red Banner was probably recognition of Staros and Berg's wartime espionage exploits. There was some precedent for giving foreign KGB agents the Red Banner. Kim Philby, one of the KGB's most effective spies ever, and George Blake, a British KGB agent whom the Soviets had managed to spring from an English high-security prison, were the most famous Western KGB agents to receive it. Other foreign KGB operatives given the order included John Cairncross and the American brothers Morris and Jack Childs, as well as Lona Cohen, who had been tapped by the KGB to serve as a cutout between Feklisov and Rosenberg, and her husband, Morris Cohen.[24]

The year they were honored with the Red Banner awards, Staros and Berg started three routines that they maintained for over a decade. First, they returned home to their wives for lunch and a catnap almost every day. Second, Tuesday afternoons were set aside for an extended session at the library of the Academy of Sciences in central Leningrad, where they took advantage of the right, denied to the vast majority of people living in Russia, to read foreign publications without restriction. They devoured technical journals in electronics, engineering, physics, and related fields, as well as the *New York Times, Time,* and *Popular Mechanics.* There were no copying facilities, so they had to take notes on anything of particular interest.

SL-11 also subscribed to a number of foreign journals, and Staros had a firm rule that no one could meet with him to discuss a technical topic unless he had already researched how the Americans were approaching the issue. Ironically, while SL-11's engineers were aware of the latest developments abroad, the high level of domestic secrecy prevented them from discovering what was happening at, or learning from the experiences of, other Soviet closed facilities. Staros and Berg were more familiar with the activities of computer designers in Armonk, New York, and of chip developers in San Jose, California, than with similar work that was being conducted in Moscow and Kiev.

Staros and Berg's third routine was a Thursday-night dinner at the Hotel Evropeyskaya, a palatial nineteenth-century building with a baroque exterior and plush art nouveau interiors, located in the center of town, on Nevsky Prospekt, Leningrad's version of New York's Fifth Avenue. The Evropeyskaya was one of the few places in the city that was dedicated exclusively to foreigners. Burly guards at the entrance ensured that ordinary Russians stayed out. The Thursday-night dinners were one of the few venues where the two old friends could speak English with each other in public. Anna Staros sometimes joined them, and at one of these dinners in the late 1950s they engaged some American tourists at a nearby table in conversation. The next day, one of the KGB security officers assigned to SL-11 warned Staros and Berg not to contact foreigners again. The weekly dinners at the Evropeyskaya continued, but the diners were more circumspect about whom they spoke with.[25]

Like many Russians, Berg and Staros assumed they were under KGB surveillance, as undoubtedly they were. Whenever someone interrupted a telephone conversation with Berg by saying that a certain topic wasn't suitable for discussion on the telephone, a commonly used signal that it would be better to discuss the subject in a venue less likely to be monitored by the KGB, Berg would shout loudly into the receiver: "Joseph Venyaminovich Berg has no secrets! I demand that you tell me whatever you want to say immediately."[26]

Not only were they unfazed by the lack of privacy, but also they managed to charm, if not win over, some of their minders. Berg's driver was a typical specimen of *homo KGB,* a bear of a man, easily as wide as an American refrigerator and just about as warm. Most Soviet officials sat in the back of their official black Volga sedans in stony silence, even closing the curtains that hung just behind the driver's seat, as if it were necessary to emphasize their distance from and superiority over the man behind the wheel. Berg offered his driver coffee and engaged him in conversation, inquiring about his favorite recipe for *pelmeni* (dumplings) and advice on how to make *blini* (Russian crepes).

The basic principles of semiconductor technology were no secret to Soviet scientists in 1958 — the Americans Bill Shockley, Walter Brattain, and John Bardeen had received a Nobel Prize for inventing the transistor two years previously — but there was great skepticism about the utility of semiconductor devices for defense applications, and especially for military computing. While Shockley and company were being honored on the podium in Stockholm, classified reports circulated in the USSR stating that it would be at least a decade until transistors could be used in computers. To be fair, even after Bell Labs built the first transistorized computer in 1954 there was a great deal of debate for years in the United States about the role of transistors in computing.[27]

On the basis of a close reading of the technical literature, as well as their own experience, in the summer and autumn of 1958 Staros and Berg became convinced that the future path of computing would be paved with semiconductors. Their search for allies to overcome opposition to abandoning vacuum tubes brought them to the famous aircraft designer, Andrei Tupolev. The meeting was arranged by Admiral Berg, who had covertly conspired with Tupolev for over a decade to evade the Communist Party's ban on cybernetics, which party ideologists branded a "pseudo-science." The campaign reserved its most potent vitriol for Norbert Wiener, the MIT professor who had coined the term "cybernetics." The basic ideas for the new science came to Wiener when he was working on the mathematics for what would become the M-9 Predictor, the fire-control computer that served as the inspiration for the analog anti-aircraft computer that Staros and Berg created in Prague.[28]

Tupolev and Aksel Berg went to great lengths to hide their effort, meeting on short notice in locations where the KGB was unlikely to have prepositioned bugs, and giving their airborne computer a cover name ("technical route calculator"). Eventually, a prototype technical route calculator was built, but it was a grotesque mockery of a useful airborne computer, a bookshelf-sized behemoth crammed with so many vacuum tubes that it turned the room where Tupolev inspected it into a sauna. When the famous aircraft designer criticized the machine, the engineer who had built it cried out: "Get rid of these dogmatic fools who have dared to give an entire realm of new knowledge the epithet 'pseudo-science.' Give us freedom of action. Organize the production of transistors and microcomponents. Train the programmers, and — I swear to you — we will do what you need within a year."[29]

Soon after the disastrous demonstration, one of Admiral Berg's aides visited Tupolev "along with two Czechoslovakian engineers, Staros and Berg," Tupolev's assistant remembered. They presented themselves as "lifelong Communists [who] had fled when Hitler occupied Czechoslovakia" and were researching semiconductors in Russia. The pair of engineers reported to Tupolev that they had created transistors that could replace vacuum tubes in radio circuits "and were now looking for an influential person capable of overcoming the inertia of our state bureaucrats. In their opinion, Tupolev was that person."

The aircraft designer was impressed. "After seeing the miniature parts that would replace the unreliable and capricious electron tubes, Tupolev gave an immediate assessment of their work. 'Magnificent,' he declared on the telephone to Admiral Berg. 'How can I help?' The admiral recommended that Tupolev see [Alexander] Shokin," an official who was responsible for industrial applications of transistors. Tupolev visited Shokin the next morning to express support for Staros and Berg.[30]

Tupolev was happy to lend his prestige to help the two "Czech" engineers get their project off the ground. He also gave them some insights into the brutal history of the Soviet aerospace industry, describing his unjustified arrest in 1937 as an "enemy of the people," his imprisonment in one of the harsh labor camps administered by the Gulag, and the secret prison design bureau (*sharashka*) he'd headed until Beria arranged his release. Tupolev also mentioned that he had saved the life of Sergei Korolev by convincing the authorities to transfer the future founder of the Soviet space program from imprisonment in the Kolyma gold mines, one of the deadliest, most hopeless spots on Earth, to Tupolev's *sharashka*. Tupolev was outspoken in his denunciation of Stalin, of Communism in general, and of the Soviet state in particular.

Berg felt that the aircraft designer's experiences were the result of unfortunate misunderstandings and mistakes perpetrated by specific individuals, not evidence that Communism or the Soviet system was irredeemably flawed. He and Staros were, however, extremely impressed by Tupolev's apparent ability to make such statements without fear of retribution. They attributed his "untouchable" status to the level of recognition Tupolev had earned. In a state that valued the collective over the individual, he had come to be considered nearly indispensable. For almost two decades, Staros was obsessed with achieving the status of a Tupolev or a Korolev, men whose technical accomplishments and political skills allowed them to build sovereign feudal estates where they enjoyed degrees of autonomy that were otherwise unattainable in the USSR. Staros seemed blind to the fact that his models had risen to their positions only after enduring terrible physical deprivation and humiliation, and to the fact that his status as a foreigner probably precluded his becoming a nationally recognized figure.[31]

In November 1958, Staros was invited to make a presentation on his ideas about technology to an unusual joint board meeting, a *kollegiya*, of the leaders of the GKAT and the GKRE (State Committee on Radioelectronics). Speaking to a room full of senior officials, Staros summarized recent international advances in electronics, in the process introducing a new word into the Russian language: *mikroelektronika*. He described basic components of the emerging field of microelectronics, such as thin-film transistors and new memory technologies. Staros also called for the abandonment of a number of technologies that were leading Soviet industry away from microminiaturization. Soviet military leaders had been primed to hear Staros's pitch; reports warning of a serious gap in military electronics capabilities had been circulating for years. The top echelons of the party and military industry had received a report during the Korean War attributing the ability of F-86 aircraft to hold their own against the more powerful MIG-15s to American onboard computers.[32]

Staros presented a vision for restructuring the Soviet electronics industry to take advantage of the opportunities created by microelectronics. The rigid separation of component manufacturing from the design and construction of the devices such as computers that incorporated them must be scrapped, he said. The emphasis should be on miniaturizing and standardizing components to reduce the size, power consumption, and complexity of hardware. In computing, the priority should be mass production of small programmable devices. This approach seems obvious today, but it ran against the grain of conventional thinking in 1958. At the time, computer designers favored elaborate, custom-made machines, the bigger the better.

Staros concluded his presentation by proposing to apply his principles to the creation of a new computer. The UM-1 would be the first Soviet digital computer small enough and sufficiently reliable to be placed on military aircraft. The name was a play on words. Officially, UM was short for *upravlyayu-shchaya mashina,* or control computer, but in Russian *um* means "intellect." SL-11 started work on the UM-1 in late 1958, before it finished the potentiometer project. The thirty-member staff, which included twenty-four technical specialists, was organized in a manner that set it apart from most other Soviet R&D institutes, which were narrowly focused on a particular technology, such as transistors. From the start, Staros conceived of it as the core of a much larger endeavor, an organization that when scaled up would have all the skills necessary to be the USSR's premier microelectronics and computer design enterprise. There were five departments at SL-11 — computer, memory, design and technology, physics, and chemistry — each consisting of from one to five individuals. The departments reported through Berg to Staros. The computer department, which had overall responsibility for designing the UM-1, was charged with developing digital circuitry, as well as interfaces between the computer and the outside world (digital-to-analog and analog-to-digital converters). The computer department also contained a software programming section, an innovation for the period.[33]

There were wide gaps between Soviet researchers and the engineers who attempted to apply their discoveries, and between the organizations that designed complex equipment and their suppliers. The lack of communication and integration forced designers to simply make the best of whatever components they could scrape together. There were also disconnects between designers and users; Staros's emphasis on developing software along with hardware was exceptional.

The success of SL-11's memory department illustrated the merit of Staros's approach by tackling a particularly difficult problem in a way that probably could not have been achieved in conventional Soviet design bureaus. Most other Soviet computer developers would have had to build the memory from whatever components outside organizations could supply. These organizations had no way of knowing the specific requirements of the end users, and in the unlikely event that they were interested, it would have taken a great deal of time to translate a computer designer's requirements into new components.

"In those days, computer memories were made exclusively from small ferrite cores," Berg recalled. "However, the available cores were relatively large, required a lot of power, and were very difficult to assemble. We decided to develop an integrated ferrite memory using a small ferrite plate, in which after firing at high temperatures we drilled 256 0.4-millimeter holes using ultrasonic drilling and a specially designed tool with 256 holes." The resulting ferrite memory cube was an elegant, innovative solution that was more advanced than analogous American designs. It was the subject of Soviet patent number 151507, awarded to I. V. Berg and F. G. Staros in 1962, the first of scores of Soviet patents bearing their names as co-inventors.[34]

UM-1 achieved a number of Soviet firsts, including the incorporation of thousands of off-the-shelf germanium transistors, which forever disproved the assertions of experts who had deemed Soviet transistors inappropriate for computing uses. The first prototype was assembled in July 1959, less than eight months after the project had been approved. The little computer was a dramatic example of what could be accomplished by applying Staros's design principles. In contrast to the room-sized monsters produced by other Soviet computer designers, the UM-1 was small enough to fit on a kitchen table, light enough for one person to lift, and required about the same power as a light bulb.[35]

The diminutive computer attracted a great deal of attention. A month after the first UM-1 prototype was finished, Ustinov, the VPK chairman, visited SL-11, dragging the head of the Soviet Air Force and other top military brass into the attic of the Volkovskaya Street laboratory to meet Staros and Berg and see the first desktop computer made in the Soviet Union. The UM-1 prototype, which had been working perfectly before the visit, consistently operating for over 200 hours without interruption, inexplicably crashed the moment the important visitors arrived. A couple of quick-thinking engineers saved the day by connecting the UM-1's indicators directly to a multivibrator "so that they blinked and twinkled as if the UM-1 was actually working." Staros and Berg, unaware of the ruse, continued with the demonstration.[36]

Ustinov pushed for field trials of the UM-1 aboard aircraft, but the resistance of the military and caution on the part of the aviation technology bureaucrats, who feared that failure would retard the development of microelectronics, scuttled the project. In fact the computer was much more valuable to the bureaucracy as an interesting prototype than it would have been if it had been put into production. The successful demonstration of a new design brought prestige to the GKAT, bolstering its chances for more military orders, but under the Soviet system manufacturing the computer would have brought nothing but innumerable complications and difficulties to the organization.

A month after the UM-1 presentation, the Soviet Union staged a more public demonstration of technology, slamming a missile into the moon on September 14, 1959, two weeks before Khrushchev was scheduled to tour the United States. The not-so-subtle message was that a nation capable of putting a metal sphere on the moon could easily lob a nuclear warhead a quarter of the way around the Earth. Coming two years after the Sputnik success, it also reinforced Khrushchev's notion that scientific and technical achievements enhanced the Soviet Union's stature as a superpower, partially by distracting attention from humiliating failures in more mundane spheres such as agriculture. At a time when he was slashing the size of the armed forces by a third and cutting spending on all but the most important budget items, Khrushchev happily funded high technology.

For Berg and Staros, like other scientists in the Soviet Union, the early Khrushchev years were a time of tremendous optimism. Space successes made slogans about socialism "catching up and surpassing" the West seem credible. Not only did it look as if Staros's 1945 prediction about a man walking on the moon by his wife's fifty-fifth birthday would be proved accurate, but it seemed likely that the space traveler would have a Communist Party card in his wallet.

On September 21, 1959, during his first visit to the United States, the Soviet leader toured a plant in San Jose, California, that was making IBM 305 Random Access Method of Accounting and Control (RAMAC) computers. He gave two workers on the IBM assembly line medals commemorating the first rendezvous of a manmade object with a heavenly body. Khrushchev returned to Russia apparently more impressed by the company's cafeteria than by its technology, lecturing his Politburo colleagues about the wonders of Formica tables. But although Khrushchev didn't comprehend the details of the RAMAC computer, the trip reinforced Soviet respect for American technology. Khrushchev's mind was primed regarding the importance of computers: if the United States made such a fuss over IBM, these devices must be important.[37]

The successful completion of UM-1 launched Staros and Berg on an upward path. In November 1959, Ustinov reshuffled the electronics industry, giving some functions to the GKRE that had previously been in the purview of the GKAT, and vice versa. Several GKAT components responsible for avionics and radar R&D, including SL-11's parent (Experimental Design Bureau, P.O. Box 998), were combined into a huge organization, a closed "mailbox" operation, that was given to GKRE. SL-11 was elevated in stature, acquiring the designation Special-Purpose Design Bureau 2 (SKB-2), and was granted independence from OKB-998.

The newly christened SKB-2 moved into the Palace of Soviets. An enormous edifice, the largest office building in Leningrad, and one of the biggest in the Soviet Union, the Palace of Soviets was intended to be the centerpiece of a new downtown when it was built in the late 1930s, but was orphaned after plans to abandon the historic city center were dropped. Every workday morning, Berg and Staros would drive the short distance to work — each had been given the right to purchase a car, a commodity beyond the reach of most Soviets at that time — and park in an enormous square in front of the building. Passing guards who took their jobs much more seriously than the old codgers at Fort Monmouth, they crossed a gleaming marble lobby and rode small, creaky elevators to the third floor.

Elevators were a constant reminder of the disparities between military and civilian industry. The USSR had beaten America into space and built world-class jet fighters, but engineers like Berg and Staros who valued design and craftsmanship were offended by the knowledge that it never produced a decent elevator, washing machine, or domestic appliance.

Staros occupied a corner office with a balcony; a secretary controlled entrance. Two telephones sat on his desk, one connected to a personal line, the other shared with Berg, whose office was around the corner. They were careful to speak Russian in the presence of employees, but behind the closed doors of Phil's office, they would talk and joke in English, Joe's loud voice and laughter bursting through the door and into the hallway.

Staros and Berg's organization went by several names over the years, but its structure didn't change significantly from the earliest days of SL-11. It did, however, grow, from a head count of about 50 when it moved into the Palace of Soviets to almost 2,000 several years later. As it grew, SKB-2 retained its character. "The organization which we headed was unique in the Soviet Union," Berg recalled. "In contrast to other firms in the Soviet Union, which were profiled in a narrow area, we attempted to cover the whole field of electronics from design of elements to building complete systems. It was, in fact, a miniature corporation similar to IBM." Although there were other design bureaus with similarly broad missions, they were rare and secret, so Berg didn't know about them. And none of them had the distinctly un-Soviet ambiance that Berg and Staros created.[38]

Like the American companies it emulated, SKB-2 launched a broad range of initiatives, simultaneously pursuing short-term goals and researching highly speculative areas. When SKB-2 conceived of a new project, Staros and Berg would estimate how long it would take to accomplish, shave a bit of time off, and present the estimate to various organizations that were in a position to authorize it. This was normal practice in the United States, where success depended on a company's ability to land a contract and everyone understood that salesmanship sometimes necessitated the presentation of hopes as promises, but it was the exact opposite of standard Soviet practice.

"We had been successful in organizing our organization not as a typical Soviet organization," Berg recalled. "The typical Soviet organization was run from Moscow. They were given plans that they were supposed to fulfill, and the plan was handed down from above. We, on the other hand, proposed the plans. We went out on a limb, presenting plans for research and development which we had no guarantee of fulfilling. This was absolutely against the typical Soviet method of the director accepting a plan which he knew in advance was going to be fulfilled."

Berg got a picture of the typical R&D enterprise in late 1959:

> We became friendly with the chief engineer of an enterprise in Leningrad which was responsible for resistors and condensers and other electronics parts. He told us how things were done. The basic policy was to accept a plan for research and development and production of elements which he had already spent years researching, developing, and putting into production. He never went out on a limb. He always was sure that what he committed to do the next year was already done. It was an incredible situation which guaranteed him the position of chief engineer for life, and it worked. He died in office as chief engineer.
>
> I remember him taking a resistor which he had already developed out of a drawer, and he said, "See this resistor? Now we are supposed to develop this resistor in the next Five-Year Plan. My department that is responsible for designing, researching, and putting this resistor into production has already built a machine, an *avtomat* [assembly line], for building this resistor, and they are producing it in quite big volumes already. But I haven't taken on the job."

The chief engineer went on to explain that when the time for setting goals for the next plan came around, he would arrange for Moscow to require that his plant produce these resistors in about five years. He would then unveil them in three or four years, getting credit for fulfilling the plan ahead of schedule. In the meantime, his research team was working on designs that would become commitments for a future plan. This strategy, the chief engineer was pleased to say, ensured that he would never fail to fulfill the plan — and, to Berg's horror, it also ensured that his organization's technology would always be obsolete. "This system, which guarantees the viability of the organization but has absolutely no connection with trying to get ahead of the West or at least keeping up, explains the reasons for the Soviet failure on the world market. There were no organizations in Russia that were competing with" the chief engineer, Berg recalled.[39]

The chief engineer stood as a vivid illustration of the swamp that doomed Soviet industry to mediocrity. The basic problem as Berg saw it was that the men — almost without exception, military-industrial decisionmakers were male — responsible for deciding how state funds would be invested were selected for their political reliability, not for their technical knowledge. They reported to men who were even less qualified to make technical decisions, who ultimately reported to the Central Committee, which with a few exceptions was composed of poorly educated political operatives. At the same time, failure was harshly punished. The Stalinist days when officials who failed to fulfill a plan were sent to the Gulag were only a memory, but under Khrushchev and subsequent leaders there was little tolerance for management failures. Careers were ended, Communist Party memberships revoked, access to a wide range of perks withdrawn if a manager was deemed to have committed an error.

The risk-reward ratio in Soviet industry was infinite. The Soviet system provided no rewards for innovating, and the risk was complete. There were no second chances: managers knew that their lives would be ruined if they were caught making what was considered a mistake.

In this environment, there was very little incentive to innovate. Managers who weren't competent to judge between competing proposals adopted a simple stratagem: invest only in technologies that had already been proven in the West, particularly in the United States. The smarter officials, particularly those responsible for military industry, however, realized that this would doom the Soviet Union to being several steps behind its adversary, and as the pace of technical change quickened, the gap would continually widen. They then seized on another tactic, perhaps inspired by the activities of agents like Julius Rosenberg and Joel Barr in the 1940s: obtain the plans for important technologies at an advanced development stage, before they had been put into production. The KGB ramped up its technical espionage activities, stealing plans for new computers and other equipment fresh off the drawing boards, sometimes years before they were manufactured in quantity.[40]

Relying on purloined American technology obviously had its limitations. It would be possible to snatch only a relatively small quantity of information; Soviet industry would have to keep up with the West in order to manufacture it properly; and, perhaps most important, the strategy doomed the USSR to perpetual second-class status. The appearance of Staros and Berg on the scene must have appeared to Ustinov a wonderful solution to this dilemma. If acquiring American technology was an effective shortcut for modernizing Soviet industry, acquiring two American technologists could be even better.

The move to the Palace of the Soviets and the military's increased interest in microelectronics plunged SKB-2 into the middle of a power struggle between Staros's immediate superior, Valentin Smirnov, and Smirnov's boss, Alexander Shokin, the first deputy chairman of the GKRE. Smirnov wanted SKB-2 to pursue areas of research that would reinforce his reputation, to support his campaign to join the small circle of elite chief designers. Displaying a degree of self-confidence that reflected his close association with Ustinov and other senior government officials, Staros defied Smirnov, who in turn threatened to disband SKB-2.

Shokin also sought to use SKB-2 to enhance his career, but his goals were more closely aligned with Staros and Berg's. Shokin wanted desperately to become a government minister. His strategy was to convince Ustinov and other higher authorities that microelectronics was a large enough field, and of sufficient importance to the state, that a new ministry should be created to oversee its development. Shokin showered praise on Staros and Berg, supported them in their battles with Smirnov, and did his best to ensure that SKB-2's projects were funded. In exchange, Shokin asked Staros to brief top military and government leaders on the importance of microelectronics, a task he performed enthusiastically. Staros was a talented and convincing speaker.[41]

With Shokin's backing, SKB-2 started work on an enhanced, civilian version of the UM-1, which Staros and Berg named the UM-1NKh; NKh was supposed to be short for *narodnoye khozyaystvo* (people's industry), but it was not a coincidence that the initials matched those of the first secretary of the Communist Party of the Soviet Union, Nikita Khrushchev. For a Soviet enterprise, building a computer specifically for nonmilitary uses was an unusual and, as it turned out, brilliant decision.

Success whetted their appetites, and Shokin, backed by Staros and Berg, continued to bombard higher authorities with reports and plans, all aimed at enlarging the scope of his empire. "We kept well informed of the latest developments in electronics in the West by reading the main technical journals, and we knew that reducing the size and power of electronic equipment by many orders of magnitude was absolutely possible and would create a revolution in the field of electronics. Theoretically there were practically no limits to the size and power of the future computers," Berg remembered later. "In a report to the Soviet government in 1960, we showed that in ten years there would be millions of computers in the world, and that this would only be the beginning of a new revolution in industry. The tool that would make this possible was a new concept in science and technology called microelectronics." The report, which predicted the personal computer, was greeted by more than a little skepticism. Few people in 1960 could envision that computers would become ubiquitous.[42]

The leaders of SKB-2 were convinced that they were on an elevator headed to the top. They were more certain than ever about the future importance of microelectronics, and that the socialist system's comparative advantages over the West — its ability to centralize industrial decisionmaking, to create and implement rational planning, and to mobilize men and resources with unparalleled speed — could make the Soviet Union a computer superpower. Staros and Berg felt they were creating the technological infrastructure for Soviet prosperity and the basis for world preeminence — economic and military.

Joe Berg and Phil Staros marched together in the May Day parade in 1960 with their families. The four Staros and three Berg children were bundled up against the cold, wet Leningrad air. Despite the fact that the weather in Leningrad was rarely anything to celebrate, May Day was one of Berg's favorite holidays, just as it had been two decades before in New York, and he never missed the opportunity to march alongside posters of Lenin, Marx, and Engels.

Four hundred miles south and west, Khrushchev was also in a festive mood as he stood atop Lenin's mausoleum in Red Square, reviewing the Moscow May Day celebration. The day had started badly for the Soviet leader, when aides woke him with the news that an American spy plane, in the latest in a series of flights that he viewed as humiliating provocations, had crossed the border and was cruising from one sensitive military site to another. Powerful radar, which had been designed and manufactured under Admiral Berg's supervision — assisted by data from the United States, such as the specifications Joel Barr had slipped Alexander Feklisov in a Manhattan cafeteria years earlier — detected the intruder minutes after it took off from an airfield in Pakistan, just before it crossed the Soviet-Afghan border.[43]

When the CIA first proposed U-2 overflights of the USSR to President Eisenhower, it was confident that Soviet radar wouldn't be able to track it. On the basis of a study of Soviet World War II–era radars and tests using contemporary American radar equipment, the president had been advised that the Russians probably wouldn't even know their territorial sovereignty was being violated. At the worst, the CIA told Eisenhower, Soviet radar would pick up vague traces of the U-2; the Russians certainly wouldn't be capable of tracking it closely enough to shoot it down. The CIA had incorrectly assumed that the Russian radar program, which had been virtually nonexistent at the start of World War II, could not have advanced to a level comparable to or beyond that of the best U.S. technology.[44]

After several bungled attempts to down the American plane, an order was given to launch three SA-2 missiles as it approached Sverdlovsk. Another foul-up caused two to abort, but one missile streaked into the sky, emitting radio waves from a small device in its nose as it soared to 75,000 feet. Four and a half hours into what had been a routine flight for the American pilot Francis Gary Powers, his twenty-eighth U-2 surveillance mission and the second deep

into Soviet territory, he felt a tremendous blast that immediately sent his plane
into a freefall. The concussion came seconds after one of the radio signals
bounced off his plane, triggering a switch that detonated a powerful explosive
charge. It was the first time a Soviet-made proximity fuse — a direct descendent
of the device Julius Rosenberg had cleverly slipped out of Emerson Electronics
and handed Feklisov as a Christmas present in 1944 — shot down an enemy
aircraft.[45]

Staros and Berg told colleagues vaguely that they'd had some connection
with the U-2 shootdown, but didn't provide a detailed explanation.

In late 1960, before the UM-1NKh prototype was completed, Staros and Berg
decided that the time was ripe to leapfrog into the next generation of computers. They envisioned an airborne computer that could, with minor varia-
tions, be used by every branch of the armed forces, working equally well in
airplanes, in spacecraft, on ships, missile-launch platforms, and submarines.
The new computer, the UM-2, would incorporate state-of-the-art components, including many that SKB-2 would have to create, and radical new
design concepts.

SKB-2 launched a number of research efforts to develop the new technologies that Staros envisioned for the UM-2 computer, including the creation
of a new threadlike microresistor that would be mounted on microminiature
flat modules that SKB-2 also designed. The modules were mounted on standard boards fitted with microwired interconnections that could be easily
replaced.

Because they had to overcome limitations that their Western counterparts
didn't face, such as shoddy materials and a paucity of computing power,
Soviet engineers often came up with novel solutions. The space program was a
good example of this phenomenon. Russian aerospace engineers devised practical, low-tech methods for achieving goals that were accomplished in the
United States using expensive, sophisticated equipment. In this spirit, Staros
and Berg contributed an important innovation to Soviet technology, the principal of multicascade component protection.

Soviet electronic components were notoriously unreliable. Designers typically blamed poor-quality components when their devices failed to perform
properly; they also claimed that unreliable materials made it impossible to
emulate the far more advanced equipment that was manufactured in the West.
Staros argued that good engineering could overcome inferior components.
Multicascade protection presented an alternative to encasing a component,
for example a transistor, in a thick jacket intended to protect it from dirt and
moisture that made it overheat. Instead it should be placed in a thin covering

and placed in a subsystem that was insulated from the elements. This subsystem would, in turn, be located in a device designed to keep its innards safe. The responsibility for reliability shifted from the transistor manufacturer to the system designer.

To prove the validity of his theory, Staros insisted on using caseless microtransistors in SKB-2's new computer. A special order from Shokin was required to convince a defense factory to produce the components for the UM-2 because the plant's management, which was convinced they wouldn't work reliably in a computer, didn't want to be blamed for the project's failure. In the end, Staros's principle was validated: the design was sufficiently robust to allow the microtransistors to function flawlessly.

The UM-2 was designed to have its own microclimate. The computer was hermetically sealed and was connected to a refrigeration unit that maintained a constant internal temperature of about 20 degrees Centigrade. Creating a microclimate removed one of the Soviet military's prime arguments against the use of computers. The generals had claimed that while it might be possible to put a computer in a missile in the temperate climate of the United States (conveniently ignoring places like North Dakota and Wyoming, where the weather is almost as extreme as in Siberia), it would be impossible to do so on the steppes of Kazakhstan, where temperatures range from minus 50 degrees Centigrade in the winter to plus 50 in summer. "Of course, Shokin, since he was responsible for elements instead of computers, was always against the wall," according to Staros's disciple Henry Firdman. "People were saying, 'Why don't we have elements that can withstand those temperatures?' That's why Shokin liked what Staros did so much. Because he said, 'Why do we need that? We have microclimate in the computer.' "[46]

Shokin's and Staros's briefings of military industry leaders and lobbying paid off. In early 1961 the Kremlin, convinced that microelectronics, like applications of nuclear technology, was a critical field, approved the creation of the GKET (State Committee of Electronic Technology), the equivalent of a new ministry. As he had hoped, Shokin was appointed chairman. He repaid his allies by removing SKB-2 from Smirnov's control and elevating it to an independent design bureau. Staros was made director and chief designer, and Berg chief engineer and principal scientist, of Subscriber Box 155. Unofficially, box 155 was called Design Bureau 2 (KB-2). The name was an allusion to KB-1, the huge, enormously influential design bureau that Sergo Beria had run in Moscow until his father, Lavrenty Beria, was arrested and shot in 1953.

Shokin, Staros, and Berg began plotting their next jump up the ladder, an accomplishment that, like the creation of the GKET, would give Shokin a great deal more political authority while increasing the resources available to his two protégés by several orders of magnitude. They identified the organizational flaws holding back the development of microelectronics and computers and conceived of a framework for correcting them. The idea was to create something like the U.S. companies Berg and Staros were familiar with, but on a Soviet scale. At its heart there would be a massive R&D enterprise, similar to Bell Laboratories, tightly coupled with manufacturing enterprises, like Western Electric. There would also be affiliated educational institutions, from undergraduate to Ph.D., training the microelectronics workforce of the future. All controlled by a Center for Microelectronics.

The team needed a high-profile success to prove that microelectronics was more than a passing fad. A prototype of the UM-1NKh machine was completed in early 1962, and it was immediately clear that it was a step forward for Soviet technology.

The UM-1NKh was nothing special compared to contemporary American computers — it used discrete transistors, but its designers decided that Soviet integrated circuits were not ready for prime time — but it was a major breakthrough for Soviet industry. It required one-thousandth of the power used by other Soviet control computers, was ten times lighter and smaller, and cost less than half as much. Quite a bit of original engineering went into the machine, including an upgraded version of the ferrite memory pioneered for the UM-1 and a sort of cache memory that speeded up the computer's operations. Of even more interest to its users, the UM-1NKh was more reliable than its competitors, working in tests for 250 hours without a failure. Breaking from standard Soviet practice, KB-2 considered the needs of the computer's users and built a multiplicity of input-output features so it could be relatively easily plugged into industrial applications.[47]

Staros and Berg envisioned the UM-1NKh as the first of a line of tabletop computers. They coined the word *miniputer* to describe the small, flexible, and inexpensive computers they were confident would be mass-produced in the near future. The term never caught on; the world came to call the kinds of machines that Staros and Berg envisioned by different names: microcomputers and personal computers.

As Staros and Berg were riding the wave of success that followed completion of the UM-1NKh, they didn't notice the storm clouds gathering on the horizon. Like the management of every other Soviet enterprise, KB-2's leaders had to answer not only to the government, but also to a parallel structure, the Communist Party. The party's tentacles reached into KB-2 through a party committee (*partkom*), which operated independently of Staros's or Berg's control. The *partkom* secretary acted as the Leningrad party organization's eyes and ears in KB-2. The *partkom*'s official responsibilities included ensuring discipline and morale among employees, as well as what today would be called "political correctness." The *partkom* had powerful tools for exerting control: salaries, bonuses, and promotions all had to be approved by its secretary.

KB-2 was in a constant state of tension with the Leningrad branch of the party, which was run by two particularly odious apparatchiks, Vassily Tolstikov and Grigory Romanov. Both were reactionary, xenophobic, and anti-Semitic. Tolstikov and Romanov resisted Staros's efforts to expand the size of KB-2 and pressured him to hire fewer Jews. Staros, believing that he was under the protection of Ustinov and other top Soviet leaders, did not pay local party officials the deference they expected from a man in his position. While his star was ascending, local party officials were an annoyance, but they did not seem to present a major threat to Staros and KB-2.[48]

In March 1962, Staros and Berg embarked on what by then had become a routine trip to Moscow to brief senior government officials about micro-electronics. Driving into the city from the airport, they stopped near a village called Kryukovo at a spot where some workers were digging in the mud. The construction site manager recalled that a fast-talking, excited man who "looked a little bit like a Georgian, with a black moustache," walked up and started asking a lot of questions with an air of authority, without introducing himself. "I said, excuse me, who am I speaking with? He showed an ID, he was the General Director of an enterprise in Leningrad."

The site manager reported that there were plans to build a satellite city near Kryukovo, but the project was stalled because of a typical bureaucratic snafu. The ministry that had ordered a ball-bearing factory and a plant for assembling clocks and associated housing built in the new city didn't have budget authority, while the ministry that controlled the purse strings wasn't interested and hadn't provided funds.

Staros asked if something like the Center for Microelectronics could be built on the site. The construction chief replied that the project Staros described was far too small to be of interest. Staros "jumped up" and declared: "'We are going to see Shokin now.' I didn't know who Shokin was. He wrote down my home phone number and called that night, saying that Shokin was waiting for me the next day."[49]

The idea for a small institute morphed overnight into one for a huge campus with laboratories, a university, factories, and housing for the tens of thousands of people who would work in them. The construction chief learned that Shokin was a minister, and a very smooth operator. He readily agreed to Shokin's order to suspend work on the ball-bearing and clock factories—there was no money to finish them anyway—and to start laying plans for a much bigger project in synch with the satellite city that Soviet designers envisioned for Kryukovo. Still, he was skeptical. What they were asking was far from standard operating procedure. Something like this would require backing from the highest levels; Shokin couldn't order it on his own authority. Don't worry, the minister and the impetuous man with the black moustache said; the project would receive support from the top levels of government.

About this time, KB-2 received a visit from a young engineer working for Vladimir Chelomei, one of the Soviet Union's leading missile designers. KB-2 was doing some work for Chelomei, designing components for intercontinental ballistic missiles (ICBMs). Their visitor was responsible for creating the guidance system for a new weapons system, the cruise missile, that military leaders hoped would compensate for the Soviet Union's lack of aircraft carriers. He was interested in finding out if KB-2 could design some devices for the flying bombs. Ordinarily, a department head would have handled this kind of inquiry, but there was something extraordinary about this twenty-seven-year-old engineer that prompted KB-2's director and chief engineer to give him the royal treatment, showing off their most exciting projects. His name was Sergei Khrushchev, and as the son of Nikita Khrushchev he was as close to royalty as existed in the USSR in 1962.

Sergei Khrushchev, one of the few people in the Soviet Union who knew at the time that its leaders were defectors from the "main adversary," was impressed by KB-2. He told his father about the UM-2 computer and explained that the design bureau was doing interesting work that could have far-reaching implications for Soviet technology. "Father was a very curious man and he liked innovation. He met with many different kinds of scientists, engineers, aircraft designers, so when he heard from me that it was interesting, he decided to visit," Khrushchev recalled.[50]

8

Zelenograd, the Soviet Silicon Valley, 1962–1965

A long-planned May 4, 1962, visit to the Leningrad shipyards to launch a new cruiser provided an opportunity for Nikita Khrushchev to drop in on KB-2. The visit, originally intended to be a low-key affair, mushroomed into a major state visit as one official after another managed to get himself added to the entourage, hoping to absorb some of the reflected prestige.

In the spring of 1962 Khrushchev was at the center of the Soviet firmament; the inertial force of an empire stretching from the Gulf of Finland to the Sea of Japan was the only check on his power. He combined the roles of commander-in-chief of the military, head of state, and pope of the secular religion. Soviet industry was organized as if it was a huge conglomerate, so in addition to his other roles, Khrushchev was the CEO of the biggest corporation on earth. Rarely in history has so much power been aggregated in the hands of an individual so poorly equipped to wield it. The concentration of power and lack of accountability created ridiculous circumstances, such as imposing the literary or artistic tastes of the nation's ruler on hundreds of millions of citizens, or requiring that Khrushchev, a man with four years of formal education, personally decide which of two rival missile designs the state would trust for its defense. Ironically, a system that presented itself to the outside world as the most rational, scientifically planned society in history often based important decisions on the whims of ill-informed leaders and the outcomes of highly personal bureaucratic turf battles.[1]

Staros and Berg spent an almost sleepless week finalizing the preparations for a day they believed could change the course of their lives. In addition to testing and retesting the UM-2 prototype—no one wanted a repeat of the UM-1 crash that had occurred during Ustinov's 1959 visit to Volkovskaya Street—the engineers of Design Bureau 2 were pressed into overtime duty preparing colorful posters illustrating the advances that investment in microelectronics would make possible: networks of military satellites spying on the United States, antimissile defenses, high-precision bombing, and industrial automation.

Just as Shokin, Staros, and Berg had rehearsed the day before, after the initial introductions, Khrushchev was ushered into a room adjacent to Staros's office. This was the private lab reserved for the director and chief engineer. Two objects had been placed on a green baize table: a Rodina (Motherland) radio receiver, a familiar battery-powered shoebox-sized model weighing twenty-eight pounds that could be found in almost every Russian household; and beside it a small box holding what looked like a hearing aid. Staros explained that the tiny device, weighing only a few ounces, performed the same function as the much larger one, and that the reduction in size and mass had been made possible by the techniques of microminiaturization that KB-2 was pioneering. The sight of a radio small enough to wear in your ear isn't surprising today, but in 1962, especially in the Soviet Union, where consumer electronic items were always clunky, it was startling.

"I helped Nikita Sergeivich put the receiver into his ear and suggested that he rotate the volume regulator of the Rodina. The microreceiver was tuned to Moscow, as was the Rodina [so he could hear that they were picking up the same broadcasts]. The relation of mass and sizes of both receivers was impressive," Staros recalled. He informed Khrushchev of the broader implications of this kind of miniaturization, for example, "for the creation of a nuclear missile shield."[2]

Berg was delighted as the Soviet leader stopped several times during the tour to tinker with the volume control on the receiver in his ear and marveled aloud about it. When his partner had first proposed the project, Staros had sneered that it was a mere toy, hardly worth the time of a design bureau that was engaged in projects at the cutting edge of technology. Berg persevered, creating the microreceiver with a team of five engineers working part-time. Later Staros admitted that the little receiver had won the first secretary's heart and played a major part in the success of the visit.[3]

Speaking fluently and confidently in flawless, unaccented Russian, Staros guided Khrushchev—followed by an ensemble that included Admiral Gorshkov; Marshal Ustinov; the GKET chairman, Shokin; the head of the State

Figure 9. Nikita Khrushchev's visit to Design Bureau Number 2 (KB-2), May 4, 1962. Seated, left to right: Alexander Shokin, chairman of the State Committee of Electronic Technology (GKET); Philip Staros, director and chief designer, KB-2; Joseph Berg, chief engineer and principal scientist, KB-2, in Staros's office a few moments before Khrushchev arrived. (Source: Joel Barr's personal papers, photo album inscribed to Philip Staros; photo by unknown official Kremlin photographer.)

Committee on Aviation Technology, Pyotr V. Dementyev; Leningrad party boss Vassily Tolstikov and his deputy Grigory Romanov; and a gaggle of senior military and civilian officials — through rows of gleaming lab counters where young women in white smocks manipulated tiny bits of metal under microscopes. The scene evoked Leskov's story of the smith creating shoes for a mechanical flea. The fact that it looked a great deal like the labs he'd seen at IBM in California was probably even more impressive to the Soviet leader, who was obsessed with a desire to "catch up and surpass" the technical accomplishments of the capitalist world, as the slogan plastered on factory walls in those days exhorted. The similarity to an American high-tech company would have been particularly evident to Khrushchev, one of the few people

Figure 10. Nikita Khrushchev's visit to Design Bureau Number 2 (KB-2), May 4, 1962. Left to right: Admiral Sergei Gorshkov, commander-in-chief of the Soviet Navy and deputy minister of defense; Dmitri Ustinov, deputy chief of the Soviet Council of Ministers; Alexander Shokin, chairman of the State Committee of Electronic Technology (GKET) and minister of the USSR; Philip Staros, director and chief designer, KB-2; Nikita Khrushchev; Joseph Berg (standing to Khrushchev's right, wearing glasses), chief engineer and principal scientist, KB-2; Yevgeny Zhukov, senior engineer, KB-2; Nikolai Averin, director, Special Design Bureau 998. (Source: Joel Barr's personal papers, photo album inscribed to Philip Staros; photo by unknown official Kremlin photographer.)

who knew the path Staros and Berg had taken from Fort Monmouth to Leningrad.

Staros spoke freely, admitting that Soviet industry was behind the West's, but confidently predicting that with socialist planning it could jump ahead. He held his tongue, however, when Khrushchev asked if the Leningrad party was supporting KB-2 appropriately. Tolstikov stepped forward to assure Khrushchev that of course *tovarischi* (comrades) Staros and Berg had the full backing of the Leningrad party, a statement that several of the men in the room knew was a lie.

Figure 11. Nikita Khrushchev's visit to Design Bureau Number 2 (KB-2), May 4, 1962. Philip Staros briefing Nikita Khrushchev. The metal case in the left foreground holds the UM-2 computer. Admiral Sergei Gorshkov (far left) and Joseph Berg (far right) look on. (Source: Joel Barr's personal papers, photo album inscribed to Philip Staros; photo by unknown official Kremlin photographer.)

The delegation was treated to a demonstration of the UM-2 computer, which Staros explained would expand the capabilities of military aircraft and automate life-support systems for cosmonauts. The ability of computers to store and manipulate information would also make them powerful tools for automating industry and improving the efficiency of government, he predicted. Khrushchev was charmed when the *umnyi* (clever) computer, responding to simple queries, printed out his name, titles, and decorations.

Staros's main theme, that microelectronics would make weaponry far more accurate and deadly, was carefully calibrated to support Khrushchev's contention that missiles and other high-tech machines had made huge, expensive standing armies, as well as aircraft carriers, obsolete. Khrushchev was constantly battling the military, demanding that it cut back to free up money and manpower for civilian needs. Shokin and Ustinov confirmed Staros's claims that the UM-2 could help Soviet aviators navigate better, ensure that its cosmonauts survived the rigors of space travel, and guarantee that submarine-launched torpedoes hit their targets.[4]

The all-important pitch was saved for the end of the visit. Staros guided his audience to an easel with posters depicting an entire city dedicated to researching, developing, and manufacturing microelectronics. A fifty-two-story building dominated low-rise industrial buildings, while apartment buildings, clustered around ponds and surrounded by birch trees, were scattered around the periphery. The skyscraper, which Staros assured Khrushchev would rival the most impressive American corporate headquarters buildings, would house the Center for Microelectronics. The Center would coordinate a massive program, ranging from educational institutions to computer design and manufacturing, all aimed at catapulting the Soviet Union ahead of capitalist countries, which were not capable of concentrating so many resources in such a short period on a single goal. The gap between research and manufacturing, responsible for the shoddy quality of most Soviet products, would be closed by tightly coupling the work of basic research institutes, design bureaus, and manufacturers.

The scheme wasn't limited to the new city that would sprout from the muddy fields near the village of Kryukovo, or even to Russia. "Since it was impossible to transport specialists from the whole of the Soviet Union to the Center, we presented a system of subsidiary organizations. They were located in the capitals: Kiev, Riga, Vilnius, Tbilisi, Minsk, Yerevan," Berg remembered. "The most important element of this proposal was to create the base for the new computers that were going to appear on the scene. Our first job was to build the basis for these new machines, the integrated circuits and the logic."

Staros and Berg's ideas, especially their insistence that microelectronics would be based on silicon semiconductors and that computers would become cheap and ubiquitous, went against the stream of contemporary Soviet technology. "We were organizing what turned out to be the future of microelectronics, that is, solid-state electronics based on silicon semiconductors. This line was very much argued about. There were many people against it. At the time when we proposed it, silicon was not being made in the Soviet Union," Berg recalled.[5]

Khrushchev couldn't have understood the details of Staros's explanations of microelectronics or sensibly arbitrated the disputes between KB-2 and other design bureaus over which technologies the Soviet Union should invest in. But he trusted the short, dark-haired engineer and his tall, intellectual-looking partner. The fact that they were Americans probably helped, both because

Khrushchev and most Russians had tremendous respect for U.S. technology, and because the flip side of Russian chauvinism was an inferiority complex that led its leaders to distrust any technical innovations that hadn't already been validated by American industry. In addition, foreigners were unlikely to be pursuing political goals or trying to scam money out of the state.

Khrushchev consistently opposed virtually all construction projects except housing, so his support for the American engineers' plan to build a new city sent a powerful signal of his support for the project and its leaders. Khrushchev's assent was all the more remarkable because he was struggling at that moment with a rapidly deteriorating economic situation that forced him to pare government expenditures to the bone. While he was listening to Staros's request for facilities that would cost hundreds of millions of rubles, Khrushchev knew that decrees were being prepared for his signature that would attempt to shore up the government's finances by increasing the retail price of food while decreasing the salaries of factory workers. Since Stalin's time, the Soviet system had promised workers that progress toward Communism meant that prices would be continuously lowered. In addition to running the risk that lowering living standards would create civil unrest, the decrees constituted a painful admission that the Soviet Union was not exempt from the laws of economics, that it wasn't true, as Berg and other Communists around the world had believed, that only decadent capitalist countries experienced inflation.[6]

The Soviet leader didn't give any indication that he was concerned about the cost of creating a world-class microelectronics industry. On the contrary, Khrushchev hugged Staros and Berg after the presentation and promised full support. Warning the two American engineers that the bureaucracy would try to scuttle or hijack their project, he invited them to contact him directly, through his assistant, Grigory Shuisky, with any problems.

The visit had been even more successful than Staros and Berg had imagined possible. It left them giddy, almost drunk with happiness. Under their direction, the world would finally see what socialism could achieve! The ideas that Berg had enthused about to his fellow CCNY students in the late 1930s, the ability of a planned economy to harness the fruits of technology, were being proved correct. And two men who had been unable to obtain a small contract from the U.S. Navy to get Sarant Laboratories off the ground would be Communist tycoons, masters of vast resources.

Khrushchev signed the *postanovlenie,* or official decree, on August 8, 1962, authorizing the establishment of a center of microelectronics, to be called the "Scientific Center," near Kryukovo rail station. The *postanovlenie* specified that the Scientific Center would be the lead organization in the USSR for microelectronics. It was described as a "self-contained entity, consisting of a complex of scientific research institutions and production plants for the development and production of integrated circuits."

The Soviet leader also signed another document that was a prerequisite for Staros's appointment to a top position. Papers making the Greek-American a full member of the Communist Party of the Soviet Union bore the signature of Nikita Khrushchev. This was unusual — most people went through a lengthy induction process, including a formal probationary period — but given everything that had happened to him, it was par for the course. Philip and Anna Staros, and by extension their children, had also been made citizens of the Soviet Union. Vera refused to adopt Soviet citizenship, so for the time being the Bergs remained foreigners.

For the next two years, while Zelenograd was under construction, Staros and Berg shuttled back and forth between Leningrad, where they retained leadership of KB-2, and Moscow. Gifts of chocolates from the Red October factory for the girls behind the reception desk ensured that a room was always available at the Metropol Hotel; even senior officials had to share rooms in Soviet hotels. Their informal Moscow headquarters was located around the corner from the KGB's nerve center in the Lubyanka, and a short walk from Red Square and the Moskva Hotel, where Berg and Staros had been reunited in 1951. The Metropol was also across the street from an institution that was important for fathers with large families: Detsky Mir (Children's World), the Russian equivalent of F. A. O. Schwartz, the nation's biggest toy and children's clothing store. The hotel management knew that Staros and Berg were authorized to purchase foreign publications, so they often read day-old copies of the *International Herald Tribune* over chicken Kiev in the Metropol's restaurant.

Berg drove his car to Moscow and kept it there for him and Staros to use in the capital region, and they shared Staros's car in Leningrad. They had a raging debate over the best way to travel between the two cities. Staros insisted that a sleeping compartment on the Red Arrow, a train that pulled out of Leningrad's Moscow Station around midnight and arrived at Leningrad Station in Moscow just before dawn, was best. (The stations are identical, including matching busts of Lenin, so passengers leaving one see the same sight when they pull into the other.) Despite the hour or so wasted on each end traveling between downtown and the airport, Berg insisted that the forty-five-minute plane ride was far more efficient.

Berg had just settled into the window seat of an Ilyushin Il-18, one of the most elegant airliners built in the Soviet Union, on the morning of May 30, 1962, when a thin blonde beauty took the aisle seat next to him. He quickly established that her name was Elvira Valueva and that she was twenty-two years old, an engineer on a business trip to a factory near Moscow. Berg insisted on driving his new acquaintance to her hotel. He scribbled the telephone number of the Metropol on the back of his business card before they parted, making her promise to call in a few hours so he could return to take her to a concert that night. Staros answered the call, speaking with Elvira briefly before passing the phone to his partner, who blushed like a teenager.

Tickets for the concert, the first performance in the USSR by an American swing band, were as scarce as strawberries in a Siberian winter, but Berg managed somehow to snag two. On the way in, he and Elvira passed a thousand people who, unable to get tickets, stood close to the theater, hoping that some of the sound would leak out. Nikita Khrushchev led the thunderous applause that erupted as soon as the bandleader removed the clarinet from his mouth, signaling the end of "Let's Dance," the first piece. Benny Goodman and his orchestra continued, blowing pure joy into the warm Moscow evening. Joe beamed at Elvira as the band played "Mission to Moscow," a piece written especially for the historic tour. It was one of the warmest moments in Khrushchev's cultural "thaw," a hopeful sign for the world that the frigid relations between the USSR and the United States were improving, and, for Berg, the start of a relationship that endured for the rest of his life.

When Elvira joined Joe and Al for breakfast at the Metropol the next morning, she asked for a ride to the train station, but Berg insisted on driving the 200 kilometers to the factory where she was working. They stopped on the way to tour the house where Anton Chekhov had lived and worked, and at Yasnaya Polyana, Leo Tolstoy's estate, arriving at the factory after midnight. The next weekend Joe drove out and took her back to Yasnaya Polyana, where they cooked a meal over a fire in the woods. He talked about the city that was being built on the outskirts of Moscow according to his Staros's and his instructions, about a future in which millions of computers would do all the boring, repetitive jobs, freeing humans to write music and poems. Elvira recited pages of Pushkin from memory. The next week, Joe picked her up again, and they stopped on the way to Moscow to camp overnight, pitching a tent near Kryukovo, in the middle of the spot that was destined to become the headquarters of the Center for Microelectronics. He showed off the sites on the edge of a pond that he and Staros had selected to build private villas. Sitting by the fire, Berg confessed to Elvira: "I love you, but I have a family and children." He would never, ever do anything to hurt the kids, so leaving Vera was out of the question, he said. She also had a confession. A year earlier, she'd met an Aeroflot engineer at Sochi, a resort on the Black Sea. Desperate to get away from her father, a party boss in Sverdlovsk, she had married him three days after they met.[7]

When they returned to Leningrad, Elvira introduced Berg and Staros to a bohemian circle. The parties were like the musicales they remembered from their earlier life in Greenwich Village. Staros played the guitar and sang, accompanying two young men who later became very well-known bards, Yury Kukin and Evgeny Kliachkin. The dissident poet Joseph Brodsky, already on his way to becoming a Soviet counterculture icon, dropped in a few times to read his poetry. The thaw turned out to be fleeting, but for the moment Russia seemed on the right track, getting the government out of people's private lives, moving from success to success in space, reorienting the economy to focus on making life more comfortable for ordinary people, and exposing Stalin's crimes. Alexander Solzhenitsyn's *One Day in the Life of Ivan Denisovich* was published in November 1962, and over a million copies were distributed.

Other, less famous dissidents frequented the parties; one later died in a Siberian labor camp, where he'd been imprisoned for publishing *samizdat* (self-published) literature. Whenever political subjects came up, Berg always argued in favor of the Communist system. "Joe would say, 'I'm Communist number 1.' He accepted the system; he thought it was right," Elvira recalled years later. "He had an idealistic way of looking at it. It was technical progress. Bureaucratism was a problem — it was in the way of real Communism — but it would go away. He thought things should be better, that better people should be in charge. The system was good, but the wrong people were in charge." Berg cited approvingly Khrushchev's 1960 pledge that within twenty years the Soviet Union would achieve Communism, most people would be living rent-free in high-quality housing, the stark contrast in living standards between rural and urban areas would be eliminated, and Soviet economic performance would be far ahead of the capitalist nations'. He also appreciated the party's renewed assault on organized religion.[8]

In November 1962 the Central Committee of the Communist Party decided to dramatically expand electronics production, a development that was noted with particular interest by the U.S. Central Intelligence Agency. In April 1963, the CIA issued a secret report titled "Big Boost in Soviet Military Electronics by 1965." On the basis of statements in the Russian press, the American intelligence agency was concerned that the USSR would achieve the kinds of advances that Staros and Berg had envisioned when they conceived of the Center for Microelectronics, renamed the Scientific Center. By 1965, "Soviet military/space programs could represent expenditures for electronics about as large or larger than those currently forecast for US military/space programs in 1965," the CIA predicted. It estimated that the USSR would spend the equivalent of $15 billion on electronics in 1965. (Subsequent CIA reports about

Soviet microelectronics and computing were more sober, accurately pointing out that the USSR was so far behind the United States that it was unlikely ever to catch up.)[9]

The CIA report didn't mention that a big chunk of the increased electronics budget would be spent in a new scientific center devoted to microelectronics, nor did it contain a hint that any Americans were playing major roles in the Soviet electronics industry. The CIA and FBI were looking for Sarant and Barr, but no one in the U.S. government had a clue about their whereabouts. In the winter of 1962, the Bureau sent the U.S. legal attaché in Rio de Janeiro on a wild goose chase, based on faulty intelligence suggesting that Barr might be in Brazil. In New York, G-men interviewed Barr's brothers at least once a year, monitored all mail arriving at his relatives' homes, and kept Sarant's ex-wife, Louise, under periodic surveillance. Customs offices at all entry points to the United States were periodically instructed to be on the lookout for Barr and Sarant, or anyone resembling them.[10]

At about this time, the U.S. government ignored the first of several clues it received over the years about the fate of the missing engineers. Morton Nadler, the CCNY graduate whom Staros and Berg had met in Prague, spotted an article by Staros in a Russian computer journal. Seeking to ingratiate himself with the government in the hope that it would help his effort to recover U.S. citizenship, Nadler brought the article to the attention of officials at the American embassy in Paris. Staros was an American who, given his status and treatment in Czechoslovakia and the Soviet Union, might have been a Soviet spy before he defected, Nadler said. The State Department officials were not impressed, and there is no evidence that anyone thought to mention Nadler's report to the FBI or CIA.[11]

The wheels were set in motion to begin mass production of the UM-1NKh in 1962. The following year, the Leningrad Electromechanical Factory built the first of over 200 of the machines. At a minimum cost of 50,000 rubles, the little computers were five times more expensive than KB-2 had hoped, but the high cost did not prevent their widespread adoption. The control computers were used to automate more than 100 different industrial operations, ranging from papermaking to electricity generation. Berg traveled to Siberia to help install an UM-1NKh in the control room of the Beloyarsk nuclear power plant. The UM-1NKh was also installed at one of the largest steel plants in the Soviet Union, located at Cherepovets, where it controlled blooming and pressing operations.

In the summer of 1964, *Soviet Union,* the glossy propaganda magazine the USSR published in English and numerous other languages, featured an interview with the designer of the UM-1NKh, identified only as "Flippov." A photo on the inside cover — adjacent to photos of Khrushchev's recent trip to Egypt — showed Henry Firdman and two other young KB-2 engineers with the computer, but not even the mysterious Flippov's shadow. The pseudonym was probably employed because security officials feared that a Greek-sounding name like Staros could lead American intelligence to think of Sarant.

Alongside photos of an assembly line producing the computer, an article written by Staros summarized the rationale behind the UM-1NKh in terms very much like those he had used in briefings to the Soviet leadership. "The problem of 'cybernetisation' of industry has developed in some backroom boys in this field a kind of cybernetic megalomania. Carried away by the breath-taking opportunities of computer technology, they would like to see computers working faster and faster, with larger and larger 'memories.' They see them as Jacks of all trades. This tendency leads to the development of expensive, unique installations. What industry needs, however, is thousands of light, portable, efficient computers. Our machine answers these requirements."

Staros continued: "Our first consideration in designing it was that very many manufacturing processes have no need for a super-fast control mechanism capable of storing vast quantities of information. Hence, we can make our machines simpler, better and more compact."

The director of KB-2 reported that he and his team "gradually pictured in our mind's eye the kind of machine we needed. Our ideas have been implemented in this compact control device designed for use in many industrial spheres."

Staros did not neglect the political aspect, noting that the "ability of control machines [to control industrial operations] makes them especially valuable in a planned, socialist economy. And conversely, only in a planned economy can all the advantages of 'electronic brains' be revealed and exploited to the utmost." He also forecast the future of computing, predicting that "in six or seven years such machines will be a must not only at any industrial enterprise: hundreds and thousands of them will be working in offices, big and small, all over the country. There will develop a system of interconnected machines which will feed information into a few specialized computer centers. In those centres, which will have to handle tremendous amounts of information, exclusively designed giant machines, with huge storage capacities and capable of making tens of millions of computer operations a second, will come in handy."[12]

A full-page graphic showed a photo of the UM-1NKh along with typical industrial applications, including controlling atomic power production, steel and iron production, radio and electronic engineering, and healthcare.

The UM-1NKh also attracted attention in the United States. An article in the American journal *Control Engineering* said it was comparable in speed to the H-290, Honeywell's first transistorized computer, and to an IBM control computer that had first been marketed in 1963. It added that the UM-1NKh was "remarkable for small size and low power usage." The article concluded that the UM-1NKh and other Russian control computers were "technically behind ours, but not by much." Clearly, at this point in the game the USSR was in a position to stay close to the world level in computing, and Staros and Berg's dream of jumping ahead of the United States was not science fiction.[13]

The U.S. intelligence community also took note of the UM-1NKh. A secret CIA report distributed in 1966 ranked it among the "most important" special-purpose computers disclosed in open Soviet publications. It added that the UM-1NKh "is particularly interesting because of its small size."[14]

As its first mass-produced computer started to roll off the assembly line, KB-2's leaders were focused on cementing their role in the future of the micro-electronics industry. Staros was invited to drive the first symbolic stake into the ground at an August 1962 ceremony marking the start of construction work on the Scientific Center. The dream of a fifty-two-story building had been dismissed as impractical, but top-level architects who favored Futurist styles were commissioned to design the public buildings. The city's layout was quite pleasant, particularly by comparison with other Soviet cities of the same era, and remains so today.

The satellite city was officially named Zelenograd (Green City) on January 15, 1963, by a decree of the Moscow Executive Committee. The first planned city in the Soviet Union, it was designed to accommodate about 65,000 people. Its designers had been influenced by the British New Town movement. Unlike in other Soviet industrial centers, where apartment buildings were often built adjacent to belching industrial smokestacks, living areas and factories were located in separate areas. The standard four- and five-story non-descript apartment blocks were given generous allotments of green space. Zelenograd was supposed to be the first of ten similar-sized satellite cities where factories that clogged and polluted the center of Moscow would be relocated, but this grand idea was later abandoned.

Located twenty-five miles north of the Kremlin, Zelenograd was declared a part of Moscow. This designation provided a powerful recruitment tool because employees who accepted positions in Zelenograd automatically received a Moscow *propiska,* the coveted document that allowed an individual or family to live in the capital city. In those days people went to extreme lengths, including sham marriages, to acquire a Moscow residency permit. Arrangements were made for Zelenograd's residents to have access to superior supplies of food and consumer goods. Theaters, ice rinks, and other cultural amenities were built. All these incentives, plus the opportunity to work in an exciting field with greater possibilities for promotion than were offered in older, better-established areas, would have been enough to attract the best talent in the Soviet Union. In addition, the Center was authorized to surpass the pay rates available elsewhere in the Soviet electronics industry.

The administrative details for the Scientific Center began to take shape as the buildings were going up. Staros personally recruited and appointed the heads of the R&D institutes that were slated to be located in the new city. The plan was for these institutes to conduct basic research on the entire spectrum of microelectronics-related topics, from solid-state physics to integrated circuits to software, following a plan established by the Center's director.

The institutes at Zelenograd were to be coupled with design bureaus sprinkled throughout the Soviet Union charged with translating the institutes' breakthroughs into working prototypes. KB-2 would occupy a privileged position, concentrating on the most exciting areas, including innovative computers. Other design bureaus would be responsible for developing microelectronics manufacturing equipment, integrated circuits, and microelectronic devices such as telemetry systems to be used in satellite communications. The design bureaus would in turn work closely with manufacturing plants. Staros and Berg also interviewed candidates to run the subsidiary centers in the capitals of Ukraine, Estonia, Byelorussia, Armenia, and Georgia.

Staros and Berg were looking forward to moving into their adjoining villas in Zelenograd. Their tiny Leningrad apartments had become intolerably cramped. Tensions were inevitable when Joe and Vera slept in one room and their four children slept, played, and lived in the only other room; and the Staroses lived in similar tight quarters. Relations with local party officials were also growing increasingly testy.

As KB-2's prominence increased, so did the challenge its defiance posed to the Leningrad Regional Party Committee (Raicom). About 40 percent of KB-2's staff was Jewish, leading Leningrad party bosses to refer to it as a "nest of Zionists."[15]

Staros knew that his hiring policies were creating turbulence. "I'd come to Staros and say, 'We need to hire this guy,' and Staros would look at me with his big brown eyes and say, 'Jewish again? Wait a minute, how many do you have?' I'd say, 'What do you want from me?' — there was no expression 'politically correct' but that's what it was — 'do you want me to be politically correct or do you want me to get the job done?' And he'd say, 'Why would I have you, otherwise, if not to get the job done?' So I'd say, 'Okay, then give me some leeway.' And he'd say, 'Okay, but this is the last time.' And that was probably fifteen times. He was very untypical in that respect, and that's why he was hated also," Henry Eric Firdman, who was Jewish, remembered.[16]

Romanov, the second secretary of the Leningrad Raicom, a notorious anti-Semite, had become increasingly obstreperous, demanding that KB-2 adhere to his hiring policies — no more Jews, and more working-class party members. There was a fight over every new employee or promotion, and KB-2 didn't always win. Staros was effectively thumbing his nose at Romanov, believing he'd soon be based in Zelenograd, where he'd be free of the Leningrad Raicom and its small-minded bosses.

Although they were resolute Communists, Staros and Berg found the party's intrusion into KB-2's operations, and the lives of its employees, irritating and unnecessary. They never got used to the party's habit of monitoring people's private lives. Staros insisted on strictly linking rewards and responsibility to an individual's talent and accomplishments, but party officials sometimes overruled him. The party could deny a promotion to someone who was committing adultery or otherwise failing "to be a good Communist."

Staros and Berg never gave even a hint in public that they questioned some of the party's more eccentric practices. KB-2's party cell established quotas for its "patriotic contributions to agriculture," as the enforced "voluntary" service on collective farms was called. Like other educated people, Berg, Staros, and their families weren't exempt from the requirement to go every year to the countryside to pull potatoes out of the cold mud, pack eggs into boxes, or perform some other unpaid menial labor.

Staros and Berg felt more comfortable in Moscow, near Khrushchev, Ustinov, and other senior officials who they felt could be relied upon. They were pleased to see Zelenograd grow rapidly, from the earliest days, when newcomers were assigned apartments near the entrances of otherwise-empty apartment buildings in an effort to prevent looting by local villagers, to a population numbering tens of thousands within a couple of years. Roads, shops, offices, schools, and clinics sprouted like mushrooms. It was an example of how quickly men and resources could be mobilized in the Soviet Union, an auspicious beginning for the Scientific Center, Berg felt.

Staros and Berg had strong support from Khrushchev, Ustinov, and some others at the top, but they faced strong opposition from mid-level officials, especially as word spread that they would be in charge of the Scientific Center. Romanov wasn't the only Russian rankled by the idea of two foreigners — one of them a Jew — heading an important and high-prestige project with an annual budget of 100 to 150 million rubles. With his take-no-prisoners style, Staros in particular created a lot of ill will among rivals. By this time it was openly stated that Staros was a Canadian, and rumors circulated that he and

Figure 12. The Scientific Center at Zelenograd, headquarters for the Soviet microelectronics industry, winter 2003. (Photo by Givi Adzharsky, with permission.)

Berg were actually Americans. The Soviet Union was a closed, xenophobic society dominated by ethnic Russians. There were plenty of people, especially in the military, who didn't trust foreigners.

Confident that his position at the head of the Scientific Center would afford him the "untouchable" status he longed for, Staros had been acting like a drunk, ignoring the conventions of society and offending the sensibilities of those around him, oblivious to suggestions that he'd be better off taking things slower and easier. He sobered up rapidly in February 1963, when he received the shocking news that another man, Fyodor Lukin, an engineer and scientist who had succeeded Sergo Beria as chief engineer at KB-1, had been appointed general director of the Scientific Center. Staros was stunned to learn that he had to settle for the number-two position, deputy director of research and development, the job Berg had assumed he'd get. Berg never received an official appointment at the Center, though he had an office there and acted on Staros's behalf.

In an effort to sooth the ego of a man who had Khrushchev's personal blessing, Shokin told Staros he was being spared the burden of an administrative job, that his scientific talents would have been wasted as director. Although he didn't have the total control over the Center or the emerging industry he felt entitled to, institutes employing over 20,000 researchers with advanced degrees were reporting to Staros. He continued to believe that the director's job was within grasp; all that was required to push Lukin out, he thought, was a major technical success. A small team that was working on the UM-3, an airborne computer that was far more advanced than anything that had been produced to date, had been moved from KB-2 to the Center. They were supposed to quickly finalize a prototype of the machine, which was renamed the Zelenograd. The project foundered, however, because it proved impossible to build hybrid thin-film integrated circuits that were to be essential elements of the computer.

UM-2 was running into problems that were even more nettlesome. Technical obstacles could always be overcome, or a project like the UM-3/Zelenograd computer could be scrubbed and the lessons learned applied to the next project. The problem with the UM-2 wasn't that it didn't work, but rather that it might work very well. The prospect of a common computing platform applied in several branches of the armed forces seemed like a sound idea to Staros, Shokin, and Ustinov, but it threatened a lot of people, including some who were in a position to block its adoption. "If successful, it would become a standard in Soviet airborne computing, to be applied in army, air force, navy, space, and missile systems. Consequently, since their jobs were at stake, all of the people involved in designing such systems, computing devices, and subcomponents were vehemently opposed to the UM-2. The chief designers of airborne systems, for example, believed its success might mean the end of their monopoly on airborne computers for specific applications," Firdman noted.[17]

In an effort to derail the UM-2, critics demanded that the computer be proved reliable in at least two, and preferably three, different types of airborne platforms. This process was guaranteed to take a great deal of time, as it would be necessary to find design bureaus willing to take a chance on an unproven computer and to work with KB-2 to adapt the UM-2 to the needs of specific weapons.

Staros decided that the best way to promote the UM-2 was to collaborate with powerful chief designers who would be pleased to have their projects enhanced by an efficient, reliable computer, and who wouldn't feel threatened by a rival's success. He and Berg visited Tupolev, winning a commitment to incorporate a customized version of the computer, the UM-2T, in a long-range bomber that was under development. They were far more excited, however, by a meeting in late 1963 with the chief of OKB-1, the design bureau responsible for the Soviet Union's proudest accomplishments in space, from the Sputnik to the first manned space flight. The fact that they were permitted to discuss collaboration with OKB-1 is evidence of the Soviet regime's trust in Staros and Berg. OKB-1's activities were so secret that even the name of its director, Sergei Korolev, was a strictly kept secret.[18]

Korolev awarded two contracts to KB-2, for the production of the UM-2M and UM-2S computers. The former was intended as a test model and a tool for writing and debugging software. The UM-2S was to be used in the Soyuz spacecraft currently under development. Korolev was quite secretive about how the computers would be used, insisting that his own engineers would write all the applications software.

The orders for UM-2 versions were positive steps for KB-2, but they also meant that the government's formal acceptance of the computer could take years. In the meantime, Staros and Berg felt that they were losing momentum, that Zelenograd wasn't panning out as expected, and that there was a risk that everything they'd accomplished would unravel. As they saw it, they had come to a fork in the road: the choices were to retreat to Leningrad and focus on making KB-2 a success, or to try to put the Center in Zelenograd back on the course they had originally intended, which meant getting Staros to its helm.

Berg, skeptical about the ability of foreigners to win a fight against highly placed Russians, counseled the more conservative approach, but Staros insisted on pressing forward. He was convinced that the Zelenograd project, and along with it the chance to attain technological superiority over the United States, was headed for ruin and that the only way to save it was for him to gain complete control. Staros rejected peace overtures from Lukin, refusing to countenance anyone else in the director's office.[19]

Ironically, the American engineers were frustrated because Russia wasn't Soviet enough. Rather than submitting to the direction of a central administration, each of the institute directors in Zelenograd wanted to act autonomously. Seeking to increase their head counts — the primary measure of success for the director of a Soviet enterprise — they were starting to add on design and manufacturing capabilities, to morph into little semiautonomous companies that lacked the critical mass required to achieve real breakthroughs. The vision of a centralized, disciplined conglomerate bringing the resources of the entire Soviet state to bear on microelectronics was slipping away, apparently to be replaced with a multiplicity of feudal baronies.

Staros was particularly galled that the institute directors, men he had handpicked, were going over his head to Lukin, who was doing little to force them to adhere to the original ideal of a tightly organized enterprise. "For the idea of the Center of Microelectronics to function as we envisioned it, there had to be a director who was technically qualified. There had to be one director with the power to decide in which direction electronics would go," according to Berg.

"There was a minister who was responsible for the development of electronics in the Soviet Union, but he [Shokin] was not sufficiently technically erudite to decide concretely in a particular case, for example, should we make vacuum-deposited schematics, should we make solid circuits, or should we make hybrid circuits. We therefore demanded that the head of the Center be given the power to determine the direction for the development of microelectronics in the country. And this was denied. This was considered not a Soviet method of directing. We were told it had to be more democratic."[20]

The two American engineers considered their connection to Khrushchev their ace in the hole, and in the summer of 1964 they decided it was time to play it. They demanded a meeting with Khrushchev and, hearing that he was on an extended vacation, requested an audience with whoever was making decisions in his place. Surprisingly, a meeting was arranged for Staros and Berg with the Politburo member in charge of military industry. Staros presented his case for gaining control of Zelenograd and complained about the Leningrad party's interference with KB-2.

"You don't understand how our Soviet system works yet," Leonid Brezhnev, then second secretary of the Central Committee, told Staros and Berg. No action would be taken in response to their complaints, he brusquely informed them. Even more than the fact that Brezhnev rudely brushed them off, the thing that stuck in Berg's mind about the meeting was that he wore diamond cufflinks and a diamond stickpin in his tie. A Communist leader wearing diamonds! It was sacrilege for Berg, who, despite his continuing fealty to the Soviet Union and easygoing manner, harbored an abiding hatred for Brezhnev following this incident. Brezhnev and Romanov were probably the only two individuals he really detested.[21]

Staros and Berg didn't give up hope. They were confident that Khrushchev would return from the Black Sea soon and set everything straight. Remembering that Khrushchev had instructed them to communicate with him through his aide, they drafted a letter outlining their grievances and addressed it to him via Shuisky. The letter, sent in the first week of October 1964, reminded Khrushchev of his visit to KB-2 and his offer to be of assistance if the bureaucrats got in the way. "You were absolutely right when you told us the bureaucrats in both the Central Committee and Ministry of Electronic Industry would try to impede our progress. In fact, they have been preventing us from accomplishing what we promised you," the letter, which was signed by Staros alone, stated. It complained of the "lack of support from the Minister of Electronic Industry, comrade Shokin," and attacked Romanov, saying that his interference in KB-2's operations, especially in its hiring policies, was jeopardizing the design bureau's ability to fulfill its potential.[22]

Shuisky wrote back to Staros indicating that he'd received the letter and would pass it on to Khrushchev when he returned from his vacation.

Staros and Berg were breakfasting at the Metropol on October 16 when they learned that Khrushchev wasn't going to answer their letter, ever. A terse article in *Pravda* reported that the man whose support they were counting on—whom they had heard on the radio two days before clowning with a trio of cosmonauts orbiting the Earth—had resigned because of "advancing age and deteriorating health." The images they saw as they discussed the situation in the privacy of the icy streets of central Moscow were even more troubling. Two oversized photos had replaced the giant portrait of Nikita Sergeevich Khrushchev on the outside of the Hotel Moskva. One was of Aleksei Kosygin, who had become prime minister, and the other was the new party leader, their diamond-adorned nemesis, Leonid Brezhnev.

Staros and Berg drove out the Leningrad Highway to Zelenograd, their hearts in their shoes, not knowing what to expect but fearful that something awful was waiting. It was a relief to find that the guards let them into the building. Except for the stunned expression on everyone's face, apparently, nothing had changed.

Behind the scenes, however, some changes were being prepared for the two engineers who had the hubris to believe they could go over the heads of a minister and the Leningrad party leadership. When Khrushchev was placed under house arrest, Brezhnev and his supporters cleaned out the safe that served as the former ruler's in-basket. Staros's letter was discovered, and copies were forwarded to Shokin and Romanov, who no doubt read it with great interest.

Shokin went into action immediately, ordering a full investigation of KB-2. Staros and Berg had been lulled into a false sense of security and expected nothing out of the ordinary when a request came for them to attend a *kollegiya,* or board meeting, of the GKET in December. Two top KB-2 managers, Firdman and Mark Galperin, accompanied the design bureau's director and chief engineer to what they expected would be a routine discussion of administrative topics.

As soon as the *kollegiya* started, it became apparent that it was far from an ordinary meeting. Instead, it was basically a trial, except Staros and Berg were not expected to put up any defense. Shokin had gathered people from every station who had interacted with KB-2, from unskilled workers to technical experts and customers. The minister led and directed the denunciations, accusing Staros and Berg of squandering state funds and failing to fulfill commitments specified in official plans—very serious accusations in the Soviet Union. They were castigated for real mistakes, such as the UM-3, and minor errors were blown up into examples of major malfeasance. The trial-and-error process from which the stepping-stones of all scientific and technological progress are built was presented as evidence of gross incompetence.

Staros and Berg were paying the price for attempting to graft an American-style management culture onto the trunk of Soviet industry. Where they came from, it was perfectly acceptable, even routine, to overpromise. A company would often announce a new product when it was conceived, and there was rarely any outcry if it took years for it to be manufactured or even if it never made it onto the market.

The proceedings verged on the ridiculous. For example, opprobrium was piled on them for insisting on building "houses inside houses," their accuser's term for clean rooms, which are essential for assembling microelectronic devices. Another "expert" said that clean rooms were "an invention of American imperialism." Shokin moderated the abuse only once, when an overeager accuser, employing an outmoded formulation from the Stalin era, excoriated Staros and Berg for participating in an international Zionist plot.

Berg went along with the program, staying quiet or humbly admitting errors. Staros, his Greek blood boiling, was defiant. The criticisms of Shokin and Romanov in the letter to Khrushchev, which had been read to the *kollegiya*, were impetuous mistakes, he acknowledged, but the letter should be understood in the context of all of his and Berg's achievements. They had brought microelectronics to the Soviet Union, had conceived the Scientific Center, and had made tremendous contributions to the nation's industry and defense.

Shokin was visibly angered by his former protégé's self-aggrandizing remarks. "Philip Georgeivich, it seems to me that you are under the strange fantasy that you are the creator of Soviet microelectronics. This is wrong. The creator of Soviet microelectronics is the Communist Party, and the sooner you realize that fact, the better it would be for you," Shokin said. He also tried to disabuse Staros of the notion that he had conceived of the Scientific Center. The author of that idea, it turned out, was not the Communist Party of the Soviet Union (CPSU), but Shokin himself.[23]

The unrelenting stream of abuse, which flowed for hours, was all the more humiliating for Staros and Berg because their employees, Firdman and Galperin, witnessed it. As he sat listening to his character, loyalty to the Soviet Union, and technical competence being shredded, Berg felt as if everything was lost. He imagined that men with handcuffs were waiting outside the room, that he and Staros would be arrested as enemies of the state, just as Tupolev and Korolev had been a generation earlier.

After about five hours, when every blemish on KB-2's record had been exaggerated to the point that it appeared to be a cancerous tumor, one of

Ustinov's men, a representative of the defense ministry, took the floor. He said that while it was true that Staros and Berg had made grave mistakes, in light of their previous contributions to the Soviet Union, they would be given a second chance. At the time, it seemed like a spontaneous reprieve. The two old friends stumbled into the cold night stunned and drained, feeling like condemned men who had been saved from the noose at the last moment, but who faced an uncertain future.

Looking back on it, Berg was convinced that Shokin had prerehearsed the entire event, just as he'd walked through Khrushchev's visit to SKB-2. He also believed that the outcome of the meeting, including their pardon, was preordained. Subsequent events supported the notion that Shokin and Ustinov's goal was to clip the foreigners' wings by removing them from Zelenograd, but to make sure that the USSR continued to benefit from their technical skills.[24]

On paper, Staros retained his job at the Scientific Center, but it was clear that he would have no further role there. He was officially stripped of the deputy director title in early 1965. Meanwhile, he and Berg were left in charge of KB-2.

Soon after their return to Leningrad, a twenty-page letter outlining Staros and Berg's alleged mistakes and faults was read aloud to all the employees at KB-2. The humiliation, shame, and disappointment were too much for Staros. He suffered a mental and physical breakdown and was committed to a sanitarium outside Leningrad. In his absence, Berg ran KB-2, which had been made subordinate to the Scientific Center.

Staros returned to KB-2 after six months. He moved ahead resolutely, determined to make the best of the situation, to use the resources at hand to prove that he was a great scientist and engineer, that his small team could do things the far bigger Center in Zelenograd, with its less competent leadership, couldn't accomplish. Things were never the same, however, for Staros and Berg. Although they never stopped trying to break into the elite group of top-ranked chief designers, to become the Soviet version of captains of industry, it was always from the position of underdogs. They never recovered the status of rising stars that Khrushchev's blessing had conferred. From this point on, KB-2 was subject to the same constraints that all other design bureaus struggled with; the unique background of its directors, once a major asset, was if anything a liability. As foreigners, they were suspect, and as individuals closely identified with the disgraced former ruler, they were stigmatized.

Following Staros's breakdown, his relationship with Berg changed. Privately, he blamed Berg for the disastrous letter to Khrushchev, telling Firdman that "Joe screwed up my whole life, not only once, but twice." Firdman, who was almost an adopted son to Staros, didn't know at the time what he was talking about. Decades later he understood that the first "screwup" was his recruitment during World War II as a spy. Over time it became clear that although the second screwup, the letter to Khrushchev, precipitated Staros's downfall, Brezhnev's accession to power made it inevitable. The KB-2 director occasionally criticized, even ridiculed, Berg in front of their employees, something he had never done before their Zelenograd debacle. Berg accepted this treatment with complete equanimity, astonishing people who observed him closely by his subservience to Staros.[25]

Despite his critical attitude toward Berg, Staros continued to rely on his partner to run day-to-day operations at KB-2, to lead teams developing new technologies, and to solve difficult engineering problems. Their families remained close, with Joe playing the part of the boisterous, kindly uncle to the Staros children.

To no one's surprise, Romanov's attacks on KB-2 intensified. Even if they hadn't already done a great deal to antagonize the Leningrad party officials, anyone closely identified with Khrushchev would have been marked for retribution. Berg was surprised to find that Shokin, the organizer of his and Staros's fall from grace, backed the design bureau and its management against the Leningrad party. Shokin had intended to wound, not destroy them; the two foreigners could still make important contributions to Soviet microelectronics and, not incidentally, to Shokin's career.

Leningrad Design Bureau, 1965–1973

Like a cardplayer who rearranges a losing hand in the futile hope that a winning combination will emerge, Leonid Brezhnev launched a reorganization of Soviet industry in October 1965. Shokin was shuffled into a higher position, as head of one of nine ministries responsible for military industry. The newly created Ministry of Electronic Industries incorporated the old GKET and several other entities. Now he was responsible not only for designing new electronic products, including those that came out of Staros and Berg's labs, but also for manufacturing them. The requirement to actually squeeze products out of Russia's sclerotic factories significantly dulled Shokin's ardor for innovation, especially when it involved new, difficult-to-produce, high-tech products.

The KGB decided about this time to turn the nomenclature for secret organizations inside out. Whereas the names of entities like design bureaus had been secret and their mailbox addresses public, henceforth new secret addresses would be assigned and entities would be referred to by proper names. KB-2 came to be known as the LKB (Leningrad Design Bureau) but was identified in classified documents as P.O. Box G-4783.[1]

While UM-1NKh's were finding homes throughout the Soviet Union, the emphasis at LKB was literally on getting the UM-2 off the ground. The design bureau's engineers were particularly excited by the possibility that their computer would be launched into space. It was an opportunity for them to acquire prestige, probably a state prize, raises, and other perks. Creating the UM-2S posed significant engineering hurdles, particularly paring it down to less than half the size and mass of the UM-2 prototype. It also presented a political challenge. Just as Khrushchev's imprimatur had helped the LKB win orders before 1964, association with the fallen leader made it difficult to retain them or win new orders.

Sergei Korolev, who had lost half his teeth and most of his health in the labor camps, had good reasons to be distrustful of authority. The chief designer of OKB-1 was usually extremely autocratic, especially with suppliers, but he was warm with Berg, and especially with Staros. Korolev and Staros had compatible personalities. Both were workaholics. Despite his many successes — no individual in the twentieth century came close to contributing as much to the manned exploration of space — Korolev also felt he was an underdog. He was constantly on guard to ward off attacks from Vladimir Chelomei and other rival missile designers. Like Korolev, Staros was driven by a vision bigger than himself. Korolev and Staros were what today would be called "control freaks," convinced that progress would be made in their respective fields only if a single individual had dictatorial control, and they were confident of their own qualifications for the position.[2]

The UM-2S got a boost in mid-1965 when Berg found the specifications for an IBM computer that was used aboard the American Gemini spacecraft published in American technical journals. "It was a very simple calculator for navigation problems," Berg recalled, while the UM-2S "was much more serious." Berg and Staros translated the article and showed Shokin and Korolev that the UM-2 was superior in every respect to the IBM computer that flew onboard the Gemini.[3]

"The chief designer, Korolev, told us that there was a big fight [within OKB-1] because our computer weighed about 25 kilograms, and each kilo of weight meant you had to have an additional 1,000 kilos of fuel," Berg recalled. "Twenty-five kilograms for this computer would mean that 25 kilograms of other equipment couldn't be put on board." In early January 1966, Korolev told Staros and Berg that he'd resolved the conflicts and had drafted an order that would ensure that the UM-2S would be incorporated into the Soyuz craft. Korolev told Berg that the UM-2S would be used to maintain the environment aboard the Soyuz, to automate navigation, and for other purposes. He promised to sign the order in about two weeks, after he recovered from minor surgery. The Soviet space program, and the LKB, suffered a major blow on January 14, 1966, when Korolev unexpectedly died on the operating table.

"The new chief designer was more careful, to put it mildly, and didn't want to take a chance" on the UM-2S, Berg remembered. "The point that to me is very, very significant is that if we had succeeded in getting into space with Korolev, we probably would have been what I call 'untouchable.' We would have been in a position where the leadership of the party and the government would have been, practically speaking, unable to control us. They could not have demoted or removed us from our positions as directors" of the LKB.[4]

The UM-2S was delivered to Korolev's successor in 1966, but it was never installed in a spacecraft.[5]

The collaboration with Tupolev's design bureau wasn't working out either. Although the chief designer was on good personal terms with the two "Czechs" he had met and vigorously endorsed a decade earlier, his subordinates were less than enthusiastic. There was great resistance to adding to the risk of a new airplane design by incorporating an unproven computer. Relations between the LKB and Tupolev's design bureau gradually petered out. The order for the UM-2T was canceled in 1967.

After its attempts to get the UM-2 tested in space or aboard an aircraft failed to get off the ground, the LKB began a long-term collaboration with the Navy in 1966 that ultimately led to military use of its "airborne computer" in an equally demanding environment, deep under the sea. When it received a contract from a Navy unit based in Peterhof, a Leningrad suburb, the LKB team initially thought the UM-2 could be installed on submarines with only minor modifications; but just as the need to overcome gravity had forced the LKB to slim down its computer for extraterrestrial applications, the tight spaces in a sub's control room necessitated a complete redesign to reduce the size of the Uzel (Knot), as the naval version of the UM-2 was called, and to design completely new display hardware. The LKB also faced challenges in writing software for navigation and for aiming torpedoes.

Foreign citizenship was a burden for Berg, restricting him to Intourist hotels when he traveled and sometimes making it difficult to gain access to military bases where Uzel R&D was being conducted. It was clear that Russia was his home — he'd been a Soviet patriot since the 1940s — so Berg eagerly became a citizen of the Soviet Union in 1965. In accord with the legend he'd lived under since arriving in Prague, "English" was written on space in his internal passport indicating nationality. Vera continued to insist on retaining Czechoslovakian citizenship, and she ensured that each of their children was registered as a Czech.

Berg never attempted to teach his children English. Czech, the only language they heard at home, was literally their mother tongue. They started school completely unaware of the Cyrillic alphabet that is used in Russian but not in Czech. The four Berg youngsters were sent to a special school in Leningrad that provided two hours of instruction in music at the end of the regular school day. Each studied a different instrument (flute, violin, cello, piano), and Joe dreamed that someday the Berg Quartet would travel the world performing classical music to great acclaim. The combination of inherited talent, a home environment in which music was played, appreciated, and discussed, and world-class instruction succeeded. Each of the children graduated from the Leningrad Conservatory and, to their father's great pleasure, pursued the kind of musical career he had dreamed of for himself.

In the spring of 1966, Berg was informed that he finally was close to achieving one of his lifelong goals, admission into the Communist Party of the Soviet Union. A special meeting of the party cell at the LKB was convened to formally determine the fate of his application. The protocol called for the candidate to state his autobiography, which ostensibly would serve as the basis for his peers to determine if he was suitable material for the party. Berg gave a twenty-minute speech, larded with Soviet-style platitudes. These speeches usually were rooted in a person's actual life story, salted with insincere rhetoric about class struggle, and peppered with bits of the Marxist-Leninist dogma that every child absorbed in school.

Because of the need to stick to his KGB-supplied legend, Berg's story was even more fictional than most. It began with a description of how he first became aware of social inequality as a teenager in Johannesburg, followed by a creative digression regarding the role Maxim Gorky's novel *Mother* had played in raising his consciousness about the class struggle. The plight of the blacks in South Africa and the powerful images of the novel brought the young Berg to the realization, he explained in a theatrical manner, that he must devote his life to the victory of Communism all over the world. The desire to help build socialism, he said, brought him first to Prague and then to Leningrad.[6]

As soon as Berg concluded his speech, the inevitably unanimous vote to accept him as a probationary member was held. To mark the occasion, *tovarisch* Berg was given the privilege of chairing the remainder of the meeting. One of the happiest moments of his life, it was, as was typical for Berg, marked by laughter. He read some kind of resolution that the meeting was supposed to vote on, and then in a loud voice called out the familiar refrain: "*Kto za?*" (who is for?), "*Kto protiv?*" (who is against?) — of course nobody was against; but when he meant to ask "*Kto vozderzhalsya?*" (who abstains?), instead he asked "*Kto zaderzhalsya?,*" which means "who is late?" His comrades burst out laughing. Despite this slip of the tongue, in December 1966 Berg was very pleased to receive his red Communist Party membership booklet, with a gold-embossed hammer and sickle on the cover and spaces for the party secretary to record monthly dues payments.

Figure 13. Joseph Berg's Communist Party booklet, noting his birth in 1917 and acceptance into the party in December 1966. Berg's monthly salary and payment of party dues are recorded at right. His base salary at this time, in 1974, was 650 rubles, more than a deputy minister's, while bonuses boosted it to an average of 837 rubles, an enormous sum at a time when many engineers were paid less than 200 rubles per month. (Source: Joel Barr's personal papers; photo by Anton Berg, with permission.)

The following year, the Berg and Staros families received a prize that from a practical standpoint was far more rewarding. With the exception of their very large salaries and cars, the two foreigners had received few perks during their decade in Russia. In 1966 Berg finally applied for larger apartments, and in 1967 both families moved into sprawling six-room apartments in nine-story buildings a few blocks apart. Soviet apartment buildings were generally built according to standard designs that didn't include such large apartments. The Staroses' and Bergs' unusually large dwellings were created by joining two three-room apartments.

In the process of unpacking in the new apartment, Kristina Staros, then fifteen years old, found two letters in Anna's belongings that gave her an inkling of the tragedy of her mother's life. The letters, which had never been mailed, were addressed to Bruce Dayton. Anna wrote that she'd never intended to leave forever. She asked Bruce to make sure that their son and daughter, Eric and Derry, never forgot her, and to tell them that she loved and missed them terribly. Confronted with the letter, Anna told her children that she'd had another husband in the United States and had been forced to leave him and her children behind.

Anna and Phil admitted that they were Americans, not the Canadians they'd pretended to be, but they didn't reveal that they'd once had different names or explain how they came to be in the Soviet Union. The subject was too painful to discuss in detail, so it was many years before Anna's Russian children learned more details about their American siblings. Anna frequently said she hoped that somehow, someday she would be reunited with her children, but the likelihood of this fantasy's being fulfilled seemed extraordinarily remote.

Moving to new apartments put the Berg and Staros children, for the first time in their lives, in different buildings. Phil and Anna spoke English at home, but their children responded in Russian and, unlike the Bergs, considered themselves Russians. At the same time, they were conscious that they were different from their classmates. They ate American food at home and didn't adopt many typical Russian customs and mannerisms.

While the Bergs went to Czechoslovakia for the summer, the Staroses were sent to Young Pioneer camp, the somewhat militarized Soviet versions of Scout camps. Phil rarely discussed his work or his connections with prominent politicians and scientists in front of the children, so it came as a huge surprise to Kristina Staros when her father was invited one summer in the 1960s, as an eminent person, to address the children at her Pioneer camp.[7]

Berg requested an apartment on the top floor in the new building on Budapestkaya Street, close to the roof, where he planned to test his ideas about hydroponic techniques for growing strawberries and tomatoes in the inhospitable Leningrad climate. He turned one room of the apartment into a musical instrument. Inside, there was an amplifier, a messy, monstrous-looking contraption Berg had built from scratch and stuffed with huge vacuum tubes, which, belying its ungainly appearance, produced a clean, powerful high-fidelity signal, far better than anything available on the Soviet market. This device was connected to a pair of enormous speakers, the type used in cavernous Russian movie theaters, mounted in two doors on opposite sides of the room, pointing inward. Even at low decibels, a person sitting in the room felt the vibrations of the music as much as heard it. To the discomfort of the prosecutor and his family living below, Berg liked to crank up the volume, in part to compensate for the deafness in his left ear, but also to add a tactile dimension to the music.

Berg collected and carefully cataloged thousands of classical records. As word of the collection spread in Leningrad's music circles, students from the

Leningrad Conservatory would visit the Berg apartment to listen to a particular piece of music, for example, a specific Sibelius symphony. As soon as he heard that electric organs were being produced in the Soviet Union, Berg ordered one from the factory in Riga. "It was the size of a regular organ. Of course he modified it immediately," replacing the amplifier with a more powerful one, his son Robert recalled. Later Berg rushed out to buy one of the first color television sets the moment he learned that they were available.[8]

Staros also built a stereo system that reflected his personality. The amplifier was transistorized, housed in a polished, neat metal case that was hooked up to a reel-to-reel tape recorder. Staros's cataloged music collection was smaller than Berg's but wider ranging. It included bootlegged tapes of the Beatles and other Western popular musicians whose works were officially banned in the Soviet Union.

To outsiders, it seemed as if Berg and Staros lived inside invisible bubbles where the rules governing Soviet society didn't apply. Staros ran the LKB with a combination of informality and rigor that was completely out of phase with typical Soviet enterprises. In contrast to the ubiquitous rigid seniority system, he quickly promoted talented young people to highly responsible positions. While most men in comparable positions in military industry had more political and managerial than technical talent, Staros greatly preferred speaking with engineers to meeting with people who managed engineers, and he and Berg were intimately involved in the details of the LKB's work. Their names were on scores of patents not because as the bosses they had the right to claim authorship to other people's ideas, but because they were actively leading the research. Staros also pushed his employees to work harder and in a more disciplined manner than was common in Soviet enterprises. He and Berg replaced the usual pattern, in which the employees felt oppressed by their bosses and therefore conspired against them, with the sense that the LKB was struggling against the entire system of Soviet industry. Many of the employees felt that they had something special at the LKB that was worth fighting to preserve.

It was quickly evident to Russians that the LKB and the two foreigners who ran it were unique and distinctly non-Soviet. Berg was particularly cavalier about restrictions. For example, friends and associates were surprised by his behavior when he was pulled over by traffic police, a common occurrence given his erratic driving habits. Whenever a cop asked for his driver's license, Berg would put on a performance, slowly pulling a Communist Party booklet and government commendations out of his wallet and piling them up on the dashboard, all the while talking a blue streak. Often the bemused policeman, not sure if he was dealing with an important dignitary or a madman, would let Berg go. If he persisted, Berg declined to make the customary arrangement, which was a small bribe discreetly slipped to the officer. Instead, he would insist that a ticket be issued and that a hole be punched in his driver's license. The holes worked like the points that are assessed against licenses in the United States; a certain number of holes in a license rendered it void. Asked why he risked losing his right to drive rather than pay a small bribe, Berg would laugh and reveal that he'd made several copies of his license (putting the photography skills he had practiced in Greenwich Village to good use). When one started to get too many holes, he simply threw it away and used another one.

Berg frequently told acquaintances that he'd heard a piece of news on the BBC or Voice of America, a revelation that shocked Russians. It was illegal to listen to shortwave broadcasts, which were sometimes audible despite Soviet jamming, and although many people listened, very few admitted it publicly. Berg would quickly point out that he listened in English, and thus was protected by the same authorization that gave him free access to foreign publications. He used the information gleaned from the radio and American newspapers to point out the inequities of the capitalist world, emphasizing the fate of the poor, racism, crime, and other seamy sides of American society.[9]

Because they were exposed to both Soviet and American media, Berg and Staros were acutely aware of the Cold War, and they had no doubts about which side was the aggressor. "We always felt that all of the wars that occurred had been started by capitalist countries, that the leaders of the United States had demonstrated absolutely without question that they would stop at nothing to fulfill their ambitions," Berg recalled. "We knew the Cold War was getting hotter all the time. We had seen what the American leaders could do, and that they would stop at nothing to preserve the system." Truman's decision to drop the second atomic bomb on Nagasaki "left an indelible impression in our mind," confirming the ruthlessness of the United States, Berg said. This view was bolstered by America's role in conflicts from Korea to Vietnam.[10]

When called upon to make toasts at weddings and birthdays, Berg often expressed the hope that the celebrants would get rich. If he was scolded that these were rude, possibly dangerous remarks, Berg would reply that it was proper to aspire to be rich because under real Communism everyone would be wealthy beyond imagination. After all, Lenin and Khrushchev had both predicted that living standards would be higher under Communism than they had been under capitalism.

On most Sunday mornings, Berg woke early and cooked stacks of pancakes — not paper-thin Russian blini, but thick, American-style pancakes, made from flour he'd create by putting buckwheat into a coffee bean grinder — and invited neighbors and friends over. During breakfast, Berg played Bach's organ music and proudly showed off gadgets he'd made or modified. On weekend afternoons the family usually went to the countryside for a picnic, creating an unusual public spectacle. Four youngsters, in a society in which one child was the norm and almost no family had more than two, and a bulldog in the back of a black Volga, the large sedan reserved almost exclusively for government motor pools, Vera in the passenger seat, and, in the behind the wheel, where people expected to see a brooding official driver with a cap, Joe bounced along, smiling broadly, gesturing expansively, plotting an erratic course. Even if he had acquired a perfect accent, the smiling would have given away his foreign origins. Russians rarely smile in public; they consider it a sign of stupidity.

Berg was a devoted, proud papa, who unlike his own father was extremely close to his children. He made toys for them and was very proud of their accomplishments. He doted particularly on his first son, Robert, shooting home movies of his first steps. At the same time, Berg inhabited a parallel world that his family knew nothing of.

Employing the psychological compartmentalization he'd honed as a secret Communist and Soviet spy during World War II, Berg maintained a separate life with Elvira, and was able to switch back and forth apparently without effort. He was passionate about her, but refused to even consider leaving Vera. Berg never gave Elvira money, telling her that "only prostitutes get money. Love is love, but wallets are separate." They remained close from the day they met to his death.[11]

On more than one occasion, Joe left his apartment on a weekend evening, saying that he was going to the garage to work on the Volga, which was always in need of repair. Elvira, who had a key to the garage, would be waiting for him with a bottle of sweet Georgian wine. They would hop in the back seat and, as Joe called it, "do the business." Then he'd step out of the tiny garage, make sure none of his neighbors were walking by, and give Elvira the all-clear signal, indicating that she could return to her family while he went back to his. He also secretly arranged for her to accompany him on business trips to Moscow, Odessa, and other cities, sometimes for weeks at a time.[12]

Elvira became pregnant three times from such encounters. The first baby died during delivery in the summer of 1963, but later she gave birth to two girls. Elvira told Joe that her husband believed he was the father of her girls, even after an incident in which he returned home unexpectedly and caught Joe in his bed with Elvira. The infuriated husband dragged Berg, who had hastily dressed, by the collar to the nearest *militsia* (police) station. The cops assured the distraught husband they would deal with the miscreant harshly, but sent Joe on his way a few minutes later, cheerfully admonishing him to be more careful in the future. Berg was certain Elvira had set up the drama as part of a plot to force him to divorce Vera and marry her.

Berg spent a great deal of time with Elvira during the long summer vacations that Vera and the kids spent in Czechoslovakia. In the summer of 1968, Elvira joined Joe in Latvia, where he was working on a project for the Navy. The day after she arrived, he drove her out of Liepaja and parked in a lonely spot, under pine trees. They parted the strands of a wire metal fence, climbed to the top of a sand dune, and, spotting the sea, stripped and rolled in each other's arms down to the water.

For Vera and the Berg children, trips to her family's home in Mnichovice were joyous homecomings, chances to hike and play in the forests and visit Prague, less than an hour away, which seemed infinitely freer and more cosmopolitan than Leningrad. They were staying with Vera's father as usual when on August 20, 1968, Warsaw Pact tanks rolled across the border and Russian paratroopers battled civilians in Prague. Like virtually all Czechs, Vera was horrified by the unprovoked occupation, which validated her family's long-standing hatred of Communism and disdain for Russia.[13]

Most communications to Czechoslovakia were cut, but after a couple of days Joe managed to get through via a telephone in Shokin's office. Vera insisted that there was no way she or the children were returning to Leningrad, while he shouted into the line that they must come at once. It took several weeks, but eventually Shokin and a contact at the KGB helped Joe arrange for his wife and children to be ferried back to Russia on a special flight with two other Soviet families.[14]

Despite his wife's scornful skepticism, Berg stubbornly believed the official Soviet line, that German troops had been colluding with the reformist Czech leaders to invade the country and forcibly tear it from the socialist camp. The Czech Communist reformer Alexander Dubèek was a fool and a traitor who had forced the Soviet Union to act, Berg said.

Over the years, Berg and Staros had scoured the newspapers for information about the Rosenberg case and about their families. They'd seen some references to themselves, including Senator Joseph McCarthy's hysterical assertions that the espionage ring they were associated with was still operating at Fort Monmouth in the late 1950s. They also read reports about friends and relatives — Louise Sarant, Vivian Glassman, Max Elitcher, and others — being forced to testify to grand juries and later to Senator McCarthy's subcommittee. The only personal news gleaned from the press was evidence that Sarant's brother's business was thriving; advertisements for Sarant Motors appeared almost every week in the *New York Times.*

One morning in late January 1969, Staros put down his copy of the *International Herald Tribune*, turned to the companions who were breakfasting with him at the Metropol in Moscow, and uttered a single enigmatic sentence: "By now, I could already be free." He didn't explain the remark, and the young men from the LKB who were with him didn't think to scan the newspaper for clues. If they had, they would have seen an article on the front page, under the headline "Morton Sobell Free as Spy Term Ends," reporting: "Morton Sobell, sentenced to 30 years for a wartime espionage conspiracy to deliver vital national secrets to the Soviet Union, was released from prison yesterday after serving 17 years and 9 months." The article quoted Sobell's son, Mark, as saying, "It's about time — my father was innocent," and noted that David Greenglass had already completed his fifteen-year sentence. Staros calculated that if he had stayed behind, he would not have served more time than Sobell.[15]

Staros never expressed regret about his decision to flee the United States, but while in Russia he constantly strived for the kind of recognition he and Berg imagined they would have achieved had they remained in the capitalist world. In the spring of 1969, the LKB submitted its tabletop computer, the UM-1NKh, as a candidate for the State Prize, formerly called the Stalin Prize, the second-highest award in the Soviet Union. Just as their hopes of winning were soaring, Berg and Staros learned that the Leningrad Raicom had refused to forward the application to the commission in Moscow. "[Grigory] Romanov was very worried about the fact that we were becoming absolutely out of his control. Of course, all of the higher-ups in the [electronics] ministry and the engineers and specialists who worked in microelectronics knew there were two foreigners working at a high level in Leningrad. There had been many, many meetings in which we had spoken. We became very well known in the industry as foreigners who were heads of one of the key organizations in Russia. Romanov understood what would have happened if we had still further successes. We would not be under his control," Berg remembered. "When we heard that the Leningrad Party had refused to approve our entry for the State Prize, our mood sank. We knew that without the support of the Leningrad party organization, it was impossible for a State Prize to be given to us."[16]

Having given up hope, Berg was astonished on the morning of November 9, 1969, when he received a telephone call at home from someone who had seen his name in *Pravda*. He, Staros, and several of their employees had been awarded the State Prize for the UM-1NKh. Somehow, their application had bypassed the Leningrad party and found its way into the hands of the nominating commission in Moscow. The prize was approved and their commendation signed by Mstislav Keldysh, president of the Soviet Academy of Science.

Staros and Berg were elated by the recognition, but they quickly discovered that it was effectively a kiss of death. Leningrad party officials had also been surprised to read about the recipients of the State Prize; unlike the engineers at the LKB, they weren't pleased. "We were close to the point of being untouchable," Berg recalled. "The possibility of the international community knowing that two foreigners had been working in the Soviet Union and were responsible for the level of microelectronics in the country was too much for the party to tolerate. We were called in by Romanov and practically given a command to hand in our resignation. My partner and I decided that we were not going to do that, although we knew that this was an impossible situation, that sooner or later we'd be kicked out. We determined to fight it to the end. We fought it technically by convincing everybody, including the minister [Shokin], that we had new ideas on the drawing board that had the potential for getting ahead of the United States and Japan."[17]

Surpassing the West, particularly in high technology, however, was no longer a compelling, or realistic, goal for the Soviet leadership. The grim economic realities that Khrushchev had hoped brilliant technological feats would camouflage had become impossible to ignore, while America had reacted forcefully to the USSR's early lead in space. Apollo 11's July 1969 mission signaled the end of the race to put men on the moon. The Soviets continued to invest in space missions, but Brezhnev and company were far less willing than Khrushchev had been to pour money into projects aimed at boosting the USSR's image. A year and a half after the Apollo II lunar landing, the world hardly noticed when a Soviet spacecraft landed on the moon's surface and returned to Earth with a sample of lunar soil in September 1970. Berg ruefully noted that the Americans had continued to develop space applications of computing, so the Apollo had a sophisticated onboard computer, while the Soviet craft's computer was far less powerful than the UM-2.

In the late 1960s and early 1970s, the Soviet Union adopted a policy that infuriated Staros, Berg, and those who worked under them at the LKB: to reverse-engineer the best products manufactured abroad, most notably in Japan and the United States. Only imitations of designs already proven in the West would be funded; it became almost impossible to get anything innovative approved unless its designers could point to an American analogue.

An LKB engineer ran across an example of this mentality when trying to convince a group of technical experts in the Ministry of Electronic Industry to fund the development of one of the world's first computer-aided design (CAD) systems, which was to be applied to all stages of integrated circuit (IC) design. "I made a presentation at the ministry," Henry Firdman recalled, "and those high-level people sat there and said, 'This is great!' And then one of them, the highest one, a department head at the ministry, asked me, 'Do the Americans do that?' When I said I didn't know, he said, 'Son, remember, if they don't do something, it isn't worth doing.' "[18]

The policy was a desperate response to the technological revolution that occurred in the West when civilian manufacturers enthusiastically adopted technologies originally developed for space and military applications, particularly in microelectronics. As long as the competition was confined to the military sphere, the USSR's military contractors could keep within sight of their competitors in the United States, but when the race was opened to all comers, the pathetic Soviet civilian manufacturing sector couldn't even get out of the starting blocks.

It was obvious, even to Soviet bureaucrats, that copying products that had already been manufactured in the West could only cause their industry to fall ever farther behind, especially as the pace of innovation was increasing. They hit on what appeared to be a sounder strategy: steal late-stage plans for cutting-edge technology and rapidly put products based on them into production.

The biggest reverse-engineering project undertaken in the Soviet Union was a copy of NASA's space shuttle. The USSR invested billions of rubles to build what amounted to an enormous white elephant that flew a single unmanned mission before being permanently grounded. Today it sits in a Moscow park, perhaps the most expensive piece of playground equipment in history.[19]

In the 1960s, the Soviet bloc launched a project based on this strategy that was reminiscent of Stalin's order to copy the B-29 bomber. This time the target was the IBM 360/370 series of computers, and the idea was somewhat subtler. Rather than make a bolt-for-bolt copy, a functional equivalent capable of running the same software would be built. Like the TU-4, it took a massive effort to build the Ryad, as the IBM 360 clone was called, and the teams working on the project in the USSR and each of the Soviet-bloc countries were forced to develop new skills. There were two other important similarities: both projects were helped by the KGB's acquisition of proprietary information, and in both cases the end result was a serviceable, obsolete product.[20]

In 1963 the LKB received documents stamped "strictly confidential" in two languages. The English classification had been imposed by IBM, which didn't want commercial rivals to see the information, and the Russian classification was required by the KGB. The confidential papers were technical documentation for the IBM 360, which was unveiled to the public a year later. The LKB didn't play a major role in the Ryad, although Staros, Berg, and other LKB engineers reviewed copies of purloined IBM specifications; but it did have a leading part in a similar effort, a crash program to make facsimiles of one of the first and most dramatic examples of the civilian use of space microelectronics.[21]

When North American Rockwell Corporation began producing metal oxide semiconductor large-scale integration (MOS LSI) chips for the Apollo program in 1969, most experts expected that consumer applications were years in the future. Later that year, Sharp surprised its rivals and engineers around the world by launching the Microcompet, a calculator based on four Rockwell LSI chips, each packing thirty times more electronic components onto a 3-millimeter square piece of silicon than had been fitted onto any previous chip.[22]

The responses to the Microcompet in the USSR and Japan foreshadowed the next thirty years of high technology. Sharp made a million Microcompets in 1970, sparking a fierce war among its Japanese rivals, which competed with one another to build smaller, better, faster, and ever cheaper calculators. The Soviet Union launched a crash program in 1970 to copy the Microcompet; by the time it succeeded in creating a single prototype, the Japanese had leapt far ahead.[23]

The LKB and two other organizations were given the challenge of reproducing the Microcompet. The LKB's rivals attacked the problem by attempting to make an exact copy, an approach that even if successful would be of limited value because it would not create the technological base for designing and manufacturing other types of LSI chips. Staros accepted Shokin's challenge to design and set up a production facility that could mass-produce MOS LSI chips, including chips compatible with those used in the Sharp machine as well as other designs, and to provide detailed instructions for integrating them into a functioning calculator. At the time, the best Soviet ICs had about 40 elements on a chip about the size of the Rockwell LSI chip, so the challenge of creating chips with 1,875 components was quite serious. It was made even more acute by imposing a March 30, 1971, deadline so that the calculator could be put on display at the start of the Twenty-fourth Party Congress the following month. In honor of the occasion, it was to be called the Elektronika-2471.

The density of IC chips was only one measure among many that together indicated that the gap between Soviet and American computing, about two or three years when the UM-1 was built, had stretched to a decade by 1970. An American computer scientist who was allowed to spend half a year at the Soviet Academy of Sciences in 1971 analyzed the problem in words that could have come out of Staros's or Berg's mouth. "What the Russians need is a centralized computer development program headed by a tough-minded, pragmatic technical man like those who headed development of the Russian rocket and space program." He predicted that if they found such a person, "they have the raw technical potential to achieve something near parity in computing with the United States in ten years." He didn't know, of course, that by pushing Staros aside, the Soviet Union had rejected someone who met those specifications.[24]

A secret 1971 CIA report also painted a picture of the Soviet microelectronics industry that was startlingly similar to those of the LKB's director and chief engineer: "Superficially, the tardiness of the Soviet electronics industry in mastering silicon technology is explained by its overlong concentration on the development and production of devices based on germanium. But this explanation reduces to a tautology. The true reasons are more complex and are deep-rooted in the psychology and organization of an economic system that discourages creative, innovative activity and adapts to change slowly. A few of the more obvious factors that have perpetuated obsolescence in the electronics component sector are: a cumbersome planning system, lack of incentives for factory workers and built-in resistance to change at the factory management level, faulty coordination between plants and between plants and research and development institutes; and disharmony between component designers and equipment designers."[25]

The report noted that "limited quantities of integrated circuits (ICs) apparently are being manufactured at the Radio Parts Plant in Voronezh, in plants of the Svetlana Production Association in Leningrad, and in unidentified facilities in the Moscow suburbs of Kryukovo and Zelenograd." At the time, the CIA was dimly aware of Zelenograd but was under the mistaken impression that there were separate microelectronics facilities at Kryukovo.

Three years later, another secret CIA report cited an unnamed "source" who was well informed about the Soviet electronics sector. The agency's analysts described Zelenograd as "the leading scientific center in the USSR for the advancement of silicon semiconductor state-of-the-art" and noted that the first Soviet silicon epitaxial-planar transistor and the first monolithic IC based on silicon had been produced there in 1965.[26]

The CIA's source apparently did not mention that two Americans had started Zelenograd, or that the "firsts" cited in its report were the results of R&D projects they had initiated.[27]

The Soviets were so confident that the American origins of Zelenograd were secret that they invited President Richard Nixon to tour the satellite city when he visited Moscow to sign the arms-control treaty SALT I in May 1972. The visit was to include a tour of the "chicken farm," as Shokin's deputies referred to the Mikron semiconductor manufacturing plant in Zelenograd. It was a popular spot on tours of Moscow for visiting dignitaries like Fidel Castro and Nicolae Ceausescu.[28]

The KGB and U.S. Secret Service went over the exact route Nixon would take to Zelenograd. Just as he had walked Staros and Berg through Khrushchev's visit to their Leningrad lab in 1964, Shokin rehearsed plans for Nixon's visit with plant managers in Zelenograd. Preparations for scrutiny by the world's press included repaving Zelenograd's main street and refurbishing buildings along the motorcade's route. "The residents of Zelenograd had never seen such a large amount of street building machinery. Some old-timers still called the main prospect Nixon Street" as late as 1999. The irony of the Soviet leadership's boasting to President Nixon and the world of the wonders of a semiconductor plant and a planned community that had been inspired by two American spies was narrowly missed when treaty negotiations ran late on May 26, forcing cancellation of the visit to Zelenograd. When several members of Nixon's party toured Zelenograd, they didn't hear a hint about its American origins.[29]

Some of the LKB's innovations were described in the Western media, of course with no mention of the identity of the design bureau's leadership. In 1971 the Pskov Radio Components Plant began manufacturing a civilian version of the UM-2, significantly upgraded from the original prototype. The Elektronika K-200, which used the first generation of Soviet-made integrated circuits, startled American experts on the Soviet computer industry. The editors of the *Soviet Cybernetics Review* were surprised that the brochure describing the computer, written in flawless English (almost certainly by Staros and Berg), provided detail "beyond that commonly found even in the specification pamphlets for Western computers. For the Soviets, it is unprecedented to provide so much information, especially on a new machine." They correctly deduced, on the basis of its compact size and low power requirements, that the computer had originally been designed for use onboard an aircraft or spaceship. The Americans noted that the K-200 incorporated a number of "design features [that] would not be considered unusual in Western practice, but their appearance on a Soviet computer is unusual."

Staros and Berg would have been particularly gratified if they had read the journal's assertion that the K-200 "may even indicate some fundamental shifts and improvements in Soviet design policies." One of these shifts was the simultaneous release of hardware and software. "Few, if any, Soviet computers have ever reached the production stage with even a minimally acceptable, but checked-out, software package. Only in the past few years has it become common to even attempt to provide the software as part of the manufacturing process. The completeness of the software package claimed for the K-200 is quite remarkable," the American journal noted. The authors were also impressed by the steps taken to ensure dependability: "By Soviet standards, it is an exceptionally reliable machine (assuming the accuracy of the brochure). A key feature in this regard is total element-by-element redundancy, a design criterion previously unknown in the Soviet Union and almost never used in the West."

Soviet Cybernetics Review concluded: "The Elektronika K200 may or may not be a product of military/space technology. Nevertheless, everything we know about it suggests technological transfer: transfer of technology from a qualified, capable (by Soviet standards) design and production environment to an application environment long thwarted by unreliable, inappropriate, and scarce computational equipment. The K-200 is the first Soviet production computer that can be fairly characterized as well engineered. It may not be up to Western standards, but it easily surpasses anything else known to be currently available in the Soviet Union for process control automation."[30]

In October 1970, Brezhnev gave the Leningrad party chief, Vasily Tolstikov, the thankless task of representing the Soviet Union in the People's Republic of China as part of an effort to heal the rift between the Communist giants. When they heard that Romanov was to take his place at the head of the Leningrad party operation, the LKB's director and chief engineer braced themselves for an all-out assault. It wasn't long in coming. Yet another bureaucratic reorganization provided Romanov with a lever to pry the LKB out of its independent perch in the Palace of Soviets and place it under the control of a more pliable organization.

Romanov was the USSR's most visible proponent of the creation of science-production associations (NPOs), organizations that were intended to speed innovation by combining basic research institutes, design bureaus, and manufacturing enterprises into entities resembling capitalist companies. The authorities in Moscow suggested that local authorities amalgamate smaller entities into NPOs for all areas of industry, but they mandated it only for one field: electrical engineering.[31]

When the LKB was merged into the Pozitron NPO in late 1970, Staros and Berg immediately clashed with its leadership. For the first time since arriving in the Soviet Union in 1956, the Americans had to report on a daily basis to a boss, and they didn't like it. Pozitron's general director revived the old canard about "houses within houses" and the allegedly "American imperialist" origin of clean rooms. He ordered Staros to dismantle two clean rooms and to abandon another that was under construction.

The LKB's leaders appealed directly to Shokin, who as a minister was several levels in the hierarchy above Pozitron's general director. They insisted that it would be impossible to build the LSIs for the Elektronika-2471 microcalculator if the LKB remained under the control of Pozitron, citing the irrational opposition to clean rooms among other constraints. Staros and Berg also told colleagues that they had appealed to their "comrades and sponsors" at the KGB for assistance.[32]

The tactics worked in the short term: Pozitron's managers were told to back off, and the LKB was permitted to keep its clean rooms, and even to implement a system of performance bonuses that was unusual for the Soviet Union. The LKB developed a computer-aided design system, probably the first in the Soviet Union, and computerized automated testing equipment based on the UM-1NKh. The project succeeded, both in delivering a functioning prototype microcalculator to Brezhnev's desk just before the Twenty-fourth Party Congress and in jump-starting Soviet LSI production. The next year a factory in Leningrad began producing EKBM 24–71 calculators.[33]

Staros and Berg held a party to celebrate the LKB's success in creating LSIs. To the surprise of his employees, Staros minimized the importance of the EKBM 24–71. "This microcalculator stuff is nothing. Today, we are opening a new era for mankind, the era of personal computers." He predicted that in five to ten years everyone would be able to afford a computer as powerful as the BESM-6, the Soviet Union's most advanced computer. The prediction seemed outrageous to Firdman and other engineers at the party, but it turned out to be conservative.[34]

In addition to their responsibilities in Leningrad, which included completion of the Uzel, a new generation of Elektronika-300 computers, and numerous microelectronics projects, Staros and Berg spent several days a week in Moscow desperately trying to relocate the LKB. Their goal was to get out from under the control of Pozitron's management and into a situation in which their lives wouldn't be subject to the whims of either Romanov, the Leningrad party boss, or Shokin, whom they viewed ambivalently as both a potential ally and the cause of their torment.

Staros seized on a solution that he thought would create security for himself and for his team. He lobbied hard to be elected a member of the Soviet Academy of Sciences and to have the LKB transferred from the military-industrial sphere to the Academy of Sciences, preferably in a location distant from Leningrad and Moscow. Election to the Academy, which conferred the title Academician, was the highest honor a scientist could achieve in the Soviet Union. In addition to prestige, Academicians received significant material rewards for themselves and their families. Staros also believed that dissociation from the military sector would insulate him and the LKB from political infighting.

From their usual base at the Metropol, Staros and Berg met with a virtual who's who of Academicians, including the president of the Academy of Sciences, Mstislav Keldysh, and his successor Anatoly Alexandrov; one of the

USSR's most prominent spacecraft designers, Vasily Mishin; Tupolev; as well as Vadim Trapeznikov and Boris Petrov, two pioneers of Soviet computing. They also met with their "comrades and supporters" at the KGB, the heads of several ministries, and anyone else who could conceivably help their case.[35]

In the end, these meetings yielded little other than unfulfilled promises of support. Even eminent scientists and chief designers would not intentionally antagonize either Shokin or Romanov by helping Staros and Berg escape from their grip. The lobbying did convince Shokin to remove the LKB from Pozitron. The era of independent design bureaus headed by politically powerful chief designers was over, so it is unlikely that he could have given Staros and Berg the autonomy they craved, even if he had wanted to do so. Throughout the USSR, the independent design bureaus and experimental design bureaus of the Stalin and Khrushchev eras were being merged into larger organizations, and as the colorful, dynamic scientist-politician chief designers of the previous era retired or died, they were replaced by gray apparatchiks.

The LKB was moved in 1972 from Pozitron to an enormous electronics conglomerate, NPO Svetlana. For the LKB, it was like being thrown from the frying pan into the fire. Founded in 1889, Svetlana was a large, well-established enterprise with 30,000 employees, which under the new NPO structure had been given control over a dozen design bureaus and basic research institutes. It would, Staros and Berg worried, be virtually impossible to operate independently inside such a behemoth.[36]

Ambitious for higher office, Romanov had vowed to make the defense industry in Leningrad, and particularly the electronics sector, a showpiece for Brezhnev's reforms. Having foreigners who openly violated party discipline in charge of a highly visible military microelectronics R&D operation didn't fit in with his plans. Romanov "instructed Filatov, General Director at Svetlana, to cancel LKB's operation and oust its leaders within one year," a former chief engineer later said.[37]

At first, things at Svetlana went well enough for the LKB. Having successfully produced prototype LSI chips, Staros and Berg appealed to Shokin for a photorepeater, an essential piece of equipment for making the photomasks used to make integrated circuits. Without it, their yields were too low to take LSI fabrication from the hobbyshop scale to mass production. The fact that photorepeaters were on the list of restricted equipment that Western countries had agreed not to export to the Soviet bloc presented only a minor inconvenience.[38]

It took three months from the time in 1973 when the LKB convinced Shokin to order a state-of-the-art photorepeater, manufactured by the David W.

Mann Company in Lincoln, Massachusetts, for the device to arrive on Svetlana's loading dock. The machine was purchased by a cooperative West German company that quickly resold it, at a profit, to a Yugoslav company, which marked it up again and sent the sensitive equipment on its way to Leningrad. With the critical piece of equipment in hand, the LKB dramatically increased LSI yield. This was fortunate, because the LKB had been assigned responsibility for meeting Svetlana's LSI production targets, a tricky proposition for Staros and Berg, who hadn't been involved in manufacturing for the two decades since they had left Western Electric and Bell Labs.[39]

Meanwhile, after seven years, the Uzel, originally envisioned as a quick project, was finally nearing completion.

In early 1973, Staros overcame claustrophobia to squeeze into a space that he was almost certainly the first American to visit. The CIA would have risked a great deal to be in Staros's shoes as he joined a small group of admirals and senior officers in the control room of a Soviet Tango-class submarine (known in the Soviet Union as "Project 641B") that plunged under the Baltic Sea near Liepaja. The largest diesel-electric submarines ever built, the Tangos were a source of great alarm to Western militaries in the 1970s. Coated with special sonar-absorbing tiles, the sixty-man craft was designed to hunt American submarines, particularly to defend the USSR's home waters, or "bastions," areas in the Barents and Okhost Seas where the Soviet Navy stationed submarines equipped with nuclear missiles.[40]

Staros watched as the Uzel, the first digital computer used aboard a Soviet submarine, correlated information from sonar, the engines, and sensors to plot the craft's location, as well as the locations of a half dozen potential targets, on a green display that the LKB had designed specifically for the Navy. In addition to helping navigate the submarine, the Uzel took input from sonar and, like the antiaircraft computers Staros and Berg had worked with in the United States and Czechoslovakia, automatically calculated the coordinates of targets, predicted their future positions, and determined how the sub's torpedoes should be aimed and when to fire them.[41]

The Uzel may be Staros and Berg's most enduring legacy. It could be found into the twenty-first century lurking under the Indian Ocean, the Mediterranean and Black Seas, and the Pacific and Atlantic Oceans in the fleets of a half-dozen navies, including those of several potential adversaries of the United States. If Iran decides to send oil tankers to the bottom of the Persian Gulf, if Chinese submarines attack Taiwanese shipping, or if India opts to scuttle Pakistani cargo ships—all plausible scenarios—the torpedoes will probably be aimed by Uzel fire-control systems. Each of these nations, along with Poland, Algeria, and Romania, has purchased Project 877, "Kilo-class" in NATO's nomenclature, submarines from the Soviet Union and Russia.[42]

An attack submarine capable of functioning in a variety of situations, including shallow water, the Kilo was one of the quietest and most successful submarines designed in the Soviet Union. The Uzel system in Kilo subs uses three of the LKB-designed computers to feed information to two consoles. It can simultaneously track five targets and automatically calculate the ballistic data needed to attack three of them. It also controls automatic reloading of torpedoes. Ironically, an Uzel system was operating as late as 2004 inside the hull of a NATO-flagged submarine, the Polish ORP *Orzel,* which participated in NATO exercises in 2001 and 2002.[43]

The Navy awarded Staros the Order of the Submariner and invited him and Berg to a banquet to celebrate the successful 1973 Uzel test. Staros and Berg dreaded these types of events, which were quite predictable. There would be tables loaded with caviar, dozens of cold dishes ranging from smoked fish and cured meats to elaborate salads, and pungent black bread. They would be expected to eat generous portions of the cold foods; then soup would be served, followed by a massive portion of some kind of meat and potatoes. The hours-long event would be punctuated by dozens of toasts, which became increasingly difficult to understand as the evening progressed because the vodka that accompanied them caused the speakers to slur their words. Sharp eyes always watched the foreigners to make sure their glasses were drained after each toast, so it was difficult to escape having consumed less than a third of a liter of vodka. Berg had never been a heavy drinker, and Staros was, by Russian standards, a teetotaler.

On the evening of the celebratory dinner, the two LKB leaders arrived with their wives at the Rossiya Hotel, a building near the Palace of Soviets that resembles an enormous ice-cube tray turned on its side. The Staroses were seated next to Admiral Gorshkov, the head of the Soviet Navy. Everything proceeded according to custom, with the sole exception that Staros and Berg drank from a bottle of cognac that they had brought themselves. Midway into the festivities, the vodka bottle in front of one of the admirals seated next to Anna ran dry. He reached across her and helped himself to a glass of the LKB director's cognac, took a swallow, and spat it out, along with a powerful Russian expletive favored by sailors. He had inadvertently discovered Staros and Berg's secret: the "cognac" was actually strong tea. For the Russians, this was the ultimate insult: it was bad enough that the foreigners had declined to drink with the Soviet officers, but the fact that they'd fooled them, that they'd wanted to remain sober while others allowed the alcohol to loosen their hearts and tongues, was intolerable. After this scandalous event, the LKB never won another order from the Soviet Navy, and Gorshkov, who had intervened to protect the design bureau from the local party organization, was no longer willing to do so.[44]

In April 1973, at age fifty, Romanov was made a candidate member of the Politburo, meaning that he was one step away from joining the narrow circle of individuals who actually ran the Soviet Union, and from whom all the nation's dictators had been drawn. He was a veritable youth in the old men's club at the Kremlin, prompting talk of a second Romanov dynasty.[45] Romanov retained control of the Leningrad party while gradually acquiring a portfolio of national responsibilities that included control over military industry. Thus, he sat atop the two chains of command with ultimate authority over the LKB. There were only a handful of men in the Soviet Union who could defy Romanov's will, and probably only one, Brezhnev, who could challenge his authority over defense contractors operating in Leningrad.

The end of Staros's and Berg's careers as senior managers in the Soviet microelectronics industry came quickly after Romanov's promotion. In May, Svetlana's general director, citing the LKB's failure to fulfill its LSI manufacturing quota, which had been set at an impossible level, removed Staros and Berg from their leadership positions. The LKB was merged into Svetlana and renamed the Leningrad Design and Technological Bureau (LKTB). Staros was named deputy director for science and research at the new entity; Berg was not given any specific title or duties, but continued to draw a supersized salary. Staros and Berg appealed to Ustinov, who refused to see them. The two American Communists had spent just about all of their political capital.

10

The Minifab, 1975–1990

Philip Staros's life was marked by abrupt shifts and huge gambles: agreeing to become a Soviet agent; fleeing the United States with the FBI in pursuit, abandoning a wife and two small children; moving from Prague to Leningrad; and trying to leap from heading a small design bureau to leading an industry employing tens of thousands of scientists. He left homes, family, friendships, and careers behind several times in order to start over. In 1974, Staros laid plans to again rip his life out by the roots, to move as far away from Leningrad as possible while remaining in the Soviet Union. He negotiated a job with the Far Eastern Branch of the Soviet Academy of Sciences in Vladivostok, nine time zones away from European Russia.

The Academy of Sciences had just started to create a series of academic research institutions in the Russian Far East. Although they were intended to develop native talent, the opportunity to avoid the scrutiny of politicians in Moscow and Leningrad attracted scientists from throughout Russia, just as the Academic City (Akademgorodok) carved out of the Siberian wasteland a generation earlier had been colonized by some of the country's best minds. Staros's move was recommended and facilitated by Piotr Kapitsa, a friend who had achieved the independence Staros constantly sought. The combination of tremendous scientific stature and strength of character allowed Kapitsa, one of the world's most famous living physicists, to defy Stalin and his successors, first by refusing to work on nuclear weapons and later by openly supporting the dissident scientist Andrei Sakharov. Kapitsa introduced Staros to his son, Andrei Kapitsa, the director of the FESC (Far Eastern Science Center).[1]

The Kapitsas helped arrange for Staros to be named director of a new artificial intelligence laboratory at the Institute of Automation and Control Processes, part of the FESC; to be appointed to a position on the Presidium of the FESC; and to receive an appointment at the Far Eastern University in Vladivostok. The deal came with two promises that were particularly attractive to Staros: it would make him a full member of the Soviet Academy of Sciences, and it would enable him to purchase a yacht that he could sail in the Pacific near Vladivostok.

Staros tried to convince his LKB team to move to Vladivostok, but for most it was too far away and the risk of failure too great. Berg was the first to refuse to go, although Staros, knowing that it would be virtually impossible to convince Vera to move 5,000 miles from Prague, didn't press him hard.

Berg told Staros that he was crazy to leave Leningrad; they had to stay and fight to rebuild their reputations and careers, not run away, he argued. Berg, who had always been Staros's loyal deputy, was angry that his friend was deserting him and uncertain about how to proceed on his own. Although he retained his salary, car, apartment, party membership, and access to restricted foreign publications, it was clear that without Staros standing up for him, Svetlana's management wouldn't restore Berg's status.

In contrast to his career in Russia up to that point, which had involved managing teams of several hundred engineers, having access to large amounts of hard currency to purchase equipment, and meeting with world-class scientists and engineers, Berg was reduced to reporting every day to an empty room. He had no staff, no budget, and few responsibilities. Determined to turn his predicament into a positive experience, Berg spent a great deal of time reading American technical literature, especially on chip-manufacturing technology, and began sketching out ideas for inventions that could propel the Soviet Union — and himself — into the forefront of microelectronics.

Henry Firdman was the only one of the LKB team willing and able to leave Leningrad, Russia's second-largest city, for the Far East. Upon arriving in Vladivostok, Firdman quickly found that things weren't as well arranged as Staros had expected. Staros's immediate superior at the Institute of Automation, who ridiculed artificial intelligence as a pseudoscience, refused to provide laboratory space. The rector of the Far Eastern University had a similar attitude. So instead of directing a well-staffed, fully equipped laboratory as he had imagined, Staros spent months begging for space. He met with scores of party, industry, and military officials, but none was interested in sponsoring an outcast who had incurred the displeasure of top party leaders in Leningrad and Moscow.[2]

Andrei Kapitsa provided some space, but it was too small to accommodate the crates of equipment that started pouring in and the scores of researchers whom Staros planned to recruit. Eventually Staros made a deal with the director of a boarding school who thought it would benefit his students to be in the proximity of scientists. So Staros started over in 1975, much as he had in 1956, only this time his team worked in basement classrooms instead of in an attic. Unlike during the early days in Leningrad, it was difficult to sustain the idea that this was a way station on the road to much bigger and better places. Staros, however, was upbeat, telling the men he'd recruited that "Henry Ford began his factory in a barn. Above all, we have equipment and can start to work."[3]

Although they were on opposite sides of the Eurasian continent, Berg and Staros responded to their fortunes similarly. Staros organized a music salon at the Science Workers' House, playing classical music records as well as bootlegged Beatles tapes. Berg organized concerts and lectures about music in the House of Scientists (Dom Uchenyh), a magnificent palace on the banks of the Neva River that had once belonged to Grand Duke Vladimir. Even in Soviet times, when many of Leningrad's architectural treasures were desecrated or allowed to crumble, the House of Scientists was maintained in its prerevolutionary splendor.

Berg was able to connect with creative people of any age, but especially with young people. Although he didn't care much for popular music, starting in the mid-1970s Berg often held sessions, first at the House of Scientists and later at his apartment, during which he translated the lyrics of British and American rock. It was very unusual for a loyal member of the Communist Party to openly display interest in a musical genre that Brezhnev derided as the "belch of Western culture," but Berg seemed to have an intuitive sense of how far he could stray from orthodoxy without suffering negative consequences. Much of the censorship of expression and action in the Soviet Union was self-imposed; Berg acted as if he did not have an internal censorship mechanism.[4]

In addition to classical musicians from the conservatory, Berg invited jazz, rock, and avant-garde musicians to play and discuss their music at the House of Scientists. He managed to skirt the edges of the politically acceptable until one memorable evening, when he hosted a young artist named Sergei Kuryokhin. Kuryokhin started off playing a Japanese synthesizer, the first that most people in the audience had ever seen, but then switched to the Dom Uchenyh's old, venerated grand piano. Gradually whipping himself into a frenzy, the artist started throwing objects onto the strings: coins, keys, batteries, and finally a chair. That was the end of Berg's use of the House of Scientists, but not of his friendship with Kuryokhin, who went on to become a famous underground artist, attracting so many people to his illegal performances that the authorities were once forced to shut down a Leningrad subway station to reduce the size of the crowd. Through Kuryokhin, Berg met the legendary Russian rocker Boris Grebenschikov at about the time Kuryokhin and Grebenschikov cofounded Aquarium, the Soviet Union's most influential underground band.[5]

Through the concerts at the House of Scientists and his broad contacts with intellectuals and avant-garde artists, Berg became widely known in Leningrad. He was a bohemian splash of color against the drab landscape of the Brezhnev years.

Throughout their years in the Soviet Union, Staros and Berg occasionally bumped into Americans in hotels or theaters, but while they were responsible for the LKB they took care not to say anything to foreigners that might compromise their official legends. Later, perhaps sensing that the authorities had lost interest, they relaxed, taking fewer precautions to camouflage their origins. After his children finished high school and entered the Leningrad Conservatory, whenever Berg met foreign music students he invited them home. After Staros left Leningrad, the KGB began to behave as if it didn't care if Western intelligence agencies figured out who he and Berg were, as if it couldn't be bothered with trying to hide them any longer.

Anna Staros, who still bore a striking physical resemblance to the woman who had left Ithaca twenty years before, was permitted with her daughter Kristina to host a popular television program in Vladivostok called *Do You Speak English?* The city, home to the Pacific fleet, was closed to foreigners, so it was unlikely that visiting Americans would recognize her. But the Berg and Staros families engaged in other activities that posed bigger risks to their covers. Berg and Staros received KGB clearance to attend international conferences in the Soviet Union at which they would be exposed to American scientists, among whom were certainly CIA informants or agents. In 1975, for example, the two American expatriates traveled to Tbilisi, the capital of Soviet Georgia, for an international conference on artificial intelligence, mingling with delegates from the United States and Western Europe.

Berg had much more extensive interactions with Americans the next year, at an international conference in Tashkent, Uzbekistan. He befriended an American scientist and his wife, responding to their questions about his background with his official biography. Queried about his accent, Berg gave his stock answer, that he had grown up in an American neighborhood in Johannesburg. After the conference, the American couple flew to Leningrad for a planned two-month visit.[6]

They were surprised one day to receive a telephone call from Berg, who drove with his daughter Vivian to the hotel to invite them to his home for dinner. At Berg's apartment, the Americans were introduced to Vera Bergova (the feminine form of Berg in the Czech language) and Anna Staros. Joe spooked the scientist by asking well-informed questions about computer technology. His queries revealed a familiarity with very recent technical developments, including some that the U.S. government preferred to keep secret. The scientist deflected the questions and asked a few of his own.

In the course of the evening, Mrs. Staros revealed that she was visiting from Vladivostok, where her husband conducted research on artificial intelligence at the Soviet Academy of Sciences. Abandoning her official legend, Anna also told the strangers that she and her husband were Americans who had been forced to flee anticommunist persecution in the United States. Remarkably, she described their flight to Mexico, including the role of the Polish trade mission in facilitating their clandestine cruise to Europe.

Anna and Joe disagreed in front of their guests about the merits of the Soviet system. While she admitted to being disillusioned by the realities of socialism, he said that life in Russia was for him far better than anything the capitalist world could have provided. Berg extolled the benefits of socialism primarily in material terms: he earned an enormous salary relative to most workers — "more than a deputy minister" — had a car and a large, comfortable apartment, and his children had received first-class educations that would have cost a fortune in the United States.

Perhaps even more surprising than Joe Berg and Anna Staros's candor to relative strangers is the fact that officials in the U.S. consulate in Leningrad were not interested in hearing about them. As a result of the consulate's indifference, the American scientist did not include any mention of his interaction with the strange South African with a Brooklyn accent, or his female American friend, in a report about the trip submitted to the government upon his return to the United States. Asked about it a decade later, the scientist reported that "the cool attitude of the American consul in Leningrad had led him to believe his encounter with Berg was not of any particular interest." The consul was wrong; it would certainly have been of interest to the FBI.[7]

In fact, American intelligence was still trying to solve the riddle of Barr's and Sarant's disappearing acts. In June 1974, FBI Director Clarence Kelly sent a memo to the CIA requesting any information it had regarding Barr. The letter stated that Barr "had left the U.S. in 1948 and was living in France on the date of the arrest of David Greenglass in New York, namely 6/16/50. On that date he disappeared from his French residence and we have developed no information indicating his location since that date."[8]

At the time, there were lookout notices for Joel Barr and Alfred Sarant at every U.S. port of entry. The information Anna provided in 1976 would have allowed the FBI to deduce that Staros was Sarant—how many American Communist scientists had fled with a blonde woman to Mexico in the early 1950s and then disappeared? From there, it wouldn't have been difficult to connect Berg to Barr.

The total absence of information about Barr and Sarant led the FBI to give up the hunt a year later. In September 1977, the FBI canceled requests to the State Department to be on alert for attempts by Sarant or Barr to renew their passports, and withdrew instructions to look for them at border crossings. Twenty-seven years after they disappeared, FBI headquarters noted in the file that its investigations of Barr and Sarant had been "RUC'd": referred upon completion to office of origin, Bureau-speak for "case closed."[9]

Soon after Staros got his institute up and running, with one group conducting basic research on silicon as part of a long-term plan to build three-dimensional integrated circuits and another, under Firdman's direction, working on artificial-intelligence software, things started to fall apart. As had happened so many times previously during his life in Russia, Staros's fate was tied to that of his sponsor. Andrei Kapitsa was ousted as head of the Far Eastern Science Center, and his replacement had no faith in Staros's artificial-intelligence project. On a visit to the lab in the boarding school where Staros's team was experimenting with various kinds of solid-film technology in vacuum chambers, the new director of the Far Eastern Science Center suggested that they work on more practical applications, such as electroplating silverware.[10]

Staros became obsessed with the desire to become an Academician, convinced that the prestige associated with the title would ensure funding for his projects, attract talented researchers, and validate his status as the father of Soviet microelectronics. In March 1978, he traveled to Moscow for the Academy's annual elections, confident that Piotr Kapitsa (who was about to receive the Nobel Prize) and other friends had arranged everything. Instead of the expected victory celebration, Staros left Moscow deeply disappointed. Shokin, Staros learned, had blocked his election. The minister had received one "Hero of Socialist Labor" award and was eager to get a second, which would trigger the erection of a monument in the city where he'd been born. Staros's election would have made it impossible for Shokin to take sole credit for conceiving of Zelenograd and the Scientific Center, the accomplishments he hoped would be the basis for a second Hero award.

The following March Staros returned to Moscow, assured again that the members of the Academy would vote to admit him. Berg had flown from

Leningrad to Moscow to meet his old comrade. He was waiting at the Metropol on the afternoon of March 12 when the telephone rang. Berg was expecting to hear Staros's cheerful voice saying that he was in the lobby, but the call was from a hospital, and the news was devastating: Staros was dead. He had suffered a massive heart attack while driving in a taxi to meet Berg and died on Leninski Prospekt, en route to the hospital.

Izvestia announced Staros's death in a March 16, 1979, obituary:

> Soviet science has experienced a heavy loss. In his sixty-third year of life, a member of the Presidium of the Far Eastern subsidiary of the Academy of Science of the USSR, laureate of the State Prize, doctor of technical sciences, Professor Philip Georgeivich Staros unexpectedly died. The death took from our ranks a tireless scientist, a talented organizer who for many years gave all his strength and bright talent to the development of Soviet science and technology. The head of an electronics industry design bureau for twenty years, chief designer Philip Georgeivich Staros made a large contribution to the establishment and the development of domestic microelectronics. He is the originator of several cornerstone ideas which received acclaim and which were implemented by several enterprises and organizations of our country. In his last years, Philip Georgeivich Staros headed a team of scientists of the Far Eastern subsidiary of the Academy of Sciences of the USSR. Up to his end he was at the forefront of domestic science. The kind memory of Philip Georgeivich Staros will forever live in our hearts.

The obituary was signed by the Presidium of the Academy of Sciences of the USSR, the Kollegiya of the Ministry of Electronics Industry of the USSR, the State Committee on Science and Technology of the USSR, and the Far Eastern subsidiary of the Academy of Science of the USSR.

Berg was shattered by the loss. If he had been able, Berg said, he would gladly have died in his friend's place. He often said that a part of him died with Staros.

Heartbroken, Berg organized the funeral ceremony at a Moscow crematorium. Staros's ashes were interred in a Leningrad cemetery under a platinum pyramid that Berg designed. The grave doesn't mention the name Sarant or hint at his American origins.

After Phil's funeral, Anna moved back to Leningrad with her children. Berg devoted himself to the Staros family, moving heaven and earth to get Anna an apartment. He also managed to arrange for her to receive Phil's pension, despite the fact that they had never married.

Soon after she arrived in Leningrad, Anna's son Kolya, twenty-seven years old, began insisting that the family make contact with their relatives in the

United States. Anna didn't have any idea of how to reach her former husband Bruce Dayton, but she remembered that Philip Morrison, an old friend of Phil's and of Bruce, was the book editor of *Scientific American*. She and Kolya wrote a letter to Bruce, enclosing it in an envelope in a letter to Morrison. Somehow the letter got through. Morrison tracked down Dayton and forwarded the letter to him. Dayton sent a copy to his and Anna's children, Eric and Derry, who had grown up with the idea that their mother was dead.

A couple of months later, in early 1980, Anna was astonished to find a letter in her mailbox from the United States written in a cramped script, filling only three-quarters of a single sheet. It was from her ninety-five-year-old mother, who Anna had assumed was long dead, writing to say that she was ecstatic to find her daughter. Over the years, she wrote, she had drifted into sleep in tears on countless nights worrying about her girl's fate.

Anna begged her contact at the KGB for permission to travel abroad to see her mother, but it was denied. She learned of her mother's death a year later in a letter from her daughter Derry, who was living in Canada. Derry wrote that she had grown up believing that her mother was dead, was thrilled to discover her alive and well, and wanted to meet her. Bruce also wrote, but he wasn't ready to see the woman who had deserted him and their two children.

Remarkably, in 1981 Anna's KGB contacts, who treated her with the affection and respect they felt for Phil, allowed a reunion between Anna and her American family. It was the height of the Cold War, just a year after the United States boycotted the Moscow Olympics. The authorities may have arranged the meeting because they feared that otherwise Anna would contact the American embassy or newspapers, or the Staros family may be correct in believing that the KGB felt it had to honor the sacrifices she and Philip Staros had made for the Soviet Union. The government of the Soviet Union surreptitiously contacted Eric and Derry in Canada, arranged for them to be granted visas, and paid to fly them to Prague. A third relative, Jeremy Sarant, Louise and Alfred Sarant's son, joined Eric and Derry Dayton, traveling at his own expense. Louise Sarant and her two sons had stayed in touch with Bruce Dayton and his children after their father disappeared, and Jeremy, who lived in the United States, was as hungry for information about his missing parent as were Eric and Derry.

The FBI, CIA, and Canadian intelligence authorities were completely unaware of the visit.

After thirty-one years, Anna had to face the consequences of her impulsive decision to help Alfred Sarant escape. She had just ten days to explain to the grown-up children why they had been abandoned, and why she had never contacted them. She told her son and daughter that she had not intended to leave them for so long, and that she had never forgotten them. They struggled to connect with a stranger who was their mother.

When she returned to Leningrad, Anna told her Russian children, Kolya, Mila, Kristina, and Tonya, that Derry, thirty-nine years old, felt like her daughter, but that Eric, forty-three, had kept his distance. She also explained a great deal more about her past than she'd ever revealed previously. The Staros children were shocked and angry when their mother admitted that the stories she and their father had told them about their pasts had been lies, legends created by their KGB "contacts."[11]

Berg's family still had only a murky idea of his real identity. Philip Staros told Vera in 1975 that her husband was an American, not a South African of English descent as she had believed. Joe wasn't happy to have the secret revealed. He rarely spoke with Vera about his American past and didn't say anything at the time to his children.

During their years at SL-11, KB-2, and the LKB, Staros and Berg had worked frenetically, never taking the two months of annual paid vacation to which they were entitled. After he was transferred to Svetlana, Berg started taking vacations. He adopted the habit of leaving Leningrad each year in late August, while it was still warm, and returning in the icy short days of October. Almost without fail, at the end of summer, Berg steered his car south, spending weeks in the southern fringes of the Soviet Union, driving a Volga that over the years became increasingly dilapidated.

The car got to be in such bad shape — the front fender attached with wire at an angle like a French artist's beret and the body pockmarked with holes patched with epoxy — that police often stopped Berg and threatened to impound it as a hazard. Once he bartered a digital watch manufactured by Svetlana for permission to continue his journey through Georgia. On his return to Leningrad, Berg came up with a more creative, less expensive solution. The next time a traffic cop questioned the roadworthiness of his car, Berg dug through the glovebox for a neatly typed piece of paper bearing an official-looking stamp. It stated that Dr. I. V. Berg was conducting a scientific experiment on the durability of this particular model of Volga and that he appreciated the cooperation and courtesies of the traffic police.

Elvira or Berg's son Robert accompanied him on several of these road trips, which were filled with adventures, often comical, involving car breakdowns, collisions with camels, the kindness of strangers, and the outwitting of petty officials. One year Berg was driving a new car that didn't happen to have license plates or registration documents. He made some documents and got someone at Svetlana's "first department" (the security branch operated by the

KGB) to stamp them. "We drove all the way to Baku, and everything went fine," Elvira recalled. "Then we decided to go to Astara, a city that is half in Azerbaijan and half in Iran. We got our tent out and went to sleep, but in the middle of the night the border guards came and arrested us because we were in a prohibited border zone. They took us to their office and started calling to Leningrad. They couldn't believe anyone was so crazy. In the end, it was easier for the border guards to let us go than to sort everything out."[12]

Relatively few individuals in the Soviet Union owned personal cars, and the idea of traveling long distances by car for pleasure was completely alien. In many of the places Berg visited there were no hotels or restaurants. Petrol stations were scarce, so he bartered vodka for diesel from truckers who siphoned it from their tanks. He usually cooked over a primus stove and camped in a tent, but some nights peasants invited him to stay in a hut or yurt. Wherever he was, Berg delighted in engaging strangers in conversation. As a result, he experienced a slice of the Soviet Union that few Russians, and even fewer foreigners, ever saw.

"My vacations consisted mostly of getting in the car with some companion and living in the wilderness, in the woods, and sometimes we would meet people. It was on one of these vacations down south," Berg remembered, "when I met a couple. The wife told me an incredible story — it really astonished me — of her daughter coming home one day, a six- or seven-year-old girl, and saying, 'Mama, I love Brezhnev more than I love you.' The kid set off a situation for this woman that was untenable. She went to the school and created a scandal. She became a virulent anti-Soviet person. I think she was put in jail."

Berg was astonished at the sense of helplessness felt by the ordinary people he encountered, and at the defenses that the engineers and intellectuals he worked with erected to protect themselves from the intrusions of the state into their private lives. He was particularly impressed by their ability to tune out the intellectual garbage that was thrown at them from every form of communications media, even in the ubiquitous slogans that adorned rooftops and bulletin boards. "The Russians inured themselves and tried their best not to pay attention to it. They just lived, took it in their stride. And this is an element of the Russian character, to be immune to the tremendous political and cultural pressure in the newspapers, on the radio, on the television programs. They became impervious to this propaganda. I had many, many conversations with Russian intelligentsia, and I often told them that there is this split between what they read in the papers — how their society is flowering, that it is the best society in the world — and reality. I'm not going to say it was absolute horror, it was not Orwell's *1984*, but there was an element there where you just couldn't put the [official version of reality and one's own experiences] together," Berg recalled.[13]

Berg never complained about the Soviet government, even to his children, who tried in vain to get him to read *samizdat* literature that exposed the barbarism of the Soviet system. Although he kept his thoughts to himself until after the dissolution of the Soviet Union in 1991, Berg understood the material and spiritual toll that Soviet conditions took on individuals and families. "It is difficult for anyone, particularly Americans, to understand what it was like to share a kitchen for years and years and years," Berg said, looking back on the communal apartments that were common in the Soviet period (and are still home to hundreds of thousands in St. Petersburg). "To have one room in which four or six or eight people lived. When we talk about sex in the Soviet Union, there was practically no sex" in the communal apartments. The "sexual prison" created by communal living "changed the character, the personality of the Russian people."

Berg felt that the country's experience mirrored his own, that the Soviet experiment took a wrong turn in 1964. He vividly remembered Khrushchev's five-hour speech in 1960 "in which he presented to the world and the Russian people a picture where we have finally come to a point in Soviet history where in twenty years we would be living in Communism. What did this mean? Well, he even had the figures. In every field—food, clothing, shelter—the Soviet Union would have a per-capita level that would be better than any country in the world. Now it appeared, twenty years passed, and where were they in 1980? Everybody forgot about that. In 1980 Brezhnev was in. It was even forbidden to discuss this question. That is, why aren't we living the life the party said we would in 1960? Not that you were considered an enemy of the people, but certainly, if you valued your freedom, you wouldn't go out and start a campaign saying, 'They are lying to us all the time.'"[14]

Berg was also acutely aware of the significant role that ethnicity played in Soviet life. Being characterized as a Jew was a two-edged sword for most Russians. Although Jews were bullied and insulted from childhood, and severely restricted in their educational and professional opportunities, they had one tremendously valuable privilege starting in the 1970s: because of political pressure from the United States, Jews were among the very few Soviet citizens permitted to emigrate. There were many jokes about this. For example, a quotation from a popular novel, "an automobile is not a luxury, but a means of transportation," was changed to "a Jewish wife isn't a luxury, but a means of transportation."[15]

"I must admit that most of my friends, the engineers, the scientists, the physicists, were Jewish," Berg remembered. "Really, this is a fact, I cannot deny it. Why was this? Well, I don't think it is because I actively searched and became friendly with the Jews. I think it was the other way around. When it became clear right from the beginning that I was a foreigner, and that I had been going to Czechoslovakia, the Jews in Russia looked on me as a road to getting out, to Czechoslovakia or to the West. It was an incredible situation where, by an accident of birth, a Jew had the possibility of leaving whereas others didn't." That possibility was not open to him, Berg hastened to add. During the Khrushchev years he had no thought of leaving, and during the Brezhnev regime he was certain that the KGB would never let him leave the Soviet bloc.[16]

In the late 1970s Berg hit on an idea for an invention that he believed could revolutionize microelectronics. The idea was to shrink the basic functions of silicon-chip making, which normally take place in ultraclean rooms housed in multi-billion-dollar factories, or "fabs," so that they could be accomplished by a device small enough to fit onto a desktop. Lithography and other functions would all take place in hermetically sealed containers. The idea was inspired by the microclimate that he and Staros had developed for the UM-2 computer. Such desktop fabs, or "minifabs," would be economical for creating custom chips, such as application-specific integrated circuits (ASICs), Berg believed. If the minifabs were cheap enough, they would become as common as bread-boards, the devices that engineers use to build prototypes of electronic systems.

The minifab idea was elegant and relatively simple to describe, but creating a working prototype would require a great deal of original engineering. New, miniature versions of most of the basic elements of IC manufacturing would have to be created, and tiny robots would have to replace the young women in bunny suits who worked in conventional fabs. As Berg envisioned it, the minifab would consist of six to twelve modules, each with its own air-filtration and climate-control system, with a sealed mechanism to transport materials from one module to another. A silicon wafer would go in one end, and about twenty minutes later a single custom chip would be ejected from the other end. For the first time, it would be practical to make one or two unique chips, and to make them on a laboratory desktop or factory floor.

As Berg elaborated his ideas for the minifab, he began requesting lab space, funding, and staff. He grew increasingly frustrated by Svetlana's indifference. Finally, despite the disastrous consequences of the letter Staros had sent Khrushchev in 1964, Berg decided to use the tactic again. In 1981 he wrote to Brezhnev, Ustinov, and a KGB contact, explaining that he had emigrated to the Soviet Union to help build socialism, and complaining that his talents were being wasted. The letters briefly explained the minifab concept, stressed that it was far in advance of anything existing or even contemplated in the West, and requested resources. The response was swift; this time it was positive.

"*Tovarisch* Berg, there was no need to go over my head. In the future, just let me know what you need, and it will be taken care of," Svetlana's general director said. Berg was given a budget, including hard currency to import foreign equipment, and the right to recruit staff. Several experienced engineers who had worked for him at the LKB joined the minifab project. By the time he had assembled the entire team, nearly 100 engineers and technicians, Berg noticed something that he found strange and somewhat unsettling: almost every one of them was Jewish. He wasn't sure whether they had been attracted by the opportunity to work on cutting-edge technology, or whether they expected that association with him would improve their chances of emigrating.[17]

In 1985, with the minifab project under way and his professional life on an upward path for the first time in years, an earthquake fractured Berg's private life. It arrived in the form of a small envelope, slipped into the Berg family's mailbox, addressed to Vera. The short note, which Joe believed had been written by a nosy neighbor, informed Vera that her husband had been having an affair for over a decade and that his mistress lived in the family's apartment when Vera and the children were away. Vera flew into a rage and demanded a divorce. At first Joe defended himself, saying that at their age — Joe was sixty-nine, Vera was fifty-nine — and with four children to consider, it would be silly to break up. But she was determined, and he agreed reluctantly.

Since they had been married in Czechoslovakia as Czech citizens, there was quite a bit of confusion about whether Soviet or Czech law should be applied. In the end, Soviet law was used, and, as was standard, a sum equal to approximately one-third of Berg's salary was automatically deducted from his pay every month for Vera. She stayed in the apartment with Berg for almost two more years, until their youngest son, Anton, graduated from the conservatory, and in 1987 moved back to the house she had grown up in near Prague. The four Berg children also moved to Czechoslovakia.

Alone for the first time in a quarter-century, Berg decided to return to his bohemian roots by creating an informal nightclub, a meeting spot for Leningrad's intelligentsia. He applied to the local authorities for permission to turn three of his six rooms into one large space, but they refused to allow him to knock down any walls. After all, the apartment was state property. Undaunted, he got a sledgehammer and pounded them down anyway. This exploit was easier than getting rid of the old walls; there were no Dumpsters or trash-hauling services.

At first, Berg threw the debris into the garbage chute, but his neighbors became incensed when the pipe got stopped up and the entire building started to stink of rotten food. Forced to develop a new disposal technique, Joe and Elvira packed the rubble into large bags, hauled them down in the elevator, and, once outside, poked holes in the bottoms of the bags. Together they walked around the neighborhood, leaving a trail of concrete, plaster, and dust, returning home with empty bags and sore backs.

Having disposed of the walls, Berg set about transforming the large room that remained. He covered the floors and walls with stained, shellacked plywood squares, then built a one-meter-wide bench, topped with foam and fabric, along three of the walls. The bench seat was hinged, providing a storage area and Berg's bed. The result was a strikingly unique space, a funky marvel in a city filled with millions of indistinguishable apartment blocks composed of nearly identical apartments filled with identical floral-print wallpaper and similar furnishings.

As he was building this space, Berg came across a ruined prerevolution grand piano in an alley outside a club. The club manager didn't have the legal right to sell it, but Berg's assurance that he would give the instrument a fine home — plus a generous financial contribution, paid in cash — persuaded the manager to make a permanent loan to comrade Berg. Joe provided a similar financial inducement to a couple of strong men to borrow a truck from their workplace to haul the monster to his building and, because it was far too large for the tiny elevator, muscle it up nine flights of stairs. A teacher from the conservatory restored the piano, which was placed in the center of the apartment, to its former glory.

Berg loved to challenge first-time visitors to his renovated apartment to find the refrigerator. They looked in vain for the white box, less than half the size of a standard American version, found in all Soviet apartments. The more persistent guests opened a closet door and discovered the secret. Berg had taken the compressor from an ordinary refrigerator, placed it on the balcony, run a pipe into the closet, and insulated the door. The cold air dropped to the bottom, causing the closet floor to serve as a freezer, while food stored on shelves at waist level was cold; the top shelves were perfect for things like butter and fruits that needed only slight chilling.

When nature called, Berg directed guests to the bathroom, the only room walled off from the main space. Then he waited, depending on the character of his visitor, for a scream for help or for an embarrassed person to emerge and ask for assistance. The toilet had been replaced by a kind of throne. Invariably, newcomers didn't notice the absence of a flush mechanism until it was too late. Berg would joyfully clear up the mystery: one flushed by leaning back on the seat or pressing on the throne's back.

Other inventions were more obvious. One was a Rube Goldberg–like rotisserie device for cooking chickens that had been constructed from a fan. Another was a meter-deep bathtub that covered half the floor space in the bathroom. In its initial incarnation, the tub had a much larger footprint, but the first time he filled it up, Berg learned that the floor couldn't support it. He repaired the floor and paid for the damage to the ceiling, furniture, and carpets of the family who lived on the eighth floor. His inventions looked a little strange, but they worked, and in a country where there were no rotisseries or hot tubs, it made perfect sense to Berg to make his own versions.

Two or three times a week, Berg held musicales in the apartment. Thirty or forty people usually came for conversation (which Berg dominated), food, wine, and, most of all, live music, which was usually provided by students from the conservatory or members of the Leningrad Philharmonic.

Berg stayed in close touch with his children, who were working in Czechoslovakia as musicians. With an active social life, a continuing relationship with Elvira, and the minifab project progressing rapidly, he was quite happy.

Unlike Berg, Anna Staros never adjusted to Soviet life, nor did she ever get used to being separated from her children. The meeting in Prague and a trickle of letters didn't come close to satisfying Anna's desire for contact with her two youngest children. She pressed the KGB for permission to visit them in Canada. Rather than allow her to leave the Soviet Union, in 1987 the KGB permitted Derry to travel to Leningrad with her five-year-old daughter and fourteen-year-old son. She stayed with Kristina Staros, and the half-sisters spoke, in English, late into the night, discussing each other's very different lives. The Staroses learned that Derry's father, Bruce, had been devastated by his wife's departure. After it had become clear that she wasn't returning, he had moved as planned to Boston to take up a postdoctoral position at MIT, where he had written several papers about cosmic rays that were published in prestigious journals. When the postdoctoral appointment was completed, Bruce couldn't find another academic position, despite his excellent scientific credentials. He had the misfortune to be sending applications at the peak of Senator Joseph McCarthy's influence, a time when academic institutions were afraid to hire a physicist who was publicly associated with the Rosenbergs.[18]

As the FBI tried to expand the scope of atomic-espionage prosecutions beyond Harry Gold, David Greenglass, the Rosenbergs, and Morton Sobell, Dayton was summoned to testify before several grand juries. The Bureau believed it had sufficient evidence to convict him for perjury when he denied knowing Bill Perl or having ever visited Sarant's Morton Street apartment. Buttressed by lab logs documenting his presence in Ithaca on dates the FBI said he was in Greenwich Village, Dayton vigorously rejected the accusations. An

FBI informant claimed to have seen him at Morton Street in pajamas, but Dayton said he'd stopped sleeping in them as a teenager. The Justice Department never indicted him, and no evidence has emerged to suggest that Dayton had any involvement in, or knowledge of, espionage.[19]

Unable to find a research position in the United States, in 1954 Dayton accepted an offer to resume his research on cosmic rays at the Tata Institute of Fundamental Research in Bombay, India. The invitation came from Bernard Peters, a close friend of Dayton's and Carol's and a former student of J. Robert Oppenheimer, who had been fired from a teaching position in Rochester, New York, when newspapers printed stories alleging his membership in the Communist Party.[20]

The State Department refused to issue a passport to Dayton, citing secret information provided by the FBI that, it asserted, linked him to subversion. When Dayton sued to obtain a passport, Secretary of State John Foster Dulles described some of the FBI's evidence in an affidavit. The information the government was willing to release amounted to an accusation of guilt by association: Dayton's friends included Alfred Sarant and Peters, both of whom the State Department branded as suspected Communist espionage agents. The affidavit claimed that Dayton had visited the Morton Street apartment, which it said had been "used for microfilming material obtained for the use of a foreign government." The State Department asserted that it had more derogatory information about Dayton which it could not reveal publicly. The affidavit concluded that Dayton planned to travel "abroad to engage in activities which will advance the Communist movement."[21]

Lower courts upheld the State Department's decision in Dayton's case, but on June 16, 1958, Supreme Court Justice William O. Douglas wrote in a majority opinion that the government did not have the legal authority to deny someone a passport on the basis of allegations of Communist activity.[22] The next week the State Department announced that it would no longer ask passport applicants if they had ever been members of the Communist Party.[23]

Derry told her newfound half-sister that her father had remarried, about the family's move from the United States to Bombay, and how after a few years Dayton followed Peters to Europe. In the 1970s, Dayton returned to the United States, where he made fundamental discoveries about the physics of cosmic rays while teaching at several universities before settling at California State University.

Another link to Anna and Phil's past arrived in Leningrad in 1987. The man whom Dayton had followed to India, Bernard Peters, and his wife, Hannah Peters, visited and stayed with the Staroses.

The decision to allow Derry and the Peters to visit the Staros family in

Leningrad was a remarkable gesture, made possible in part by the Staros and Dayton families' discretion. Gorbachev was in power, *perestroika* and *glasnost* were already worn clichés, but the Soviet Union was still a repressive police state. The American media didn't learn of Derry and Eric Dayton's earlier visit to Prague, and there was no evidence that the FBI or CIA had been informed. The KGB probably calculated that everyone involved would keep quiet out of fear that any publicity would cause a permanent break in communication between the Staroses and Daytons, and possibly some unpleasant repercussions for the Soviet side of the family.

The Czechoslovakian government, like those in other Soviet satellites, responded to *glasnost* by battening down the hatches. Prague, for years a much freer, more open city than Leningrad, became stifling as the old guard struggled to suppress change. The Czech government quashed any sign of spontaneous culture, for example, jailing the organizers of a jazz club as dangerous enemies of the state. Distrust of Gorbachev's reforms was so great that for the first time since 1948, Czech newspapers did not print copies of a Soviet leader's speeches. Intellectuals had the sense that the dreary Stalinist regime would persist forever.[24]

Berg's son Robert decided that he couldn't stand Prague any longer. While traveling with a Czechoslovakian musical group in 1988, he presented himself to officials at the U.S. embassy on Via Veneto in Rome saying that he wanted refuge in America. Defecting was not a trivial act in those days; it entailed making a complete break with relatives and friends who remained behind. As far as they were concerned, someone who was in Europe or the United States could just as easily be on the moon. It was assumed that they would never be seen again. And if something went wrong and one was caught, the consequences would be extremely unpleasant.

Before leaving Prague, Robert had asked Vera for Joe's real name, so he was able to tell the American embassy officials that he was the son of an American named Joel Barr. When they asked for proof of his father's American citizenship, Robert remembered Joe coming home one day in November 1985 in a state of excitement and telling how during his usual Tuesday-afternoon library session, he had seen an incredible article in an American journal, *Physics Today*. Berg had managed to copy only a portion of the article into his notebook before the library closed for the day. He reported that under a photograph of KB-1's old home, the Palace of Soviets, the headline read: "The American connection to Soviet microelectronics." Berg didn't mention that it also revealed in smaller, bold type: "A former Soviet physicist solves a longstanding mystery about the identity of two Americans who disappeared during the Rosenberg spy case and engaged in technology transfer for the Kremlin."[25]

Mark Kuchment, a physicist educated in the Soviet Union who was working as a science historian at Harvard's Russian Research Center, had been hearing stories for years from Soviet émigré scientists about two foreigners named Staros and Berg. Kuchment spent eighteen months trying to make sense of the clues his Russian sources had provided about Staros, as well as the sketchy details provided in Soviet reference works, but they didn't add up. Staros's official Soviet biography, in the 1970 yearbook published by the *Great Soviet Encyclopedia*, stated that Staros had graduated in 1941 from a university in Toronto, but Kuchment discovered that no university in Toronto had a record that anyone by that name had ever attended.

During the summer of 1983, Kuchment interviewed several Czechoslovakian émigrés in Europe, hoping to glean more information about Staros, but none of them had heard of him. "The night of my return home to Cambridge, I relaxed with a copy of the *New York Review of Books*. Suddenly, there it was: a review of a book about the Rosenbergs that mentioned their friends who had probably disappeared behind the Iron Curtain," Kuchment reported in the *Physics Today* article. He "ran to Harvard Square, bought a copy of [*The Rosenberg File*] and found the name Sarant. All the pieces of the puzzle soon fell into place." Kuchment showed photos of the Soviet engineer named Staros to Morrison and to Sarant's sister, Elektra Jayson, both of whom identified him as Sarant, while Firdman, Staros's protégé who had emigrated to the United States in 1981, told Kuchment that an old photo of Sarant was the man he had known in Russia as Staros.[26]

Incredibly, Kuchment had succeeded in solving the mystery of Barr's and Sarant's fates, a task that the FBI and CIA, with infinitely greater resources, had pursued fruitlessly for decades. Two of his best sources of information had tried to interest U.S. government officials in Staros and Berg but had been rebuffed. One was Morton Nadler, who failed to interest officials in the U.S. embassy in Paris in his theory that the partners he met in Prague in 1955 were Soviet spies. The other was Firdman.

A team of CIA analysts had debriefed Firdman for a week, but the interrogators were interested only in details about Soviet microelectronics technology. "They didn't ask about Staros and Berg. I told them, and they weren't interested. I didn't know they were in the Rosenberg case, but I knew they were Soviet spies. I told them I worked for people who I believed were Soviet spies, and they just were not interested," Firdman recalled.[27]

Kuchment's article had prompted Berg to tell his wife and children a bit about his life and family in America. He didn't mention the Rosenbergs, nor did he give even a hint that he'd been a spy. The day after spotting the article, Berg returned to the Academy of Sciences library to finish copying it, but it was gone.

The State Department had more luck procuring a copy of the *Physics Today* article. Robert, however, couldn't establish to the State Department's satisfaction that he really was Joel Barr's son, nor could he prove that Barr had retained his U.S. citizenship. Sympathetic government officials explained to Robert that without a great deal more information, it would be impossible to grant him citizenship. Instead, they quickly approved Robert's application for refugee status, and he flew to the United States in June 1988.

There were tremendous ironies in Robert's defection. He was risking a great deal, including permanently severing connections with his parents and siblings, in order to leave Czechoslovakia and the Soviet bloc, just as his father had risked everything to defect to Czechoslovakia and the Soviet bloc, and as Berg's own father had given up his old life in Ukraine to emigrate to America 100 years before.

Joe didn't appreciate the irony. Normally ebullient, he uncharacteristically went ballistic when he learned about Robert's defection. It was a repudiation of everything he believed in. Furthermore, Joe was certain that the Czech authorities would make his other children's lives hell, and he was afraid that Svetlana would fire him, a typical fate for a defector's relatives, or put someone else in charge of the minifab project. He wrote a letter demanding that Robert return and sent it to Anton, his youngest son, who lived in Prague, requesting that he forward it to Robert. Anton never sent the letter, however.

It turned out that Berg's worries were unjustified. Probably because Robert was a citizen of Czechoslovakia, the Soviet authorities took no apparent interest in his defection. Within two months of Robert's arrival in New York, Joe's daughter Vivian and her husband managed to drive to Germany, where they applied for asylum in the United States. They were placed in a refugee camp while the U.S. authorities considered their applications. Unlike her brother, Vivian wasn't put on a fast track. As the weeks of waiting turned into months, she decided to claim U.S. citizenship on the basis of the fact that she was the daughter of a citizen. She was, however, unable to provide any documentation to prove that her father was in fact a U.S. citizen, and her sister Alena and brother Anton, who remained in Prague, pleaded with Joe to step forward and help Vivian.

The U.S. embassy in Prague received an unusual request in May 1989, almost a year after Vivian's arrival in Germany. Someone claiming to be an American citizen wanted to speak with an embassy official, but he was afraid to be seen entering the embassy. A consular official agreed to a meeting in a car parked several blocks from the embassy. During an initial conversation in the car and a subsequent meeting in Alena's apartment, Berg explained that he wanted to establish his U.S. citizenship in order to help his daughter receive an American passport.

Berg told the skeptical U.S. official that his real name was Joel Barr, that he had decided to go to Czechoslovakia in 1950 when "all his friends," including the Rosenbergs, had been arrested in the United States. He declined to describe in detail his careers in Czechoslovakia and the Soviet Union. Berg provided a copy of Kuchment's *Physics Today* article, which he described as "very accurate," and showed copies of his Soviet passport, South African birth certificate, and Czechoslovakian passport. He had no documents with the name Barr, and the only evidence that he'd ever lived in the United States was his Brooklyn accent. He started to complete a citizenship questionnaire, but refused to give it to the consular official, saying he needed more time to think things over. He was afraid that he might write something on the form that would get him into hot water in Russia if it leaked, and he was also concerned that he might inadvertently jeopardize his prospects for someday returning to the United States.[28]

The consulate sent copies of Berg's fingerprints to Washington. The Prague embassy sent copies of its report about Berg to the consulate in Munich, which was adjudicating Vivian's citizenship claim, to the embassy in Moscow, and to the FBI in Washington.

While U.S. authorities were pondering Berg's tale and determining Vivian's fate, Anna Staros also decided that the time was right to contact the American government. She was clearer about her goals than Berg had been. She wanted a passport in order to return permanently to the United States. Unlike Berg, she was able to substantiate her amazing story. When she met with consular officials in 1989, Anna Staros gave them a battered old California driver's license with her picture, thumbprint, and maiden name, Carol Dorothy. Sympathetic officials in the consulate, a couple who by coincidence were friends of her son-in-law, helped Anna/Carol fill out the necessary forms and pressed Washington to reinstate her citizenship. They cautioned that it could take a long time to resolve the case.

While the American government was considering whether it should grant Anna's claim to citizenship, Soviet authorities granted her a visa to travel to Denmark. She was working in Bernard and Hannah Peters's garden in 1990 when Bruce Dayton called his old friends on the telephone. Bruce didn't speak with her, but the news that his ex-wife was free to travel was startling. After a couple of weeks, Anna quietly returned to Leningrad with a suitcase full of European gardening equipment.

As the winds of *perestroika* and *glasnost* reached Zelenograd in the late 1980s, the scientists and engineers who worked in the Scientific Center were pleased by the removal of hoary Communist slogans from the city's rooftops, even if the giant statue of Lenin remained in front of their building, and celebrated when the Communist Party was forced to move out of their building. Berg, however, was saddened. It was, he predicted, the beginning of the end of Soviet science and technology. But although he lamented the decline of Communist power, he was enthusiastic about one manifestation of the new economic policies.

In 1987 the Scientific Center at Zelenograd sponsored a competition that was designed to identify truly innovative microelectronics projects. The idea was to reverse decades of risk aversion that had limited investments to concepts that had been validated in the United States. The best ideas, those that presented realistic opportunities to advance beyond the best Western technology, would receive sufficient funding to bring them to the prototype stage, after which it was hoped Soviet or foreign companies would license and manufacture them.

As one of the first cohort of finalists, in 1989 Berg was given funding and staff to complete a detailed feasibility study of the minifab. He later defended the concept at a final round of competition and, helped by endorsements from prominent scientists including Zhores Alferov, a future Nobel Laureate, received a commitment for sufficient funding to complete a working prototype. He was given authority to hire a staff of up to 800 and, just like two decades previously, began shuttling between Leningrad, where he retained his position at Svetlana, and Zelenograd. Berg started to think about the next step, getting the minifab into production, and concluded that it would be nearly impossible to squeeze enough money out of the Soviet government. Maybe, he thought, it would be possible to find an American investor.[29]

The American embassy in Prague heard from Berg again in May 1990. Vivian had managed, after almost two years of detention in Munich, to enter the United States as a refugee. This time Berg came in his own behalf, indicating that he was "interested in establishing his identity as Joel Barr, in obtaining a B-1 visa in the near future to permit him to travel to the United States on behalf of his employer, Svetlana Electron Device Manufacturing Corporation in Leningrad, and eventually in establishing his claim to U.S. citizenship," according to a cable signed by American Ambassador Shirley Temple Black. The cable, which was sent to State Department headquarters, included a heads-up note for the Leningrad consulate: "Berg will probably be contacting you in the near future. Reftels [reference telegrams], which were sent to Moscow, detail Berg's flight from the United States, naturalization as a Czech and later Soviet citizen." The cable concluded that the State Department "reports it has no [passport] records or loss of citizenship record for either Josef Berg or Joel Barr."[30]

A couple of months later, while browsing in a bookstore in New York, Robert Berg picked up a copy of *The Rosenberg File,* coauthored by Ronald Radosh, a historian who started investigating the Rosenberg case certain that Julius and Ethel were innocent and ended up convinced of their guilt.

Robert was horrified to discover that his father and Philip Staros had been spies for the Soviet Union. Suddenly everything made sense: the huge salary, the large apartment, his father's "connections." He was so upset that he missed a scheduled audition for the New York Philharmonic. Robert rushed home, found Radosh's number in the Manhattan telephone directory, and called him. "Hello, I'm Robert Berg," he said.

"Yes, what can I do for you?"

"Don't you recognize my name? I'm Joel Barr's son."

Radosh was floored. It was like speaking with the son of a ghost. He answered Robert's questions about Joel Barr and Alfred Sarant, and heard Robert's description of his family's life in Soviet Russia.

A few days later it was Radosh's turn to floor someone with an unexpected telephone call. He dialed the telephone number in Leningrad that Robert had provided.

"I'm Ron Radosh, is this Joel Barr?"

"You finally found me!" Barr exclaimed. He had read about *The Rosenberg File* and knew who Radosh was. Barr denied that he'd been involved in espionage, but "acknowledged that his disappearance and failure ever to contact family or friends looked sinister, and that he had a great deal of explaining to do," according to Radosh. Barr provided one startling piece of information: he planned to return to the United States soon. The U.S. consulate had refused to issue an American passport, so he would be traveling with Soviet documents, as Iozef V. Berg.[31]

The Strange Case of Iozef (Josef) Berg AKA
Joel Barr, 1990–1998

Joseph Berg was nervous for the entire flight, imagining that he'd be met by police with handcuffs, or by flashing cameras, bright television lights, and reporters, or, worst of all, that at the last minute he'd be turned back. The biggest surprise, however, was that there were no surprises when he landed at JFK airport on an Aeroflot flight from Leningrad on October 25, 1990. To hide his anxiety, Berg joked in Russian with the attractive, pencil-thin, vivacious young woman who stood at his side in the queue for noncitizens.

Berg's companion was Valerie Valueva, the younger of his and Elvira's two daughters. Although they lived a few miles from each other in Leningrad, it was at a party only a couple of weeks before his return to the United States that Berg had met Valerie and her sister, Julia, for the first time since they were toddlers. Elvira and Joe hadn't discussed revealing their secret to their daughters, and Elvira assumed that Joe would be content to see them without saying anything about their relationship. She was almost as shocked as Julia and Valerie when Joe impulsively told them that he was their biological father. Seeing the girls beside Joe, there could be no doubt that it was true. Valerie not only looked like him but also had a similarly bubbling personality. To Elvira's surprise, the sisters quickly got over their astonishment and accepted Joe as a second father.[1]

Berg wasn't planning to travel with Valerie, but after learning that the daughter he'd recently become acquainted with also had plans to visit the United States, they decided to go together. True to her genes, Valerie was a musician, a singer, and she dreamed of finding fame and fortune in America.

Berg handed over his Soviet passport to the immigration officer, who flipped to the page where the Leningrad consulate had stamped a B-1 (business) visa, added his own stamp, and pushed it back without a word.

Father and daughter emerged into the crowded terminal, grinning and staring with amazement. It had been forty-two years and ten months since Berg left the United States. The first thing in America that really impressed him was the public restroom. He could hardly believe the automatically flushing urinals, and he played with the automatic faucets on the sinks like a kid. Picking up the *New York Times*, Berg skimmed the headlines: "Gorbachev's Economic Plan Approved"; "Berlin Police Raid Ex-Communists"; "Bush Describes Himself as 'Determined' on Kuwait." The impending war in the Persian Gulf reinforced his conviction that the United States was an imperialist power that sought global hegemony.

The newsstand also had a copy of the *New Republic*. Berg didn't pick it up at the airport, but a few days later he read the article on page nine, "Socialist Heroes." It described new revelations from Nikita Khrushchev's memoirs confirming that the Rosenbergs had helped the Soviet Union acquire the atom bomb. Of more interest to Berg, the article suggested that with the Cold War drawing to a close, "perhaps the one man still alive who can shed light on the activities of the Rosenberg spy ring will feel able to tell his story. That man is Joel Barr." Incredibly, the first news for decades about Barr in an American magazine, except for the *Physics Today* article and a few similar stories Mark Kuchment had written in popular periodicals, appeared the week he returned. The article, by Rosenberg biographer Ron Radosh, revealed that Barr had lived for more than forty years in the Soviet Union under the name Joseph Berg and that he planned "to visit America traveling on a Soviet passport."[2]

A Moscow-based American consultant who hoped to broker the licensing of the minifab to a U.S. company had paid Berg's plane fare. Another American who wanted to profit from Berg, a television producer working on a documentary about the Rosenbergs, had found someone to host Valerie and Joe in New York.

Joe expected to need a place to stay for a night or two, until he reconnected with his family. It had never occurred to him that the Barr family would be anything other than delighted to see their long-lost relative. When he met his brothers Bernard and Arthur they would embrace, maybe share a bottle of wine, and spend days catching up on four decades of news, Joe imagined. The stories he'd tell! And of course, his brothers and baby sister, Iris, would come to Leningrad, where he'd throw a musicale in their honor and take them to Moscow for a tour of Zelenograd.

Joe was trembling with excitement when he called Bernard Barr on the telephone, but the conversation with his older brother didn't go as expected. Bernard sounded strange, hostile. He only reluctantly agreed to a meeting in Manhattan; there was no invitation to his house. Joe attributed his brother's cold response to shock at hearing from him after so many years of silence. Surely, everything would be fine once they met. His next call was to Arthur Barr, the younger brother whose birthday he'd appropriated.

The first time Joe called, Arthur hung up, thinking it was a prank call. The second time, he demanded proof that it really was his long-lost brother. "If you're Joel, tell me how I got the scar on my forehead."

"Jesus Christ, Artie! For Christ's sake, it's me, Joel! Jesus, Artie, how the hell can I remember something like that after all these years?" Berg screamed. Then it came to him. "It was on the sled! You banged your head when the sled crashed!" Convinced that it really was his brother, Arthur agreed to a meeting in California.

The reunion with Bernard was even worse than the telephone call. He blamed Joel for their mother's death in 1959. The stress caused by his disappearance had done her in, Bernard said. The family had decided in the early 1950s that Joel had probably died in an accident, and Bernard made it clear that as far as he was concerned, it would be better if that had happened. He wanted nothing to do with his brother.

Vivian Glassman, Joe's old girlfriend, received him much more warmly, although their relationship had very nearly landed her in jail. Eighteen months after she and Joe had embraced in front of the S.S. *America* in January 1948, Vivian was visited by a mysterious Russian who claimed to be a friend of Joel's. Following the Russian's instructions, she carried $2,000 he gave her to Bill Perl in Cleveland, along with the KGB's instructions on how he was to flee to Mexico. Afraid that it was a provocation, Perl rebuffed Glassman and reported the incident to the FBI. Glassman gave a vague story about the incident to the FBI in August 1950 but, after consulting an attorney, refused to say another word about it. She cited her constitutional right to avoid self-incrimination when questioned by grand juries and by Senator McCarthy's committee about her relationships with Barr, Sarant, and Perl, as well as her knowledge of or involvement with Soviet espionage.[3] The FBI never uncovered solid evidence to support its suspicion that Julius Rosenberg had microfilmed documents in Glassman's apartment and that she had played an active role in supporting Barr's espionage activities. She wasn't indicted, but the publicity associated with her testimony before the McCarthy committee got her fired and made it very difficult to find a job.[4]

In 1950 Vivian married Ernest Pataki, a Communist engineer who worked at the Federal Telephone and Radio Corporation Laboratory, but she never forgot Barr, nor did she give up the political ideals they had shared in the 1940s.[5] When Glassman and Berg compared notes, he realized that they had almost crossed paths twenty years before. She had visited Leningrad twice in the 1970s during tours of the Soviet Union taken with progressive political groups. The groups had stayed in hotels that Berg had sometimes visited, hoping to run into foreigners at the bar. Now that they were reunited, Vivian suggested that they take a vacation together in China, but Berg was far more interested in reacquainting himself with the United States.

Having narrowly avoided indictment for her activity in the Rosenberg espionage ring, and with memories of the McCarthy period still fresh, Glassman strongly urged Berg to maintain a low profile. She screamed at him in exasperation when Berg said he was considering writing a book about his life or giving a series of lectures promoting the benefits of socialism. For his own sake, as well as for the benefit of the Rosenberg children — who changed their last names to Meeropol after Abel and Anne Meeropol adopted them in 1954 — and everyone else associated with the Rosenbergs, he should keep quiet, she insisted.[6]

The future had always been more attractive for Berg than the past, but in New York he was forced to spend time attending to his history, reexamining actions taken as a young man, and deciding how to present them to his relatives, friends, the authorities — and himself. He received advice from Marshall Perlin, an attorney who had represented the Rosenbergs during their final attempts to avoid execution and then worked tirelessly for their codefendant, Morton Sobell, and the Meeropols. Perlin insisted that Berg not breathe a word about any connection to espionage or to the KGB during his life in the United States, just as he strongly advised the Meeropols not to reveal that they were gradually coming to believe that although he had been unjustly convicted, their father had probably been a spy for the Soviet Union.

Perlin brought Berg to the library at Columbia University Law School, where hundreds of thousands of documents related to the Rosenberg case, primarily FBI files released as a result of a Freedom of Information lawsuit that Perlin brought against the U.S. government, were deposited. Burrowing through the files, Berg learned for the first time that the FBI had known he was an active Communist Party member when Sperry Gyroscope fired him in 1948, and that it had narrowly missed locating him in France in the summer of 1950. Berg smiled when he came across an FBI document that quoted a former supervisor at Sperry calling him a "brilliant engineer," and was upset to see that his brother-in-law had volunteered on his own initiative to help the FBI track him down. After hours of peering into his life's paper trail, Berg found what he had come for: the number and date of issue of the passport he'd turned over to the KGB in Prague, crucial information for convincing the State Department to provide a replacement.[7]

Like a modern Rip van Winkle, Berg walked the streets of New York, finding them at once familiar and bewildering. A Brooklyn tenement his family had occupied in the 1930s hadn't changed much; it was still filled with very poor people, but they were all black. The neighborhood synagogue retained its stained-glass Star of David, but it had been transformed into a Baptist church. The cheap diners and automats where he had once met with KGB agents were gone, replaced by McDonald's and Burger King restaurants.

In Russia, Berg stood out because he thought and acted like an American. In America he also seemed out of place, not completely American. Things that everyone around him accepted without a second thought were puzzling or disturbing. Why were there thirty-eight kinds of mustard at the grocery store when in Russia people had been content with one? If capitalism was so efficient, why were so many different kinds of cars manufactured? Surely it would be better, Berg said, if someone planned things!

Berg spoke a petrified 1940s version of English, peppered with expressions and corny jokes that had long since drifted out of usage. Sometimes he substituted Russian words, especially for things that hadn't existed when he left New York. For example, he used the word *magnitofon* instead of "tape recorder."

The two weeks allotted for their visit to New York seemed to fly by, and on November 9, Valerie and Joe flew to Los Angeles, where he fulfilled the ostensible purpose of the trip by attending the Western Electronic Show and Convention (WESCON) in Anaheim. The reunion with Arthur, in a Los Angeles hotel, wasn't much more satisfying than the encounter with Bernard. After an awkward meeting, "Artie shoved a sweaty wad" of twenty-dollar bills into his brother's hand and ran away, Berg remembered bitterly. Joe, who was almost obsessively concerned about his children, couldn't comprehend how Arthur and Bernard could reject their own brother. He felt that they should have got over the way he had left; after all, the only other choice had been to be arrested. The annual visits from FBI agents asking if he'd been in contact didn't seem like a big deal, especially not compared with regaining a brother.

Berg realized that he had overreacted to Robert's defection, and during the trip he reconciled with his son and started urging all his children to emigrate to the United States. He struggled to explain to them why he'd left in 1948, and tried to convince them that his dream of a planned society, of Communism, was realistic and worthwhile. At the same time, he stressed the importance of individual achievement.

"I think the secret of happiness is very much connected with creativity. I'm absolutely convinced that the happiest people are those that create," he wrote in a letter to his daughter Vivian. "I know this, in a small way, from my own experience. Some of my happiest moments in life have been when I got some technical idea." Berg signed the letter, which was sent as Vivian was creating her new life in the United States, "Your loving, bad Papa, Joe, or Joel (which I like much better)."[8]

After a couple of days in southern California, Valerie and Joe flew to northern California, where they met Sobell, still recognizable under a beard and ponytail. Until shortly before their reunion, neither had expected ever to see the other again. For nearly two decades Sobell had been behind bars, and for more than twice as long Berg had lived behind the Iron Curtain, his travel restricted to the Soviet bloc.

Time hadn't mellowed Sobell. Defiant and unrepentant, he lived in San Francisco, where daily life often took him to places with clear views of Alcatraz, the rocky hell that had been his home for five of the eighteen and a half years. Sobell had resumed political activism after leaving prison, but unlike during his younger days, there was no longer any need for secrecy. In the mid-1980s he had traveled to Hanoi to set up an assembly line to produce hearing aids. His activities there had been funded by a political activist linked to illegal technology transfers to the Communist country until the latter was murdered. In April 1986 Sobell had been arrested at a demonstration in Manhattan against U.S. aid to Contra rebels in Nicaragua.

Proud that he had never "cracked," Sobell pressed Berg to deny vociferously any connection with espionage. It was, Sobell said, the only way to honor the Rosenbergs. Advancing "the cause" and maintaining the struggle against capitalism were more important than telling the truth, Sobell stressed.[9]

Berg returned to Leningrad on November 16, taking care to leave the United States before his visa expired; he wanted to avoid any action that could jeopardize his chances of obtaining another visa. Valerie stayed behind to make a life in America.

One of Berg's first stops at Svetlana was at the Communist Party office, to pay his monthly dues and have his party book stamped, as he had done faithfully for nearly a quarter of a century. It was the last time. Even after the end of the Cold War, U.S. visa applications asked about Communist Party membership, and Berg thought it would be best if he could truthfully deny membership in the Communist Party of the Soviet Union. Berg left the party by default and with a heavy heart, not by renouncing it as many of his colleagues had done, but by simply allowing his membership to lapse. He dropped out for purely pragmatic reasons and never stopped considering himself a Communist.

Leningrad, like the rest of the Soviet Union, was in a state of disarray in the winter of 1990. Gorbachev's "reforms" had succeeded in wrecking the old economic system, but not in creating functioning markets to replace it. There was a tremendous shortage of everything except lines. The engineers who were supposed to be working on the minifab hadn't been paid in months, and many of them spent the time they were supposed to be working queuing for milk or meat, or searching for opportunities to emigrate. Some of the offices at the Scientific Center in Zelenograd were devoted to Arabic classes for engineers who hoped to find work in the Middle East. Work on the minifab had stopped, and it was obvious to Berg that the project could never be completed without foreign funds.

Emboldened by his initial trip to the United States, his fears of arrest having proved groundless, Berg decided to return, primarily to find an investor for the minifab. He also started to think more seriously about regaining U.S. citizenship. The opportunity to revisit America presented itself in early 1991, when Berg was invited to head a delegation of Soviet scientists to an international conference on semiconductor technology in San Francisco.

Preparations for the trip started with a visit to the American consulate in Leningrad to apply for a visa. The consulate promptly sent a cable to Washington with a subject line reflecting the staff's bemusement with Berg: "Visa application and identity/citizenship determination: The strange case of Iozef (Josef) Berg AKA Joel Barr." It noted the *New Republic* article's claim that "Berg is Joel Barr, an Amcit [American citizen] who was involved in the espionage ring of Julius and Ethel Rosenberg," and reported his response. "Berg said he had read the article, and described the allegations of espionage as 'crap.'" Berg also told the American diplomats that "he went to Prague in 1950 to avoid possible detention by U.S. authorities in connection with the investigation into the Rosenberg espionage case."[10]

Realizing that it could take considerable time to resolve Berg's citizenship claim, the Leningrad consulate issued him a second B-1 visa. He flew to New York in February, where, as loyal Soviet citizens, he and the other scientists in the delegation checked in with the Soviet consulate. They continued to San Francisco, with Berg acting as the head of the delegation and translator. The speech he delivered to the conference describing the minifab and soliciting partners or investors was mentioned in the trade press, but there was no suggestion of his real identity. After the conference, Berg met individually with Gordon Moore, the cofounder of Intel Corporation, telling him that he and Staros had often cited "Moore's Law" (that the number of transistors per square inch of integrated circuit would double roughly every year) to the

Soviet leadership. Berg was unsuccessful in his effort to entice Intel to invest in the minifab.[11]

The Soviet delegation returned to Russia, while Berg traveled back to New York, where he met with literary agents to discuss the possibility of working with a professional writer on an autobiography. The William Morris agency contacted several publishers, receiving a bid of a $150,000 advance, which Berg rejected because it was contingent on his working with a writer who demanded the entire sum. Berg wanted his story told, but he wasn't going to sit by getting nothing while someone else made six figures.

In July 1991, Berg applied for a U.S. passport in New York. He wrote on the form that he had lost a passport in Prague in 1950; that he had never applied for, but had been granted Czechoslovakian and Soviet citizenship; and that he had accepted the former in order to marry Vera and the latter because it was required for him to work in the Soviet Union. To his surprise and delight, a couple of weeks later, a shiny new American passport bearing the name Joel Barr arrived in the mail.[12]

When Berg returned to Leningrad at the end of the summer, Svetlana forced him to retire on the grounds that he had overstayed the three weeks allotted for the trip. The Soviet government began paying a generous pension. Berg couldn't resist telling all his friends about the passport, adding that it was a secret. Of course, the news spread in a flash. Hundreds, maybe thousands, of people learned that Berg had an American passport, an extremely uncommon and valuable possession for a Soviet citizen. The KGB provided him with a document certifying that Berg and Barr were the same individual.

Anna Staros was also in the process of reacquiring her former name, as well as her passport. The application submitted two years earlier was finally nearing the end of its trip through the State Department decisionmaking machinery. On Friday, August 16, 1991, the vice-consul sent a cable to Washington requesting final permission to grant the passport. It was the last message from the Leningrad consulate to Washington before the weekend. At 6:30 on Monday morning, the official TASS news agency announced that an "Emergency Committee" had taken control of the government because Mikhail Gorbachev had "serious health problems" and could no longer govern. It looked as if the coup's leaders were plunging the Soviet Union back into dictatorship.

Anna and her children spent Monday glued to the television and radio, terrified that the coup would slam shut the window that Gorbachev had opened to the West, that after coming so close to leaving, they could be trapped in Russia. On Tuesday, when it was far from clear that the coup would be reversed quickly, the consulate called with the news that the passport was ready. The three Staros children living in Leningrad, Kristina, Kolya, and Mila, immediately started the process of applying for U.S. citizenship.

One of Anna and Philip Staros's children was already in the United States. Tonya had been accepted into a master's degree program by Pennsylvania State University. She arrived in the United States, carrying a bright red Soviet passport and speaking fluent English, on Labor Day 1989. After graduating, she moved in the summer of 1991 with her husband, a world-famous mathematician from Leningrad, to Berkeley, California, to pursue a Ph.D. at the University of California. Soon after she arrived in California, Tonya called her mother's former husband, Bruce Dayton, who was also living in the San Francisco Bay area, suggesting that they meet.

The moment he glimpsed Tonya, Bruce was dazed and almost overwhelmed with emotion. Tonya looked exactly like Carol when he had last seen her at the Ithaca bus station in July 1950. It was, he later said, an "out-of-body" experience, as if he were hovering in space above, watching himself together with the woman who had disappeared so many years before.[13]

In November 1991 Anna traveled to California, where she resumed her life as Carol Dorothy. Bruce was reluctant to see Carol, but they met in early 1992 and quickly found that after all the years and pain, there was still a spark between them. Later she moved into a guest cottage behind Bruce's house to help him care for his second wife, Betty, who had Alzheimer's disease. After Betty moved into a nursing home, Bruce and Carol resumed their life together, as a couple at the center of an unusual, close-knit family composed of their two children, a daughter from Bruce's marriage to Betty, Carol and Phil Staros's four children, and several grandchildren. Al and Louise Sarant's two children and Joe and Vera Berg's four children remain close to the Staroses.[14]

In 1992, Carol flew to Washington to be interviewed for a television documentary that ABC's *Nightline* program was filming about Joe Berg. He had agreed to participate, believing that the show would focus on East–West technology transfer and would serve as a platform to market the minifab. Before Joe and Carol met in Washington, ABC sent crews to Berg's apartment in St. Petersburg, where they filmed one of his musicales, and to Prague to interview Vera and his son Anton.

To Berg's naive astonishment, the interviewer, Ted Koppel, focused almost exclusively on the Rosenbergs and spying. Berg denied that he or the Rosenbergs had been involved in espionage of any sort. Afraid that candid answers would somehow harm his children, who were living in California, he feigned conversion to capitalism (and religion), telling Koppel: "I get down on my hands and knees every evening and praise the Lord" that he had been able to

Figure 14. (From left to right:) Elena (the author's wife), Steven Usdin, Maxime Usdin, and Joel Barr, fall 1995, near Washington, D.C. (Photo in author's possession; photographer unknown.)

return to the United States. Berg concluded the interview truthfully, however. "What I'm interested in is tomorrow, and my minifab."[15]

Retired FBI agents and conservative politicians were infuriated by Berg's comments and by the way he was being treated by the U.S. government. Not only had he received an American passport, but Berg also was not shy about exercising his rights as a citizen. In 1991 he applied for and started to receive payments from the Supplemental Security Income (SSI) program, administered by the Social Security Administration for people with low incomes. He voted in the April 1992 New York Democratic presidential primary, picking Jerry Brown because he was the most radical candidate in the race.

"If I were running things in Washington, Joel Barr certainly would never be allowed back in the United States. Barr is a spy and a traitor, and I don't see any reason why . . . a man who has devoted his life to the cause of the Soviet Union, including running a research laboratory for them, should ever be allowed back in the United States," Robert Lamphere, a retired FBI agent who had led the investigations of the Rosenberg ring, said on the *Nightline* program.

After the *Nightline* broadcast, several members of Congress criticized the government's handling of Berg. "Thanks to some no-name bureaucrat, Barr is living in Brooklyn and receiving Social Security at the expense of American taxpayers," Representative Sam Johnson of Texas fumed. "Words cannot express my outrage over a man who admittedly helped the Soviets develop the very technology that may have been responsible for losing seven years of my life in Vietnam," said Johnson, who had been shot out of the sky by a Soviet antiaircraft weapon during the Vietnam War. At a Capitol Hill press conference, Representative Dana Rohrabacher, a California Republican, asserted that Barr "most likely . . . committed treasonous acts against the United States of America and cost the lives of American servicemen." A trial for treason was in order, Rohrabacher maintained, suggesting that "if Mr. Barr is found guilty of treason, he should be sent on to join the Rosenbergs." Twenty-two members of Congress signed a letter to Attorney General William Barr demanding an investigation. To Berg's relief, the hubbub died down rapidly, and no law-enforcement agency ever contacted him or made any attempt to impede his travel between the United States and Russia.[16]

The politicians who signed the request would probably have been astonished by the chutzpah Berg displayed in his contacts with another member of Congress, Representative Stephen Solarz, a Democrat who represented Brooklyn's 13th Congressional District. Berg traveled to Capitol Hill to meet with Solarz's staff several times seeking help obtaining back Social Security benefits. He had started to receive the SSI payments at age seventy-five, ten years after he became eligible. The law limits back payments to six months. Berg argued that it would have been impossible for him to apply for benefits during the Cold War, when he lived in Leningrad (and received a Soviet salary), and asked Solarz to introduce legislation to compel the Social Security Administration to pay him $30,000 in missed payments, plus interest. Despite Berg's vote for him, Solarz was defeated in the 1992 primary, and Berg did not contact any other members of Congress about the issue.

For the rest of his life, Berg split his time about equally between St. Petersburg and the United States, where he stayed for weeks or months at a time with his children in California, with friends in New York, and at the author's home in Washington, D.C. In Russia he continued to use the Berg identity and to collect a government pension, while Social Security checks for $290 were deposited monthly into his Citibank account.

Rampaging inflation turned what was at first a healthy pension into a miserable sum. Like millions of Russians, Berg was bitter that after a life of work, which in his case had been very highly compensated, his monthly payment was barely enough to buy cabbage and potatoes. By allowing the rubles to pile up while he was in the United States, Berg had enough to live on during visits to Russia. Except for his musicales, he lived relatively quietly, attracting little attention in either St. Petersburg (the pre- and postcommunist name for Leningrad) or the United States.

Interest in the fate of Joel Barr revived on July 11, 1995, when the news media were invited to the Central Intelligence Agency headquarters near Washington, D.C., for an extraordinary ceremony. It was the first public acknowledgement of the codebreakers who had transmuted into intelligible text the seemingly random numbers sent over Western Union cables between Soviet intelligence operatives during World War II. Not only were Meredith Gardner and his colleagues from the Arlington Hall cryptography operation celebrated, but also a large batch of the Venona decryptions was released to the public. The first documents released demonstrated to the satisfaction of all but the most determined conspiracy fantasists that Julius Rosenberg had been an important espionage agent for the KGB. They made it clear that Joel Barr and Alfred Sarant had been Soviet agents as well.

Despite the Venona evidence, Berg felt that nothing good could come from a public confession. The notoriety could hurt his children, who had been mortified by the Koppel show, damage the reputations of the Rosenbergs, and hurt the cause of Communism. Privately, while he never frankly admitted what he'd done, he did say *why* someone would transfer information to the KGB. He, Sarant, and the Rosenbergs had been certain that the United States was planning to destroy the Soviet Union by allowing the Nazis to conquer it. When the USSR triumphed over Germany, his circle had become convinced that the capitalists would use their nuclear monopoly to blast Communism off the face of the Earth. Looking back on his life in 1992, he said that during World War II he had felt just as a Jew would have in Nazi Germany. Regarding his flight, and Sarant's more dramatic escape, Berg explained: "We were under the influence of socialist psychology. We knew that there were fascist elements in the American government, in the FBI. In Germany, would anybody think anything [negative] of someone trying to get out of the country during the fascist dictatorship?"[17]

Although he had stopped paying dues to the party, the destruction of the Soviet Union strengthened Berg's loyalty to the Communist ideal. He criticized Soviet leaders for behaving as dictators and conceded the need to provide financial incentives to workers, but he clung to the idea that a planned economy would be far superior to the chaos of capitalism. He wrote a friend that history would have unfolded very differently if, after the launch of the first Sputnik, "instead of 5 percent of the Soviet economy being spent on the civil sector, Khrushchev's proposed 10-fold increase" had been put into action.

"Then what would have happened? American tourists coming to the Soviet Union would have seen an incredible sight. A standard of living much higher than in any capitalist country." The disintegration of Russian science and technology under Gorbachev and Yeltsin as the river of rubles that had flowed into research institutes dwindled to a trickle, and the looting of natural resources that enriched a tiny, criminal elite sickened him. To Berg, it seemed a massive overreaction to discard the sacrifices of generations of Communists, as well as his and Staros's struggles, in order to correct mistakes made by Brezhnev and his successors.

In October 1993 Berg sent a letter to the Chinese consulate in St. Petersburg describing his and Staros's careers in the Soviet Union and offering to move to Beijing to perform similar services for the Chinese Communist government. There was no reply.

Although he deplored Russia's abandonment of central planning and the dismantling of its social welfare programs, Berg was surprised to discover that during his years in the Soviet Union some of the raw edges had been smoothed from American capitalism. During one of his stays with the author's family, he arrived home for dinner waving a small plastic card and shouting, "I've found Communism in America!" His excitement was over a Medicaid card signifying his eligibility for free medical treatment. Berg was only half joking: to him, getting services from the government was a big part of Communism.

Technology, especially advances in computers and telecommunications, continued to fascinate Berg. He started working with a friend on an "Encyclopedia of the Future," imagining how life would look at the end of the twenty-first century, and talked constantly about ideas for new inventions. He learned to operate a personal computer in his late seventies and became a prolific e-mailer. Until he was eighty, Berg rode around Washington on a ten-speed bicycle, attending congressional hearings on high technology, including the first Senate hearing on cloning; giving lectures on Bach at a local library; and presiding over "evenings of music and merriment," as he called the parties he organized. The neighbors were surprised on a muggy evening in the summer of 1994 to see an old man—Berg—sitting in front of a campfire behind an apartment building in a Washington residential neighborhood with a group of people less than half his age, drinking vodka from plastic cups, singing in Russian, and listening as a professional saxophonist improvised jazz riffs well past midnight. That winter Elvira flew from St. Petersburg to spend a month with him in Washington.

In conversation, Berg talked about Communism with a joking smile, as if his comments were ironic and he didn't expect them to be taken seriously. But in e-mails he was more direct, boasting about voting for the Communist candidate in the 1996 Russian presidential election. "I do my little bit wherever I go, and I guess I got a lot of votes for the Communists in the elections," Berg e-mailed a friend. "You have to understand that the former Communist apparatus is still intact. And, even more important, the psychology of the people has not basically changed. All the Communists need to get back into power is a charismatic leader." He detested the return of religion to Russian political life, writing that "the Communist atheistic position was one of the greatest victories in the history of mankind."

Berg was contemplating moving permanently to the United States, but he hesitated to leave St. Petersburg, which was pulsing with political change. "I am fascinated by the political situation here in Russia. It's like sitting in the front row of the most dramatic Shakespearian play he never wrote, because no one in his right mind would have ever been capable of conceiving such a plot. It involves the fate of millions of people and nations right now and for the centuries to come," he wrote in an October 1996 e-mail.

That year a St. Petersburg television station broadcast one of Berg's musicales. A Russian writer published a novel loosely based on Berg and Staros, and several newspaper articles appeared in Russia describing his unusual life.[18]

Further evidence of Staros and Berg's espionage emerged in March 1997 from a surprising source, one that was more difficult to ignore than the lifeless Venona decryptions. Alexander Feklisov came forward to announce that he had been Julius Rosenberg's KGB case officer, as well as Joel Barr's and Morton Sobell's. Feklisov told his story first in an American television documentary and later in a book. His words had more weight than those of other retired KGB officers because they were spoken from the heart—Feklisov said he couldn't bear the thought of dying without having informed the world that Julius Rosenberg was an antifascist hero—and because he was speaking in defiance of the Federal'naya Sluzhba Bezopasnosti (FSB), the Russian foreign intelligence agency.[19]

Feklisov tried to reach out to Berg and Sobell, urging them to join him in setting the historical record straight. "I know that you do not approve my decision to go public and tell the true story in the Rosenberg case. But we, Julius's surviving comrades-in-arms, have one mutual mission in the face of which we have to put all our differences aside—the mission to rehabilitate our dear friends Julius and Ethel Rosenberg. For this sake me, Alexander Feklisov, you, Joel Barr, and Morton Sobell should form a united front with the Rosenberg sons, Michael and Robert," Feklisov wrote in a January 22, 1998, letter to Berg. "And for this noble purpose you should be as courageous as you were in the years of our mutual struggle against fascism and come out and tell the true story of Julius Rosenberg's helping America['s] war-time ally." Feklisov concluded the letter by pleading with Barr "to stand up and go into the records of history as a courageous person and reliable friend. Please, write me a line."

Sobell received a similar letter from Feklisov, noting their "reunion in Moscow." The retired KGB officer wrote that he admired and appreciated Sobell's "courage in standing firm during the trial and in doing time." According to Feklisov, Morton Sobell visited Moscow with his wife, Helen, after he was released. Feklisov claims that Sobell was treated like a hero during the visit, and that the KGB politely declined Sobell's offer to resume his work for Soviet intelligence. Sobell vigorously denies that the visit to Moscow ever took place.

Determined to stick with their stories, Berg and Sobell reacted with mock outrage. Berg threatened to sue Feklisov for libel, claiming that he had never met Feklisov and had never spied, and even solicited the FSB's assistance. Privately, Berg had acknowledged that Rosenberg had "done something for the Soviets, but not the atomic stuff" he was charged with.[20]

On June 30, 1998, Berg, who was in St. Petersburg, sent an e-mail to friends describing the contentious political scene in Russia and airing his view that advocates for socialism were being muzzled. "I don't want to be dramatic, but if I go public here in Russia with my progressive political views in the present situation where honest journalists are assassinated every day, I may become a martyr, and strange to say, I love the idea. Imagine my statue in Red Square next to Marx and Lenin." He added: "I have already at 82 years of age become a little reconciled to dying."

The e-mail also mentioned that Berg was going to Moscow soon to be interviewed for a movie that a Swiss director was making about the idea of Utopia. He spent the last evening before his departure with Elvira, reminiscing about their lives. In the morning he flew to Moscow, carrying a single bag as usual. He was planning to sell his St. Petersburg apartment and move to the United States before winter.

In the second week of July, Berg complained of severe throat pain and was admitted to a Moscow hospital, diagnosed with a serious infection. He lay in bed, helpless, as both the infection and diabetes raged out of control. The physicians eventually beat the infection, but they neglected the diabetes. As his condition worsened, Vivian and Robert Berg rushed to Moscow from California, hoping to stabilize their father and bring him to the United States, where he could receive better medical care, but he was too weak to travel.

On the morning of August 1, 1998, Berg asked Vivian to get him an American hot dog and a coke. Those were his last words.

Iosef V. Berg's funeral was held in the same Moscow crematorium where he had presided over Staros's ceremony nineteen years before. His ashes were interred in a graveyard near Vera Bergova's house in the Czech Republic, alongside those of her father, Anton Krcmarov, a man who opposed everything Berg lived for.

Krcmarov's stubborn refusal to heed Berg's recommendation that he sign over his land to the state was validated after the Czech "velvet revolution." Individuals who had voluntarily transferred their property to the state received no compensation, while those like Krcmarov who had refused to go along with expropriation were eligible for compensation. Bergova managed to regain ownership of her family's land.

Each of Joe and Vera's children embraced their father's love of music, becoming talented professional musicians. Four of Joe Berg's six children have decided to build their lives in the United States. All of them have rejected his lifelong dedication to Communism.

Notes

Chapter 1. Initiation

1. Interview with Joel Barr, March 17, 1997.
2. William Taubman, *Khrushchev: The Man and His Era* (New York: Norton, 2003), 541.
3. Sergo Beria, *Beria, My Father: Inside Stalin's Kremlin* (London: Duckworth, 2001).
4. Irving Howe, *The World of Our Fathers* (New York: Simon and Schuster, 1976), 6.
5. Ibid., 327.
6. Interview with Joel Barr, March 17, 1997.
7. Ibid.
8. Walter Duranty, "Free Trade in Food Allowed in Russia; Grain Collections Completed before Dec. 31 for the First Time in Soviet History; Big Export Surplus Seen, Amount for Reserve and Shipment Abroad Is Put at 7,000,000 Tons," *New York Times,* Dec. 17, 1933, 32; idem, "Soviet Holds 1933 a Year of Victory," ibid., Jan. 1, 1934, 19; Thomas Fleming, *The New Dealers' War: FDR and the War within World War II* (New York: Basic Books, 2001), 289–290.
9. Lionel Abel, "New York City: A Remembrance," *Dissent,* summer 1961, 255.
10. In 1932 the Communist Party's presidential candidate, William Foster, received 103,000 votes. In 1948 and 1952 the Communist Party endorsed Henry Wallace's Progressive Party, which drew 1.2 million and 140,000 votes, respectively.
11. The loyalty pledge requirement in New York City schools was instituted in 1918 in response to draft dodgers and pacifists. The graduating class's reluctance to sign the pledge and subsequent decision to accept it were described in the *New York Times:*

"Pledge of Loyalty Rejected by Pupils," June 15, 1933, 12; and "Students Sign Pledge," June 17, 1933, 15.

12. Morton Sobell, *On Doing Time* (San Francisco: Golden Gate National Parks Association, 2001), 25; interview with William Danziger, Feb. 23, 2003.

13. From an interview conducted by the Public Broadcasting System for the film *Arguing the World,* 1999.

14. Howe, *The World of Our Fathers,* 283; interview with William Danziger, Feb. 23, 2003; "Five-Cent Hot Dog Returns to Alcoves," *The Campus,* Nov. 2, 1936, 1.

15. Leon Wofsy, *Looking for the Future: A Personal Connection to Yesterday's Great Expectations, Today's Reality, and Tomorrow's Hope* (Oakland: I. W. Rose, 1995).

16. Sam Roberts, *The Brother: The Untold Story of Atomic Spy David Greenglass and How He Sent His Sister, Ethel Rosenberg, to the Electric Chair* (New York: Random House, 2001), 41.

17. Interview with William Danziger, Feb. 23, 2003; Sobell, *On Doing Time,* 26.

18. Ronald Radosh and Joyce Milton, *The Rosenberg File,* 2nd ed. (New Haven: Yale University Press, 1997), 51.

19. David Ramsey, "Laboratory and Shop; Science Goes to Bat for Big Business," *Daily Worker,* July 4, 1934, 5.

20. *The Microcosm, 1937* (New York: City College of New York, 1937), 25; interview with Joel Barr, March 17, 1997.

21. Roger Baldwin, "Freedom in the USA and the USSR," *Soviet Russia Today,* Sept. 1934, 11. On actual conditions in the Soviet Union, see Myroslava Sokolova, "Unknown Chroniclers of Manmade Famine," *Vinnytsia* (The Day), Kiev, Dec. 3, 2002; Samuel Totten, *Century of Genocide: Eyewitness Accounts and Critical Views* (New York: Garland, 1997), 95.

22. Baldwin, "Freedom in the USA and the USSR."

23. Interview with Joel Barr, March 17, 1997. The *Kim* attracted public attention on another occasion, when it brought cash that probably was used to fund KGB espionage. In February 1940 more than 160,000 ounces of gold bullion, worth $5.6 million at the time, were unloaded from its hold and taken to the USSR's account at the Chase National Bank; "Soviet Ship Brings $5,600,000 Gold to U.S. to Replenish Commercial Balances Here," *New York Times,* Feb. 8, 1940, 1.

24. Roberts, *The Brother,* 42: "Julius and his friends staged [the] raid on the *Bremen.*" In a personal communication with the author, Roberts attributed this information to David Greenglass. Bill Bailey, a Communist longshoreman, described the storming of the *Bremen* in his autobiography, *The Kid from Hoboken* (San Francisco: Circus Lithographic Prepress, 1993), as having been organized and conducted by tough seamen, not CCNY students; Lucy S. Dawidowicz, *The War against the Jews: 1933–1945* (Toronto: Bantam, 1986), 66.

25. Interview with Joel Barr, March 17, 1997. There was more truth to this than Barr could have known. Some of the president's closest advisors went beyond sympathy to the Soviet Union to spying for the KGB. For example, Laughlin Currie, a close advisor of President Roosevelt, and Harry Dexter White, a senior Treasury Department official, were Soviet espionage agents. Christopher M. Andrew and Vasili Mitrokhin, *The Sword and the Shield: The Mitrokhin Archive and the Secret History of the KGB* (New York:

Basic Books, 1999), 106–109; John Earl Haynes and Harvey Klehr, *In Denial: Historians, Communism, and Espionage* (San Francisco: Encounter, 2003), 169–192, 212–219; John Earl Haynes and Harvey Klehr, *Venona: Decoding Soviet Espionage in America* (New Haven: Yale University Press, 2000), 138–150; Allen Weinstein and Alexander Vassiliev, *The Haunted Wood: Soviet Espionage in America — the Stalin Era* (New York: Random House, 1999), 48, 106, 90, 157–169, 243, 265–267, 274.

26. Roberts, *The Brother,* 42; "Police End Harlem Riot," *New York Times,* March 21, 1935, 1.

27. Maurice Isserman, *Which Side Were You On?: The American Communist Party during the Second World War* (Middletown, Conn.: Wesleyan University Press, 1982), 10.

28. Harvey Klehr, *The Heyday of American Communism: The Depression Decade* (New York: Basic Books, 1984), 314.

29. *Teacher and Worker,* April 1935, 1.

30. Interview with Joel Barr, April 18, 1992.

31. Elijah Wald, *Josh White: Society Blues* (New York: Routledge, 2002), 83.

32. Ron Eyerman, *Music and Social Movements: Mobilizing Traditions in the Twentieth Century* (Cambridge: Cambridge University Press, 1998), 58. Joel Hagglund, a Swedish emigrant who called himself Joe Hill in the United States, was a union organizer and songwriter. His songs, as well as the Alfred Hayes/Earl Robinson song about him, inspired generations of radical folk singers. "Joe Hill" quickly traveled from Camp Unity to Spain with members of the Abraham Lincoln Brigade and was adopted by a new generation three decades later when Joan Baez sang it at Woodstock.

33. Louis F. Budenz, *Men without Faces: The Communist Conspiracy in the U. S. A.* (New York, Harper, 1950), 99.

34. *The Campus,* Oct. 30, 1936.

35. *Teacher and Worker,* May 6, 1936, 1; June 1938, 1.

36. Ibid., summer session, 1937, 5.

37. Henry Petroski, *Remaking the World: Adventures in Engineering* (New York: Alfred A. Knopf, 1997), 3–11; Robert Slater, *The New GE: How Jack Welch Revived an American Institution* (Homewood, Ill.: Business One, 1993), 4, 6, 8; Ronald R. Kline, *Steinmetz: Engineer and Socialist* (Baltimore: Johns Hopkins University Press, 1992).

38. Carroll W. Pursell, *The Machine in America: A Social History of Technology* (Baltimore: Johns Hopkins University Press, 1995), 252–253; William E. Akin, *Technocracy and the American Dream: The Technocrat Movement, 1900–1941* (Berkeley: University of California Press, 1977).

39. "Stop Them Short," *The Integrator,* CCNY Tech. YCL, Oct. 1937, 1.

40. *The Campus,* Jan. 31, 1938.

41. Sobell, *On Doing Time,* 27.

42. *Sunday Worker,* May 1, 1938, 1.

43. "94 on Prize List at City College," *New York Times,* June 21, 1938, 19.

44. Interview with Joel Barr, March 17, 1997; *Daily Worker,* July 6, 1939.

45. G. E. R. Gedye, "Reich and Soviet in 7-Year Treaty," *New York Times,* Aug. 21, 1939, 1.

46. Sobell, *On Doing Time,* 31.

47. Evidence pieced together from archives in the former Soviet Union, KGB messages decrypted by the U.S. Army, and the revelations of defectors leave no doubt that Browder made the subtle switch from subversion to espionage when he returned to the United States and Moscow appointed him to lead the CPUSA; James G. Ryan, *Earl Browder: The Failure of American Communism* (Tuscaloosa: University of Alabama Press, 1997), 138–139; Weinstein and Vassiliev, *The Haunted Wood,* 302–303.

48. Weinstein and Vassiliev, *The Haunted Wood,* 75, 157, 277; James G. Ryan, "Socialist Triumph as a Family Value: Earl Browder and Soviet Espionage," *American Communist History,* 1, no. 2 (2002): 125–142; Andrew and Mitrokhin, *The Sword and the Shield,* 108.

49. Cacchione's name was struck from ballot by a state court on October 13, 1939, on a technicality. The state legislature had recently amended the election law, slightly changing the affidavit form to be used by witnesses who certified the authenticity of petitions, and Cacchione's witnesses used the old form. A week later a higher court put the Communist candidate back on the ballot, but this decision was reversed on appeal the next day. Even without a place on the ballot, Cacchione received 24,132 write-in votes; two other Communist candidates who were forced off New York City ballots received another 25,000 write-in votes. Cacchione finally was elected to the New York City Council in 1945, along with another Communist in Manhattan, he was one of first openly Communist Party candidates to win elections in the United States.

Chapter 2. Washington, Spring 1940

1. Interview with Joel Barr, March 17, 1997.

2. Larry Hannant, "Inter-war Security Screening in Britain, the United States and Canada," *Intelligence and National Security,* 6, no. 4 (1991): 721.

3. Interview with Joel Barr, March 17, 1997.

4. John Earl Haynes and Harvey Klehr, *Venona: Decoding Soviet Espionage in America* (New Haven: Yale University Press, 2000), 326–327. In a September 1944 message to KGB headquarters in Moscow, the New York KGB office mentioned that a background check of a FAECT member had revealed that he was not suitable, so the officers "intend to find another candidate in FAECT"; Venona no. 1340, New York to Moscow, Sept. 21, 1944. The U.S. Army Security Agency's Signal Intelligence Service (SIS) launched a secret program in February 1943 that eventually succeeded in decrypting parts of about 3,000 wartime Soviet diplomatic communications. The project was codenamed Venona. Venona documents are available on the Website of the SIS's successor, the National Security Agency, at http://www.nsa.gov/venona/index.cfm. During the war the Roosevelt administration, leery of its ties to Communists, asked the FAECT to refrain from organizing at the Berkeley Radiation Laboratory, which was performing research on the Manhattan Project.

5. Interview with Joel Barr, March 17, 1997.

6. Andy Marino, *A Quiet American: The Secret War of Varian Fry* (New York: St. Martin's, 1999), 203–205; Stephen Schwartz, "The Mysterious Death of Walter Benjamin," *Weekly Standard,* June 11, 2001.

7. FBI serial 65-58236. FBI serials refer to FBI documents obtained by the author under the Freedom of Information Act.

8. "Dies Sounds Warning of 'Fifth Columns'; Tells House Hitler and Stalin Have Big Organizations Here," *New York Times,* May 18, 1940, 6.

9. Hannant, "Inter-war Security Screening," 718.

10. For example, the FBI had files on most members of the Rosenberg ring in the early 1940s, and Julius Rosenberg, Joel Barr, and Alfred Sarant were fired at various times in the 1940s because of suspicions that they were Communists, but they all managed to continue working for the Soviet cause. Jacob Golos, one of the KGB's top case officers in the United States, kept running agents for years after the attorney general publicly identified him as a Soviet spy.

11. Katherine A. S. Sibley, "Soviet Military-Industrial Espionage in the United States and the Emergence of an Espionage Paradigm in U.S.-Soviet Relations, 1941–45," *American Communist History,* 2 (June 2003): 37.

12. Christopher M. Andrew and Vasili Mitrokhin, *The Sword and the Shield: The Mitrokhin Archive and the Secret History of the KGB* (New York: Basic Books, 1999), 107. In 1939, KGB operations in the United States netted 18,000 pages of technical documents, 487 sets of designs, and 54 samples of new technology. In May 1941, the KGB had 221 agents in the United States, and the GRU (Soviet military intelligence) had a separate network.

13. Interview with Joel Barr, April 18, 1992.

14. Interview with Morton Sobell, Aug. 14, 1999; Morton Sobell, *On Doing Time* (San Francisco: Golden Gate National Parks Association, 2001), 29.

15. Interview with William Danziger, Feb. 23, 2003; Sobell, *On Doing Time,* 30.

16. Sobell, *On Doing Time,* 31.

17. FBI serial 101-1632-94.

18. FBI serial 101-1632-66.

19. For example, Julius Rosenberg paid party dues through Bernard Schuster for years after he had severed all overt ties with the CPUSA.

20. Sobell, *On Doing Time,* 29.

21. FBI serial 101-2483-17.

Chapter 3. Fort Monmouth, 1940–1942

1. Ellen Schrecker, *The Age of McCarthyism: A Brief History with Documents* (New York: Palgrave, 2002), 18.

2. Interview with Joel Barr, April 18, 1992.

3. Stephen Schwartz, *From West to East: California and the Making of the American Mind* (New York: Free Press, 1998), 332–335; "C.I.O. Union Hits 'Reds,'" *New York Times,* July 26, 1940, 20; "Reds Responsible for Vultee Strike, Jackson Declares," ibid., Nov. 24, 1940, 1; "Congress Stirred as Strikes Spread to Check Defense; Surprise Tie-Up of Big Plane Plant in California Hits 20% of Nation's Production," ibid., June 6, 1941, 1..

4. Russell B. Porter, "Reds Here Shift in Stand on War," *New York Times,* July 27, 1941, 17.

5. The FBI later found that the New York City Police Department, including Special Squadron No. 1, had no record of Joel Barr; FBI serial 65-14872, 6, 13; "Four Red Orators Speak at Same Time," *New York Times,* Sept. 5, 1940, 16.

6. FBI serial 101-2483-17.

7. Dulany Terrett, *The Signal Corps: The Emergency* (Washington, D.C.: Office of the Chief of Military History, Department of the Army, 1986), 221–223; "13 Army Pigeons Killed by Hawks at War Games," *New York Times*, Aug. 25, 1939, 10; "Army Registering Homing Pigeons for Conscription in an Emergency," ibid., Jan. 6, 1941, 17.

8. Terrett, *The Signal Corps*, 42.

9. The term did leak out, however; "The Value of Armament to Merchant Ships," *New York Times*, Oct. 2, 1941; "Navy Seeks Radio Technicians," ibid., Nov. 18, 1941. The latter mentions a Navy campaign "to recruit men for training and maintenance of the radio device known as 'Radar,' which is used to locate ships and aircraft that are hidden by fog or darkness." See also Terrett, *The Signal Corps*, 129; Louis Brown, *A Radar History of World War II: Technical and Military Imperatives* (Philadelphia: Institute of Physics, 1999), 83–92.

10. Telephone interview with Samuel Stine, former security officer, Fort Monmouth, Sept. 13, 2003. According to declassified FBI files, Gunther Rumrich, a Nazi spy, "drove up to the main gate at Fort Monmouth, where supposedly top-secret experiments were being conducted. A bored sentry simply waved the Nazi spy through the entrance and went back to reading a comic book. Rumrich, a friendly, engaging fellow, meandered around the post unchallenged, striking up conversations with army officers and scientists alike. He had no trouble locating the site of the secret experiments: he had merely asked a captain where the radar tests were taking place." Rumrich "was able to collect an enormous amount of intelligence on radar research and experiments. Moreover, he obtained information on other secret tests: infrared detection, and an antiaircraft detector for searchlight control and automatic gun sighting"; William B. Breuer, *Secret Weapons of World War II* (New York: John Wiley, 2000), 12.

11. Asked by the prosecutor at the trial of Julius and Ethel Rosenberg and Morton Sobell (United States v. Julius Rosenberg, Ethel Rosenberg, and Morton Sobell) "Did [Julius] Rosenberg tell you how he got into espionage?," Max Elitcher replied: "He told me that a long time ago he decided that this is what he wanted to do, and he made it a point to get close to people in the Communist Party, until he was able to approach a Russian." Ruth Greenglass testified at the trial that Julius Rosenberg had told her that "for two years he had been trying to get in touch with people who would assist him to be able to help the Russian people more directly other than just his membership in the Communist Party." She also testified that "Julius had said they spent two years getting in touch with people who would enable him to do work directly for the Russian people, that his friends, the Russians, had told him that the work was on the atomic bomb, that the bomb had dangerous radiation effects, that it was a very destructive weapon and that the scientific basis, the information on the bomb should be made available to Soviet Russia." Rosenberg had other connections with Spanish Civil War veterans in addition to Osheroff. After graduating from CCNY, he was briefly employed on a freelance basis by Paul Williams, an Abraham Lincoln Brigade veteran who flew in the Loyalist Air Force during the Spanish Civil War (FBI serial 100-332133-2). Anton Fokker had invented the basic technology of synchronizing a machine gun's stream of bullets with the rotation of propeller blades during World War I, so the idea wasn't new. It is possible that Rosenberg had access to a novel or improved method, or that he overestimated the value of the information he had acquired. The anecdote about Julius Rosenberg importuning Os-

heroff to assist him in committing espionage comes from a surprising source: the younger of the Rosenbergs' two sons, Robert Meeropol, who has devoted much of his adult life to redeeming his parents' reputations; Robert Meeropol, *An Execution in the Family* (New York: St. Martin's, 2003), 224.

12. Interview with Joel Barr, April 18, 1992.

13. "19 Classes Elect at Cooper Union," *New York Times,* Nov. 25, 1937.

14. *Executive Sessions of the Senate Permanent Subcommittee on Investigations of the Committee on Government Operations, Eighty-third Congress, First Session, 1953* (Washington, D.C.: U.S. Government Printing Office, 2003), vol. 3, 2705.

15. Interview with Joel Barr, March 17, 1997.

16. Ronald Radosh and Joyce Milton, *The Rosenberg File,* 2nd ed. (New Haven: Yale University Press, 1997), 54–55. Before their marriage, "Julius Rosenberg would visit Ethel frequently at [her apartment]. This apartment was littered with copies of the *Daily Worker* and Communist Party literature. Julius and Ethel became violent Communists between 1932 and 1935 and after that maintained that nothing was more important than the Communist cause. They were very insulting toward anyone who disagreed with their views"; FBI serial 94-3-4-317-348x, 5; Sam Roberts, *The Brother: The Untold Story of Atomic Spy David Greenglass and How He Sent His Sister, Ethel Rosenberg, to the Electric Chair* (New York: Random House, 2001), 274.

17. FBI serial 65-58236-3.

18. "Anti-War Pickets to End White House Vigil Today," *New York Times,* June 21, 1941, 9; "White House Pickets Quit," ibid., June 23, 1941, 28.

19. "Welles Says Defeat of Hitler Conquest Plans Is Greatest Task," ibid., June 24, 1941, 1; interview with Joel Barr, April 18, 1992.

20. Allen Weinstein and Alexander Vassiliev, *The Haunted Wood: Soviet Espionage in America — the Stalin Era* (New York: Random House, 1999), 177.

21. Elizabeth Bentley, *Out of Bondage* (London: Rupert Hart-Davis, 1952), 79.

22. Ibid., 170–171; Kathryn S. Olmsted, *Red Spy Queen: A Biography of Elizabeth Bentley* (Chapel Hill: University of North Carolina Press, 2002), 20–21.

23. *Soviet Russia Today,* Aug. 1934.

24. Louis F. Budenz, *Men without Faces* (New York: Harper, 1950), 41; Anthony Cave Brown and Charles MacDonald, *On a Field of Red* (New York: Putnam, 1981), 341.

25. Bentley, *Out of Bondage,* 84.

26. Ibid., 97.

27. "Red Agency Indicated Here," *New York Times,* Mar. 14, 1940, 17; Bentley, *Out of Bondage,* 87–88.

28. Christopher M. Andrew and Vasili Mitrokhin, *The Sword and the Shield: The Mitrokhin Archive and the Secret History of the KGB* (New York: Basic Books, 1999), 109–111.

29. Weinstein and Vassiliev, *The Haunted Wood,* 177.

30. Lionel Abel, *The Intellectual Follies* (New York: Norton, 1984), 66.

31. Athan Theoharis, *Chasing Spies: How the FBI Failed in Counterintelligence but Promoted the Politics of McCarthyism in the Cold War Years* (Chicago: Ivan R. Dee, 2002), 112.

32. FBI serial 101-2483-17.

33. FBI serial 65-58236-3.
34. Interview with Joel Barr, March 17, 1997.
35. FBI serial 65-14872.
36. "Clip and Save This Map for Use during President's Broadcast Tonight," *New York Times,* Feb. 23, 1942, 12; "The President's Address," ibid., Feb. 24, 1942, 1.

Chapter 4. Western Electric, 1942–1945

1. *Executive Sessions of the Senate Permanent Subcommittee on Investigations of the Committee on Government Operations, Eighty-third Congress, First Session, 1953* (Washington, D.C.: U.S. Government Printing Office, 2003), vol. 3, 2801.
2. FBI serial 65-14872, 13.
3. FBI serial 65-159392-120.
4. FBI serial 65-58236-3.
5. FBI serial 65-59453-3.
6. The advisability of espionage agents' severing all overt ties to the party is so obvious that for decades historians incorrectly assumed that the Rosenberg group's covert activities started after 1944, after Julius canceled his *Daily Worker* subscription and ceased all political activities; Ronald Radosh and Joyce Milton, *The Rosenberg File,* 2nd ed. (New Haven: Yale University Press, 1997), 56–57; Ralph de Toledano, *The Greatest Plot in History* (New York: Duell, Sloan, 1963), 197.
7. FBI serial 65-56402-220, 106; Elizabeth Bentley, *Out of Bondage* (London: Rupert Hart-Davis, 1952), 155.
8. Allen Weinstein and Alexander Vassiliev, *The Haunted Wood: Soviet Espionage in America — the Stalin Era* (New York: Random House, 1999), 217–218; *Executive Sessions of the Senate Permanent Subcommittee,* vol. 3, 2514. Max Elitcher testified that Sobell reported the following regarding a conversation with Julius Rosenberg: "Yes, and he said something that was, Juley says it is all right, he had spoken to Elizabeth Bentley on the phone, or he had spoken to Elizabeth Bentley on the phone at one time, but that she didn't know who he was, and everything was all right, and not to worry about it."
9. Elizabeth Bentley's testimony at United States v. Julius Rosenberg, Ethel Rosenberg, and Morton Sobell; Bentley, *Out of Bondage,* 86.
10. Weinstein and Vassiliev, *The Haunted Wood,* 174.
11. In Venona nos. 1163 and 1164, New York to Moscow, July 18, 1943, and 784, May 26, 1943, Browder sent messages to Moscow via Golos; the latter's disdain for the ability of Russian officers to handle American agents is described in Bentley, *Out of Bondage,* 168. "During his last months, Bentley recalled in 1944, Golos's only bright moment seemed his friendship with [Browder]"; Weinstein and Vassiliev, *The Haunted Wood,* 92–93.
12. Akhmerov's disdain for Zarubin is described in Weinstein and Vassiliev, *The Haunted Wood,* 178. An espionage officer who served under Zarubin painted a flattering picture of him in his memoir; Alexander Feklisov, *The Man behind the Rosenbergs* (New York: Enigma Books, 2001), 49–52, 106–107.
13. Christopher M. Andrew and Vasili Mitrokhin, *The Sword and the Shield: The Mitrokhin Archive and the Secret History of the KGB* (New York: Basic Books, 1999), 108, 111.

14. FBI serial 65-4307-1-B-18(7); *Internal Security Annual Report for 1957: Report of the Committee on the Judiciary, United States Senate, Eighty-fifth Congress, Second Session, Made by Its Subcommittee to Investigate the Administration of the Internal Security Act and Other Internal Security Laws Pursuant to S. Res. 58, 85th Congress, 1st Session, as Extended* (Washington, D.C: U. S. Government Printing Office, April 28, 1958), app. D, 245–246.

15. Pavel Sudoplatov and Anatoli Sudoplatov with Jerrold L. Schecter and Leona P. Schecter, *Special Tasks: The Memoirs of an Unwanted Witness, a Soviet Spymaster* (Boston: Little, Brown, 1994), 48.

16. Feklisov suggests that prior to meeting with Semyonov, Rosenberg had not been spying (Feklisov, *The Man behind the Rosenbergs, 108*). This claim is contradicted by a memo that Semyonov wrote in 1944 stating that Rosenberg was giving Golos purloined information in 1941 (Weinstein and Vassiliev, *The Haunted Wood*, 177–178); by Elizabeth Bentley's testimony at the Rosenberg/Sobell trial regarding her encounter with "Julius" in the summer of 1942 (Bentley, *Out of Bondage*, 86); by one of the KGB's top-ranking officials, Pavel Sudoplatov, who asserted in his memoir that the Rosenbergs were recruited by Gaik Ovakimian before the spring of 1941 (Sudoplatov et al., *Special Tasks,* 117); and by a June 1942 cable from KGB headquarters to its New York office that mentioned Rosenberg (Weinstein and Vassiliev, *The Haunted Wood*, 174).

17. *Internal Security Annual Report for 1957*, 245.

18. Feklisov, *The Man behind the Rosenbergs,* 109.

19. Bradley F. Smith, *Sharing Secrets with Stalin: How the Allies Traded Intelligence, 1941–1945* (Lawrence: University Press of Kansas, 1996), 72–73, 128.

20. Weinstein and Vassiliev, *The Haunted Wood,* 276.

21. FBI agents who tailed Anatoly Yatskov, a KGB agent who operated under the cover name Anatoly Yakovlev, reported in 1947 that he had a curious habit: he almost always carried a newspaper folded under his arm. The report didn't indicate that its authors suspected why the Russian was so fond of carrying newspapers; FBI serial 100-346193-18. Robert Lamphere stated to interviewers for the PBS program *Red Files:* "I remember following [Yatskov] on one instance to a Soviet — to a Russian theater, just off of 42nd Street on the West Side. Two of us were watching him from four or five seats back, watching a film of a victory parade in Moscow. All of a sudden he was gone. We looked in horror around, and he had moved from a good seat to a bad seat further up. Years later we knew that he had actually used the message from underneath the seat."

22. Feklisov, *The Man behind the Rosenbergs,* 117; FBI serial 65-15324-1B. The American KGB courier and agent handler Harry Gold told the FBI: "In all my meetings with Soviet agents from the very first I was told that they would pay for any meals which we happened to have together and that I was never to attempt to take a check. I was also told in my meetings with sources of information in America, that I was to use the same technique. I was to pay for the meals. The same applied to any occasions when we took cabs"; FBI serial 100-346193-37. Semyonov used Childs as a rendezvous point for at least one other American agent, Harry Gold.

23. For more-detailed descriptions, see John Earl Haynes and Harvey Klehr, *Venona: Decoding Soviet Espionage in America* (New Haven: Yale University Press, 1999), 25–28; Robert Louis Benson and Michael Warner, eds., *Venona: Soviet Espionage and the American Response, 1939–1957* (Washington, D.C.: National Security Agency, CIA, 1996).

24. Feklisov, *The Man behind the Rosenbergs,* 80.

25. FBI serial 65-59453-95. One of Rosenberg's agents, referred to in KGB cables by the cover name "Nil," has never been identified. The decrypted cables indicate that Nil was a longtime friend of Rosenberg's who was known to Ethel. Both Savitsky and Sussman fit the profile; FBI serial 65-15360-1099. David Greenglass told the FBI he suspected that Sussman was one of Rosenberg's agents, but didn't provide solid evidence to substantiate the claim; ibid. Other sources of Greenglass information are FBI serials 65-1524-1B and 65-4307-1B-18.

26. Robert Buderi, *The Invention That Changed the World: How a Small Group of Radar Pioneers Won the Second World War and Launched a Technological Revolution* (New York: Simon and Schuster, 1996), 155, 196–216.

27. George Raynor Thompson and Dixie R. Harris, *The Signal Corps: The Outcome (mid-1943 through 1945)* (Washington, D.C.: Office of the Chief of Military History, U.S. Army, 1966), 324.

28. FBI serial 65-59453-116 lists some of the radars Barr worked on or had access to, including many of the most sophisticated airborne and ground-based radars developed during World War II; Buderi, *The Invention That Changed the World,* 153–159.

29. Anthony Cave Brown, *Bodyguard of Lies* (New York: Harper and Row, 1975), 258; Buderi, *The Invention That Changed the World,* 155; William Kahan, "How Blabber-Mouth U-Boats Got Sunk in World War II," 19, paper prepared for presentation to the Electrical Engineering and Computer Science Undergraduate Honor Society HKN, March 7, 2001; Thompson and Harris, *The Signal Corps,* 303.

30. Thompson and Harris, *The Signal Corps,* 303, 485–486.

31. Buderi, *The Invention That Changed the World,* 31; Smith, *Sharing Secrets with Stalin,* 152.

32. Barr did not directly acknowledge that he had provided such information to the KGB, but in a conversation with the author, he answered the question indirectly. He said that until the question was posed to him in 1992, it had never occurred to him that anyone providing the Soviet Union with intelligence in World War II could have compromised the safety of the United States or its allies.

33. For a few years in the mid-1930s, the USSR had the world's most advanced radar technology. The promising early start was frozen in 1937 when leading radar engineers were thrown into prison camps; Louis Brown, *A Radar History of World War II* (Philadelphia: Institute of Physics Publishing, 1999), 85–89.

34. The amazing story of how Soviet aircraft designers, many working in prison workshops, overcame both wartime privations and their own government, is recounted in L. L. Kerber, *Stalin's Aviation Gulag: A Memoir of Andrei Tupolev and the Purge Era* (Washington, D.C.: Smithsonian Institution, 1996). Some of Mutterperl's research was published in technical bulletins that circulated internally at NACA and were available on a restricted basis to companies that were producing military aircraft. For example, Mutterperl was a coauthor of "The End-Plate Effect of a Horizontal-Tail Surface on Vertical Tail Surface," NACA TN-797, Feb. 1941, 25.

35. Feklisov, *The Man behind the Rosenbergs,* 139.

36. CIA memorandum for the file "COMRAP," Feb. 6, 1948, in Benson and Warner, *Venona,* 105–115.

37. FBI serial 100-203581-5421.

38. The author of the document was clearly an insider with intimate knowledge of the KGB. He was also obviously mentally unbalanced. The main premise of the letter was that Zarubin was an agent of the Japanese government, while his wife worked for Germany. Decades later, American counterintelligence learned that the author was Vassily Mironov, a KGB agent posted to the Washington embassy who detested Zarubin. Mironov made similar accusations to senior KGB officials. He and Zarubin were recalled to Moscow, where the KGB rapidly sorted things out. Zarubin was appointed deputy chief of foreign intelligence while Mironov was first sent to a labor camp and later shot; Andrew and Mitrokhin, *The Sword and the Shield*, 123–124. Lamphere told a PBS interviewer: "It wasn't until we received an anonymous letter in about 1943 . . . that it galvanized the FBI into opening many investigations on suspected Soviet agents. Prior to that, most of our manpower had been against the Japanese, the Italians, and the Germans. This letter showed us clearly that there was a major effort being launched against the United States to develop information"; http://www.pbs.org/redfiles/kgb/deep/interv/k_int_robert_lamphere.htm.

39. The CIA memo of Feb. 6, 1948, summarizing the FBI's response to the anonymous letter, noted that it "was impossible to substantiate the allegations concerning" Semyonov; Benson and Warner, *Venona*, 111.

40. The surveillance net caught at least one group of agents, though they were small fry compared with the spies who continued to operate unmolested. The August 1943 anonymous letter mentioned that Andrei Shevchenko, who worked for Amtorg in Buffalo, was actually an intelligence agent. Keeping a sharp eye on Shevchenko led the FBI to three agents who were feeding the Soviets information from NACA. The FBI persuaded them to switch their allegiance to the United States and to feed Shevchenko from NACA and Westinghouse information that had been carefully screened. Because of the KGB's compartmentalization, they did not know that another NACA employee, Bill Perl, was also spying for mother Russia.

41. Athan Theoharris, *Chasing Spies* (Chicago: Dee, 2002), 70; FBI serial 65-59453-4.

42. Elizabeth Bentley testified at Rosenberg's trial that the last call was in November 1943. "Once the 'Julius' caller roused [Bentley] early in the morning because he had 'lost his Russian contact and wanted to enlist Golos's aid in getting re-established' "; Robert J. Lamphere and Tom Shachtman, *The FBI-KGB War: A Special Agent's Story* (New York: Berkley, 1987), 39.

43. Feklisov, *The Man behind the Rosenbergs*, 110.

44. Ibid., 113–114.

45. By 1951 the Soviet Union was manufacturing IFF systems based on U.S. designs to which Barr had access; CIA, *The Electronics Industry in the USSR (SC RR 101)*, CSI-2001-00001 (Langley, Va., June 1, 1955; declassified Jan. 24, 2001); all declassified CSI documents are available at http://www.foia.cia.gov.

46. Feklisov, *The Man behind the Rosenbergs*, 117; Venona no. 1340, New York to Moscow, Sept. 21, 1944.

47. Venona no. 196, New York to Moscow, Feb. 9, 1944; James G. Ryan, "Socialist Triumph as a Family Value: Earl Browder and Soviet Espionage," *American Communist History*, 1 (Dec. 2002): 132; Weinstein and Vassiliev, *The Haunted Wood*, 302.

48. Weinstein and Vassiliev, *The Haunted Wood*, 277; Venona no. 1251, New York to Moscow, Sept. 2, 1944.

49. FBI serial 65-58236-X6; Ronald Kessler, *The Bureau: The Secret History of the FBI* (New York: St. Martin's, 2002), 63.

50. As Athan Theoharis has noted, "Of the 2,900 Soviet consulate messages deciphered under the Venona Project, 29 record that Soviet agents were aware that FBI agents were monitoring their activities and some of their American recruits." And in "reporting this FBI surveillance to their Moscow supervisor, KGB [officers] evinced no concern that their espionage activities and recruitment of American sources had been compromised. The Venona messages instead display a sense of assurance"; Theoharris, *Chasing Spies*, 47–48. On April 29, 1944, the KGB's New York *rezidentura* mentioned in a message to Moscow (Venona no. 584) that "for the time being" officers Kvasnikov and Semyonov "are not being shadowed any more but shadowing of [Feklisov] has started. One is forced to the conclusion that the Hut [FBI] is carrying out 'trial' surveillance." The KGB's conclusion was absolutely correct.

51. In April 1941, 49 of the KGB's 221 agents in the United States were described as "engineers," a broad classification that included anyone with access to technical information; Andrew and Mitrokhin, *The Sword and the Shield*, 107, 128.

52. Venona no. 976, New York to Moscow, July 11, 1944; a December 13, 1944, Venona message (nos. 1749, 1750) reported that "LIBERAL's shortcomings do not mean that he will be completely useless for photography. He is gradually getting used to photography."

53. Venona no. 628, New York to Moscow, May 5, 1944.

54. FBI serial 65-1664.

55. FBI serial 65-1664-722.

56. Viola Brothers Shore became a well-known screenwriter, and her granddaughter, Dinah Shore, was a famous actress and singer; FBI serials 65-15360-2, 65-15360-3, 65-15360-4.

57. FBI serial 65-15360-3.

58. Feklisov, *The Man behind the Rosenbergs*, 133.

59. Venona no. 1600, New York to Moscow, Nov. 14, 1944; Venona no. 1715, New York to Moscow, Dec. 5, 1944.

60. Feklisov, *The Man behind the Rosenbergs*, 134.

61. Ibid., 131.

62. Ralph B. Baldwin, *The Deadly Fuze: The Secret Weapon of World War II* (San Rafael, Calif.: Presidio Press, 1980), 14.

63. Feklisov, *The Man behind the Rosenbergs*, 135. Baldwin, *The Deadly Fuze*, 6: "The Soviets, of course, tried to steal the secret of the [proximity] fuze, but we were careful to ensure that they did not. On one occasion, Gen. Sir Frederick Pile's office (commander in chief of the air defense of Great Britain) requested that a gaggle of Russian officers be escorted on an inspection tour of our AA defenses, the gun belt facing the V-1s coming from France. Telephone calls made in advance assured that all proximity fuzes were hidden and no talk about them was permitted."

64. Feklisov, *The Man behind the Rosenbergs*, 122, 135; Venona no. 1314, New York to Moscow, Sept. 14, 1944, mentioned that Perl "deserves remuneration for material no

less valuable than that given by the rest of the members of LIBERAL's group who were given a bonus by you. Please agree to paying him 500 dollars."

65. Feklisov, *The Man behind the Rosenbergs,* 149.

66. Morton Sobell, *On Doing Time* (San Francisco: Golden Gate National Parks Association, 2001), 36, 39.

67. Sobell acknowledged in his memoir that he owned a Leica at this time; ibid., 45; Feklisov, *The Man behind the Rosenbergs,* 149; FBI 65-15396, p. 22.

68. Venona no. 1053, New York to Moscow, July 26, 1944, mentioned that Julius Rosenberg "was sent by the firm for ten days to work in Carthage [Washington, D.C.]. There he visited his school friend Max Elitcher, who works in the Bureau of Standards as head of the fire control section for warships [that mount guns] of over five-inch caliber. He has access to extremely valuable materials on guns." It noted that Elitcher had graduated from CCNY in 1939, was a party member, was married to a party member, "is an excellent photographer and has all the necessary equipment for taking photographs." The message requested permission to recruit Elitcher. This message corresponds to the accounts Elitcher gave the FBI; Elitcher's testimony in United States v. Julius Rosenberg, Ethel Rosenberg, and Morton Sobell.

69. Elitcher's testimony in United States v. Julius Rosenberg, Ethel Rosenberg, and Morton Sobell.

70. Ruth Greenglass told the FBI that Julius Rosenberg had been very upset when his old friend Marcus Pogarsky (Mark Page) refused to join his espionage network. The FBI speculated that Pogarsky might have refused because he was already working for a parallel Soviet espionage network. It noted that he had joined the CPUSU in 1935, was a member of an "underground" Communist group in 1948, and while employed by Westinghouse had attempted to get reassigned to work on a secret Navy contract, even though it would have resulted in a sixty-dollar-a-week decrease in salary; FBI serial 100-332133-2.

71. Winston Churchill, *The Second World War,* vol. 2 (New York: Houghton Mifflin, 1948), 295.

72. Michael Aaron Dennis, "Secrecy and Science Revisited: From Politics to Historical Practice and Back," Occasional Paper no. 23, Oct. 1999, in *Secrecy and Knowledge Production,* ed. Judith Reppy (Ithaca: Peace Studies Program, Cornell University, 1999).

73. Baldwin, *The Deadly Fuze,* 5, 6; Bradley F. Smith, *Sharing Secrets with Stalin* (Lawrence: University Press of Kansas, 1996), 128.

74. Omar N. Bradley, *A Soldier's Story* (New York: Modern Library, 1999), 434; George Raynor Thompson and Dixie R. Harris, *The Signal Corps: The Outcome (mid-1943 through 1945)* (Washington, D.C.: Office of the Chief of Military History, U.S. Army, 1966), 297–298.

75. N. R. Kellog, *I'm Only Mr. Diamond* (Adelphi, Md.: U.S. Army Laboratory Command, Army Materiel Command, 1990); Patton to Levin Campbell, Chief of Army Ordnance, December 29, 1944, quoted in James Phinney Baxter III, *Scientists against Time* (Cambridge, Mass.: MIT Press, 1968), 236.

76. "Navy Discloses Radio Shell Fuze," *New York Times,* Sept. 21, 1945, 4.

77. "Bombing Methods Upset by New Fuse," ibid., May 9, 1946, 16.

78. Feklisov, *The Man behind the Rosenbergs,* 125.

79. FBI serial 65-58236-X6.

80. Weinstein and Vassiliev, *The Haunted Wood,* 205–207.

81. Smith, *Sharing Secrets,* 215.

82. Venona no. 732, New York to Moscow, May 20, 1944; interview with Richard P. Hallion, the historian for the United States Air Force, conducted by the PBS television documentary series *NOVA,* http://www.pbs.org/wgbh/nova/barrier/history.html.

83. Feklisov, *The Man behind the Rosenbergs,* 144.

84. Ibid., 147.

85. Ibid., 136.

86. Venona no. 1969, Washington to Moscow, Aug. 13, 1943.

87. FBI serial 65-59453-116.

88. Louis Brown, *A Radar History,* 265, 452; V. A. Pheasant, *The Sixteenth Anniversary of Window, 1943–2003* (Salisbury, Wilts.: Chemring Group, 2003); Anthony M. Thornborough and Frank B. Mormillo, *Iron Hand: Smashing the Enemy's Air Defences* (Phoenix Mill, Gloucestershire: Sutton, 2002) 24; Istvan Toperczer, *MiG 17 and MiG 19 Units of the Vietnam War (Osprey Combat Aircraft 25)* (Wellingborough, Northants.: Osprey, 2001), 22.

89. FBI serial 65-59453-116.

90. Feklisov, *The Man behind the Rosenbergs,* 148, 149.

91. CIA, *National Intelligence Estimate 31: "Soviet Capabilities for Clandestine Attack against the US with Weapons of Mass Destruction and the Vulnerability of the US to Such Attack (mid-1951 to mid-1952)"* (Langley, Va., Sept. 4, 1951); Walter J. Boyne, "The Early Overflights," *Air Force,* June 2001, 60; William E. Burrows, *By Any Means Necessary: America's Secret Air War in the Cold War* (New York: Farrar, Straus, 2001), 72.

92. Kerber, *Stalin's Aviation Gulag,* 257.

93. Von Hardesty, "Made in the U.S.S.R.," *Air & Space Magazine,* Feb./March 2001.

94. FBI serial 101-2483-118.

95. Kerber, *Stalin's Aviation Gulag,* 253.

96. In October 1946 the CIA estimated that it would take the USSR until 1954 to develop radar equivalent to that produced in the United States in 1945; CIA, *Soviet Capabilities for the Development and Production of Certain Types of Weapons,* CSI-1999-00020 (Langley, Va., Oct. 31, 1946; declassified Jan. 18, 2000). In June 1955 the CIA reported that the Soviet Union was producing some types of radar in greater quantity than the United States; moreover, "Since World War II the Soviet electronics industry has progressed from the position of a secondary sector of the electrical machinery industry, poorly equipped and of extremely limited capacity, to the status of the second largest electronics industry in the world, with generally modern plant equipment"; CIA, *The Electronics Industry in the USSR.*

97. Bill Gunston, *The Osprey Encyclopedia of Russian Aircraft* (Oxford: Osprey, 2002), 188.

98. Richard E. Stockwell, "The German Legacy," in *The Soviet Air and Rocket Forces,* ed. Asher Lee (Westport, Conn.: Greenwood, 1976), 229–240; Jim Bussert, "Russian Airborne Computers," *Avionics Magazine,* Sept. 2001.

99. Interview with Richard P. Hallion, the historian for the United States Air Force, conducted by the PBS television documentary series *NOVA,* http://www.pbs.org/wgbh/nova/barrier/history.html.

100. Interview with Joel Barr, March 17, 1997.

101. Sarant to Navy, March 19, May 11, and June 27, 1945; Navy to Sarant, April 7 and July 1, 1945, file A 13-(3) (660d), (660e-9), Bureau of Ships, Department of the Navy.

102. *NASA Technology Utilization Report SP-5005,* http://americanhistory.si.edu/scienceservice/007007.htm.

103. Interview with Joel Barr, April 18, 1992.

Chapter 5. Sperry Gyroscope, 1946–1948

1. Interview with Joel Barr, March 17, 1997. For example, Ruth Greenglass told the FBI that Barr helped the Rosenbergs financially and "that she did not think that JOEL BARR was working with JULIUS ROSENBERG because BARR seemed to have money and to be on the same level with JULIUS ROSENBERG"; FBI serial 65-59453-67.

2. Louis F. Budenz, *Men without Faces: The Communist Conspiracy in the U.S.A.* (New York: Harper, 1950), 112.

3. Interview with Joel Barr, March 17, 1997.

4. FBI serial 65-1664-27.

5. Alexander Feklisov, *The Man behind the Rosenbergs* (New York: Enigma Books, 2001), 134; interview with Joel Barr, March 17, 1997.

6. FBI serial 65-59334-105; telephone interview with Vivian Glassman Pataki, May 19, 2003; FBI serials 65-59312-40, 65-59334-19; Robert J. Lamphere and Tom Shachtman, *The FBI-KGB War: A Special Agent's Story* (New York: Berkley, 1987), 196.

7. Joseph W. Bendersky, *The "Jewish Threat": Anti-Semitic Politics of the U.S. Army* (New York: Basic Books, 2000); Athan Theoharis, *Chasing Spies* (Chicago: Dee, 2002), 139–169.

8. In general, however, the Soviet Union was extraordinarily diligent regarding cryptographic security. The efficiency of the KGB's cryptography operations, particularly their ability to maintain secrecy, impressed both the Nazis and the Americans. Despite firm orders to destroy all cryptographic materials, the U.S. armed forces seized about five tons of documents relating to German codes during the war, while the Germans never managed to get their hands on any comparable Soviet materials; Armed Forces Security Agency memo, "Russian Cryptology during World War II," ca. 1951, in Louis Benson and Michael Warner, eds., *Venona: Soviet Espionage and the American Response, 1939–1957* (Washington, D.C.: National Security Agency, CIA, 1996), 164.

9. Allen Weinstein and Alexander Vassiliev, *The Haunted Wood: Soviet Espionage in America — the Stalin Era* (New York: Random House, 1999), 89–90.

10. FBI serial 94-3-4-317-348.

11. There were other instances in which the KGB had agents match torn pieces of paper to demonstrate their bona fides. An American who gave the USSR military aircraft secrets later told the FBI that in 1940 his handler "took a picture of Shirley Temple, tore it in half, and said my new contact, upon contacting me, would provide the half which [the handler] was retaining in order to identify himself." The new contact was William Weisband, an American KGB agent who later infiltrated the Army Security Agency; FBI serial 121-13210.

12. Gold told different versions of this story to the FBI. Initially he thought the recogni-

tion signal was "Greetings from Ben in Brooklyn," but later he insisted that it had been "I come from Julius;" David Greenglass, transcript of Elitcher's testimony in United States v. Julius Rosenberg, Ethel Rosenberg, and Morton Sobell; FBI serial 65-4307-1-B-16.

13. Christopher M. Andrew and Vasili Mitrokhin, *The Sword and the Shield: The Mitrokhin Archive and the Secret History of the KGB* (New York: Basic Books, 1999), 137–138; Lamphere and Shachtman, *The FBI-KGB War*, 32.

14. FBI Director J. Edgar Hoover notified the White House about Gouzenko's revelations in a Sept. 12, 1945, memo. He reported that one of the GRU's agents was Dr. Allen May, who had worked on uranium separation at the University of Chicago and had given the Soviets a sample of uranium-233 that "was flown directly to Moscow." "It has also been definitely determined by the Royal Canadian Mounted Police that Dr. May, in the first part of July 1945, advised the Office of the [Soviet] Military Attaché in Ottawa, that the United States Navy was using radar-controlled projectiles against Japanese suicide planes and that the tubes and batteries within the projectile were finished with a special plastic protective device against the shock of firing, which the American authorities have not furnished to the British." Hoover's memo is reprinted in Benson and Warner, *Venona*, 61–62.

15. Bentley's defection may have been precipitated by news in October 1945 that Louis Budenz had defected. An editor at the *Daily Worker* familiar with the KGB's U.S. operations, Budenz knew that Bentley was involved in Soviet intelligence activities. His defection was widely publicized, e.g., "Budenz Names the 'Secret Head' of Communists in United States," *New York Times*, Oct. 18, 1945, 1.

16. Kathryn S. Olmsted, *Red Spy Queen: A Biography of Elizabeth Bentley* (Chapel Hill: University of North Carolina Press, 2002), 94.

17. Weinstein and Vassiliev, *The Haunted Wood*, 102–103, 108; Olmsted, *Red Spy Queen*, 94.

18. Olmsted, *Red Spy Queen*, 100.

19. FBI serial 65-14603-738; Lamphere and Shachtman, *The FBI-KGB War*, 131; FBI serial 65-56402-8.

20. Weinstein and Vassiliev, *The Haunted Wood*, 104.

21. Feklisov, *The Man behind the Rosenbergs*, 287.

22. Weinstein and Vassiliev, *The Haunted Wood*, 217.

23. Many commentators on the Rosenberg case have asserted that Ethel was completely innocent of any involvement with espionage. The record indicates that she played a supporting role, recruiting agents and facilitating the transfer of information to the KGB, but did not steal secrets or manage agents. She may have known about Julius' espionage activities from the start: it is difficult to imagine that on several occasions he slipped out of their apartment around 1:00 A.M. to call Elizabeth Bentley without his wife's noticing, or that he covered up with convincing lies. KGB cables indicate that she wasn't an active participant in her husband's network, but she knew that Julius, together with Barr and at least one other close friend, was spying for the Soviet Union. A November 1944 cable from the KGB's New York branch to headquarters in Moscow (Venona no. 1657) states that Ethel "knows about her husband's work and the role of [Joel Barr] and [an unidentified agent]. In view of delicate health does not work. Is characterized positively and as a devoted person." Ethel recruited her brother, David, to spy on the Manhattan Project.

24. Weinstein and Vassiliev, *The Haunted Wood*, 217.

25. Feklisov, *The Man behind the Rosenbergs*, 158; Andrew and Mitrokhin, *The Sword and the Shield*, 143; Weinstein and Vassiliev, *The Haunted Wood*, 307.

26. Feklisov, *The Man behind the Rosenbergs*, 160.

27. FBI serials 100-34619-8, 100-34619-37, 100-34619-64; Lamphere and Shachtman, *The FBI-KGB War*, 180.

28. FBI serial 65-15392-245.

29. FBI serial 59453-120.

30. FBI serial 65-15360-59; Katherine A. S. Sibley, "Soviet Industrial Espionage against American Military Technology and the US Response, 1930–1945," *Intelligence and National Security*, 14 (summer 1999): 105; Venona no. 959, New York to Moscow, July 8, 1942. No documents have surfaced demonstrating that Louise Ross was aware of Sarant's espionage or that she worked for the KGB; FBI serial 65-1664-569. However, "Jerome Tartakow, a cellmate of Rosenberg's and a confidential informant [of the FBI] advised on March twenty second, nineteen fifty one [that] Julius Rosenberg states that a woman who resides in Ithaca, NY with the name of Sarant was also an active Russian agent and her husband is now in Europe. There can be no doubt as to the identity of this woman and she is, in all probability, Louise Ross Sarant" ibid.

31. The FBI devoted a great deal of attention to investigating Morrison, Bethe, and Feynman, who were on the political left, including their connections with Sarant, but never obtained evidence that they had committed espionage.

32. FBI serial 65-59453-178.

33. In May 1948, when a KGB operative codenamed "August" resumed contact with Rosenberg, he reported to Moscow that despite firm instructions to halt espionage activities and to cut ties with his old agents, Rosenberg had in 1946–47 "continued fulfilling the duties of a group handler, maintaining contact with comrades, rendering them moral and material help while gathering valuable scientific and technical information"; Weinstein and Vassiliev, *The Haunted Wood*, 122, 217. Rosenberg stayed in touch with Barr and his other informants. As early as the spring of 1945, Feklisov reported that Rosenberg had to be restrained from spying, and that he complained that he missed the action; Feklisov, *The Man behind the Rosenbergs*, 155. At the end of December 1946, Julius and Ethel joined Barr, Al Sarant, Sobell, Perl, and Max Elitcher for a meal at a restaurant in New York, after which the group all went to the Rosenberg's apartment; FBI serial 65-59453-95.

34. FBI serial 65-15360-5.

35. FBI serial 65-58236-3.

36. Interview with Joel Barr, April 18, 1992.

37. Feklisov, *The Man behind the Rosenbergs*, 288; FBI serial 15392-668.

38. FBI serials 65-59453-95, 65-15392-668; Feklisov, *The Man behind the Rosenbergs*, 288.

39. Interview with Joel Barr, April 18, 1992.

40. FBI serials 65-59334-27, 65-5934-19.

41. Telephone interview with Vivian Glassman Pataki, May 19, 2003.

42. "I.D. Special Analysis Report #1, Covernames in Diplomatic Traffic," Aug. 30, 1947, in Benson and Warner, *Venona*, 93104.

43. FBI serial 65-58236-3. Mittleman again came to the attention of law enforcement in 1954, when he was arrested in connection with a horseracing betting scam. Mittleman built ingenious equipment that allowed his co-conspirators to flash results to gamblers before they were announced officially. One conspirator was equipped with a radio transmitter Mittleman had built that fitted into a bag a foot and a half long, a foot wide, and nine inches tall. A receiver the size of a cigarette case was strapped next to the body of a confederate and connected to two silver dimes that served as electrodes, delivering the Morse-code messages as slight shocks. In the 1960s, he was in the news again as a pioneer in the development of electronic eavesdropping devices. He was sentenced to a six-month jail term in 1969 for selling them to criminals; "Arrests Here Bare 'Sure Thing' Racing Fraud by Radio," *New York Times,* July 21, 1954, 1; "Issues of Morality Plague Technicians of Eavesdropping," ibid., Dec. 26, 1966, 1; "Bugging Expert, a 'Menace,' Gets 6-Month Jail Sentence," ibid., Oct. 18, 1969, 22.

44. FBI serial 65-58236-3.

45. FBI serial 65-14872.

46. Lamphere and Shachtman, *The FBI-KGB War,* 97; FBI serial 65-59453-9.

47. FBI serial 65-58236-3.

48. Venona no. 1054, New York to Moscow, July 26, 1944.

49. Lamphere and Shachtman, *The FBI-KGB War,* 95.

50. FBI serial 101-1632-94.

51. Morton Sobell, *On Doing Time* (San Francisco: Golden Gate National Parks Association, 2001), 43–44.

52. *Executive Sessions of the Senate Permanent Subcommittee on Investigations of the Committee on Government Operations, Eighty-third Congress, First Session, 1953* (Washington, D.C.: U.S. Government Printing Office, 2003), vol. 3, 2514; transcript, United States v. Julius Rosenberg, Ethel Rosenberg, and Morton Sobell.

53. Lamphere and Shachtman, *The FBI-KGB War,* 100.

54. Weinstein and Vassiliev, *The Haunted Wood,* 286, 291; John Earl Haynes and Harvey Klehr, *Venona: Decoding Soviet Espionage in America* (New Haven: Yale University Press, 1999), 48–49.

55. Weinstein and Vassiliev, *The Haunted Wood,* 222.

56. FBI serial 65-59453-18.

57. FBI serial 65-59453-54.

58. FBI serial 65-59453-25.

59. FBI serial 65-59453-106.

60. Yatskov left Paris sometime in 1948; FBI serial 100-346193-91.

61. Messiaen's students included the composers Pierre Boulez, Karlheinz Stockhausen, and Iannis Xenakis.

62. Feklisov, *The Man behind the Rosenbergs,* 288.

63. FBI serial 100-81002.

64. KGB document cited in Haynes and Klehr, *Venona,* 51–52.

65. Weinstein and Vassiliev, *The Haunted Wood,* 319; Ronald Radosh and Joyce Milton, *The Rosenberg File,* 2nd ed. (New Haven: Yale University Press, 1997), 75.

66. FBI serial 65-59453-34.

67. Weinstein and Vassiliev, *The Haunted Wood,* 221; Sam Roberts, *The Brother: The*

Untold Story of Atomic Spy David Greenglass and How He Sent His Sister, Ethel Rosenberg, to the Electric Chair (New York: Random House, 2001), 192–194.

68. Roberts, *The Brother*, 196; David Greenglass, statement to the FBI, July 17, 1950.

69. Weinstein and Vassiliev, *The Haunted Wood*, 320.

70. Roberts, *The Brother*, 198.

71. Weinstein and Vassiliev, *The Haunted Wood*, 328.

72. FBI serial 65-15392-63.

73. FBI serial 65-59453-48.

74. Roberts, *The Brother*, 219.

75. Lamphere and Shachtman, *The FBI-KGB War*, 177–182.

76. Harry Gold's remarks to FBI agents, May 22, 1950, as quoted in ibid., 157.

77. Weinstein and Vassiliev, *The Haunted Wood*, 330.

78. FBI serials 65-59453-60, 65-59453-84; Radosh and Milton, *The Rosenberg File*, 117.

79. The FBI recognized and gloated over the KGB's error. In an official summary of the Rosenberg case, the Bureau stated: "it is known that the Soviets with their stress on security will not usually allow a member of one network to know of the existence of another network so that in the event one network is detected, the other will not be compromised. It will be recalled that Gold's protestation to [Yatskov] about contacting Greenglass in Albuquerque went unheeded. The Soviets have undoubtedly found good reason to regret this error in judgment"; FBI serial 94-3-4-317-348, 43-44.

80. Radosh and Milton, *The Rosenberg File*, 80.

Chapter 6. Prague, 1950–1955

1. Interview with Joel Barr, March 17, 1997; notes in Barr's address book suggest clandestine meetings with the KGB in Paris and Prague; Alexander Feklisov, *The Man behind the Rosenbergs* (New York: Enigma Books, 2001), 288.

2. *International Herald Tribune*, June 17, 1950, A1.

3. Feklisov, *The Man behind the Rosenbergs*, 288.

4. Joel Barr's personal papers.

5. Minister of Interior of Czechoslovakia, memo, Dec. 30, 1953, Curriculum vitae of Mr. Berg written by himself, Ministry of Interior of Czechoslovakia, Prague (all documents from the Czech Ministry of Interior are from the ministry archives in Prague); notes from Barr's address book.

6. Sam Roberts, *The Brother: The Untold Story of Atomic Spy David Greenglass and How He Sent His Sister, Ethel Rosenberg, to the Electric Chair* (New York: Random House, 2001), 196; David Greenglass, statement to the FBI, July 17, 1950.

7. After initially attempting to shield his sister, Ethel Rosenberg, Greenglass cooperated closely with the prosecution, providing evidence that was crucial to the case against her and Julius.

8. The complaint is at FBI serial 65-15392-1; the lookout notice is at FBI serial 65-15392-66.

9. FBI serial 65-59453-57.

10. Feklisov, *The Man behind the Rosenbergs*, 132.

11. FBI serial 65-59453-200.

12. Philby was contemptuous of Lamphere, whom he called "puddingy," and of Eisenhower: "Eisenhower explained his refusal to reprieve Ethel Rosenberg on the grounds that, if he did, the Russians would in future use only women as spies. It was an attitude worthy of the most pedestrian of United States' presidents"; Kim Philby, *My Silent War: The Autobiography of a Spy* (New York: Modern Library, 2002), 164.

13. Bruno Pontecorvo became a leader of Soviet theoretical physics and, like Barr and Sarant, had a gregarious personality and a wide range of interests. He introduced Russians to snorkeling. Pontecorvo's wife had a breakdown shortly after the family arrived in Russia and spent the rest of her life in a mental institution. One of their sons, Tito, started one of the first private businesses in the Soviet Union, a horse-breeding company that is still thriving in Dubna.

14. FBI serial 65-59453-225. An FBI document recorded that the Bureau "believed [Barr] to be presently active in espionage or as a courier for the Russians in Europe, although his exact whereabouts is not presently known since he fled Paris in 1950 at the time when GREENGLASS and ROSENBERG were arrested." The document also asserted that Barr was "a dangerous individual who could be expected to commit acts inimical to the national defense and public safety of the US in time of emergency."

15. Interview with Joel Barr, April 18, 1992.

16. File memo on interview with Joseph Berg, Nov. 13, 1953, Third Administration Department, Ministry of Interior of Czechoslovakia; interview with Joel Barr, March 17, 1997.

17. Summary of Nov. 8, 1952, deposition of Joseph Berg, Third Administration Department, Ministry of Interior of Czechoslovakia; interview with Joel Barr, March 17, 1997.

18. Interview with Joel Barr, April 18, 1992; FBI serial 65-1664A-1A53.

19. FBI serial 65-1664A-1A53.

20. Ibid.

21. FBI serial 65-1664A-1A49.

22. FBI serial 65-59312-27. According to Feklisov, the KGB agents posted to New York after he departed "were no longer go-getters like Yatskov or myself, and were thinking more of their own status than about their responsibilities." They were risk-averse, and as a result Sarant "had to fend for himself. His arrest could come at any time and if he wished to avoid it he had to escape"; Feklisov, *The Man behind the Rosenbergs,* 289.

23. Interview with Kristina Staros, Feb. 11, 2004.

24. Ibid.

25. FBI serial 65-153060-182.

26. Venona no. 628, New York to Moscow, May 5, 1944.

27. Memo from A. H. Belmont to L. V. Boardman, Feb. 1, 1956, posted online at http://foia.fbi.gov/venona/venona.pdf, 61. In February 1956 the FBI outlined the obstacles to using Venona decryptions in court. In addition to concerns about alerting the Soviets to the extent of the ASA's success in breaking their codes, the memo noted legal and political constraints. If the government attempted to introduce decryptions in a court, a "defense attorney would immediately move that the messages be excluded, based

on the hearsay evidence rule. He would probably claim that neither the person who sent the message (Soviet official) nor the person who received it (Soviet official) was available to testify and thus the contents of the message were purely hearsay as it related to the defendants." The memo concluded that an exception to the hearsay rule could be obtained if the cryptographers who deciphered the messages testified to their authenticity. The use of cover names and gaps in the decrypted messages would pose additional legal problems. "Assuming the messages could be introduced in evidence, we then have a question of identity. The fragmentary nature of the messages themselves, and the questionable interpretations and translations involved, plus the extensive use of cover names for persons and places, make the problem of positive identification extremely difficult." The memo stated that while it might be possible to overcome these problems, the courts could allow the defense to have private cryptographers examine the original messages, and might require the government to make unacceptable disclosures about its codebreaking techniques and practices to help in their efforts. The defense could also reasonably argue that the messages that NSA had been unsuccessful in breaking could, if decoded, exonerate their clients. The memo also warned that "disclosure of the existence of [Venona] information at this time would probably place the Bureau right in the middle of a violent political war. This is an election year and the Republicans would undoubtedly use disclosure of the [Venona] information to emphasize the degree of infiltration by Communists and Soviet agents into the U.S. Government during the 1940s when the Democrats were in power. At the same time, the Democrats would probably strike back by claiming that the FBI had withheld this information from the proper officials during the Democratic administration and at the same time would salvage what credit they could by claiming that the messages were intercepted and deciphered during the course of their administration and under their guidance. The Bureau would be right in the middle."

28. FBI serial 65-1530-78.

29. FBI serial 65-1664-91.

30. Robert J. Lamphere and Tom Shachtman, *The FBI-KGB War: A Special Agent's Story* (New York: Berkley, 1987), 198; FBI serial 65-15360-134.

31. FBI serial 65-15360-187.

32. Interview with Kristina Staros, Oct. 13, 2003; interview with Carol Dayton, April 1992.

33. Morton Sobell, *On Doing Time* (San Francisco: Golden Gate National Parks Association, 2001), 48.

34. Lamphere and Shachtman, *The FBI-KGB War*, 199.

35. FBI serial 65-1664A-1A37.

36. FBI serial 65-1664-350.

37. FBI serial 65-15360-306.

38. FBI serial 65-1664-209.

39. FBI serial 65-1664-214.

40. FBI serial 65-1664-275.

41. FBI serial 65-1664-289.

42. FBI serial 65-15360-308.

43. FBI serials 101-2483-80, 101-2483-991.

44. FBI serial 65-15360-133.

45. Feklisov, *The Man behind the Rosenbergs,* 291.

46. Sobell, *On Doing Time,* 58; Mark Kuchment, "Beyond the Rosenbergs: A New View from Russia," *Boston Review,* Sept. 1985, 24.

47. Interview with Kristina Staros, Oct. 13, 2003; FBI serial 65-1664-392.

48. Interview with Joel Barr, March 17, 1997.

49. Hans Bethe told Mark Kuchment that "he believed Sarant to have a lack of ability"; letter from Robert Lamphere to Special Agent Gray Morgan, Jan. 22, 1985, box 2, folder 10, Lamphere Collection, Georgetown University.

50. Alexander Dolgun with Patrick Watson, *Alexander Dolgun's Story: An American in the Gulag* (New York: Alfred A. Knopf, 1975). Foreigners and people with foreign connections were especially vulnerable to the irrational arrests and executions that characterized the purges. Alexander Dolgun, the son of American engineers who emigrated to the USSR to help build socialism, is one example. He was arrested in 1948 and spent five years in prison camps, surviving only through tremendous determination; John Earl Haynes and Harvey Klehr, *In Denial: Historians, Communism, and Espionage* (San Francisco: Encounter Books, 2003), 119–121, 235–247. Many American Communists who tried to contribute their skills and labor to the USSR were executed during the Stalin years.

51. Memo to Svoboda, chief of Third Administration Department, Nov. 14, 1953, Ministry of Interior of Czechoslovakia.

52. Jan G. Oblonsky, "Eloge: Antonin Svoboda," *Annals of the History of Computing,* 2 (Oct. 1980): 284–291; Antonin Svoboda, "From Mechanical Linkages to Electronic Computers: Recollections from Czechoslovakia," in *A History of Computing in the Twentieth Century: A Collection of Essays,* ed. N. Metropolis, J. Howlett, and Gian-Carlo Rota (New York: Academic, 1980), 579–585; idem, *Computing Mechanisms and Linkages* (New York: McGraw-Hill, 1948).

53. Henry Eric Firdman, *Decision-Making in the Soviet Microelectronics Industry: The Leningrad Design Bureau, a Case Study* (Falls Church, Va.: Delphic Associates, 1985), 2.

54. Interview with Joel Barr, March 17, 1997.

55. Interview with Vera Bergova, Aug. 1, 2002.

56. Ibid.

57. Memo to Svoboda, chief of Third Administration Department, Nov. 14, 1953; interview with Vera Bergova, Aug. 1, 2002.

58. Interview with Vera Bergova, Aug. 1, 2002.

59. The program is on display at the Museum of Communism in Prague.

60. The next time the site was put to use was in 1996, when a thirty-three-foot inflatable plastic statue of Michael Jackson occupied it for several weeks to promote a concert appearance in Prague.

61. "2 Former Aides Sentenced," *New York Times,* Aug. 23, 1963, 6. Prchal was convicted by a Czechoslovakian court in August 1963 of fabricating evidence in political trials, including Slansky's, and sentenced to six years' imprisonment; Jonathan Brent and Vladimir P. Naumov, *Stalin's Last Crime: The Plot against the Jewish Doctors, 1948–1953* (New York: HarperCollins, 2003).

62. Peter Meyer, Bernard D. Weinryb, Eugene Duschinsky, and Nicolas Sylvain, *The*

Jews in the Soviet Satellites (Syracuse: Syracuse University Press, 1953), 155: "The fall of Slansky precipitated a great purge in which hundreds and perhaps thousands of Communist leaders, officials, army and policy officers, diplomats, economic administrators, and managers were removed, and in most cases, expelled from the party and arrested. Not all the victims were Jews; but the purge of Jews was so thorough and complete that there can be no doubt of its constituting a principal feature of the campaign."

63. Lamphere and Shachtman, *The FBI-KGB War,* 278. FBI Director J. Edgar Hoover recommended against a death sentence for Ethel Rosenberg, as did Robert Lamphere. Speaking at a conference on Venona in Washington, D.C., in October 1996, Lamphere explained that the recommendations were based on the paucity of evidence against her as well as consideration for her two young sons. In his memoir, Lamphere expressed a sense of "grim responsibility" for the deaths of Julius and Ethel Rosenberg.

64. Joseph Albright and Marcia Kunstel, *Bombshell: The Secret Story of America's Unknown Atomic Spy Conspiracy* (New York: Times Books, 1997).

65. Letters from Feklisov to Berg, Morton Sobell, and Michael and Robert Meerepol, copies in author's possession; Philip Knightley, introduction to Philby, *My Silent War,* xv.

66. File memo on interview with Berg, Nov. 13, 1953, Third Administration Department, Ministry of Interior of Czechoslovakia.

67. Michael Aaron Dennis, "Secrecy and Science Revisited: From Politics to Historical Practice and Back," Occasional Paper no. 23, Oct. 1999, in *Secrecy and Knowledge Production,* ed. Judith Reppy (Ithaca: Peace Studies Program, Cornell University, 1999). Michael Aaron Dennis has argued that the designers of similar technologies in the United States utilized secrecy as a management tool: "Secrecy might also be considered an essential element of the design process regardless of whether a nation is at war. The design and development of new technologies is marked by initial periods of contestation and struggle over goals, methods, and even the very possibility of the goal. Hence, if one is developing a new technology — such as a proximity fuse, an atomic bomb, or an inertial guidance system — it might prove beneficial to restrict the sheer number of voices until the group working on the project has produced what they believe is a stable vision or version of the technology. In other words, secrecy might reduce the stress of interpretive flexibility — the inherent plastic meaning of any technology"; ibid.

68. File memo on interview with Berg, Nov. 13, 1953, Third Administration Department, Ministry of Interior of Czechoslovakia; Paid Death Notices, *Newsday,* Oct. 27, 1995, A76.

69. Meyer et al., *The Jews in the Soviet Satellites,* 155–191.

70. "Informace pro s. ministra vnitra, Pripad: Filip Staros a Josef Berg," Sv-2673/50–54, Ministry of Interior of Czechoslovakia.

71. Confidential statements by Zdenek Blazek, Jiri Benes, and Mr. Richtrmoc to the StB, July 4, 1953, Ministry of Interior of Czechoslovakia.

72. Memo, MNB–Hlavni Sprava Statni Bezpecnosti, A/III-sine/312-Rch-53, Dec. 30, 1953, ibid.

73. Joel Barr's personal papers.

74. Joel Barr's personal papers.

75. Confidential statement by Blazek, Benes, and Richtrmoc to the StB, July 4, 1953, Ministry of Interior of Czechoslovakia.

76. Memo, A-1668/01-taj-53, Nov. 26, 1953, ibid.

77. II/2/KR-8054/53, May 4, 1954, ibid.

78. Joseph Berg to Consul, People's Republic of China, Oct. 3, 1994, Barr's personal papers.

79. Feklisov, *The Man behind the Rosenbergs,* 325–327.

80. Firdman, *Decision-Making,* 2.

81. Interview with Morton Nadler, June 5, 2003.

82. Ibid.; Mark Kuchment, "The American Connection to Soviet Microelectronics," *Physics Today,* Sept. 1985, 47.

83. Joseph Berg to Consul, People's Republic of China, Oct. 3, 1994.

Chapter 7. Special Laboratory 11, 1956–1963

1. Much of the description of SL-11 and successor organizations headed by Philip Staros and Joseph Berg is based on interviews with Henry Eric Firdman, who worked for them in a series of increasingly senior positions from 1959 to 1973, and on his book, *Decision-Making in the Soviet Microelectronics Industry: The Leningrad Design Bureau, a Case Study* (Falls Church, Va.: Delphic Associates, 1985).

2. Julian Cooper, Keith Dexter, and Mark Harrison, *The Numbered Factories and Other Establishments of the Soviet Defence Industry, 1927–67: A Guide, Part I,* Soviet Industrialisation Project Series, Occasional Paper no. 2 (Birmingham: University of Birmingham Centre for Russian and East European Studies, 1999), iv–v. *Yashchiki* were called either *pochtovyi yashchik* (post office boxes) or *abonentnyi yashchik* (subscriber boxes); Sergo Beria, *Beria, My Father: Inside Stalin's Kremlin* (London, Duckworth: 2001), 162, 229. Although Berg's and Staros's positions as foreigners at the head of a Soviet research entity were unprecedented, the *yashchiki* employed many foreigners. In the late 1940s and early 1950s, tens of thousands of German scientists were working in Russia at such enterprises. One of the last contingents, a group of electronics experts, remained in Russia until 1958. The unacknowledged contributions of German scientists formed the basis for many postwar Soviet military technologies, ranging from radar to jet engines and uranium enrichment. Unlike Berg and Staros, however, most were not in Russia voluntarily, and animosities toward the Nazis made it impossible for Germans to lead Soviet scientists or engineers. Sergo Beria, the son of Laventri Beria, who headed a military design bureau, noted in his memoir that "as regards missile technology, which was my sphere, I should say that we owed 99 percent of our achievements to the German engineers"; ibid., 229.

3. Interview with Joel Barr, April 18, 1992.

4. Interview with Kristina Staros, Feb. 11, 2004.

5. "Agreement between the Government of India and the Government of the Union of Soviet Socialist Republics on Delivery as a Gift to India from the Soviet Union of Equipment for the Indian Institute of Technology, Bombay, and on Rendering of Assistance by the Soviet Union to India in the Training of Engineers," signed in Moscow on Dec. 12, 1958. Berg's and Staros's salaries were in line with those awarded to foreign specialists working temporarily in the Soviet Union.

6. Teresa Toranska, *Them: Stalin's Polish Puppets* (New York: Harper, 1987), 172.

7. The branding of individuals as Jewish in Soviet Russia was based entirely on ethnicity, or, as Russians characterize it, "nationality," not on religious beliefs. All Soviet citizens carried documents that listed their nationality. It was common for people to attempt to avoid being stigmatized as Jewish, for example by adopting the nationality of a non-Jewish relative or acquiring a Russian-sounding surname. Speculation and gossip regarding hidden Jewish antecedents was also common, as was the persecution of people who were inaccurately labeled as Jewish. Berg's internal passport listed his nationality as "English," reflecting his putative South African origins.

8. Sergo Beria, discussing how he recruited scientists and engineers for the Design Bureau that developed Moscow's antiaircraft defenses in the last years of Stalin's reign, reported: "One specialist had lost his father in the purges, another was Jewish, the third came from occupied territory. If I had applied the criteria for recruitment used by the Party's cadres department I should never have had anyone but idiots in my Institute"; Beria, *Beria, My Father*, 162. He managed to pursue an independent hiring policy because his father, the head of Stalin's security apparatus, protected him.

9. Ulrich Albrecht, *The Soviet Armaments Industry* (Langhorne, Pa.: Harwood, 1993), 189–191.

10. Ibid., 159–162; Roald Z. Sagdeev, *The Making of a Soviet Scientist* (New York: Wiley, 1994), 185–187. The name Military-Industrial Commission obviously wasn't created for public consumption; the Soviet Union often railed against the American military-industrial complex and asserted that such a nexus could never exist in a socialist state. Sagdeev, a leader of the Soviet space program, recalled that until he attained a position of considerable seniority he "had no knowledge of [the VPK, an] enormously influential hidden part of the military-industrial iceberg"; ibid., 187.

11. Firdman, *Decision-Making*, 19–20.

12. *Arnold O. Beckman: One Hundred Years of Excellence* (Philadelphia: Chemical Heritage Foundation, 2000), 230. In the 1950s Beckman Instruments opened subsidiaries that manufactured and distributed components, including helipots, to virtually every nation "excepting only Soviet allies."

13. Alexander Feklisov, *The Man behind the Rosenbergs* (New York: Enigma Books, 2001), 136; Georg Trogemann, Alexander Y. Nitussov, and Wolfgang Ernst, eds., *Computing in Russia: The History of Computer Devices and Information Technology Revealed*, trans. Alexander Y. Nitussov (Brunswick, Germany: Vieweg, 2001), 123.

14. CIA, *The Electronics Industry in the USSR (SC RR 101)* (Langley, Va., June 1, 1955; declassified Jan. 24, 2001).

15. Ibid.

16. Henry Eric Firdman, *Maverick for Life* (Bloomington, Ind.: First Books, 2004), 286.

17. Slava Gerovitch, " 'Mathematical Machines' of the Cold War: Soviet Computing, American Cybernetics and Ideological Disputes in the Early 1950s," *Social Studies of Science*, 31 (April 2001): 268.

18. The R-36 was designated the SS-9 by NATO. Berg was responsible for the R-36's "List" countermeasures system, an ingenious array of false warhead targets, stealth coverings that absorbed incoming radar waves, and "a miniature spacecraft [that] . . . flew in space far from the warhead and hindered and spoofed enemy radars"; http://www.astro-

nautix.com/lvs/r36.htm; Trogemann, Nitussov, and Ernst, *Computing in Russia,* 143, 149, 237, 240, 243; Slava Gerovitch, *From Newspeak to Cyberspeak: A History of Soviet Cybernetics* (Cambridge, Mass.: MIT Press, 2002), 205–210.

19. Gerovitch, "'Mathematical Machines,'" 268; Trogemann, Nitussov, and Ernst, *Computing in Russia,* 142–143. Kitov, an early proponent of computer networking, was thrown out of the party and his career terminated for predicting that computer networks would inevitably decentralize administrative power.

20. Interview with Morton Nadler, June 5, 2003; Mark Kuchment, "Beyond the Rosenbergs: A New View from Russia," *Boston Review,* Sept. 1985, 6.

21. Interview with Henry Eric Firdman, April 19, 2003; Walter Benjamin, *Illuminations,* trans. Harry Zohn (New York, Harcourt: 1968), 92. In Nikolai Leskov's story "The Steel Flea," Russian craftsmen convince Peter the Great that they are the equal of their European counterparts.

22. Interview with Joel Barr, April 18, 1992; interview with Henry Eric Firdman, April 19, 2003.

23. Mark Kuchment, "Active Technology Transfer and the Development of Soviet Microelectronics," in *Selling the Rope to Hang Capitalism?: The Debate on West–East Trade and Technology Transfer,* ed. Charles M. Perry and Robert L. Pfaltzgraff Jr. (Washington, D.C.: Pergamon-Brassey's, 1987), 60–69.

24. Soviet leader Leonid Brezhnev, who pinned the Red Banner medal on Morris Childs's chest during a banquet in Moscow in 1975, might have been somewhat less enthusiastic if he'd known that the Childses were double agents and that they maintained a lavish lifestyle by combining an FBI salary with Soviet funds embezzled from the CPUSA; Martin Ebon, *KGB: Death and Rebirth* (Westport, Conn.: Praeger, 1994), 186; M. R. D. Foot and Brian Harrison, eds., *Secret Lives* (Oxford: Oxford University Press, 2002), 287; Christopher M. Andrew and Vasili Mitrokhin, *The Sword and the Shield: The Mitrokhin Archive and the Secret History of the KGB* (New York: Basic Books, 1999), 6.

25. Interview with Joel Barr, March 17, 1997; interview with Kristina Staros, Feb. 11, 2004.

26. In addition to the pervasive fear that their telephone conversations were recorded, many Russians were convinced that the KGB could dial into their telephones and listen to conversations in their apartments, even when the handset was in its cradle. Before discussing one of the petty illegal activities, such as buying or selling something on the black market or bribing an official, that Soviet citizens engaged in to make life more tolerable, it was common practice to place a pillow over the telephone in the hope that doing so would block Big Brother's ears. Berg and Staros, however, did not engage in this practice.

27. The TRADIC (TRAnisitor DIgital Computer), built in 1954 by Bell Labs, Sarant's former employer, was the first fully transistorized computer.

28. Paul Duffy and Andrei Kandalov, *Tupolev: The Man and His Aircraft* (Warrendale, Pa.: SAE International, 1996); Slava Gerovitch, "'Russian Scandals': Soviet Readings of American Cybernetics in the Early Years of the Cold War," *Russian Review,* 60 (Oct. 2001): 545–568; idem, "'Mathematical Machines,'" 253–287. While Norbert Weiner and the concept of cybernetics were vigorously attacked in the Soviet popular press, the military was quick to adopt the science of cybernetics and to push ideological considerations aside.

29. L. L. Kerber, *Stalin's Aviation Gulag: A Memoir of Andrei Tupolev and the Purge Era* (Washington, D.C.: Smithsonian Institution Press, 1996), 250–251, 253.

30. Ibid., 254.

31. Sagdeev, *The Making of a Soviet Scientist,* 201.

32. Miriam R. Levin, *Cultures of Control* (Amsterdam: Harwood, 2000), 253–254; Gerovitch, *From Newspeak to Cyberspeak,* 139–140.

33. Firdman, *Decision-Making,* 48.

34. *Opisanie Izobreteniya K Avtorskomu Svidetel'stvu* (Description of Invention), *Ferritovaya plastina dlya magnitnogo zapominayushego ustroistva* (ferrite plate for magnetic memory device), Jan. 25, 1962; and successive Soviet patents.

35. It had 8,000 transistors, weighed 25 kilograms, had a volume of 70 liters, and consumed 100 watts of power.

36. Firdman, *Decision-Making,* 50.

37. Harrison E. Salisbury, "Khrushchev, in a Warm Speech, Renews Appeal for Friendship," *New York Times,* Sept. 22, 1959, 1; Sergei Khrushchev, *Nikita Khrushchev: Creation of a Superpower* (University Park: Pennsylvania State University Press, 2001), 334; "Text of Remarks by Khrushchev and I.B.M. Head at Luncheon in Plant," *New York Times,* Sept. 22, 1959, 21.

38. Interview with Joel Barr, April 18, 1992.

39. Ibid.

40. Linda Melvern, Nick Anning, and David Hebditch, *Techno-Bandits* (Boston: Houghton Mifflin, 1984), 52–57. One of the most notable results of this strategy was the Ryad computer series, clones of the IBM 360/370 mainframe computers. "IBM had assigned hundreds of programmers to the job of creating the software from the 360s — to the dismay of their Western competitors. But the Soviets, as one of the first big acts in the era of techno-piracy, simply stole some of the 360s' operating systems"; CIA, *Significance of Soviet Acquisition of Western Technology (S-6846),* CSI-2000-00005 (Langley, Va., June 11, 1975; declassified Nov. 18, 1999); CIA, *Soviet Bloc Computers: Direct Descendants of Western Technology (Sw 89-10023x),* CSI-2001-00004 (Langley, Va., June 1, 1989; declassified Jan. 1, 2001).

41. Firdman, *Decision-Making,* 26–27.

42. Interview with Joel Barr, April 18, 1992.

43. Khrushchev, *Nikita Khrushchev,* 379.

44. Gregory W. Pedlow and Donald E. Welzenbach, *The CIA and the U-2 Program, 1954–1974* (Langley, Va.: CIA, 1998), 97.

45. It was far from the last time, however. A Soviet proximity-fuse-equipped antiaircraft missile shot down a U-2 over Cuba during the Cuban missile crisis, and they were widely used in the Vietnam War and other conflicts.

46. Interview with Henry Eric Firdman, April 19, 2003.

47. Firdman, *Decision-Making,* 52–53; *Soviet Cybernetics Technology: V. Soviet Process Control Computers,* Memorandum RM-4810-PR (Santa Monica, Calif.: Rand Corporation, Nov. 1965), 21–31. The UM-1NKh was 32 inches long, 20 inches wide, and 13 inches tall, ran on 150 watts of power, weighed 60 kilograms, and sold for 50,000 rubles. Other contemporary control computers manufactured in the USSR included the Dnepr general-purpose control computer (UMShN), which cost 100,000 rubles, weighed 620 kilograms, and took up 2 square meters of floor space; the VNIIEM-1 transistorized

general-purpose control computer, which required more than 6.5 kilowatts of power; the VNIIEM-3 (3 kilowatts); the UM-1 (a control computer developed in Severodonetsk that was not related to SKB-2's computer of the same name), a room-sized monster that weighed 1,700 kilograms and cost 170,000 to 200,000 rubles.

48. Solomon Volkov, *St. Petersburg: A Cultural History* (New York: Free Press, 1995), 511–512: the "Leningrad party hacks of [the 1960s] were more reactionary and vengeful than their Moscow counterparts. This condition manifested constantly, in important decisions and trifles . . . Leningrad Party head Vassily Tolstikov was one of the most unpredictable and stupid Leningrad bosses." Sagdeev, *The Making of a Soviet Scientist,* 258: "Romanov symbolized the most anti-intellectual kind of party apparatchik."

49. V. Kabanov, "How the Site for Building the Scientific Center Was Selected; Interview with the First Architect of Zelenograd, A. B. Boldov," *Elektronnaya Tekhnika,* series 3, *Mikroelektronika,* 152, no. 1 (1998): 3.

50. Telephone interview with Sergei Khrushchev, March 31, 2003.

Chapter 8. Zelenograd, the Soviet Silicon Valley, 1962–1965

1. Sergei Khrushchev, *Nikita Khrushchev: Creation of a Superpower* (University Park: Pennsylvania State University Press, 2001), 468–480.

2. S. A. Garyainov, "Oni Byli Pervymi" (They Were First), *Elektronnaya Tekhnika,* series 3, *Mikroelektronika,* 152, no. 1 (1998): 16.

3. Ibid.

4. Khrushchev, *Nikita Khrushchev,* 69–71; Matthew Evangelista, " 'Why Keep Such an Army?': Khrushchev's Troop Reductions," Working Paper no. 19, Cold War International History Project, Woodrow Wilson International Center for Scholars, Washington, D.C., Dec. 1997; William Taubman, *Khrushchev: The Man and His Era* (New York: Norton, 2003), 379; Henry Eric Firdman, *Maverick for Life* (Bloomington, Ind.: First Books, 2004), 176.

5. Interview with Joel Barr, April 18, 1992.

6. The higher prices provoked uprisings in the summer of 1962, including one in Novocherkassk that was suppressed only when the Army fired into crowds of unarmed civilians; Khrushchev, *Nikita Khrushchev,* 352; Taubman, *Khrushchev,* 518–519.

7. Interview with Elvira Valueva, Feb. 1999.

8. Ibid.

9. CIA, *Big Boost in Soviet Military Electronics by 1965* (Langley, Va., April 9, 1963; declassified Nov. 18, 1998).

10. FBI serial 65-59453-280.

11. Interview with Morton Nadler, June 5, 2003.

12. *Soviet Union,* no. 172 (1964): 34–35.

13. W. H. Ware and W. B. Holland, "Russian Control Computers," *Control Engineering,* May 1966, 119–125; quotations on 125.

14. CIA, *Computers in Communist Countries: Production, Requirements and Technology,* CSI-2001-00001 (Langley, Va., Feb. 14, 1966; declassified Jan. 24, 2001).

15. Interview with Henry Eric Firdman, April 19, 2003.

16. Ibid.

17. Technical characteristics of the UM-2: 8 addressable registers; 512 23-bit words of RAM and 2,048 23-bit words of ROM in the base unit, expandable by adding additional modules; provision for numerous analogue-to-digital and digital-to-analogue converters and input-out devices to be added as separate modules; designed to work at 1,000 kips (addition/subtraction time of 10 microseconds); weight 25 kilograms, volume 40 decimeters, power consumption 80 watts; Henry Eric Firdman, *Decision-Making in the Soviet Microelectronics Industry: The Leningrad Design Bureau, a Case Study* (Falls Church, Va.: Delphic Associates, 1985), 57.

18. James Harford, *Korolev: How One Man Masterminded the Soviet Drive to Beat America to the Moon* (New York: Wiley, 1997), 15, 175, 23; Khrushchev, *Nikita Khrushchev*, 260.

19. Interview with Henry Eric Firdman, April 19, 2003.

20. Interview with Joel Barr, April 18, 1992.

21. Ibid.; transcript of ABC's *Nightline*, broadcast June 12, 1992.

22. A. P. Lavrentev, "Vspomnim Iosifa Berga" (Remember Joseph Berg), *Elektronnaya Tekhnika*, series 3, *Mikroelektronika*, 152, no. 1 (1998): 43–45; Firdman, *Maverick for Life*, 241.

23. Interview with Henry Eric Firdman, April 19, 2003.

24. Interview with Joel Barr, March 17, 1997.

25. Interview with Henry Eric Firdman, April 19, 2003.

Chapter 9. Leningrad Design Bureau, 1965–1973

1. Julian Cooper, Keith Dexter, and Mark Harrison, *The Numbered Factories and Other Establishments of the Soviet Defence Industry, 1927–67: A Guide, Part I,* Soviet Industrialisation Project Series, Occasional Paper no. 2 (Birmingham: University of Birmingham Centre for Russian and East European Studies, 1999), vi–vii.

2. Anne Applebaum, *Gulag: A History* (New York: Doubleday, 2003), 111.

3. *Computers in Spaceflight: The NASA Experience, Chapter One — The Gemini Digital Computer: First Machine in Orbit,* www.hq.nasa.gov/office/pao/History/computers/ch1-1.html. The Gemini's onboard computer, built at a cost of $27 million, performed no critical tasks: everything the computer did could be done manually.

4. Interview with Joel Barr, April 18, 1992.

5. Henry Eric Firdman, *Maverick for Life* (Bloomington, Ind.: First Books, 2004), 263.

6. Interview with Joel Barr, March 17, 1997; interview with Henry Eric Firdman, April 19, 2003.

7. Interview with Kristina Staros, Feb. 11, 2004.

8. Interview with Robert Berg, Oct. 11, 2003.

9. Walter L. Hixson, *Parting the Curtain: Propaganda, Culture, and the Cold War, 1945–1961* (New York: St. Martin's, 1996), 48.

10. Interview with Joel Barr, April 18, 1992.

11. Interview with Elvira Valueva, Feb. 1999.

12. Interview with Joel Barr, March 17, 1997; interview with Elvira Valueva, Feb. 1999.

13. Interview with Vera Bergova, Aug. 1, 2003; interview with Vivian Berg, Oct. 12, 2003; interview with Robert Berg, Oct. 11, 2003.

14. Interview with Joel Barr, March 17, 1997; interview with Robert Berg, Oct. 11, 2003.

15. Interview with Henry Eric Firdman, April 19, 2003.

16. Interview with Joel Barr, April 18, 1992.

17. Ibid.

18. Interview with Henry Eric Firdman, April 19, 2003.

19. Roald Z. Sagdeev, *The Making of a Soviet Scientist* (New York: Wiley, 1994), 212–213; William E. Burrows, *This New Ocean: The Story of the First Space Age* (New York: Random House, 1998) 494, 517.

20. CIA, *Soviet Bloc Computers: Direct Descendants of Western Technology (Sw 89-10023x)*, CSI-2001-00004 (Langley, Va., June 1, 1989; declassified Jan. 30, 2001).

21. Interview with Henry Eric Firdman, April 19, 2003; transcript of ABC's *Nightline*, broadcast June 15, 1992.

22. Bob Johnstone, *We Were Burning: Japanese Entrepreneurs and the Forging of the Electronic Age* (New York: Basic Books, 1999), 53–54.

23. Ibid., 53–174.

24. John Noble Wilford, "A Computer Lag by Russia Found; but U.S. Expert Discerns Potential for Parity," *New York Times,* March 14, 1971, 4; Barry W. Boehm, "Extensive Tour Yields Report on Current Soviet Computing," *Soviet Cybernetics Review,* 1 (Jan. 1971): 5.

25. CIA, *Trends in the Production of Electronics in the USSR,* CSI-2001-00002 (Langley, Va., April 1, 1971; declassified Jan. 29, 2001).

26. CIA, *Soviet Progress in the Production of Integrated Circuits,* CSI-2000-00019 (Langley, Va., Sept. 1, 1974; declassified Jan. 10, 2001).

27. Mark Kuchment, "Active Technology Transfer and the Development of Soviet Microelectronics," in *Selling the Rope to Hang Capitalism?: The Debate on West–East Trade and Technology Transfer,* ed. Charles M. Perry and Robert L. Pfaltzgraff Jr. (Washington, D.C.: Pergamon-Brassey's, 1987), 67; Henry Eric Firdman, *Decision-Making in the Soviet Microelectronics Industry: The Leningrad Design Bureau, a Case Study* (Falls Church, Va.: Delphic Associates, 1985), 65.

28. Hedrick Smith, "Nixon, Brezhnev Confer 5 Hours," *New York Times,* May 24, 1972; Igor Bystrov, *Essay No. 35, Year 1972, American Delegation in Zelenograd (April 1972),* http:/mzel.narod.ru/history/35.htm.

29. Bystrov, *Essay No. 35.*

30. Wade Holland and Willis Ware, "K-200: Space Computer or Engineering Oddity?" *Soviet Cybernetics Review,* 2 (May 1972): 19–30; quotation on 30.

31. Bruce Parrott, *Politics and Technology in the Soviet Union* (Cambridge, Mass.: MIT Press, 1983), 286–288.

32. Interview with Joel Barr, April 18, 1992; interview with Elvira Valueva, Feb. 1999; interview with Henry Eric Firdman, April 19, 2003.

33. http://www.taswegian.com/MOSCOW/soviet.html/24-71.html.

34. Firdman, *Maverick for Life,* 326.

35. Interview with Henry Eric Firdman, April 19, 2003.

36. "V&T News Visits Svetlana," *V&T News,* Jan. 1998; Svetlana corporate Website (http://www.svetlana.com/docs/who.html). Svetlana was founded in 1889 by Yakov

Aivaz. It was a cigarette manufacturer until 1913, when it started making incandescent light bulbs. In 1938 it began manufacturing vacuum tubes, and it later branched out into other areas of electronics, including semiconductors and integrated circuits. During the Soviet period, more than 70 percent of Svetlana's production went to the military. The company still exists and is a major international supplier of vacuum tubes.

37. Firdman, *Decision-Making*, 43.

38. *The Technology Acquisition Efforts of the Soviet Intelligence Services* (Langley, Va.: CIA, June 1, 1982; declassified Nov. 19, 1999), 8.

39. Firdman, *Decision-Making*, 43; CIA, *Significance of Soviet Acquisition of Western Technology (S-6846)*, CSI-2000-00005 (Langley, Va., June 11, 1975; declassified Nov. 18, 1999).

40. David Miller, *The Illustrated Directory of Submarines of the World* (London: Salamander, 2002), 296; Jeffrey Tall, *Submarines and Deep-Sea Vehicles* (San Diego: Thunder Bay, 2002), 142, 148.

41. "The first digital computer system used in Russian submarines appears to have been the Uzel, which entered service with the Project 641B ('Tango' class) diesel electric attack submarines from 1973"; "Russian Command and Weapon Control Systems," *Jane's Naval Weapon Systems*, Dec. 16, 2003. "The development of the first military information-control systems [BIUS — *boevye informatsionno-upravlyayuschie systemy*] gave an impulse to the further development of naval computing equipment. Results of the work made it possible to develop the BIUS 'Uzel,' which was widely deployed in diesel submarines. The development of the system was conducted by the LKB MEP, headed by F. G. Staros. Thanks to the close cooperation of Navy scientists and the industry, with the help of the previous BIUSes, as well as implementation of fundamentally new technical solutions, the BIUS 'Uzel' was officially deployed in 1973 and has been in use for a long period, the system being exported to India, Algeria, Iran, and other countries"; Admiral Yu. V. Alekseev and Yu. P. Blinov, "Ship Automated Control Systems," publication of the Russian Navy, http://www.navy.ru/science/rv7.htm.

42. David Miller, *Illustrated Directory of Submarines*, 297; Anthony Preston, "Submarine Command Systems," *Armada International*, 25 (Aug. 2001): 30; "Sindhughosh (Kilo) (Project 877em/8773) Class (SSK)," *Jane's Fighting Ships*, Feb. 20, 2003; Graham E. Fuller and Ian O. Lesser, *A Sense of Siege: The Geopolitics of Islam and the West* (Boulder: Westview, 1995), 71; William J. Durch, *Constructing Regional Security: The Role of Arms Transfers, Arms Control, and Reassurance* (New York: St. Martin's, 2000), 47; Bates Gill and Taeho Kim, *China's Arms Acquisitions from Abroad: A Quest for "Superb and Secret Weapons"* (Oxford: Oxford University Press, 1995), 68. The 10-kilo-class subs sold to the Indian Navy from the late 1980s through 2000 were equipped with Uzel combat information systems, according to http://www.bharat-rakshak.com, a Website maintained by a consortium of Indian military contractors.

43. "Anti-Submarine Warfare — Submarine and Surface Ship ASW Combat Management, Russian Federation," *Jane's Underwater Warfare Systems*, Aug. 21, 2003; Commander Bernd Kuhbier, "Bringing the Polish Navy up to Speed" (Northwood, Middlesex: Public Information Office, Northwood Headquarters, NATO Headquarters Allied Naval Forces North, 2002).

44. Interview with Henry Eric Firdman, April 19, 2003.

45. Romanov presented a serious challenge to Gorbachev for the Kremlin's top spot in 1984, prompting the CIA to suggest to President Reagan in 1985 that Romanov might succeed Chernenko. One of Gorbachev's first acts after outmaneuvering Romanov was to fire him.

Chapter 10. The Minifab, 1975–1990

1. Viktor Zavodinsky, "Put Dlinoyu v Dve Zhizni," *Vestnik Dalnevostochnogo Otdeleniya Rossiyskoi Akademii Nauk* (Bulletin of the Far Eastern Branch of the Russian Academy of Sciences), 1 (1993): 74–87.

2. Ibid.

3. Ibid.

4. Maurice Chittenden, "McCartney Fills Red Square with Back in the USSR," *Sunday Times* (London), May 25, 2003; Nick Paton Walsh, "Russians See Red over Macca Concert," *The Guardian*, May 14, 2003.

5. Jon Pareles, "Furtive Look at Soviet Rock Pianist," *New York Times*, July 17, 1986, C22; Roy Carr, *A Century of Jazz: From Blues to Bop, Swing to Hiphop — A Hundred Years of Music, Musicians, Singers, and Styles* (New York: Da Capo, 1997), 205; John Litweiler, *The Freedom Principle: Jazz after 1958* (New York: Da Capo 1990), 258; "Sergey Kuryokhin," entry in the iceberg.com (http://www.theiceberg.com/artist/24470/sergey_kuryokhin.html); Solomon Volkov, *St. Petersburg: A Cultural History* (New York: Free Press, 1995), 533–534.

6. Mark Kuchment, "Beyond the Rosenbergs: A New View from Russia," *Boston Review*, Sept. 1985, 23; idem, "The American Connection to Soviet Microelectronics," *Physics Today*, Sept. 1985, 47.

7. Kuchment, "Beyond the Rosenbergs," 23.

8. FBI serial 65-59453-298.

9. FBI 65-15392-747.

10. "IBM Creates New Dimension for High-Performance Chips," IBM press release, Nov. 11, 2002; Zavodinsky, "Put Dlinoyu v Dve Zhizni." A quarter-century later, the microelectronics industry was still trying to create three-dimensional ICs.

11. Interview with Kristina Staros, Feb. 11, 2004.

12. Interview with Elvira Valueva, Feb. 1999.

13. Interview with Joel Barr, April 18, 1992.

14. Ibid.

15. The Jackson-Vanik Amendment to the Trade Reform Act of 1974 imposed economic sanctions on countries that restricted emigration, prompting the Soviet Union to significantly loosen restrictions on the departure of Jews.

16. Interview with Joel Barr, April 18, 1992.

17. Interview with Joel Barr, March 17, 1997.

18. Bruce Dayton and Daniel Willard, "The Decay of a Neutral *V* Particle into Two Mesons," *Physics Review*, 91 (1953): 348–350.

19. FBI serial 65-15360-802.

20. Silvan S. Schweber, *In the Shadow of the Bomb: Bethe, Oppenheimer, and the Moral Responsibility of the Scientist* (Princeton: Princeton University Press, 2000), 119–121.

21. Dayton v. Dulles, 357 U.S. 144 (1958); argued April 10, 1958; decided June 16, 1958.

22. Luther A. Huston, "U.S. Court Backs Passport Denial," *New York Times,* Feb. 10, 1956, 5; Dayton v. Dulles, 357 U.S. 144 (1958).

23. Anthony Lewis, "Red Query Dropped for U.S. Passports," *New York Times,* June 25, 1958, 1.

24. The author interviewed several leading dissidents in Prague in the spring of 1988, including Peter Uhl, a spokesperson for the Charter 77 movement; Vaclav Havel's brother, Ivan Havel; and the future foreign minister, Jiri Dienstbier. Each of them was convinced that the Communist regime had a firm grip on power and that there was little prospect of regime change in the coming decade.

25. Kuchment, "American Connection to Soviet Microelectronics," 44.

26. Ibid.

27. Interview with Henry Eric Firdman, April 19, 2003.

28. Cable from American Embassy, Prague, to Secretary of State, May 1989, released March 20, 2001. All State Department documents obtained by author through the Freedom of Information Act.

29. Interview with Sergei Garyainov, May 29, 2001.

30. Cable from American Embassy, Prague, to Secretary of State, May 1990, released March 20, 2001.

31. Ronald Radosh, "Socialist Heroes," *New Republic,* Oct. 22, 1990, 9.

Chapter 11. The Strange Case of Iozef (Joseph) Berg AKA Joel Barr, 1990–1998

1. Interview with Elvira Valueva, Feb. 1999.

2. Ronald Radosh, "Socialist Heroes," *New Republic,* Oct. 22, 1990, 9.

3. FBI serials 65-59334-19, 65-59334-124.

4. *Executive Sessions of the Senate Permanent Subcommittee on Investigations of the Committee on Government Operations, Eighty-third Congress, First Session, 1953* (Washington, D.C.: U.S. Government Printing Office, 2003), vol. 3, 2487; FBI serial 65-59312-40; telephone interview with Vivian Glassman Pataki, May 19, 2003.

5. *Executive Sessions of the Senate Permanent Subcommittee,* vol. 5, 335.

6. Telephone interview with Vivian Glassman Pataki, May 19, 2003; interview with Robert Berg, Oct. 11, 2003.

7. FBI serials 65-59453-120, 65-59453-172, 65-59453-200.

8. Copies of this and all correspondence mentioned later in this chapter are in the author's possession.

9. "Professor Allegedly Bought Computer Parts for Vietnam," United Press International, Dec. 17, 1984; Susan Tifft, "Putting the Victim on Trial: A California Shooting Yields a Tale of Sex and Intrigue," *Time,* Jan. 7, 1985, 67; "An Aging Activist Carries On," Associated Press, Dec. 26, 1986. Edward Cooperman, a physics professor at Cal State Fullerton, funded Sobell's activities in Vietnam. After Cooperman was shot to death in his office on October 14, 1984, U.S. government officials said he had been under investigation for illegally transferring computer equipment to Vietnam; interview with Joel Barr, March 17, 1997.

10. Cable from American Consul, Leningrad, to Secretary of State, Jan. 1991; released March 20, 2001.

11. "What's Doing in Russia?: The ISSCC Lives Up to Its Global Moniker by Spotlighting Soviet Scientists," *Electronics,* Feb. 1991, 37.

12. Cable from Secretary of State to American Embassy, Prague, Aug. 1992; released March 20, 2001.

13. Interview with Kristina Staros, Feb. 11, 2004.

14. *Monterey County Herald,* Dec. 25, 2003, 85. Evelyn Elizabeth "Betty" Dayton died on Dec. 13.

15. Transcript of ABC's *Nightline,* broadcast June 12, 1992.

16. Press release from Representative Johnson, quoted in Jim Shevis, "House Pow/Mia Unit Seeks Full Story on Alleged Soviet Spy," United States Information Agency, Washington file, Aug. 7, 1992; "Cold War Turncoat Returns to US," *The Telegraph* (London), July 16, 1992; Robert W. Stewart, "Inquiry Urged on Associate of Atom Spies," *Los Angeles Times,* June 24, 1992, 3.

17. Interview with Joel Barr, April 18, 1992.

18. Daniil Granin, *Begstvo v Rossiyu* (Escape to Russia) (Moscow, Novosti: 1995).

19. *The Rosenberg File: Case Closed,* Discovery Channel, 1997; Alexander Feklisov, *Confession d'un Agent Soviétique* (Monaco: Rocher, 1999); idem, *The Man behind the Rosenbergs* (New York: Enigma Books, 2001).

20. Berg, letter to FSB, Feb. 1, 1998; interview with Joel Barr, April 18, 1992.

Index

CPSIA information can be obtained at www.ICGtesting.com
Printed in the USA
LVOW082133100113

315241LV00005B/288/P